Scott Foresman

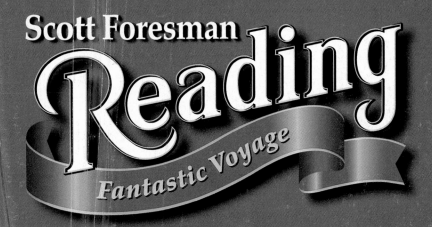

Scott Foresman Reading
Fantastic Voyage

Fantastic Voyage

Relating to Others

My World and Yours

A Job Well Done

Time and Time Again

Traveling On

Think of It!

PEARSON

Scott
Foresman

About the Cover Artist

Larry Moore started drawing when he was seven years old. His house was on a canal
with many little islands behind it. This provided plenty of wildlife for him to draw. To
this day, Moore's favorite subject to paint is nature and its creatures.

ISBN 0-328-03938-1

6 7 8 9 10 V057 12 11 10 09 08 07 06 05 04 03

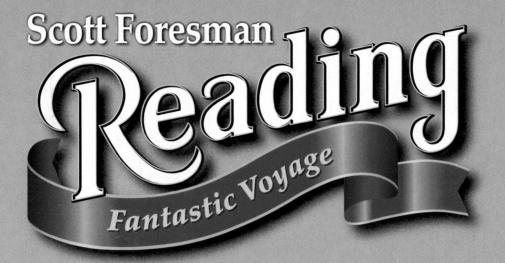

Scott Foresman Reading

Fantastic Voyage

Program Authors

Peter Afflerbach

James Beers

Camille Blachowicz

Candy Dawson Boyd

Wendy Cheyney

Deborah Diffily

Dolores Gaunty-Porter

Connie Juel

Donald Leu

Jeanne Paratore

Sam Sebesta

Karen Kring Wixson

PEARSON

Scott Foresman

Editorial Offices: Glenview, Illinois • Parsippany, New Jersey • New York, New York
Sales Offices: Parsippany, New Jersey • Duluth, Georgia • Glenview, Illinois
Carrollton, Texas • Ontario, California • Mesa, Arizona

Unit 1 • Contents

Relating to Others

Unit 2 · Contents

My World and Yours

Unit 3 • Contents

A Job Well Done

Unit 4 • Contents

Time and Time Again

Unit 5 · Contents

Traveling On

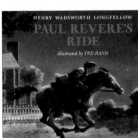

Unit 6 • Contents

Think of It!

Sharon Bell Mathis

Dear Reader,

My mother, Alice Frazier Bell, was a poet. She had three wonderful habits. She loved books and was constantly reading. She wrote poems and illustrated them with beautiful drawings. And she bought every book she could afford. Our home was filled with books by James Baldwin, Gwendolyn Brooks, Frederick Douglass, Langston Hughes, and so many others.

When I was little, I tried to copy everything my mother did. I sat with her at the kitchen table where I fashioned letters of the alphabet into what I thought were real words and drew scribbly pictures. It was fun! It was the beginning of my own desire to write.

Then I learned to read! Books were a zillion different kinds of candy and I wished to discover all the flavors. Visiting the neighborhood library—where there were hundreds of children's books—was a super treat. The five of us would trek to the library—Mama, my brother John, my sisters Patrellis and Marcia, and me. I hugged my precious books as we left our third floor apartment in the Bedford-Stuyvesant area of Brooklyn, New York. We walked to Reid Avenue and turned left. At Macon Street, we turned left and walked toward Lewis Avenue. As soon as we turned the corner onto Lewis Avenue, there it was—the Macon branch of the Brooklyn Public Library. That library opened in 1907 and is still in service after 91 years.

My excitement could hardly be contained. Books! Books! Books! Books were everywhere: on shelves, on tables, in people's hands, at the charge desk, in bins, in carts. It seemed that every book in the world was in that library. Big books with splashy colorful pages and small books with fine black and white illustrations. Skinny books and thick books. Books with pictures and books without them. I had choices to make and pages to turn.

Sadly, none of the books I remember were of children with beautiful dark skin—silky, chocolatey, satiny faces—in the rich warm colors of fudge and caramel. Where were the wide-eyed dimpled children with skin as bright as polished ebony? Where were the boys and girls who looked like me?

I discovered a favorite reading place—the fire escape outside my kitchen window. A wrought-iron castle where it seemed I could almost touch the huge tree that grew in the backyard.

It was fun to slip my feet through the iron bars and swing my long, skinny legs while I read my books. Other times, I would sit on a folded quilt. I kept company with African chieftains and talking spiders, trolls and giants, princesses and princes, kings and queens, dinosaurs and donkeys. On my wonderful windy veranda I got lost in stories of knights and jesters, huffing wolves and bears that lived in houses, clever foxes, and race-winning turtles.

On snowy nights, my father, John Willie Bell, might put a large bowl on my iron porch to catch freshly fallen snow to make snow ice cream. Who else had a place so magical? One of my first short stories for children was called "The Fire Escape."

Perched high above the backyard, in my iron library, I read books, completed homework assignments, laughed in a starry room, and grew up. I never once thought that one day another child might sit high up in the air, on a distant fire escape, and read a book that I had written.

Imagine that!

Relating to Others

What are the important things in life?

Skill Lesson

Sequence

- **Sequence** is the order in which things happen.

- Keeping track of the sequence of events will help you better understand what you read.

- Words such as *then* and *after* are often clues to the sequence. Words such as *meanwhile* and *during* show that several events can happen at once.

- By arranging events in sequence, you can see how one thing leads to another.

Read *Homer Price* from the book by Robert McCloskey.

Talk About It

1. What led Mr. Murphy to put the mousetrap on his car? Tell the events in sequence.

2. What sequence of events must happen to make the trap work?

from
Homer Price

by Robert McCloskey

"Then," said Homer, "Mr. Murphy set to work to make a *musical* mousetrap."

"That wouldn't hurt the mice?" inquired Uncle Ulysses.

"That wouldn't hurt the mice," Homer stated. "It was a long hard job too, because first he had to build an organ out of reeds that the mice liked the sound of, and then he had to compose a tune that the mice couldn't possibly resist. Then he incorporated it all into a mousetrap . . ."

"That wouldn't hurt the mice?" interrupted the barber.

"That wouldn't hurt the mice," Homer went on. "The mousetrap caught mice, all right. The only trouble was, it was too big. What with the organ and all, and sort of impractical for general use because

somebody had to stay around and pump the organ."

"Yes, I can see that wouldn't be practical," said Uncle Ulysses, stroking his chin— "But with a small electric motor . . ."

"But he solved it, Uncle Ulysses!—The whole idea seems very practical after you get used to it. He decided since the trap was too large to use in a house, he would fasten it onto his car, which he hadn't used for so long anyway. Then, he could drive it to a town, and make a bargain with the mayor to remove all the mice. You see he would start the musical mousetrap to working, and drive up and down the streets and alleys. Then all of the mice would run out of the houses to get themselves caught in this trap that plays music that no mouse ever born can possibly resist. After the trap is full of mice, Mr. Murphy drives them out past the city limits, somewhere where they can't find their way home, and lets them go."

LOOK AHEAD

In "From the Diary of Leigh Botts," Leigh invents a burglar alarm for his lunchbox. As you read, follow the sequence of events.

Vocabulary

Words to Know

cafeteria	demonstration	diary
racket	triggered	switch

Many words such as *play* have more than one meaning. To decide which meaning of the word is correct, look for clues in the surrounding sentences or paragraph.

Read the paragraph below. Does *switch* mean "a change" or "a thing that turns electricity on and off"?

Oops!

Yesterday there was a science demonstration in the cafeteria. I wrote about it in my diary because it ended in a funny way. Two kids had a model of a volcano. It was supposed to erupt with smoke and lava when they flipped a switch . But it didn't. When they moved the switch to the *on* position, it triggered an explosion. The loud racket caused everyone to cover their ears and laugh.

Write About It

Describe an experiment you've seen or done. Use as many vocabulary words as you can.

From the Diary of
Leigh Botts

from *Dear Mr. Henshaw* by Beverly Cleary

Leigh Botts writes letters to Mr. Henshaw, his favorite author. And Mr. Henshaw writes back. It was Mr. Henshaw who told Leigh to keep a diary. Leigh finds that he has lots to write about, like who's stealing food out of his lunchbag. Mr. Fridley, who works at Leigh's school, says that a burglar alarm will help catch the thief. Will it?

Thursday, March 1

I am getting behind in this diary for several reasons, including working on my story and writing to Mr. Henshaw. I also had to buy a new notebook because I had filled up the first one.

The same day, I bought a beat-up black lunchbox in the thrift shop down the street and started carrying my lunch in it. The kids were surprised, but nobody made fun of me, because a black lunchbox isn't the same as one of those square boxes covered with cartoon characters that first and second graders carry. The next day my little slices of salami rolled around cream cheese were gone, but I expected that. But I'll get that thief yet. I'll make him really sorry he ate all the best things out of my lunch.

Next I went to the library for books on batteries. I took out a couple of easy books on electricity, really easy, because I have never given much thought to batteries. About all I know is that when you want to use a flashlight, the battery is usually dead.

I finally gave up on my story about the ten-foot wax man, which was really pretty dumb. I thought I would write a poem about butterflies for Young Writers because a poem can be short, but it is hard to think about butterflies and burglar alarms at the same time, so I studied electricity books instead. The books didn't have directions for an alarm in a lunchbox, but I learned enough about batteries and switches and insulated wires, so I think I can figure it out myself.

Friday, March 2

Back to the poem tonight. The only rhyme I can think of for "butterfly" is "flutter by." I can think up rhymes like "trees" and "breeze" which are pretty boring, and then I think of "wheeze" and "sneeze." A poem about butterflies wheezing and sneezing seems silly, and anyway a couple of girls are already writing poems about monarch butterflies that flutter by.

Sometimes I start a letter to Dad thanking him for the twenty dollars, but I can't finish that either. I don't know why.

Saturday, March 3

Today I took my lunchbox and Dad's twenty dollars to the hardware store and looked around. I found an ordinary light switch, a little battery, and a cheap doorbell. While I was looking around for the right kind of insulated wire, a man who had been watching me (boys my age always get watched when they go into stores) asked if he could help me. He was a nice old gentleman who said, "What are you planning to make, son?" *Son.* He called me son, and my Dad calls me kid. I didn't want to tell the man, but when he looked at the things I was holding, he grinned and said, "Having trouble with your lunch, aren't you?" I nodded and said, "I'm trying to make a burglar alarm."

He said, "That's what I guessed. I've had workmen in here with the same problem."

It turned out that I needed a 6-volt lantern battery instead of the battery I had picked out. He gave me a couple of tips and, after I paid for the things, a little slap on the back and said, "Good luck, son."

I tore home with all the things I bought. First I made a sign for my door that said

KEEP OUT
MOM
THAT MEANS YOU

27

Then I went to work fastening one wire from the battery to the switch and from the other side of the switch to the doorbell. Then I fastened a second wire from the battery to the doorbell. It took me a while to get it right. Then I taped the battery in one corner of the lunchbox and the doorbell in another. I stood the switch up at the back of the box and taped that in place too.

Here I ran into a problem. I thought I could take the wire clamp meant to hold a thermos bottle inside the lunchbox lid and hook it under the switch if I reached in carefully as I closed the box. The clamp wasn't quite long enough. After some thinking and experimenting, I twisted a wire loop onto it. Then I closed the box just enough so I could get my hand inside and push the wire loop over the button on the switch before I took my hand out and closed the box.

Then I opened the box. My burglar alarm worked! That bell inside the box went off with a terrible racket that brought Mom to my door. "Leigh, what on earth is going on in there?" she shouted above the alarm.

I let her in and gave her a demonstration of my burglar alarm. She laughed and said it was a great invention. One thing was bothering me. Would my sandwich muffle the bell? Mom must have been wondering the same thing, because she suggested taping a piece of cardboard into the lid that would make a shelf for my sandwich. I did, and that worked too.

I can't wait until Monday.

Monday, March 5

Today Mom packed my lunch carefully, and we tried the alarm to see if it still worked. It did, good and loud. When I got to school, Mr. Fridley said, "Nice to see you smiling, Leigh. You should try it more often."

I parked my lunchbox behind the partition and waited. I waited all morning for the alarm to go off. Miss Martinez asked if I had my mind on my work. I pretended I did, but all the time I was really waiting for my alarm to go off, so I could dash back behind the partition and tackle the thief. When nothing happened, I began to worry. Maybe the loop had somehow slipped off the switch on the way to school.

Lunchtime came. The alarm still hadn't gone off. We all picked up our lunches and went off to the cafeteria. When I set my box on the table in front of me, I realized I had a problem, a big problem. If the loop hadn't slipped off the switch, my alarm was still triggered. I just sat there, staring at my lunchbox, not knowing what to do.

"How come you're not eating?" Barry asked with his mouth full. Barry's sandwiches are never cut in half, and he always takes a big bite out of one side to start.

Everybody at the table was looking at me. I thought about saying I wasn't hungry, but I was. I thought about taking my lunchbox out into the hall to open, but if the alarm was still triggered, there was no way I could open it quietly. Finally I thought, Here goes. I unsnapped the two fasteners on the box and held my breath as I opened the lid.

Wow! My alarm went off! The noise was so loud it startled everybody at the table including me and made everyone in the cafeteria look around. I looked up and saw Mr. Fridley grinning at me over by the garbage can. Then I turned off the alarm.

Suddenly everybody seemed to be noticing me. The principal, who always prowls around keeping an eye on things at lunchtime, came over to examine my lunchbox. He said, "That's quite an invention you have there."

"Thanks," I said, pleased that the principal seemed to like my alarm.

Some of the teachers came out of their lunchroom to see what the noise was all about. I had to give a demonstration. It seems I wasn't the only one who had things stolen from my lunch, and all the kids said they wanted lunchboxes with alarms, too, even those whose lunches were never good enough to have anything stolen. Barry said he would like an alarm like that on the door of his room at home. I began to feel like some sort of hero.

One thing bothers me, though. I still don't know who's been robbing my lunch.

About the Author
Beverly Cleary

In seventh grade, Beverly Cleary discovered how much she liked to write. Her teacher asked the class to write about a favorite character in a book. Ms. Cleary had so many favorites that she couldn't choose just one. Instead she wrote a story about a girl's trip to Bookland so that she could make up conversations for all her favorite characters. The next day, the teacher read Ms. Cleary's story to the class and said, "When Beverly grows up, she should write children's books." And that is just what she did!

When she was young, Ms. Cleary was like the character of Leigh Botts. She liked writing and inventing. She made stilts from big coffee cans and rope as well as perfume from crushed rose petals and water. Today she's still inventing stories and winning awards for them. Among her many awards is the 1984 Newbery Medal for the book *Dear Mr. Henshaw*, which tells the story of Leigh Botts.

Reader Response

Open for Discussion

Pretend you are Leigh. You've just finished triggering the alarm. What is running through your mind?

Comprehension Check

1. Why does Leigh start carrying a lunchbox? What probably causes him to choose a beat-up lunchbox from a thrift shop? Find details to support your answer.

2. After the students and teachers see the demonstration of Leigh's invention, what do you think they will think of Leigh? Use evidence from the story to explain.

3. Leigh feels like a hero at the end of the story. Do you think he is? Why or why not?

4. What is the **sequence** of events that lead up to the time when Leigh begins making the burglar alarm?
(Sequence)

5. Leigh brings his lunchbox alarm to school on Monday, March 5. Tell what happens next, in **sequence.**
(Sequence)

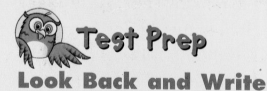

Test Prep

Look Back and Write

Leigh gets ideas and information from several places. Look back at pages 24–29. What does he learn from library books? from other people? What does he figure out by himself?

The Rampanion
by Arlene Erlbach

Alison DeSmyter knows about the problems people have in wheelchairs. Alison was born with cerebral palsy, a condition that makes it difficult to control muscles. So Alison has used a wheelchair most of her life.

One common problem for wheelchair users is crossing streets with curbs. To get her chair over a curb, Alison needed somebody to push or lift her chair. She wanted more independence. So Alison invented the Rampanion—a portable ramp that allows a wheelchair to move easily over a curb.

Alison first thought of the Rampanion when she was asked to do an invention project for school. She had just two weeks. That wasn't much time to design something as complicated as the Rampanion.

But Alison did it!

First Alison thought about making a rubber ramp, but she decided it would be too bulky to carry around. Next she considered an inflatable ramp. That wouldn't do, either—it would always need to be blown up. Finally Alison decided to make a ramp out of lightweight metal. This type of ramp could easily be folded and carried.

Alison began by building a small model of her ramp from Popsicle sticks. Once she had built the model, she thought about the type of metal she'd use for the real thing. The Rampanion needed to be light yet strong, so Alison decided on aluminum. Her father found some aluminum where he works, and he helped Alison put the ramp together. To build the ramp, they needed a lot of exact measurements, which Alison took herself.

As Alison and her father built the Rampanion, they thought of improvements they could make to its design. They added an edge to the Rampanion's sides, to keep a chair's wheels on track. They put sticky tape on the bottom, to help secure the Rampanion to any surface—even in the rain.

The completed Rampanion weighs only four pounds. When it's folded, it can be carried in its own cloth bag. The bag can be attached to a wheelchair.

Alison's Rampanion won the fifth-grade grand prize for the third annual Houston Inventors' Showcase Exposition. Her prize was a trip to Florida. The trip included visits to Disneyworld, the Kennedy Space Center, and Thomas Edison's estate. Thomas Edison was a great inventor who created many electrical devices, such as the light bulb and the phonograph.

Alison hasn't stopped inventing things for wheelchair users. She's working on a Handy Helper, which is a tray that attaches to a wheelchair. The Handy Helper allows people in wheelchairs to be served more easily in cafeterias and fast-food restaurants.

Character

- **Characters** can be people or animals in stories. When you learn about the characters, you will better understand and enjoy the stories.

- You can learn about characters by noticing what they think, say, and do.

- You can also learn about characters by thinking about how other characters treat them and what these other characters say about them.

Read "No Friends" from *Lost and Found* by Jean Little.

Talk About It

1. Would you describe Lucy's character as patient or impatient? What does Mrs. Bell say that helps you learn about Lucy?

2. What else can you say about Lucy? How do you find out about her character?

3. How would you describe the character of Lucy's mom? How do you know what she is like?

No Friends

by Jean Little

Lucy leaned her head against the glass. She blinked to keep the tears back. Then she took off her glasses and cleaned them on her T-shirt. She put them back on her nose and sighed.

"What's wrong, Lucy?" asked Mrs. Bell.

Lucy did not turn around. She did not want her mother to see how sad she was. But her voice shook.

"I wish we still lived in Guelph. I don't know anyone in this town. There's nothing to do here."

"There's a lot to do," her mother told her. "There are all these boxes to unpack. There are your books and toys to put away. I need someone to go to the store for me too. I forgot to get ice cream."

Lucy made a face.

"I don't want work to do. And I don't like putting things away. I want someone to play with. At home I had lots of friends. But here I have none. I'll never make a friend here."

Her mother shook her head.

"Lucy Bell, that's just plain silly. We only got here yesterday. It takes time to make friends. Give the girls here a chance."

"I don't see any girls here," Lucy said.

Mrs. Bell was sitting on the floor sorting through a box of sheets and towels. She got up and went to stand beside Lucy. They looked out at the street.

"Maybe they're still on vacation," she said. "Don't forget that this is the last long weekend of the summer. But school will start bright and early on Tuesday morning. They'll all be back in time for that."

LOOK AHEAD

In "Faith and Eddie," Faith has trouble making friends when she moves to her new home. As you read the story, think about what the characters are like.

Vocabulary

Words to Know

alternating	cemetery	faith
anticipation	darted	scent
retraced	withdrew	

Scent and *cent* are **homophones.** These are words that are pronounced the same but have different meanings and spellings. To understand their meanings, look for clues in the surrounding words and sentences.

Read the paragraph below. Why is *scent* used and not *cent?*

From Spain to Mexico

In 1521 Spain invaded Mexico in anticipation of gaining great riches. Spanish rule was hard, but three hundred years went by before a revolt began. In 1810, in the town of Dolores, the village priest Miguel Hidalgo retraced his usual path. He walked by the square, noticed the scent of flowers, passed the cemetery, and entered the church. His message was new—he spoke out against Spain. With faith that they could rule themselves, people darted out to join the revolution. For eleven years, Mexico fought, alternating between winning and losing. Finally, in 1821, Spain was defeated and withdrew.

Talk About It

Use vocabulary words to tell about a historical figure who is of interest to you.

Faith

and Eddie

from
Faith and the
Electric Dogs

by
Patrick
Jennings

Faith has moved from California to San Cristóbal de las Casas in Mexico with her mother, Bernice, and stepfather, Hector. Being in a new school and learning Spanish is hard, and Faith turns to her dog Eddie for comfort. Eddie is a **perro corriente,** *which in Spanish means the same as* mutt. *Eddie, who understands Spanish, English, and other languages, tells this story.*

Fetch

In the morning I was awakened by an aroma wafting from the kitchen and decided to investigate.

Milagros was there cooking eggs. Milagros is dark and broad and always wears traditional brilliant blue blouses, which she hand-embroiders herself. On the shoulder of this blouse, she'd sewn her name and surrounded it with bright yellow and pink flowers. She sang in Tzotzil while she worked.

I could smell chiles, cilantro, onions, garlic, and fresh corn tortillas. I whined.

"¡Ay, perrito!" Milagros said.

She looked down at me and I could see pity in her eyes. She had an open, friendly face. Though she was only a teenager, she looked very grown-up.

"Mi chavi 'naj?" she asked.

¡Ay, perrito!
(Spanish):
Oh, little dog!

Mi chavi 'naj?
(Tzotzil):
Are you hungry?

I nodded and gave her my beggar face. I have charming, amber-colored eyes, which, combined with my creased brow—a common electric dog trait—make for an irresistible sight. I moistened my eyes and sucked in my gut. I was completely pitiable.

She looked to the left and to the right, as Faith had done the night before, and when she'd decided the coast was clear, she opened the refrigerator and withdrew a platter of the leftover *carnitas*.

"Sssshh," she said.

I stopped panting.

She gingerly plucked a particularly gooey chunk of pork from the plate and offered it to me. I seized it, swallowed it, and sighed.

Dare I whine for more? I wondered.

I dared.

"SSSSHH!" she hissed, looking around. Without taking her eyes off the kitchen door, she snatched another piece of pork and flipped it into the air. It arched high over my head. I leaped and caught it with a stunning midflight torso twist and, once again, dispensed with it hastily.

There were indeed perks to this new lifestyle.

"*Mu 'yuk xa*," she said, replacing the platter and closing the refrigerator door.

Bernice came in minutes later and escorted me out onto the courtyard, saying, "No dogs in the kitchen, understand?"

Little did she know, dear reader, that I *did* understand.

After the family had eaten breakfast, Bernice and Hector each got ready for work. As Bernice had to leave earlier, it was left to Hector to get Faith off to school. Plainly, she did not wish to go to school.

"I hate it," she answered when Hector asked why she didn't want to go.

Mu 'yuk xa
(Tzotzil):
No more

Eventually he got her into the car despite her kicking and screaming, and off they went. Milagros got started on her housework—the dishes, the beds, the mopping, the laundry.

And I? I got down to dog's work. Marking my territory. Napping. Digging up the flower beds. Gnawing. Napping.

That afternoon, Faith rushed through the door, her eyes all red and swollen. She sank to her knees and hugged me and sobbed.

"Oh, Eddie," she said. "I hate it. I just hate it."

I pressed my muzzle up into her face and licked her cheek. It tasted salty.

"The kids at school hate me," she said. "The teacher hates me. I can't understand a thing anyone says and they can't understand me, either." She sniffled. "Diego keeps making fishy faces at me."

At that she buried her face into my neck and cried.

After a few minutes she pulled away and tried to speak, but only big spit bubbles came out of her mouth. Horrid slimy goo oozed out of her nose. She wiped it all away with a swipe of her sleeve.

"Would you like to learn a new game?" she asked, snuffling.

The game was called Fetch. She threw a stick and I retrieved it. Quite simple, really. I caught on very quickly. Soon I was catching the stick in midair. We played until Faith was called in to dinner, and then, after she'd eaten, I tugged her back outside. We played until it got too dark to see. All that night I lay awake thinking of fetching.

The next day when Faith came through the door after school, I greeted her, stick in mouth. Again, we played until dark, pausing only for dinner. I was obsessed. Dogged. Retrieval was all I could think about.

It got so that we played Fetch every afternoon and always on into the night. I was manic. I would wait for hours by the door with a stick in my mouth, drooling in anticipation.

Faith was a real trooper. She rarely denied me a toss. She'd stay up until she was fainting from fatigue, but still she threw. When finally she could go on no more, I would whine and whimper and paw. I slept with a stick in my mouth, just in case she should wake up and wish to play. I began having nightmares too.

In one, Faith threw a stick high into the air and I waited and waited for it to come down, but it never did. I just stood, poised and intent, staring skyward, waiting. I awoke in a sweat. In another, I chased down a thrown stick and just as I bent to scoop it up, it moved. Again I lunged at it, but again it danced out of reach. It began to taunt me, to tease me. Yes, it *spoke*. I chased it and chased it, but I never caught it, never retrieved.

Then, one day, as if from a dream, I saw Fetch for what it truly is: a monotonous, pointless waste of time. I remember laughing at how positively nutty I'd been.

Then she taught me Tug-of-war.

Faith Lost

Some afternoons, Faith's Spanish tutor, Socorro—everyone called her Coco—would come to the house to help Faith with her Spanish. Faith liked Coco. She liked her bright smile and glittering assortment of jewelry: woven bracelets, chain anklets, skull brooches, amber earrings. Faith liked one particular necklace very much. It was a small, shallow, silver box that had several long thin pieces of silver dangling from the bottom. The front of the box was hinged and had a clasp that you could open and close (if you had thumbs). Faith loved to open and close Coco's little silver box so much that Coco began wearing that particular necklace every time she came to visit, and she always put a little surprise inside for Faith.

There was only one thing about Coco that Faith didn't like, and that was that she kept trying to teach Faith Spanish.

"It's a physical impossibility," Faith would say.

But Coco kept trying. Each time she came she had a surprise in her necklace and a new plan of attack.

Coco didn't teach Spanish with a textbook and a chalkboard and worksheets. No, no, nothing like that. She played games with Faith—card games, board games, running games, pretending games. She was very clever.

One day, she pretended to be Bernice and Faith pretended to be Hector and they pretended to have an argument. They talked about love and money— you know, grown-up stuff. The catch was that Coco spoke almost entirely in Spanish, and that Faith barely seemed to notice.

mercado
(Spanish):
marketplace

**¡Tres pesos
por cada
papaya!**
(Spanish):
*Three pesos for
one papaya!*

Sí
(Spanish): *Yes*

Madre
(Spanish): *mother*

Padrastro
(Spanish):
stepfather

Amiga
(Spanish):
female friend

**Perro
corriente**
(Spanish):
mutt

Yo
(Spanish): *I*

On another day, Faith was a vendor in the *mercado* and Coco was a hungry customer with very little money. They both really hammed it up and, without realizing it, Faith began speaking in Spanish.

"*¡Tres pesos por cada papaya!*" Coco said.

Faith tried to look stern but ended up giggling and saying, "*Sí.*"

Once, Coco helped Faith make what Coco called a family tree. Faith drew pictures of herself, her mother, Hector, Milagros, and me on colored paper. Then she cut the pictures out and glued them onto another piece of larger, stiffer paper and wrote the names of each of us under his or her picture. It was the first time I'd ever seen "Edison" spelled out, and I felt a little proud. It's a handsome word, very tall and straight on one end and very short and curved on the other.

Then Coco wrote a word under "Bernice."

"*Madre,*" she read when she'd finished.

She wrote another word under "Hector."

"*Padrastro,*" she said.

Beneath "Milagros" she wrote, and said, "*Amiga.*"

Below my handsome name she wrote the words I'd so often heard before: "*Perro corriente.*"

And under "Faith" she wrote a short little word.

"*Yo,*" Faith read. "I know '*yo*' means 'I.' But how do I say 'Faith' in Spanish?"

"*¿Cómo?*" Coco asked, smiling.

"In Spanish?" Faith asked with a heavy sigh.

"*Sí, en español,*" Coco said.

Faith cleared her throat and said, "*¿Cómo se dice 'Faith' en español?*"

"*¡Bravo!*" Coco said, clapping her hands. "*¡Perfecto!*"

"*Gracias,*" Faith said, blushing.

"You can say 'Faith,'" Coco said. "In English or in Spanish, it's the same."

Faith seemed disappointed by this, and I think Coco sensed it.

"You can also say *'Fe,'*" she told Faith. "*Fe* is Spanish for 'faith,' like when you believe in something."

Faith smiled.

"*Fe,*" she said. "Swell!"

¿Cómo?
(Spanish): *What?*

Sí, en español
(Spanish):
Yes, in Spanish

¿Cómo se dice 'Faith' en español?
(Spanish):
How do you say "Faith" in Spanish?

¡Bravo!
(Spanish): *Bravo!*

¡Perfecto!
(Spanish): *Perfect!*

Gracias
(Spanish):
Thank you

Fe
(Spanish): *faith*

It was on one of the afternoons that Coco came by that the roof fell in.

Bernice had gone to pick up Faith from school and Coco had been waiting a long time for them to return. She kept checking her watch and walking up and down. Milagros assured her, in Spanish, that they'd be home any minute. But on and on we waited.

Finally, Coco said she had to leave. She gave Milagros a hug and said, *"No te preocupes, mi hija."* Then she got her coat, rubbed my head, and left.

The sun was nearly down and I just couldn't sit and wait any longer. I barked and barked and howled by the front gate until Milagros finally opened it, and then out into the streets of San Cristóbal de las Casas I ran, back out into those familiar, unfriendly streets to find the one who had rescued me from them.

· No te preocupes, mi hija. (Spanish): *Don't worry, my child.*

Electric Shoes

I raced through the narrow cobblestone paths of El Cerrillo, through the feet of the tourists shopping for handicrafts in the plaza of Santo Domingo, past the cathedral and the *zócalo* and the little hill (El Cerrito) in the center of town with the little church on top. The sky was darkening and the air was chilling and my heart was pounding.

zócalo (Spanish): *town square*

Old street dog chums called out as I passed but I did not acknowledge them. I had far to go and no time to lose. I crossed streets without looking. I passed food scraps without slowing. I was ignoring instincts I'd spent my whole life developing. All I could think about was finding Faith. Nothing else mattered.

When I finally crossed the small bridge that spans the stream around Faith's school, I found Bernice's funny little red car in the parking lot. Parked next to it was a police car, with flashing red and white lights.

I hurried up the path to the school, which was a cluster of round adobe huts. The lights were on in one of them. I saw Bernice through the window talking to several other people, including a police officer. She looked quite beside herself and was waving her arms about as if she was some great bird. I sized up the situation quickly: Faith was missing.

I put my nose to work and within a few minutes I was able to pick up my master's scent. It led me down a path out behind the school and through the trees. The sun had set completely now. There were no lights, except the stars above. I was at the mercy of my snout.

Her scent led me past the spot by the stream where I'd first seen her. I forded the stream and picked her scent up again on the other side. Brave girl! Brave, foolish (and probably soaking wet) Faith!

I crossed a pasture where horses stood sleeping and, in the darkness, trod in their droppings several times. I got snagged in thistle bushes. I got caught on barbed wire. But I did not lose Faith's scent.

It led me into the *panteón*.

I slipped through a hole in the fence and followed my nose past wooden crosses decorated with plastic flowers. These were the grave markings of the people of San Cristóbal de las Casas who had died with little or no money. I climbed the hill toward the more spectacular mausoleums and shrines, in which were laid the city's richer dead folk. Many of the sites were still decorated from the Days of the Dead.

panteón
(Spanish):
graveyard, cemetery

On those days—the first two days of November—the people of Mexico visit the graves of their dear departed and stay throughout the night. They bring with them the favorite foods and belongings of their loved ones to lure them from the beyond. They decorate the graves with candles and bouquets of bright orange marigolds. They sing the dead's favorite songs and the children wear masks and play with toy skeletons and eat candied skulls. The cemetery is filled with light and song and laughter. It's a party for the dead.

You see, in Mexico the dead are not feared—they are welcomed. And graveyards are lively places.

But I knew Faith was not from Mexico, and I'd heard that, to North Americans, cemeteries are spooky places. So I speeded up my search.

I tracked her scent all around the *panteón,* until I found I was covering the same ground—going around in circles. Obviously, she'd gotten lost. On the outside chance that she was nearby, I howled.

I heard back only my echo.

Fog settled in, wrapping the dimly lit *panteón* in an eerie cloak of mist. The air temperature dropped. I felt the dampness in my bones. I wondered if Faith had worn her jacket.

I howled again. Again, just my echo.

I continued the search. Round and round the gravestones I went. It seemed useless, but what else could I do? I traced and retraced my steps.

Finally, exhausted, I crawled up onto a tall sky-blue crypt to think.

The hill that the *panteón* sits atop lies between the school and town. From my vantage point, I looked down on the city nestled in the valley below, all lit up with streetlights and the headlights of cars.

The sun had set and a crescent moon glimmered behind the wispy fog. I could hear roosters crowing and dogs howling, and so, once again, I howled. I howled from deep down inside of me— from my belly.

When you're blue, there's nothing quite like howling at the moon.

I don't know how long I'd been howling when I noticed a tiny red flash of light below, down in the cow pastures that separate the *panteón* from town. Then I saw another one. Each of the flashes lasted less than a second. After the second, there was a third, then a fourth. There was a rhythm to their appearance. After a moment or two I remember deciding that there were just two lights and that they were taking turns flashing: they were alternating. One, two. One, two. One, two. It wasn't an automobile's taillights—they wouldn't alternate. They would glow together. It looked to me as if these tiny red lights were *walking.*

And that's when I remembered Faith's *zapatos eléctricos*—her electric shoes! The ones that blinked red with each and every step! (They were—and still are—commonly worn by children from the United States.)

zapatos eléctricos (Spanish): *electric shoes*

I jumped from the crypt and darted as quickly as I could down the hill, through the gates of the *panteón,* and along the dirt road toward town and Faith's blinking feet.

When I was within earshot, I began to bark. The red lights went out and I lost where she was. I guessed that she had stopped. I continued running in the same direction I'd been, and just hoped I'd bump into her.

And then the red lights began blinking again, only much more rapidly than they had before. She was running! Running away!

I barked louder but the lights only blinked faster.

"Go away!" Faith yelled. "Go away, devil dog! *¡Afuera! ¡Afuera!*"

I found—to my relief—that I run much faster than Faith and was able to gain on her fairly easily. I ran past her and headed her off. She skidded to a stop and stood heaving and sobbing and shaking (she *was* soaking wet and she *didn't* have her jacket on).

"Eh-Eh-Eddie?" she said.

I barked.

She rushed me and I jumped up and licked her salty face.

"Oh, Eddie!" she said, giggling. "Good boy! Good boy!"

About the Author
Patrick Jennings

Patrick Jennings knows what it feels like to be an outsider. Like the character Faith, Mr. Jennings moved from San Francisco to San Cristóbal de las Casas in Mexico, where he had to learn Spanish, make new friends, and try to understand new customs. His first novel, *Faith and the Electric Dogs,* is based on his experiences in Mexico. He hopes that sharing those experiences will show readers that they are not alone in facing such problems.

Mr. Jennings is fascinated with the power of language, and he tries to get others to feel the same excitement. He believes writing is like magic. "In fact, I often refer to a pen or pencil as a magic wand, capable of creating in the minds of others anything a magician can imagine," he says.

Mr. Jennings often visits schools to talk to students and teachers about what a powerful tool writing can be. "One of the most important themes in my work, and in my interactions with students, is the power language holds to excite the imagination, to express one's ideas and emotions, and to bring people closer through empathy and understanding," he explains.

If you enjoyed *Faith and the Electric Dogs,* you might also enjoy the sequel, *Faith and the Rocket Cat,* which is Mr. Jennings's second novel.

Reader Response

Open for Discussion

What did you think of reading a story from a dog's point of view?

Comprehension Check

1. First, Eddie chases after a stick. Later, he chases after Faith. What is different about the two chases?

2. When Eddie catches up to Faith on the dirt road toward town, why does she at first tell him to go away? Support your answer with evidence from the story.

3. If you could help Faith adjust to her new school and new language, what would you do? Suggest specific actions.

4. Think about Faith. How does this **character** feel about living in San Cristóbal de las Casas? How do you know? (Character)

5. How is Eddie like any other dog? How is his **character** like a person? (Character)

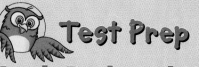

Test Prep

Look Back and Write

Look back at pages 44–45. Explain how Eddie gets humans to do what he wants. Tell about specific actions he performs and the results he gets.

Say What?

by Tracey Randinelli

Figuring Out What's on Your Pet's Mind

Carol Stark says she can tell when her dog Chauncey wants attention. Chauncey, a four-year-old golden retriever, will pick some trash out of the garbage can.

"Then," says Carol, "she prances around the living room like she's saying, 'Look what I have.' She does it even though she knows she's not supposed to."

Carol isn't the only pet owner who believes her pet's actions communicate its feelings. There are whole books that describe the meaning of animal body language. They claim if the animal's tail is up, for example, the critter is showing a certain feeling. If its ears are down, it's showing a different feeling.

But can you really know for sure what your pets are telling you? Not all pet experts think so. Dr. Linda Goodloe is an animal behaviorist in New York City.

According to Goodloe, animals' actions don't always speak louder than words.

For example, most people assume that when a dog's tail is up, it's in a friendly mood. But many dogs don't raise their tails that high to begin with. "If it's a dog that's a little more submissive," says Goodloe, "the tail may wag, but it may be a little lower. You can't say that the tail up means it's friendly. It often is, but not always."

And like people, animals may feel more than one emotion at a time. "A dog may be curious and want to greet you, but also a little fearful," says Goodloe. "Even if its tail is wagging, you could get bitten. You have to look at the situation and the individual dog."

Getting Emotional

Many pet owners are certain their pet can tell how they're feeling too. "If I'm sad," Carol said, "Chauncey comes over to me and looks into my eyes as if to say, 'It's okay.'"

But according to Goodloe, pets don't have the ability to pick up on our emotions as much as we think.

That's because animals aren't able to show the kinds of emotions people have. "People seem to need to believe that this mental connection exists," Goodloe says. "But the person may be reading something into the behavior that isn't there."

In fact, your pet may not treat you much differently than it would another human—or another dog or cat. "Dogs that want to play do a bow with their front paws down," says Goodloe. "They'll do that with a cat, with a human, or with another dog."

Carol has seen that kind of behavior in Chauncey. "If I go toward her on all fours and put my head down," she says, "she'll play rougher, like she's playing with another dog."

All in the Past

To understand how your pet communicates, it helps to know something about its ancestors. Take dogs. They are related to wolves. Wolves hunt and hang out in packs. In a group, wolves have a pecking order. Wolves let themselves be pushed around by a more dominant wolf.

Dogs act a lot like wolves. They like to be part of a family—including your family. If your dog howls when you leave him alone, it isn't necessarily feeling sad that you're not there. It may be saying, "I've been separated from the pack. I have to howl to let them know where I am."

A dog also accepts its owner as "top dog." Much of what it communicates is that you are boss. This is usually why a dog won't meet its master's eyes and why it rolls over and shows its belly, swallows, or cringes.

Pack animals have to be able to get their point across to others in their group. That's why dogs are so expressive.

So how do you communicate with your pet? The best way is to remember it's an animal—not a small human friend. "Learn how animals look at the world," advises Dr. Goodloe. "They don't see or hear the same things." When you see things through your pet's eyes, you'll really understand what it's saying.

	Happy	Frightened	Threatened	Hurt/In Pain	Possessive
Guinea Pig	Leaps straight in the air with back curved	Squeals	Rises up with stiff legs, freezes	Squeals and shrieks	Marks items with scent
Cat	Relaxes tail, slants eyes, purrs	Crouches, flattens ears	Raises tail, flicks tail tip back and forth	Purrs, pulls ears back	Rubs its head or claws on an object
Dog	Wags tail, perks up ears	Straightens or lowers tail, flattens ears	Bares teeth, stiffens legs	Growls, snaps out	Barks, snarls

Generalizing

- **Generalizing** is making a statement about what several people or things have in common.

- This is a generalization: *Many people like popcorn.* Clue words such as *many* and *most* can signal generalizations.

- A valid generalization is supported by facts and logic. A faulty generalization is not.

Read "A Special Family" from *We Don't Look Like Our Mom and Dad* by Harriet Langsam Sobol.

We
Don't Look Like
Our Mom and Dad

Write About It

1. *Many Asian children have been adopted by American families.* What helps you know that this statement is a generalization?

2. Think about this generalization: *Everyone in a family is biologically related.* Is it valid or faulty? Why?

3. What generalization can you make about families, based on what you read in the selection? Are there facts to support your generalization?

A Special Family

by Harriet Langsam Sobol

The Levins are a family. Eric and Joshua Levin are brothers. Their dog is named Melby.

Eric plays the cello, and Joshua loves to play Frisbee. Both boys are adopted, and both are Korean by birth.

The Levins adopted them when they were very young. Eric, who is ten years old, was only a few months old when he became part of the Levin family. Joshua was two-and-a-half years old and is eleven now. Eric doesn't remember anything before he came to America, but Joshua has a few memories of his Korean foster family. Eric and Joshua are brothers through adoption. Each boy has a different biological mother, but in the Levin household they are brothers.

Sometimes when the family goes out to eat or to shop, people stare out of curiosity. The boys used to be embarrassed, but they are becoming accustomed to people's questioning looks.

There are many Asian children who have been adopted by American families, but Joshua and Eric aren't aware of it, because they are the only adopted Asian children in their school and neighborhood. There are other Asian children in school—Koreans, Chinese, and Japanese—but they all have Asian parents.

The Levins are not a typical family. No one in the family is biologically related to any of the others. Nevertheless they are a family, because they choose to be one. Like other families, they live together and play together. Most important, they share work and share love.

LOOK AHEAD

LOOKING FOR A HOME
from Orphan Train Rider: One Boy's True Story

BY ANDREA WARREN

In "Looking for a Home," Lee tells his story about being adopted. Read about Lee and make your own generalizations.

Vocabulary

Words to Know

determined	suspicious	awe
horrified	panicked	bitter
select		

Words with opposite meanings are called **antonyms.** Sometimes an antonym can be a clue that helps you figure out the meaning of an unknown word.

Read the paragraph below. Notice how *calm* helps you understand what *panicked* means.

The Wright Brothers

Wilbur and Orville Wright loved working together. Before these two brothers invented the airplane, many people were <u>suspicious</u> about the idea of a flying machine. Others were in <u>awe</u>. There were <u>bitter</u> arguments. "Humans should not fly," some said. Others answered, "We would pay them to <u>select</u> us to fly." The news that a passenger was killed during a test flight <u>horrified</u> people. Some who supported the Wrights' work <u>panicked</u> and would no longer help. The brothers tried to calm the fears of the public. They were <u>determined</u> to succeed.

Talk About It

Tell about a time you tried to succeed at something. Use some or all of the vocabulary words.

LOOKING FOR A HOME

from *Orphan Train Rider: One Boy's True Story*

BY ANDREA WARREN

Between 1854 and 1930, more than 200,000 children rode "orphan trains" in this country. These trains were part of a program that found homes for children who were orphans or whose parents could not take care of them. Most of the riders came from large cities in the East. The trains took them to other parts of the country, where interested families lined up to choose the children they wanted.

Lee Nailling and his brother, Leo, were taken to an orphanage because their mother had died and their father could not take care of his seven children. Lee felt like a prisoner in the orphanage, often suffering from hunger because of a lack of food. Having his meal taken away was a frequent punishment when Lee misbehaved.

Lee was excited about going on his first train ride. But just before the train left, his father came with Gerald, his three-year-old brother. Lee was told to keep his two brothers with him and to write to let his father know where they settled.

When Lee learned that he was on an orphan train, he was angry. He started thinking about getting away to find his father.

As Lee's train continued its journey, his worrying increased. How would he ever find his way back to New York? What was going to happen to him and his brothers?

As always, whenever the train stopped so that the children could get some exercise, people gathered to watch. After a few days on the train, the matron told the children that there would be stops in several towns. In these towns, people would have the chance to select children. But none of the children was sure what this meant. Lee tried not to think about it.

The next day the train stopped at a town, and instead of being allowed to play, the children were marched to a church and seated on the stage. A crowd of people began to talk to them, touch them, and ask them questions. None of the children had written medical records, but, as the children quickly learned, people had their own ways of deciding if a child was healthy and strong.

Lee remembers a farmer in overalls coming up to him and feeling his muscles. Then the man stuck his hand in Lee's mouth to feel his teeth. Lee forced himself not to bite the man. When Lee glared at him, the farmer moved away.

That day Lee saw a small boy in the group being led away from his older brother. The little boy was screaming.

"I knew that all the family those boys had was each other," Lee says. "Just like my brothers and me. And I knew this was going to happen to us. The amazing thing was that it hadn't yet. We were healthy youngsters, and someone looking for workers was bound to pick one of us sooner or later. There didn't seem to be a thing in the world I could do to prevent it. I got back on the train that day with such a sense of dread that I felt like the world was going to end. As far as I was concerned, that might be the best thing that could happen."

Lee and his brothers had been on the train more than a week when it stopped in Clarksville, Texas. Of the fifty children who had started the trip, twenty five had not yet been chosen by people in towns along the way. As much as

Lee had liked the train in the beginning, he was tired of the swaying motion, the grim matron, and the same food. He was exhausted, dirty, and in need of a haircut.

He stepped from the train and looked around at a vast, empty horizon. The soil was reddish. There were few trees, and the late-winter air felt warm and dry. Texas was as different from upstate New York as Lee could have imagined.

As usual, a crowd was there to meet the train and walk with the children as they made their way to an old hotel on the main street of the little town. Everyone spoke with an unfamiliar accent, saying "y'all" and "howdy."

At the hotel, the children were told to sit on chairs lined up on the stage. Lee, Leo, and Gerald sat together. Just like before, people began to look them over.

Then a man and his wife stopped in front of Gerald. The woman spoke softly to Gerald and he smiled at her. When she opened her arms, he went right to her. Without a word to Lee and Leo, the couple walked away, holding Gerald. Lee wanted to run after them, to stop them, or to ask them to take him and Leo too. But he knew that the moment he stood up, he would be ordered to sit down.

Lee's little brother Gerald was about five when this picture was taken.

He choked back tears while the couple signed papers in the back of the room. As they started to leave, Gerald realized what was happening and screamed out for Lee and Leo. Lee forced himself to try to block out the sound.

Then a gray-haired couple stood in front of Leo and began talking to him. Lee remembers thinking, "Now I'm going to lose Leo." And sure enough, the couple asked Leo if he would like to come home with them.

But this time something different happened. Leo gazed into the woman's kind face and said, "I want my brother to go too." Lee could hardly believe it when the man and woman looked at each other and nodded. They motioned both boys to go with them. The couple told the committee that their last name was Rodgers, and they had nine grown children. They had planned to take only one child, but were willing to try both boys.

Outside, Leo and Lee climbed into the Rodgers' model-T Ford. As they drove into the Texas countryside, Lee felt almost hopeful. Gerald was gone, but Lee would find him. No strangers were going to raise any of them. They *would* get back to New York. In the meantime, at least he and Leo were finally off the train and away from the matron. The brothers were together and this couple seemed nice. Lee hoped they would get good food to eat at the Rodgers' house. He was sick of sandwiches and fruit.

After a few days with Mr. and Mrs. Rodgers, Leo acted as though he had lived with them all his life. He called them Papa and Mama and became a favorite with their grown children. Lee hung back, not ready to trust any adult. He kept a careful eye on Leo. Unable to forget his experience at the orphanage, he ate his meals very fast so no one could take his food away.

By the end of the week he had begun to relax. He and Leo had spent hours exploring the farm, fishing in the pond, and chasing the chickens and hogs. Mrs. Rodgers had gotten both of them cleaned up, soaking them in the bathtub for a long time. She had washed their clothes and was talking about taking them into town for haircuts. Lee knew he needed one—his hair was so long it hung in his eyes.

When he heard a knock on the front door exactly one week after he had arrived, he thought nothing of it. "But when Mrs. Rodgers opened the door and the matron from the train came in, I panicked. What was she doing there? If there was one person on this earth I didn't want to see, it was that horrible woman who had stolen my pink envelope."

Mrs. Rodgers took Leo by the hand and told him to come with her. They left Lee alone with the matron. "All I remember her saying was, 'Get your things together. Mr. and Mrs. Rodgers have decided they can only keep one boy and they've settled on Leo. I've arranged for another couple to take you.'

"I told her I didn't want to go," says Lee, "but she said I had no choice in the matter. The next thing I knew I was in her car. She wasn't even going to let me say goodbye to Leo. But as the car started to pull away, Leo came around the corner of the house. He saw me with my face pressed to the window and he started to scream."

Leo and his new family

Lee watched helplessly as Leo ran after the car. The last thing Lee saw as the car left the farmyard was Mrs. Rodgers holding Leo and comforting him. By that evening, Lee had been left with an elderly farm couple who hardly seemed to know he was there. "I was as bitter as I could be," says Lee. "The only thing I was going to allow myself to think about was getting back to my father. It didn't matter how many places they took me."

During a dinner of greasy fried greens, no one said a word. Then the farmer told Lee to come along: It was time to bed down the hens and chicks. Lee followed the farmer to the chicken yard where he explained how the brood hens and their babies went into their wire cages at night for protection. During the day they walked around outside looking for food.

"I liked those little chicks," Lee remembers. "They were tiny and innocent and very soft to the touch. The old man didn't seem to mind when I picked them up and stroked them."

When Lee woke up the next morning he wanted to see the chicks. He pulled on his clothes, sneaked out of the house, and went to the chicken yard. By the time he reached the wire cages, his shoes were soaked from the heavy dew. Since the farmer had said the chicks spent the day outside, Lee began pulling up the cage doors so the clucking hens and their babies could come out.

At breakfast he said nothing about the chicks. He followed the farmer out to the chicken yard when it was time to start chores, eager to show what he had done. But when they got to the cages, there in the dewy grass were the baby chicks—all dead!

The old man frowned at him. "Did you open the cages?" he asked angrily. "Don't you know them chicks drowned in the early dew? They wasn't to come out till the sun dried it up!" Lee was horrified that he had killed the fuzzy creatures. He had just been trying to help.

The farmer made Lee bury the chicks and would barely speak to him. The woman, as usual, was silent. Lee was miserable. When the farmer and his wife could not see him, he cried about what he had done. Late that afternoon, when the matron pulled up in her car and told him to get in, he did not even look back. He sat silent in the back seat as the car bounced over the rough Texas roads.

"I was really upset at what was happening to me," Lee recalls. "I felt terrible about killing the chicks, but I hadn't known any better. I didn't even care where I was being taken. I was nine years old and life stunk."

By the time the matron left him with another family, in the little village of Manchester, Texas, Lee had no hope that things would work out. He barely looked around at the large, comfortable house, nor would he smile at tall, friendly Ben Nailling. Ben's wife, Ollie, was short and plump and had kind eyes. She took Lee into her warm kitchen and gave him apples and milk, but he ate very little.

"I just wasn't hungry," he says. "I was willing to give them credit for at least acting interested in me, but the interest was all theirs. As far as I was concerned, the sooner I could get out of there, the better."

It was growing dark as they showed Lee around the grounds and the barns, and introduced him to the horses. Ben pointed to the woodpile and asked Lee to stack some wood for the kitchen stove on the back porch. Lee was immediately suspicious.

"I remembered that farmer who felt my muscles and teeth. It looked to me like the Naillings thought they'd found themselves a chore boy. I turned to him and said, 'Do it yourself. I didn't come here to work for you.' I think my voice was really angry because it sort of surprised me. They both looked shocked. Ben grabbed me by the arm and gave me a hard swat on the behind. He said, 'Now look here, boy, if you're going to be part of this family, you'll pull your weight. That stove has to be fed and that's to be your job and you don't ever talk to your elders like that. I think your disrespect went too far.'

"Well, that was too much for me. I refused to talk to either one of them. I figured I had nothing to lose because I wasn't going to be there in the morning, that was for sure. I meant to run away that very night."

Later that evening, Ollie showed him around his new bedroom. "Go to bed now and we'll get a fresh start in the morning," she said, smiling. Lee looked around in awe. He'd never had a room of his own before. Often he had shared his bed. But he still was suspicious. "I decided it was just a trick to soften me up before they put me to work, and I was determined I wouldn't fall for it."

He climbed onto the big feather bed and sank down into its softness. Ollie came back and sat by him. She said she knew he was tired and she hoped he would sleep well. Then she tucked the covers around him and gave him a kiss on the cheek before she left the room.

"I couldn't remember the last time anyone had kissed me," Lee says. "It rekindled a memory in me—maybe of my mother. I started to cry and I buried my head in the pillow so they wouldn't hear me. I think I cried half the night."

The next morning, he awoke to Ben shaking him and telling him to get up for breakfast. His bedroom was flooded with sunshine.

"I was so surprised that it was already morning," Lee says. "I had planned to sneak out after the house was quiet. But I felt better after a good night's sleep and figured I could run away the next night. I got dressed and went to the kitchen, following my nose to all these delicious smells."

Ollie greeted him and told him they were going to eat in the dining room. "We only eat there on special occasions," she said. The table was heaped with ham, bacon, eggs, grits, biscuits, potatoes, jams, and jellies. Lee thought company must be coming, but saw only three place settings. After Ben motioned for him to sit, Lee immediately grabbed a biscuit and started to take a bite out of it, but Ollie stopped him. "We say grace first," she said, telling him to bow his head and close his eyes.

"I did what she told me, but I was wishing she would hurry up so I could eat. That food smelled so good," Lee says.

"Then I started to listen to her. She was thanking God out loud for the beautiful day and the recovered health of a friend who had been sick, and for the bounty of food we were about to enjoy. Then she said an amazing thing: 'Father, thank you for sending our new son to us, for the privilege of allowing us to raise him. We will try to be good parents to him.'

"I'm sure my jaw dropped in amazement. Somebody was actually thankful I was there? I had always felt like a bother to adults, but this woman was acting like she was glad I was there! I stole a glance at Ben. He smiled at me and said, 'We're happy you're with us, son. Now let's eat.'"

Ben, Lee, and Ollie Nailling

Lee stuffed himself. He could not remember when food had tasted so good. The more he ate, the more pleased the Naillings seemed to be. After breakfast they said they would take him to the store they owned to get him some new clothes, and then to the barbershop for that much-needed haircut.

Lee clearly remembers the walk down the lane into the village, Ben and Ollie on either side of him. They stopped at each of the six houses along the way, and at each one they introduced Lee as "our new son" and said how glad they were that he was with them. By the time Lee was fitted for new clothes and had his hair cut, he already knew some of the villagers by name and had met several children his own age.

By the end of the day, after another home-cooked meal, he had decided to give the new arrangement a chance, at least for a little while. The Naillings' house was beginning to feel like home.

About the Author

ANDREA WARREN

Before Andrea Warren became a full-time writer, she was a history teacher who taught about the past with true stories, full of details and description. Her philosophy was, and still is, that the best way to learn history is through stories of the people who lived it—people such as grandparents and elderly neighbors. These people are our "historical treasures," she says.

One such historical treasure is Lee Nailling, whom Ms. Warren met and interviewed before writing *Orphan Train Rider*. She was inspired to write the book after hearing Lee's story and realizing that people today know very little about the orphan trains of the early 1900s. Over five hundred of those orphans are still alive today, and Ms. Warren believes that "we really need to hear their stories." After a great deal of research and interviews with dozens of orphan train riders, Ms. Warren created her book that tells history as a true-to-life story.

Reader Response

Open for Discussion

Pick words from the list that best describe your reactions to different parts of "Looking for a Home." Tell why you felt that way.

glad   surprised   excited

sad   disappointed   frustrated

Comprehension Check

1. How did Lee feel while he was at the Rodgerses' home and at the elderly couple's farm? What did he keep thinking about? Use evidence from the selection to support your answer.

2. At one of the orphan train stops, a farmer in overalls felt Lee's muscles and teeth. After Lee arrived at the Naillings' home, he thought of the farmer again. Why?

3. If you were Lee, would you be so happy with the Naillings that you would never try to find your brothers or father again? Explain, using details from the selection.

4. Now that you've read "Looking for a Home," **generalize** about how people selected children from the orphan trains. (Generalizing)

5. From this selection, can we **generalize** that most orphan train children liked their new homes? Why or why not? (Generalizing)

Test Prep

Look Back and Write

Look back at pages 73–75. How was Lee Nailling responsible for the deaths of the baby chicks? Tell about his specific actions. What happens to him because of his actions?

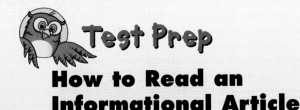

Test Prep

How to Read an Informational Article

1. Preview

- Notice that the title is in question form. What does this lead you to expect about the article itself?

- Look at the pictures and the material in boxes. What tells you that these are from the historical time the article talks about?

2. Read and Collect Information

- Read the article to find out how orphan trains operated. As you read, take notes in a chart like this:

How children were treated	Why
Some orphans were never legally adopted.	Adoption was not common in the U.S.

3. Think and Connect

Think about "Looking for a Home." Then review your notes on "What Were Orphan Trains?"

If Lee Nailling could have known the history of orphan trains, do you think it would have made his own experience any easier? Give details to support your answer.

What Were Orphan Trains?

by Andrea Warren

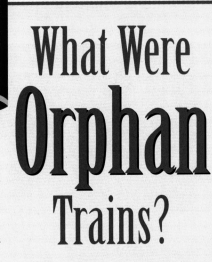

Few of the children who climbed aboard orphan trains understood what was happening to them. Once they realized why they were taking the trip, their feelings differed. If they had been passed around from relative to relative, lived on the streets, been abused by their parents, or been in an orphanage, then they were likely to be pleased at the thought of finding a new family. Others, like Lee, did not want a new family and were angry to find themselves being taken to new homes.

In the early days of the trains, the Children's Aid Society sometimes took children off the streets or out of prison, but most of them came from orphanages. A few were signed

Orphan train riders ready to leave New York City and travel to Weatherford, Texas, in October 1912

over to the society by parents who wanted their children to have a chance for a better life than they could give them. Some children found their way to the society by themselves and asked to go on the trains. Once a company of children was formed, they were bathed and given two sets of new clothes, including a hat, a coat, and shoes. Sometimes they were given a Bible. Many were taught manners—such as to eat neatly and say "thank you"—so that they would make a good impression on prospective parents. A number was pinned to their clothing to help the adults keep track of them during the trip.

Agents who worked for the Children's Aid Society looked for towns along the railroad tracks that were interested in having an orphan train stop there. Then they put up signs saying that a train was coming and set up the local screening committee—the people who would approve the families who wanted to choose a child.

Charles Loring Brace did not want families to adopt the children until it was clear that a child and a family were a good match for each other. That way the arrangement was not bound by law, and either the child or the parents could end it if it was not a success. If that happened, the society would try to find the child another home. In fact, most of the early orphan train riders were never legally adopted, even if the child and family grew to love each other. Adoption was not common in the United States until the 1900s. Still, many of the children used their new family's name.

Sometimes children lived with several families before finding one they could stay with. Claretta Carman Miller of Colorado and her two sisters were neglected by their parents, so they were taken away from their home and put on an orphan train. Claretta was chosen by a family with nine children. They did not want another child—they wanted a servant.

A society agent tried to visit each child every year, but as the program grew bigger, that became difficult. Fortunately an agent visited Claretta after only two weeks and immediately took her away from the family. She endured bad treatment in two more homes before she arrived at the Carman farm late one rainy night. Mrs. Carman was a gentle, kind woman. It took her a year to nurse the sickly little girl back to health. With the Carmans, Claretta found loving parents and a real home at last.

If the birth parents were still alive, the society would try to get their written permission before sending a child west. But some parents did not understand what they were signing. When they tried to get their children back, the parents learned they were gone and could not be traced.

Charles Loring Brace, Founder of the Children's Aid Society

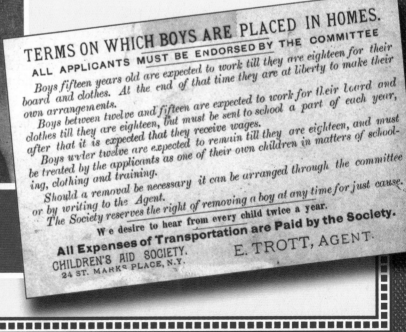

TERMS ON WHICH BOYS ARE PLACED IN HOMES.

ALL APPLICANTS MUST BE ENDORSED BY THE COMMITTEE

Boys fifteen years old are expected to work till they are eighteen for their board and clothes. At the end of that time they are at liberty to make their own arrangements.

Boys between twelve and fifteen are expected to work for their board and clothes till they are eighteen, but must be sent to school a part of each year, after that it is expected that they receive wages.

Boys under twelve are expected to remain till they are eighteen, and must be treated by the applicants as one of their own children in matters of schooling, clothing and training.

Should a removal be necessary it can be arranged through the committee or by writing to the Agent.

The Society reserves the right of removing a boy at any time for just cause.

We desire to hear from every child twice a year.

All Expenses of Transportation are Paid by the Society.

CHILDREN'S AID SOCIETY.
24 ST. MARKS PLACE, N.Y.

E. TROTT, AGENT.

At first, the Children's Aid Society had only refused to give information to parents who had abused their children. Then the society stopped letting any parents know where their children were. Brace believed it was best for children to break with the past and start a new life, so once a child left on a train, neither parent nor child knew how to find each other.

Children were not allowed to bring any keepsakes with them, although some managed to smuggle a beloved photograph or locket on the journey west. Some older children did know how to reach their parents and stayed in touch with them. Others ran away and returned to their parents.

For most orphan train riders, who either did not remember their families or did not know how to find them, being denied information about themselves and their birth families often led to anger and frustration later in life. One rider was arrested as an adult for trying to steal his records. Some agencies would give basic facts like date and place of birth or copies of birth certificates; but few would reveal reasons why the parents had given up their children.

Arthur Field Smith of New Jersey, who rode an orphan train to Iowa in 1922, feels strongly that orphans should have access to any information that exists about them: "For medical and every other reason, orphans and their families have just as much right to know about themselves as those who are not orphans. There is stigma enough attached to being an orphan," he says.

Most placements were successful, and the program grew. During the first twenty years an average of three thousand children rode the orphan trains each year. Brace continued to raise the needed money through his speeches and his writing. Railroads gave discount fares to the children, and wealthy people sometimes paid for whole trainloads of children.

Unfortunately, many children who needed homes were not allowed to go on the trains. It was always difficult to find homes for older children, and while some teenagers as old as seventeen were successfully placed, fourteen was usually the oldest a rider could be. It was always easiest to find homes for babies.

Children who were physically or mentally handicapped or sickly were usually left behind. So were children who had repeatedly committed crimes. They, too, would have been difficult to place. And almost all of the children who made the trip were white. The Midwest had been settled largely by white Europeans, mainly Germans, Scandinavians, English, and Irish. Most of the orphan train riders had those same backgrounds. The society knew that these children had the best chance of being chosen.

An advertisement in the Tecumseh, Nebraska, newspaper in 1893 announcing that an orphan train was coming to town listed children whom Brace felt would find homes. Part of it read as shown at the top of the page.

From three or four to as many as three hundred children went on one train for a trip that could last for a few days or a few weeks. Sometimes the children filled a whole car or even several cars. Older children cared for younger ones. Sometimes passengers and trainmen helped agents care for the children or gave money for food and milk. People also liked buying candy for them. At regular train stops, the children got off to play and run off energy.

Sometimes the children were lined up for people to see every time their train pulled into a station. Those not selected by townspeople got back on the train and went to the next town. But usually a company of children traveled to a specific place and children were not chosen along the way.

The success of Brace's orphan trains inspired several other groups to begin their own trains. Aside from the Children's Aid Society, the Foundling Hospital in New York City sent the largest number of children west.

Cause and Effect

- A **cause** is why something happens. An **effect** is what happens.

- When you read, sometimes clue words such as *because* and *since* signal a cause and effect relationship. Sometimes there are no clue words.

- Sometimes the author does not tell a cause, and you need to think about why something happened.

- A cause may have more than one effect, and an effect may have more than one cause.

Read "Baseball and Brothers" from "Yankee Doodle Shortstop" by Helen J. Hinterberg from *Cricket*.

Write About It

1. Meg has mixed feelings about playing baseball. What causes these feelings?

2. What causes Meg's mother to want her to sing to Charles? What effect does the song have on him?

Baseball and Brothers

by Helen J. Hinterberg

"I hate baseball."

"You love baseball."

Meg sighed. "I love it and I hate it, I guess."

Her mother was spooning strained peas into Meg's baby brother, Charles. "Don't worry, honey. It'll work out. You made the team."

Meg traced a pattern on the tablecloth with her finger. "What's the point anyway? Girls can't play in the major leagues. Might as well give it up now before I waste any more time."

Mrs. O'Malley sat down at the table and met Meg's unhappy gaze. "I know there's no professional baseball for women, honey. I knew it when I was your age. I played anyway. I loved it."

Meg smiled for the first time that day. "You still play."

"You bet I do. I'm the best player in the coed, over-35 league. I carry my team. And I still love it. Now, do me a favor and sing 'Yankee Doodle' to your brother. It'll get your mind off your problems and it'll get more peas into Charles."

Charles was thirteen months old. "Yankee Doodle Dandy" was his favorite song. It always cheered him up. Meg had sung it to him so many times that singing it was as easy as breathing. Launching into it now put a wet grin on Charles's face, but it didn't keep Meg from thinking about baseball.

If she didn't love it so much, she would walk away from it without a backward glance. But she loved every single thing about it, from the uniforms that never fit quite right, to the mouthful of dust she inhaled every time she slid into a base; from the painful sting in her hand when a line drive slammed into her glove, to the fierce jolt that leaped up her arm when she hit a ball hard.

LOOK AHEAD

In "Meeting Mr. Henry," Jason learns something new about baseball. As you read, pay attention to what happens in the story and why it happens.

Vocabulary

Words to Know

challenging corridors cut
custodian   valuable

When you read, you may come across a word you don't know. To figure out its meaning, look for clues in the surrounding words or sentences. A clue might be found in specific details given near the unknown word.

Notice how *custodian* is used in the paragraph below. Find the specific details in the same sentence. What do you think *custodian* means?

Mr. Hayes

As I walked through the school corridors, I thought about my writing assignment. Mrs. Barr had said, "I am challenging you to write about someone who has done something valuable for our town." Whom could I write about? I knew the answer when I saw Mr. Hayes, our school custodian, standing with his broom, ready to clean. Years ago, Mr. Hayes had played baseball in a major league but had gotten cut from the team. He moved to our town, joined our baseball team, and pitched one winning game after another. Mr. Hayes helped make us winners!

Talk About It

Tell about a favorite sport. Use as many vocabulary words as you can.

Meeting Mr. Henry

from *Finding Buck McHenry*

by Alfred Slote

Eleven-year-old Jason Ross has always played on the Baer Machine baseball team. During the last practice game of the spring, Jason is called out. The coach says it's because Jason daydreams about baseball cards instead of thinking about the game. The coach also says that a new Little League team will be forming and that one member of the Baer Machine will go to that team. Jason feels terrible when he learns that he's the one.

Two years ago when I was in third grade, my family moved across town. I don't go to Eberwoods School anymore, but I remembered Mr. Henry, the custodian there, real well. He was a tall, gray-haired old man who always had a friendly word for everyone as he pushed his broom down the hall. He knew every kid's name too.

I doubted he'd remember me now, though.

Mr. Henry was sitting by the back door of the school. The school's up a slight hill past center field. It was like center-field bleachers in Tiger Stadium. If Mr. Henry had been out there awhile, he probably had seen our intrasquad game.

"Hi, Mr. Henry," I said. "I got some bases for you."

"I see that, boy." He got up. "And I thank you for bringing 'em up here."

"That's okay."

He peered down at me. "Say, aren't you the one made that last out?"

I felt my face turn red all over again. This just wasn't my day. "Yes, sir."

He laughed. "Well, you sure run a lot harder picking up those bases than you run to first."

"Did *you* think I was out, Mr. Henry?"

"You were out by four feet. Four big feet. You stayed in that batter's box so long I thought the train was going to leave without you."

I laughed. It was funny how he put it. It didn't hurt. "I guess maybe I *was* out."

"You were out all right. But you got the right attitude, bouncing back like you did, running hard to pick up bases. I always said you can't keep a good man down. All right, you can give me those bases now and head on back to your team."

I looked back at the diamond. They were still there. I'd have to go back for my bike and glove. Better to hang out here till they were gone. I didn't want any more "see ya's."

"I can take the bases into the gym for you, Mr. Henry."

"That's nice of you, son. But your coach is going to be mad at you if you don't get back right away. I'll take them from you."

I held on tight to the bases. "He's not my coach anymore." I tried to sound cheerful about it. "He just cut me from the team. I don't want to go back there till they're gone."

Mr. Henry's lips pursed in a surprised silent whistle. "He cut you?"

"Yes, sir."

"For not beating out that ground ball?"

"I guess so."

His tongue made "tsk, tsk" sounds against his front teeth. "Well, that's how it goes sometimes. Sometimes they cut the best along with the worst."

"Thanks, but I'm not the best."

"You aren't the worst either." He held the back door open for me. "I've seen lots better ballplayers than you cut from ball clubs." I marched into the school with my arms full of bases. I could hear the sounds of the adult basketball game coming from the gym.

"You ever hear of Willie Mays, boy?"

"Ace 675," I said.

"What's that?"

"That's the number of my 1955 Mays baseball card. It's a pretty valuable card. It's not worth near as much as a 1952 Mickey Mantle, but it's worth a lot."

"How come?"

"How come what?"

"How come Willie Mays isn't worth as much as Mickey Mantle?"

"I don't know." Nobody'd ever asked me that before. It wasn't the kind of thing you ever thought about. It was enough to know the prices of baseball cards. They were always changing.

"Willie Mays was a greater player, wasn't he? They played the same position in the same years, didn't they? Willie Mays

92

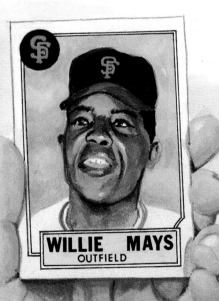

had better numbers, didn't he?" Mr. Henry was challenging me. I wondered what he was so upset about.

"I think Mays did have better stats than Mantle."

"Well, if Willie Mays had better numbers than Mickey Mantle and he was a better ballplayer, how come his card's worth less?"

"I don't know."

"You ought to find out. You've got to think about those things, young man. You've got to ask yourself how come things are the way they are."

Jim Davis, who owned The Grandstand, would know, I thought. I'd stop there on the way home and ask him.

"Willie Mays was the greatest center fielder who ever lived," Mr. Henry said emphatically.

"If he was so great, Mr. Henry, how come he got cut?"

Mr. Henry blinked. Then he laughed. "You come back with a good pitch, boy."

"Well, you said he got cut."

"He did get cut. And they were right to cut him."

"Who cut him?"

"The New York Giants when he first came into the major leagues. Willie was strikin' out all the time. He was too anxious to show the New York folks that he'd be as good up there as he'd been with the Birmingham Black Barons."

"The Birmingham who?"

"The Birmingham Black Barons. Willie played center field for them when he was sixteen." Mr. Henry's voice turned soft as he began to remember. "Willie Mays was a boy among men way

back then, but you could see the greatness in him already. He could run like a deer, hit like a mule, and throw you out from deep center field. He could do it all. It was there from the beginning. I saw it with my own eyes."

I stared at Mr. Henry. He'd seen Willie Mays play when he was sixteen?

"Willie Mays was put on Earth to play baseball. Not football. Not basketball. Just baseball. It was in his chromosomes. You know what chromosomes are, boy?"

"They're what makes us look like our parents."

"That's right. Well, Willie Mays had chromosomes for baseball."

"Wow."

"The Black Barons were good. But when he played for them, Willie made them great."

"I never heard of them."

"That right?" He didn't seem surprised. "You probably never heard of the Kansas City Monarchs neither."

"No, sir."

"Or the Homestead Grays?"

I shook my head.

"Or the best of them all. The Pittsburgh Crawfords?"

Was he making these teams up? I went on shaking my head.

"Josh Gibson caught for the Crawfords. Now I suspect you may have heard of Josh Gibson."

I was really embarrassed. "No, sir." This was kind of awful. I had over two thousand baseball cards and there wasn't a Josh Gibson on any of them. Nor a Crawford nor a Homestead Gray.

"Josh Gibson was only the greatest hitter who ever lived. That's all he was."

"Was he a better hitter than Willie Mays, Mr. Henry?"

"Yes, he was. He was better than Hank Aaron. Better than Mickey Mantle, Ted Williams. Better than Pete Rose, George Brett, Wade Boggs, your Cansecos and Strawberries. Better than

any of your players today. You name 'em and Josh was better than. Better than Ty Cobb and Babe Ruth. Why, I saw Josh hit a home run out of Yankee Stadium. Up and over and out of it. Now Babe Ruth, great as he was, and I'm not denying his greatness, Babe Ruth never did that."

Mr. Henry looked at me under my load of bases. They were getting heavy. I was hoping he'd offer to take them again. But he didn't.

"I expect you *have* heard of Satchel Paige?"

Finally I'd heard of someone beside Willie Mays. "Sure. He pitched for the Cleveland Indians." I had a 1949 Satchel Paige (Ace 129).

"Well, before Satchel pitched in the so-called big leagues, he pitched for the Pittsburgh Crawfords. And Josh Gibson was his catcher. What a pair they were. Old Josh in his rocking-chair squat and Paige firing those bullets. I tell you another great one was on the Crawfords those years. Cool Papa Bell. You hear of him?"

Here we go again, I thought. "No, sir," I said.

"Fastest man ever to play the game. Cool Papa was so fast, he'd often get hit by his own line drives."

I laughed. Mr. Henry stopped walking. He stopped so suddenly, I bumped into him with the bases. We were smack in the middle of the school where the two main corridors intersected.

"What's your name, boy?"

"Jason Ross."

"You don't look familiar. You go to school here?"

"I used to. We moved when I was in third grade. I go to Sampson Park School now."

"That's okay. It doesn't matter where you go so long as you go. Now, Jason Ross, you set those bases down."

"Here?"

"That's right. Right there on the floor."

I didn't hesitate. I set down the bases on the floor. And rubbed my arms and wrists to get the circulation back.

Mr. Henry didn't notice. He had taken a key from his big key ring attached to his belt and was unlocking a closet door that said on the front: MACK HENRY, CUSTODIAN.

"You know why you run so slow to first, Jason Ross?"

"No, sir."

"You stood there at the plate looking at where you hit the ball."

The second he said that, I knew that was just what I'd done. I'd stood there watching Art back up on my ground ball.

"Nobody in this world can run and look at the same time."

He rummaged around in the closet and came out with a long push broom.

Had I brought dirt in with my spikes? I didn't see any. Though I probably shouldn't be wearing baseball shoes inside the school. They could ruin the wax on the floors. Luckily, Mr. Henry hadn't spotted my shoes.

"You can see without looking. You've *got* to see without looking."

> "Cool Papa was so fast, he'd often get hit by his own line drives."

He unscrewed the stick from the broom and tossed it at me.

I caught it. It would have bopped me on the nose if I hadn't.

"I'm going to prove that to you, Jason Ross. That's your bat."

He picked up two of the bases, leaving one near me. He marched down the hall with the other two and dropped one of them at his feet.

"All right, Jason Ross," he called down the hall to me, "step up to the plate."

I didn't move. I wanted to know what he was going to do first.

"C'mon, boy. I haven't got all day. That's home plate there. You just step up to it."

He was standing about sixty feet from me.

"Jason, you are trying my patience. Get in there."

Still I didn't move. I don't like to do things unless I know why I'm doing them.

"Jason," he said softly, "this lesson isn't going to hurt you any. It might even do you some good. Now get up there and get your bat back."

What kind of lesson was he talking about? Well, there was only one way to find out. I stepped up to the plate. At least no one was watching.

"Good. Now get your front elbow up a bit. That's it. Now, boy, as soon as this imaginary ball arrives, you are going to hit an imaginary ground ball down that other corridor. That's where third base is. But you are not going to look once at where you hit the ball. You can see out of the corner of your eye where your ball went. You can see without turning your head to look. You are just going to run like the wind to this base, which is first base. You are going to run, Jason Ross, like there were hot coals under your feet. You understand me?"

"Yes, sir."

"Get set now. I'm throwing smoke."

And then right there in the middle of Eberwoods School, old, gray-haired Mr. Henry, the school custodian, went into a full windup.

And as he did, something strange happened. He didn't look so old. He looked tall and young and powerful as he kicked high and came down over his head with a smooth motion and fired the imaginary ball.

I swung.

"Run!" he yelled.

I ran. I didn't look down the other corridor where the imaginary ball went. I lifted my feet and ran hard and hit first base with my left shoe. The base slid far down the smooth, waxed floor.

Mr. Henry laughed and slapped me on the back. "Now, if you'd moved like that when you hit that ground ball, you'd still be on your team. You run like that and you'll be getting your share of hits and then some."

He walked back to home plate. "You know who you remind me of, son?"

I shook my head.

"Roy Campanella. You ever hear of him?"

"Sure. He played with the Brooklyn Dodgers. I've got two Ace Campanella cards."

"Well, before that, my friend, he played with the Baltimore Elite Giants and some other clubs. Just like Jackie Robinson—you've surely heard of him—played with the Monarchs before he was signed by Mr. Branch Rickey and sent to Montreal. Campy now, he was chubby like you. And he was a catcher too. And he could beat out ground balls!"

"How'd you know I was a catcher, Mr. Henry?"

"I've seen you catching."

"Well, I don't catch very much. I don't play very much."

"You will if you hit. If you hit, they've got to play you. Now you go back and tell that coach of yours to give you another chance."

Mr. Henry screwed the stick back into the broom and leaned it against the shelves of cleaning powder, wax, shelves of paper towels, toilet paper, soaps. Then he shut and locked the door that said MACK HENRY, CUSTODIAN on it. He picked up home plate.

"He won't give me another chance, Mr. Henry. I'm gonna be on a new team."

"Well then you're just going to have to come back with your new team and beat that man's socks off. Speaking of which, boy, before you take another step, you take those spikes off. You're wrecking my floor."

And with that he went off toward the gym carrying the bases as though they weighed nothing.

I had to laugh. He'd just proved that you could see without looking. I walked out of the school in my socks. The team meeting was over. The diamond was empty. I sat down on the grass and put my shoes back on. Then I raced over to my bike and glove. I wanted to get down to The Grandstand as fast as possible and check on those players and teams he'd mentioned. If they were real—those Crawfords and Monarchs and Black Barons and Cool Papa Bells and Josh Gibsons—then there'd be baseball cards for them.

Jim Davis down at The Grandstand was always saying, "Truth's in the cards." I believed that. I hurried down there.

About the Author

Alfred Slote

Alfred Slote had always been interested in sports, especially baseball. So it was not surprising that he became involved with his son's Little League teams. It was his son, John, who suggested that he write about children's sports. Mr. Slote took his son's advice and has since written many books about Little League baseball players.

Mr. Slote does not think of his novels as books about baseball. Instead he feels that he writes about young people and what happens to them. He likes to explore how his characters react to challenges and problems. Baseball just happens to be the background.

In addition to writing about baseball players, Mr. Slote has written books about hockey, tennis, and soccer players. He has also written a series of science fiction novels. Whether writing about sports or robots, Mr. Slote introduces characters many readers have been happy to meet.

Reader Response

Open for Discussion

Which scene in the story sticks out most in your mind? Why?

Comprehension Check

1. Mr. Henry says that Willie Mays had chromosomes for baseball. What does he mean?

2. What is Mr. Henry's strategy for helping Jason get more playing time in baseball games? Find details to support your answer.

3. Jason has over two thousand baseball cards, but he has never heard of Josh Gibson or Cool Papa Bell. Why do you think Jason doesn't know anything about them?

4. What **causes** Mr. Henry to help Jason practice his hitting and running skills? (Cause and Effect)

5. Mr. Henry pitches an imaginary ball to Jason. What does Jason see as an **effect** of this experience on Mr. Henry? Explain why you think this happens, using evidence from the story. (Cause and Effect)

Test Prep

Look Back and Write

Look back at pages 92–102. How important are baseball cards to Jason? Support your answer with what he says and does.

Test Prep

How to Read a Poem

1. Preview

- Sometimes the title of a poem tells you what it is about, but sometimes it does not. What kind of title do you think this is? Why?

- Some poems have rhyme, and some have rhythm. Some have both. Does this poem have either rhyme or rhythm? How can you tell?

2. Read and Listen

- Read the poem—out loud, if you can. Listen for special ways language is used.

- Jot down words and phrases you especially like.

3. Think and Connect

Think about "Meeting Mr. Henry." Look at the words and phrases you jotted down from the poem.

Which words and phrases from the poem help explain what there is about baseball that makes Jason Ross and Mr. Henry like it so much?

ANALYSIS *of* BASEBALL

by May Swenson

It's about
the ball,
the bat,
and the mitt.
Ball hits
bat, or it
hits mitt.
Bat doesn't
hit ball, bat
meets it.
Ball bounces
off bat, flies
air, or thuds
ground (dud)
or it
fits mitt.

Ball fits
mitt, but
not all
the time.
Sometimes
ball gets hit
(pow) when bat
meets it,
and sails
to a place
where mitt
has to quit
in disgrace.
That's about
the bases
loaded,
about 40,000
fans exploded.

It's about
the ball,
the bat,
the mitt,
the bases
and the fans.
It's done
on a diamond,
and for fun.
It's about
home, and it's
about run.

Author's Purpose

- **Author's purpose** is the reason an author has for writing.

- Authors often have more than one reason for writing and don't usually state their reasons.

- Four common purposes for writing are to persuade, to inform, to entertain, and to express.

Read "First Steps" from *Alesia* by Eloise Greenfield and Alesia Revis.

Talk About It

1. Discuss the purpose or purposes the authors might have had for writing "First Steps."

2. Find sentences that show one of the authors' purposes.

ALESIA
By Eloise Greenfield
and Alesia Revis

Drawings by George Ford
Photographs by Sandra Turner Bond

FIRST STEPS

by Eloise Greenfield and Alesia Revis

When Alesia Revis was nine years old, she had an accident that left her unable to walk for years. Eloise Greenfield helps Alesia tell the story of the first day she walked again.

I remember the very first time I walked by myself. My sister Alexis was in high school then. She was on the basketball team, and she was going to take me to watch her practice. She went to open the car door for me while I sat in the den, but we were going to be late, so I said to myself, "Let me help her out a little." I decided I would try to walk to the front door.

Nobody else was home, so I had to do it by myself. I was kind of scared, but I wanted to do it, so I pushed up off the arms of my wheelchair and stood up. There wasn't going to be anything for me to hold on to, because if I leaned over to hold the furniture, I would fall. So I put my mind on walking and nothing else, and I just took a step, and another one, and then about three more, and I was at the door of the den. I grabbed the wall and started smiling. I was so happy I'd made it that far. I looked up to heaven and said, "Thank you."

I stayed there for a minute and got myself together. I was hoping my knee wouldn't give out, so I practiced bending it a little bit, and then I started across the living room. I didn't look in the mirror because I knew it would make me nervous to see myself walking. I looked straight ahead, and I made it to the next wall, and I said, "Thank you" again. Then I had to walk just a few more steps to get to the door—and I did it! I said, "I made it, I made it, thank you!"

I looked out to see where Alexis was. She was coming toward the house, and I was glad she was looking down because when she lifted her head to open the door, I was standing there waving at her. She was so surprised. She burst out laughing and gave me a great big hug.

LOOK AHEAD

In her autobiography, "Eloise Greenfield," the author Eloise Greenfield tells about her own childhood. As you read, think about her purpose or purposes for writing.

Vocabulary

Words to Know

| community | applied | council |
| in-between | project | resident |

Homophones are words such as *council* and *counsel*. They are pronounced the same but spelled differently. Homophones also have different meanings. To understand the difference between homophones, look for clues in the surrounding words and sentences.

Read the paragraph below. Why is *council* used and not *counsel*?

A Playground Plan

This summer my friends and I are working to make our <u>community</u> better. We are building a playground near the <u>project</u> where many of us live. A <u>council</u> of adults is advising us. To earn money, we <u>applied</u> for a permit to sell ice cream. One <u>resident</u> gave us a one-hundred-dollar donation! Most days we're busy; we relax on the slower, <u>in-between</u> days.

Write About It

Describe a project you've worked on. Use some or all of the vocabulary words.

Eloise  Greenfield

from Childtimes: A Three-Generation Memoir

by Eloise Glynn Little Greenfield

I'm Born

*T*hey say Mrs. Rovenia Mayo delivered more than a hundred babies in and around Parmele. I was one of them.

Mama wasn't expecting me until the end of the month, but I fooled her—I was ready to see the world on the seventeenth of May. Daddy was downtown playing checkers in front of Mr. Slim Gordon's store, and Mama wanted to wait until he came home, but his mother told her, "That young'un ain't going to wait for nobody! I'm going to get Mrs. Mayo now!"

I was born at six o'clock that evening. My great-aunt Mary was there to welcome me, and both of my grandmothers, Williamann Little and Pattie Ridley Jones. My brother Wilbur was there, too, but he didn't think my arrival was anything to get excited about—Mrs. Mayo had helped him make his grand entrance just the year before.

When Daddy came home, I was all of half an hour old, and did I give him a surprise!

First Days

*I*t's the first day of my life—my remembered life. I'm three years old, sitting on the floor with Mama. Cutting out a picture for my scrapbook, a picture of a loaf of bread. Cutting it out and pasting it in my book with the flour-and-water paste I had helped to make.

As far as I know, that was the day my life began.

My school life began two years later. Mama walked my cousin Vilma and me down P Street, through the open doors of John F. Cook School, and into Mrs. Staley's kindergarten class. Vilma and I were both scared. I was scared quiet; she was scared loud. I sat squeezed up in my chair, and Vilma screamed.

A Play

When I was in the fifth grade, I was famous for a whole day, and all because of a play. The teacher had given me a big part, and I didn't want it. I liked to be in plays where I could be part of a group, like being one of the talking trees, or dancing, or singing in the glee club. But having to talk by myself—*uh uh!*

I used to slide down in my chair and stare at my desk while the teacher was giving out the parts, so she wouldn't pay any attention to me, but this time it didn't work. She called on me anyway. I told her I didn't want to do it, but she said I had to. I guess she thought it would be good for me.

On the day of the play, I didn't make any mistakes. I remembered all of my lines. Only—nobody in the audience heard me. I couldn't make my voice come out loud.

For the rest of the day, I was famous. Children passing by my classroom door, children on the playground at lunchtime, kept pointing at me saying, "That's that girl! That's the one who didn't talk loud enough!"

I felt so bad, I wanted to go home. But one good thing came out of it all. The teacher was so angry, so upset, she told me that as long as I was in that school, I'd never have another chance to ruin one of her plays. And that was such good news, I could stand being famous for a day.

Langston Terrace

I fell in love with Langston Terrace the very first time I saw it. Our family had been living in two rooms of a three-story house when Mama and Daddy saw the newspaper article telling of the plans to build it. It was going to be a low-rent housing project in northeast Washington, and it would be named in honor of John Mercer Langston, the famous black lawyer, educator, and congressman.

So many people needed housing and wanted to live there, many more than there would be room for. They were all filling out applications, hoping to be one of the 274 families chosen. My parents filled out one too.

I didn't want to move. I knew our house was crowded— there were eleven of us, six adults and five children—but I didn't want to leave my friends, and I didn't want to go to a strange place and be the new person in a neighborhood and a school where most of the other children already knew each other. I was eight years old, and I had been to three schools. We had moved five times since we'd been in Washington, each time trying to get more space and a better place to live. But rent was high so we'd always lived in a house with relatives and friends, and shared the rent.

One of the people in our big household was Lillie, Daddy's cousin and Mama's best friend. She and her husband also applied for a place in the new project, and during the months that it was being built, Lillie and Mama would sometimes walk fifteen blocks just to stand and watch the workmen digging holes and laying bricks. They'd just stand there watching and wishing. And at home, that was all they could talk about. "When we get our new place . . ." "If we get our new place . . ."

Lillie got her good news first. I can still see her and Mama standing at the bottom of the hall steps, hugging and laughing and crying, happy for Lillie, then sitting on the steps, worrying and wishing again for Mama.

Finally, one evening, a woman came to the house with our good news, and Mama and Daddy went over and picked out the house they wanted. We moved on my ninth birthday. Wilbur, Gerald, and I went to school that morning from one house, and when Daddy came to pick us up, he took us home to another one. All the furniture had been moved while we were in school.

Langston Terrace was a lovely birthday present. It was built on a hill, a group of tan brick houses and apartments with a playground as its center. The red mud surrounding the concrete walks had not yet been covered with black soil and grass seed, and the holes that would soon be homes for young trees were filled with rainwater. But it still looked beautiful to me.

We had a whole house all to ourselves. Upstairs and downstairs. Two bedrooms, and the living room would be my bedroom at night. Best of all, I wasn't the only new person. Everybody was new to this new little community, and by the time school opened in the fall, we had gotten used to each other and had made friends with other children in the neighborhood too.

I guess most of the parents thought of the new place as an in-between place. They were glad to be there, but their dream was to save enough money to pay for a house that would be their own. Saving was hard, though, and slow, because each time somebody in a family got a raise on the job, it had to be reported to the manager of the project so that the rent could be raised too. Most people stayed years longer than they had planned to, but they didn't let that stop them from enjoying life.

They formed a resident council to look into any neighborhood problems that might come up. They started a choral group and presented music and poetry programs on Sunday evenings in the social room or on the playground. On weekends, they played horseshoes and softball and other games. They had a reading club that met once a week at the Langston branch of the public library, after it opened in the basement of one of the apartment buildings.

The library was very close to my house. I could leave by my back door and be there in two minutes. The playground was right in front of my house, and after my sister Vedie was born and we moved a few doors down to a three-bedroom house, I could just look out of my bedroom window to see if any of my friends were out playing.

There were so many games to play and things to do. We played hide-and-seek at the lamppost, paddle tennis and shuffleboard, dodge ball and jacks. We danced in fireplug showers, jumped rope to rhymes, played "Bouncy, Bouncy, Bally," swinging one leg over a bouncing ball, played baseball on a nearby field, had parties in the social room and bus trips to the beach. In the playroom, we played Ping-Pong and pool, learned to sew and embroider and crochet.

For us, Langston Terrace wasn't an in-between place. It was a growing-up place, a good growing-up place. Neighbors who cared, family and friends, and a lot of fun. Life was good. Not perfect, but good. We knew about problems, heard about them, saw them, lived through some hard ones ourselves, but our community wrapped itself around us, put itself between us and the hard knocks, to cushion the blows.

It's been many years since I moved away, but every once in a long while I go back, just to look at things and remember. The large stone animals that decorated the playground are still there. A walrus, a hippo, a frog, and two horses. They've started to crack now, but I remember when they first came to live with us. They were friends, to climb on or to lean against, or to gather around in the evening. You could sit on the frog's head and look way out over the city at the tall trees and rooftops.

Clockwise from left: Weston Little and children Gerald and Eloise, Langston Terrace, Washington D.C., 1938; Pattie Ridley Jones, 1971; Eloise Little, 1932.

Clockwise from left: Eloise Little and Bobby Greenfield, 1948; Vera and Vedie Little, Langston Terrace, 1949; Wilbur Little, 1976.

Nowadays, whenever I run into old friends, mostly at a funeral, or maybe a wedding, after we've talked about how we've been and what we've been doing, and how old our children are, we always end up talking about our childtime in our old neighborhood. And somebody will say, "One of these days we ought to have a Langston reunion." That's what we always called it, just "Langston," without the "Terrace." I guess because it sounded more homey. And that's what Langston was. It was home.

About the Author
Eloise Greenfield

In addition to the autobiography you just read, Eloise Greenfield has written fiction, nonfiction, and poetry. Why does she write? She has many reasons. She likes to create what she calls "word-madness," which is that special pull that makes it impossible to put a book down. Ms. Greenfield also wants to provide literature that shows black children and their history. Ms. Greenfield says, "I want to be one of those who can choose and order words that children will want to celebrate. I want to make them shout and laugh and blink back tears and care about themselves."

Reader Response

Open for Discussion

Think about Eloise Greenfield's description of Langston Terrace. Of all the things she wrote about, which do you think are the most important for a good home?

Comprehension Check

1. Why would Eloise Greenfield call the day she cut out pictures for a scrapbook the first day of her life?

2. What kind of person do you think Eloise Greenfield was when she was in the fifth grade? Find details to support your answer.

3. What comparison could Eloise Greenfield have been making when she said, "Our community wrapped itself around us, put itself between us and the hard knocks, to cushion the blows"?

4. Find sentences in "Eloise Greenfield" that show that one of the **author's purposes** for writing was to entertain. Give reasons for your answer. (Author's Purpose)

5. Besides entertaining, what other **purpose** do you think the author had for writing this selection? Give reasons for your answer. (Author's Purpose)

Test Prep
Look Back and Write

Look back at pages 116–117. What does Ms. Greenfield mean when she says that most parents thought of Langston Terrace as an "in-between place," but that the children didn't? Explain your answer, using details from the selection.

A City Street Today

by Anne Millard

STREETS AND NEIGHBORHOODS go through changes in every city and town. Conveniences and means of transportation are constantly being improved. New inventions change the ways that people live and work. The ways that people use their leisure time change too,

A STREET THROUGH TIME
A 12,000-YEAR WALK THROUGH HISTORY
Written by Dr. Anne Millard • Illustrated by Steve Noon

Apartments

Hair salon

Church

Dentist

Café

Museum

Bookshop

Museum shop

Clothes shop

Gymnasium

Jogger

Rowboat

but many of the old ways to have fun remain. Spot modern forms of communication, such as a cell phone or computer. What other forms of modern technology can you spot? What activities are people doing that do not use modern technology? What do you imagine this street will look like 50 years from now? 100 years from now?

Crane

Office block

Artist's studio

Lawyer's office

Bank's office

Bank

Safe

Town hall

Tourists

Streetcar

Motorboat

Dredger

Curb Your Cloud

by Richard Garcia

Reeling in my kite
one day, I found
that I had caught a cloud.
It followed me home
that night, nestling about
my house, keeping me warm.

In the morning
it rose back to the sky
but still dangled
my line. "Go home," I said,
but it followed me to school.

When I tied it to the bike rack
the other kids laughed.
But after I pulled it
into the playground
and let them stroke its icy fur,
they all wanted
to catch a cloud too.

Sometimes we sit
on a hillside and watch it
do its tricks. It can do
a whale, an airplane,
and is learning
to spell our names.

Since Hanna Moved Away

by Judith Viorst

The tires on my bike are flat.
The sky is grouchy gray.
At least it sure feels like that
Since Hanna moved away.

Chocolate ice cream tastes like prunes.
December's come to stay.
They've taken back the Mays and Junes
Since Hanna moved away.

Flowers smell like halibut.
Velvet feels like hay.
Every handsome dog's a mutt
Since Hanna moved away.

Nothing's fun to laugh about.
Nothing's fun to play.
They call me, but I won't come out
Since Hanna moved away.

August 8

by Norman Jordan

There is no break
between
 yesterday and today
 mother and son
 air and earth
 all are a part
 of the other
 like
 with this typewriter
 I am connected
 with these words
 and these words
 with this paper
 and this paper with you.

You and I

and

by Mary Ann Hoberman

Only one I in the whole wide world
And millions and millions of you,
But every you is an I to itself
And I am a you to you too!

But if I am a you and you are an I
And the opposite also is true,
It makes us both the same somehow
Yet splits us each in two.

It's more and more mysterious,
The more I think it through:
Every you everywhere in the world is an I;
Every I in the world is a you!

Wrap-Up

What are the important things in life?

What's the Goal?

Create a Game

Each of the characters or people in these selections has a goal—something that he or she wants.

1. **Choose** your favorite character or person. Think about what he or she wants. Write the goal in a few words.

2. **List** actions the character or person takes to reach the goal. List obstacles, or things that get in the way.

3. **Design** a game board. Write or draw the goal at the end of a path. Along the path, write or draw the actions and obstacles. Have you ever met these kinds of obstacles?

YOU CAN RUN AT THE SPEED OF LIGHT.

On the Air

Have a Talk Show Interview

Work with a partner to choose a character from these stories. One of you can be the character, and the other can be a talk show host.

1. **Discuss** what the character has accomplished or hopes to accomplish.

2. **Brainstorm** a list of questions the host can ask the character.

3. Go "on the air." **Present** your interview for an audience.

How to Learn

Compare Learning Styles

Leigh in "From the Diary of Leigh Botts," Faith in "Faith and Eddie," and Jason in "Meeting Mr. Henry" all learn something. They learn in various ways.

1. **Choose** two of the characters. Think about what they learn.

2. **Compare** the ways they learn. Make a chart with these headings.

Character	What is learned	How it's learned

3. **Tell** how you most enjoy learning things.

A New Home

Write a Journal

Faith in "Faith and Eddie," Lee in "Looking for a Home," and Eloise in "Eloise Greenfield" all experience moves to a new home.

1. **Choose** the character or person you like best.

2. **Reread** parts of the selection that interest you. Imagine being part of that character's or person's experience.

3. **Write** a journal entry for one day soon after you have moved. Tell how you feel about your new home. Use details to make your impressions seem real.

Test Talk

Understand the Question

Find Key Words in the Question

Before you can answer a test question, you have to understand it. A test about "Say What?" pages 62–63, might have this question.

Test Question 1

How does a pet dog's behavior with its owner show that it is related to wolves? Use details from the article to support your answer.

Read the question slowly.
Ask yourself "Who or what is this question about?" The words that tell who or what the question is about are **key words.**

Look for other key words in the question.
Often the first word of the question is a key word.

Turn the question into a statement.
Use the key words in a sentence that begins "I need to find out . . ."

See how one student makes sure she understands the question.

I've read the question. What is it about? Well, it's talking about a dog's behavior and how a dog is related to wolves. **Behavior** and **related to wolves**— those must be key words.

Okay, I'm going to read the question again. There's the key word **how,** and there's the key word **show.** I need to find out how a dog's actions show something—that it's related to wolves.

Try it!

Now use what you learned to understand these test questions about "Say What?" pages 62–63.

Test Question 2

Look at the chart on page 63. What are some differences in the ways pets show they are happy?

Test Question 3

What is the main idea of this article?

Ⓐ Animals communicate differently from humans.

Ⓑ You can think of a pet as a small human friend.

Ⓒ Animals don't really communicate at all.

Ⓓ Pets can often tell how their human owners are feeling.

My World and Yours

How do we show that we care about our surroundings?

Skill Lesson

Steps in a Process

- The actions you take to make something or to reach a goal are the **steps in a process.**

- When you read, look for clues that help you follow the steps. Clues may be numbers, illustrations, or words such as *first, next,* and *last.*

- If there are no clues, think of what you already know about how the process might be done.

- Try to picture the purpose or result of the process.

Read "First-Aid ABCs" from "Do You Know Your [first-aid] ABCs?" from *Current Health.*

Write About It

1. List the steps to take if you think someone is choking.

2. How does picturing the result of the Heimlich maneuver help you remember the steps?

First-Aid ABCs

from *Current Health*

Medical emergencies or accidents can happen at any time and to anyone. If you are going to help when they strike, you need first-aid training.

You can get first-aid training from the American Red Cross or possibly your local hospital, school, or scout group.

What would you do if you had to help in an emergency before you took first-aid training? Let's look at a real-life emergency and find out.

On your way to your favorite store in the mall, you pass the food court. You see two women eating lunch. Suddenly one of them stops talking and stands up, knocking over her chair. She is clutching her throat and trying to cough. You suspect she has a piece of food caught in her windpipe and she can't breathe.

What do you do? Ask the woman if she is choking. People who have something caught in their windpipe usually cannot talk. If they cannot speak, they cannot breathe.

Have someone call the emergency medical service in your area. Most of these services can be reached by dialing 911.

The next step is to perform the Heimlich maneuver, sometimes called the Heimlich hug.

1. Wrap your arms around the victim's waist and make a fist.
2. Place the thumb side of your fist on the middle of the victim's abdomen, just above the navel and well below the breastbone, and grasp your fist with your other hand.
3. Press your fist into the abdomen with a quick upward thrust.

Many times this action will pop the food or object out of the victim's mouth. You may have to do the thrusts a few times to get results, but keep trying. The reason it works is because the air that is trapped in the lungs is put under pressure, much like a cork in a bottle. This procedure should be shown and taught by an expert and then practiced.

1   2   3

LOOK AHEAD

The Diver and the Dolphins

In "The Diver and the Dolphins," a diver goes through another medical process, a step-by-step procedure to save the life of a baby dolphin.

Vocabulary

Words to Know

hovered	doomed	injured
desperate	dolphins	
communicate	cooperate	

Words with similar meanings are called **synonyms**. You can often figure out the meaning of an unknown word by finding a clue in the words around it. Sometimes this clue is a synonym.

Read the paragraph below. Notice how *wounded* helps you understand what *injured* means.

Helpers in the Deep

Dolphins are highly intelligent sea mammals. They cooperate well with other fish and are able to skillfully communicate with humans. Many dolphins take an interest in human activities. They've been known to save injured or wounded swimmers and desperate boaters who would have been doomed otherwise. Divers have often told stories about dolphins that have hovered near them, seeming to watch out for their safety.

Write About It

Tell about a movie or TV show about dolphins. Use as many vocabulary words as you can.

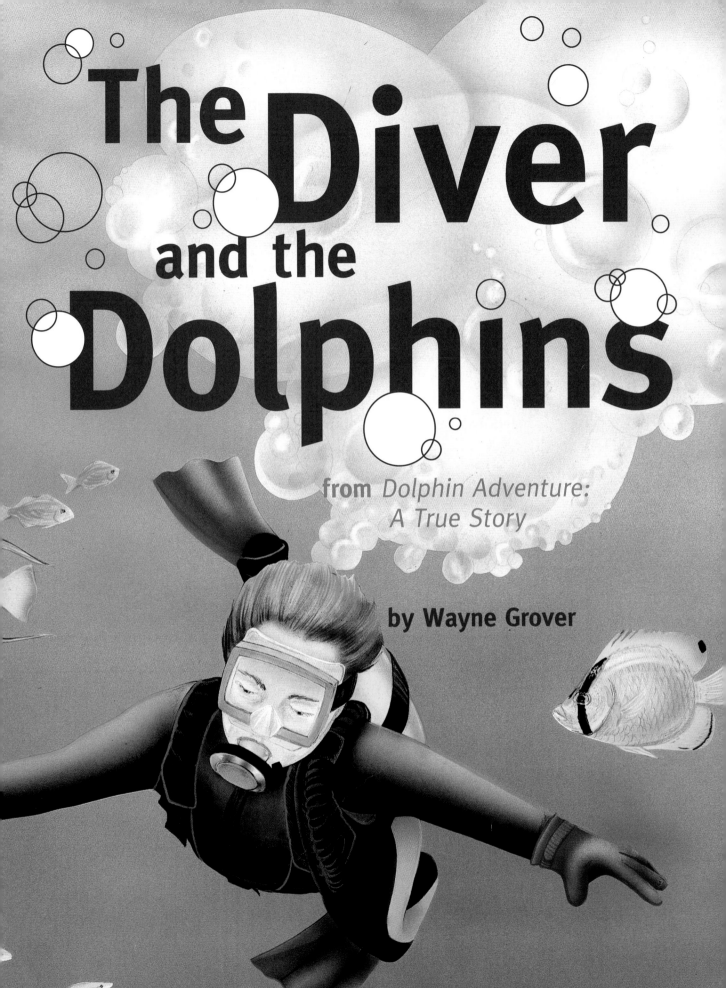

The Diver and the Dolphins

from *Dolphin Adventure: A True Story*

by Wayne Grover

One day, when diving off the coast of Florida, Wayne Grover was approached by a family of three dolphins. The baby was tangled in fishing line and had a hook snagged in its back. The parents knew that their baby's trail of blood made it a target for sharks. The dolphins came to get help. This is Wayne Grover's story of what happened.

The Dolphins

I had been diving for many years, but never before had wild dolphins come near me in the water.

As I watched, the three swam closer to me.

There was a large male, a smaller female, and a baby dolphin. As the three circled me, I could see the baby was bleeding from a deep wound near its tail where a long string of clear plastic fishing line trailed for several feet behind.

The male and female dolphins were making a clicking noise as they swam nearer to me. Then they stopped and hovered.

The clicking noise also stopped.

The baby was between its mother and father. All three looked at me with their little eyes over upturned mouths, reminding me of a human grin.

I could see the baby had become tangled in a fishing line with a big hook that had snagged it between the dorsal fin on its back and the tail fluke. The shaft of the hook was sticking out of the bleeding wound, making a trail of green in the depth.

Because all colors are filtered out in the ocean depth, the baby's red blood looked green eighty feet below the surface. My first reaction was one of awe. My second thought was worry for the baby. I knew it would either get snagged and drown or be tracked down and eaten by a shark.

Dolphins are very intelligent and are abundantly happy in their wild domain. They are loving and loyal and have close family ties, taking care of their young and their older, less able peers.

They seldom approach people in the sea and with good reason. Humans are dangerous and can cause them harm. But these dolphins were desperate.

The baby dolphin looked scared and in pain. Its little eyes rolled in their sockets as it watched me. It was afraid of me, but its parents had brought it near. I looked into the eyes of each of them as they hovered just three feet away, and thought about all the dolphins that had been needlessly killed by fishermen and their nets or caught on their hooks. All my life I have loved animals and have done my best to see they are respected and protected. Perhaps the dolphins had sensed that I was a friend. There were four other divers in the water, all armed with weapons. I was alone and unarmed.

Now we were face-to-face. This dolphin family had an injured baby. Could they have come to me for help?

I knew something most unusual was happening.

The baby dolphin would probably die without help, but what could I do? How could I do anything about the fishing hook and the plastic line?

I had only my big diving knife and no one to help me. If I didn't help, the baby was doomed. I decided I must try.

I reached out to touch the big male, who was nearest me, and all three suddenly shot away, swimming out of sight.

I felt a great surge of disappointment, thinking I'd never see them again. Had I done something wrong?

Then, within seconds, they were back. They swam around me, clicking again, but more softly. They kept their eyes on me every moment. Now I was convinced the dolphins had chosen me to help them.

I tied the rope from the float ball to a nearby rock and let myself sink to the seafloor, where I sat on my knees.

I could sense the dolphins were trying to communicate with me. As I sat there on the sea bottom looking at the three creatures, I knew it was a rare moment. They were trusting me and I was trusting them. With their great speed and strength, they could easily injure me.

They needed help, but they could not speak. I wanted them to know I would help, but I could not communicate in their dolphin language. There must be a way, but how?

I Try to Help

The clicking increased in frequency and then stopped. The three dolphins moved very slowly toward me. With their strong tail flukes barely moving up and down, they inched nearer and nearer until they were close enough for me to reach out and touch them.

The mother and father dolphin were slightly above the baby and were holding it between their flippers as they tried to place it on the sand right in front of me. At last they pushed the baby to the bottom.

The baby was frightened, and I could see it trembling. Its eyes never left mine. I slowly reached out to touch it, but when I did, it freed itself and swam rapidly away. The two parent dolphins immediately swam after it. In moments they were back, holding the baby tightly between them.

The father dolphin, hovering just inches from me, placed his nose under my arm and pushed up. My arm lifted, and I let it fall back in place. Again the big dolphin lifted it. I looked at his upturned mouth and bright eyes and couldn't help smiling. The impatient father dolphin wanted me to "get to work."

I took off my diving gloves and slowly reached out to touch the trembling baby. Its skin was smooth and silky as I ran my hand from just behind its breathing hole on the top of its head to the base of its dorsal fin in the middle of its back. I used my fingers to stroke its nose very gently, then ran them up and between its eyes.

The trembling stopped as the little dolphin began to sense that I had no intention of harming it. After petting it for a couple of minutes, I slowly ran my hand to the wounded area near its tail. The clear fishing line was wrapped around the thin part of its body, embedded into the skin, causing blood to ooze out.

The shaft of the fishhook stuck out from a bloody hole in its back that had been ripped open when the baby broke the line, freeing itself from the fisherman above.

It was in great pain and frightened. Instinctively it understood that a shark could sniff along the blood trail and find it. That would be the end of the baby dolphin, and all four of us knew it.

I knew that getting the hook out and the line loose would be painful for the baby, but it had to be done.

All I had to work with was the big diving knife I wore strapped to my right leg. It was about a foot long, and it was not very sharp.

I gently touched the hook shaft, and the baby made a high-pitched cry. It was going to be hard to help it.

Suddenly all three dolphins swam away, climbing toward the surface above. I had forgotten they had to breathe every few minutes.

Within a minute they were right back to me, this time with the baby coming along on its own. I knew I had to work fast so they could breathe when they needed to.

Surgery on the Sea Floor

I gently held the baby on the sea floor, then cut the trailing fishing line free until all that was left was the part embedded under the baby's tender skin. Getting it out with as little pain for the baby as possible was going to be the hard part.

Then, bit by bit, I started pulling the embedded line loose so I could cut it with my knife. As I pulled it up, more blood flowed out.

I looked around for sharks, not wanting to get in the way if the parent dolphins needed to protect their baby from an attack.

Seeing no sharks, I gently continued to pull some line free.

The baby cried out in pain, and the big dolphin clicked several times. It seemed as though the parent dolphins were working with me, encouraging their baby to cooperate.

Finally, all the line was cut free except for a short piece attached to the hook. This was going to be the hardest part. I touched the hook shaft, and the baby jumped and trembled. I carefully ran my finger into the deep wound, feeling its body heat within the flesh. The baby struggled to get away, but I placed my left hand on its back and pushed it down against the sand.

I felt so bad to be hurting it, but I knew if I didn't help, it would probably die.

Holding the baby dolphin with my left hand, I stuck one finger down the hook shaft until I felt the place where it turned up to form the barbed hook. It was stuck tight, hooked into the muscle tissue in the baby's tail.

I tried to wiggle it free, but it would not budge.

As the baby cried out, the mother dolphin used her nose to stroke the baby, calming its struggle. She watched my hands closely and seemed like a nurse hovering over a doctor at the operating table.

The hook had to be cut free, and I dreaded using the big diving knife to do it, but there was no choice.

Placing the blade between my fingers the way you would hold a pencil to write, I very carefully put the point into the hole above the embedded hook.

The baby cried and struggled. I could not hold it with my hand, so I placed my left leg over its body and held it down gently. I stroked its whole body for a few moments, trying to calm it.

Impatient, the big dolphin again nudged me with his bottle nose. They would need to breathe soon.

Taking a deep breath from the regulator in my mouth, I slipped the knife into the wound and gently ran it down along the hook shaft. I used my left hand to feel into the wound as I pushed the knife in. Then I hit the muscle tissue that held the hook in place. It was now or never.

I cut the barb loose, and the hook was free. I withdrew the knife and took the hook out. Blood flowed from the baby's tail, and I pushed my palm down hard on the open wound to slow the bleeding.

The Dolphin's Thanks

The two big dolphins clicked excitedly about me. I felt a great surge of relief. I had done it. My heart was filled with joy. I was unbelievably happy.

Then the big dolphin suddenly darted away downcurrent. Something had caught his attention. A pair of bull sharks were coming straight for the baby, sniffing the blood trail as it flowed toward them in the fast Gulf Stream.

The father dolphin saw them and raced for them head-on. He was so fast that even the speeding sharks could not get out of his way.

Wham! The father dolphin hit the bigger shark right behind its gill slits, knocking it aside.

Wham! He hit it again. The shark swam away with a trail of blood pouring from its gills. It wanted no more fight with the protective father dolphin.

The other shark continued swimming straight toward the baby and me. The mother dolphin exploded into action. She tore through the water and met the shark with a fierce bump to its side.

A second later the father dolphin hit it from the other side. It swam away, also trailing blood.

The father dolphin followed, making repeated attacks, ensuring they would not return to harm the bleeding baby.

The sharks were no match for the enraged parent dolphins who had saved their baby and probably me too.

I lifted my hand from the baby, and the bleeding had almost stopped. The mother dolphin had returned. She looked at the hole in its body and then at the hook lying on the sand nearby. She clicked loudly, and I heard more clicking from farther away. It was the father dolphin coming back.

He had chased the sharks far away. He was there in an instant, swimming rapidly back to his family.

I let the baby up, and it joined the parent dolphins. They all swam around me, making clicking sounds.

The father dolphin swam right up to me and looked into my eyes behind the diving mask. He nodded his head up and down in a rapid motion and then gently pushed me with his nose.

I reached out to touch his head, and he let me do so. For that brief moment, whether it was my imagination or it was really happening, I had the strong impression that he was thanking me, one father to another.

Then he made the clicking sound again, and the three swam rapidly toward the surface, leaving me alone on the bottom. I knew it was time for them to breathe again.

I looked at my air gauge and saw I had enough air to swim awhile longer. The experience that I will never forget had all happened in about ten minutes.

I kept looking for the dolphins to return that day, but they didn't.

As I climbed into the boat after I surfaced, I felt a happiness that I have never known before. The dolphins had left me with a sense of peace and a strong feeling of love.

A couple of weeks later, Wayne Grover went diving again. On the way out, several dolphins raced alongside the boat. One was a small dolphin with a scar on its back. The dolphin Wayne Grover helped had survived!

About the Author
Wayne Grover

Wayne Grover is a writer who spends much of his time around water. White-water rafting, scuba diving, and studying sharks and old shipwrecks are some of his pastimes.

All this time spent around water inspired his book *Dolphin Adventure: A True Story*. He has taken this story a step further in his second book, *Dolphin Treasure*. Unlike the true story of Mr. Grover saving a baby dolphin, the second book is a fictional account of how that baby dolphin makes its own daring rescue at sea.

Through his work in the United States Air Force, Mr. Grover has had the opportunity to travel all over the world. Now that he is retired, Mr. Grover is involved in conservation activities, marine research, and writing about underwater wonders.

Reader Response

Open for Discussion
What surprised you as you read this selection?

Comprehension Check

1. Suppose you are Wayne Grover. The dolphins need your help. What are you thinking about? Use evidence from the selection to explain.

2. How did the dolphins communicate with the diver when they wanted him to start working and when they wanted to thank him? Find details to support your answer.

3. Do you think that Wayne Grover thought about the risks to his own life when he was saving the baby dolphin's life? Why or why not?

4. After Wayne Grover pulled the embedded fishing line from the baby dolphin's wound, what **steps in a process** did he use to finish removing the fishing hook? (Steps in a Process)

5. What **steps in a process** did the mother and father dolphin use to drive the sharks away? (Steps in a Process)

Test Prep
Look Back and Write

Look back at pages 146–148. How do the parent dolphins demonstrate that they are capable of protecting their baby from sharks? Describe their specific actions and what results from them.

How to Read an Informational Article

1. Preview

- Read the title. Then read the boldfaced quotation. Look at the pictures and read the captions. Does the title fit with the information you have found so far?

2. Read and List Examples

- Look for sentences that state the main idea of paragraphs or of the article. For example,

  Some dolphins just don't get along with each other.

3. Think and Connect

Think about "The Diver and the Dolphins." Then look over your notes for "Dolphin Behavior."

What is the main idea of this article? Which examples of dolphin behavior that Wayne Grover mentions would fit as details under this main idea?

Dolphin Behavior

by Denise Herzing and Patricia Warhol

"Punchy and Big Wave still hang out together, but now Stubby only hangs out with the guys. Lil has started baby-sitting, and yesterday three of the boys chased away a bully."

Does this sound like a letter from home? Actually, it's a description of what goes on in a typical day among a group of Atlantic spotted dolphins off the Bahama Islands. Led by researcher Denise Herzing, the Wild Dolphin Project team studies these dolphins and reports back on how they live, including how they get along with each other.

For dolphins, getting along is a long-term investment in survival. Like people, dolphins need each other. They get along by doing things together—feeding, playing, resting, touching, and resolving conflicts. To study these behaviors, researchers must first identify individual dolphins by the unique forms of their dorsal fins and flukes and from the patterns of their spots. Dolphins don't all look alike! Then, following strict rules, the researchers enter the water, but they don't approach, touch, or feed these wild dolphins. They wait for the dolphins to come to them.

Once a dolphin is identified, it is given a name, like Little Gash, Luna, and Nassau. The Wild Dolphin Project has now identified over one hundred dolphins. Photos, videos, and sound recordings are made by researchers, and the fun of understanding what's really going on begins.

An Atlantic spotted dolphin, *Stennella frontalis,* for example, spends the first six months of its life by the side of its first teacher, or "Mom." Up to age three, a baby dolphin meets and plays with other infants in what researchers call a nursery group and begins to form lifelong associations and friendships. As the newborn meets other youngsters, it is introduced to the rules and games involved in being a social dolphin. These friendships are maintained in many ways. Some dolphins rub fins together, in the same way kids hold hands. Young dolphins learn about each other by watching, mimicking each other, chasing, and play-fighting. These

Like two people holding hands, rubbing pectoral fins is a way for dolphins to show friendship.

skills will be useful when they become adults.

Without the friendship of other dolphins, individuals might not survive in the wild. To stay in touch, dolphins have a complicated communications system. Each dolphin has a unique whistle, called a "signature whistle," to identify itself or to make contact. It also uses sonar clicks to find food and to navigate. Squawks, bleats, and other sounds are used for closer contact with neighbors. By identifying an individual's signature whistle, Denise and other researchers can now tell who's who among the dolphins without even seeing them.

Getting along in a dolphin society may also mean doing your job well, and one important job is baby-sitting. Young spotted dolphins often form groups of four or five individuals. A young adult (eight- to ten-year-old) male or female baby-sits. Part of the job is to stay close to the babies and to calm down any youngster that gets too excited or makes too much noise, which could attract a shark. Mothers often show up to discipline an unruly infant if the baby-sitter lets things get out of control!

Some dolphins just don't get along with each other. To communicate the message, "Leave me alone," there is a face-to-face showdown, and one dolphin opens its mouth and squawks. Grouping together is another way spotted dolphins send this message and can fend off teasing or aggressive advances of larger bottlenose dolphins.

Friends, fishing pals, baby-sitters, sparring partners, and squabblers—all are roles shared by these spotted dolphins.

Young spotted dolphins are spotless. Here Jemer, an infant female (bottom), swims with her mom, Gemeni.

Graphic Sources

- A **graphic source** is something that shows information visually. Pictures, charts, graphs, and maps are graphic sources.

- Graphic sources can help you better understand what you read because they provide a lot of information that can be seen quickly.

Read "Hurricane Seasons" from the *USA Today* weather report on the Internet.

Talk About It

1. On the bar graph find the bar for September. Run your finger up to the top of the bar. What is the number of hurricanes in September?

2. What other information about hurricanes might be given by a bar graph?

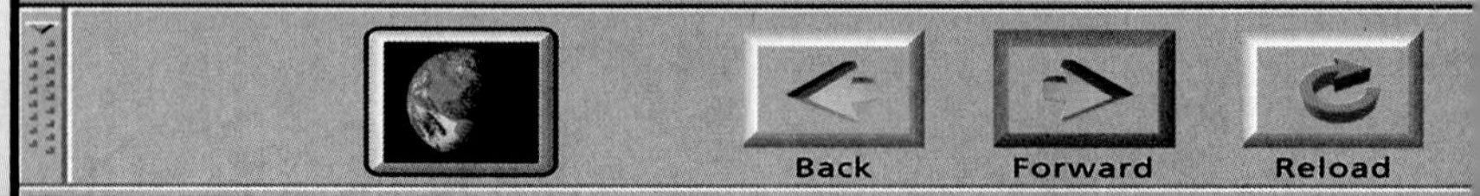

Back   Forward   Reload

Hurricane Seasons

from *USA Today*

Frequency of Hurricanes by Month
Even though the official hurricane season for the Atlantic Ocean, Caribbean Sea, and Gulf of Mexico runs from June 1 through November 30, the peak of the season is August through October. More than 80% of hurricanes occur in that period. This chart shows the total number of hurricanes per month from 1886 to 1993.

Hurricane season peaks in September

196

152

96

35

23

22

1   3   3

Jan.– May   June   July   Aug.   Sept.   Oct.   Nov.   Dec.
April

Source: National Hurricane Center

In "The Fury of a Hurricane," use different graphic sources to help you understand how hurricanes happen.

Vocabulary

Words to Know

damage	ecology	predict
hurricane	identify	pressure
mightiest	recovered	

Many words have more than one meaning. To decide which meaning of a word is correct, look for clues in the surrounding sentences or paragraph.

Read the paragraph below. Does *recovered* mean "brought back to a normal condition" or "got well"?

A Terrible Storm

One of the mightiest storms to ever hit the United States occurred in 1938. It began off the East Coast. As the atmospheric pressure dropped, the storm grew stronger. The winds picked up speed, the storm became a hurricane, and it headed toward shore. On shore, people knew that a storm was coming, but they couldn't identify what it was or predict when it would hit. The hurricane caused much damage and affected the ecology of the whole East Coast. It was many years before the area recovered and people could get on with their lives.

Talk About It

Use as many vocabulary words as you can to tell how weather affected something you did.

THE FURY OF A HURRICANE

from *Hurricanes: Earth's Mightiest Storms*
by Patricia Lauber

Galveston, Texas, was built on a low-lying island between Galveston Bay and the Gulf of Mexico. On the morning of September 8, 1900, it was a bustling port city of 40,000 people. By midnight, winds and waves of a gigantic hurricane had pounded half the city into rubble and killed 6,000 people in the worst storm disaster of U.S. history.

THE MAKING OF A HURRICANE

Great whirling storms roar out of the oceans in many parts of the world. They are called by several names—hurricane, typhoon, and cyclone are the three most familiar ones. But no matter what they are called, they are all the same sort of storm. They are born the same way, in tropical waters. They develop the same way, feeding on warm, moist air. And they do the same kind of damage, both ashore and at sea. Other storms may cover a bigger area or have higher winds, but none can match both the size and the fury of hurricanes. They are Earth's mightiest storms.

Like all storms, they take place in the atmosphere, the envelope of air that surrounds the Earth and presses on its surface. The pressure at any one place is always changing. There are days when air is sinking and the atmosphere presses harder on the surface. These are times of high pressure. There are days when a lot of air is rising and the atmosphere does not press down as hard. These are times of low pressure. Low-pressure areas over warm oceans give birth to hurricanes.

No one knows exactly what happens to start these storms. But when conditions are right, warm, moist air is set in motion. It begins to rise rapidly from the surface of the ocean in a low-pressure area.

Like water in a hose, air flows from where there is more pressure to where there is less pressure. And so air over the surface of the ocean flows into the low-pressure area, picking up moisture as it travels. This warm, moist air soars upward.

Birth of a Hurricane

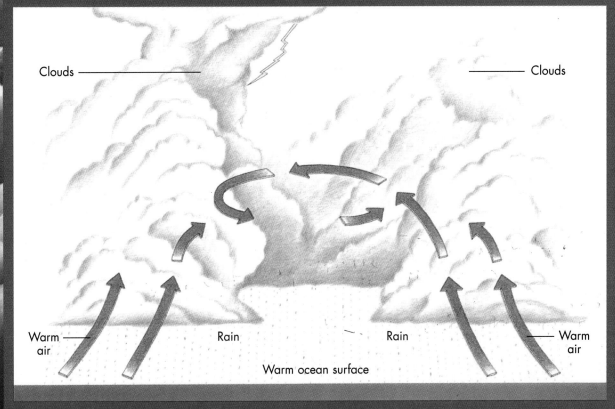

Clouds ————   ———— Clouds

Warm —— air   —— Warm air

Rain   Rain

Warm ocean surface

Warm, moist air flows into a low-pressure area. As the air rises and condenses into clouds, more warm air is drawn in over the surface of the ocean. It spirals upwards, traveling counterclockwise. Clusters of thunderstorms form.

As the air rises above the Earth, it cools. The cooling causes moisture to condense into tiny droplets of water that form clouds. As the moisture condenses, it gives off heat. Heat is one kind of energy. It is the energy that powers the storm. The clouds are the source of the storm's rain.

The low-pressure area acts like a chimney—warm air is drawn in at the bottom, rises in a column, cools, and spreads out. As the air inside rises and more air is drawn in, the storm grows.

Most of these storms die out within hours or days of their birth. Only about one out of ten grows into a hurricane.

As high winds develop, air pressure falls rapidly at the center of the storm. This low-pressure area is called the eye, and it may be 10 to 20 miles across. The eye is a hole that reaches from bottom to top of the storm. Winds rage around the hole, but within it all is calm. Winds are light. The air is clear, with blue sky or scattered clouds and sunshine above. People caught in a hurricane may suddenly experience calm air and dry skies. Sometimes they make the mistake of thinking the storm has ended, but it hasn't. The eye moves on and the second half of the storm arrives, with winds blowing from the opposite direction.

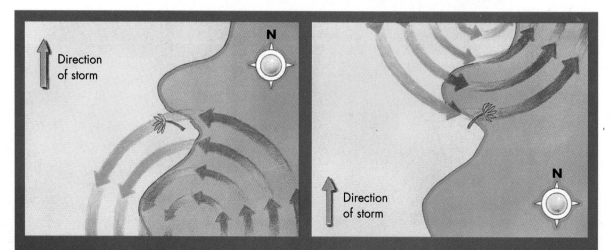

If hurricane winds first blow from the east, they will blow from the west after the eye has passed.

Inside a Hurricane

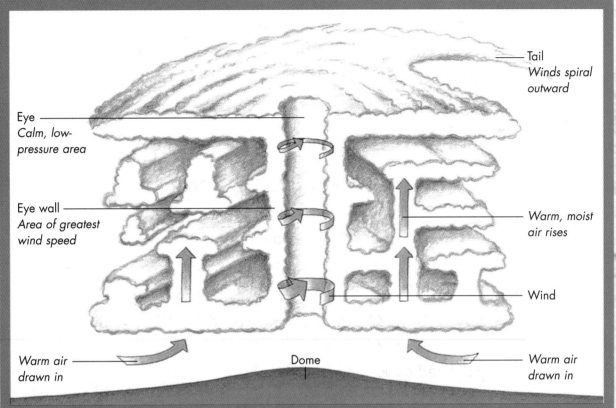

Eye
Calm, low-
pressure area

Eye wall
Area of greatest
wind speed

Warm air
drawn in

Dome

Tail
Winds spiral
outward

Warm, moist
air rises

Wind

Warm air
drawn in

High winds spiral around the eye, but within the eye all is calm. Air pressure within the eye is extremely low. Because there is less pressure on it than on surrounding areas, the sea under the hurricane rises in a bulge, or dome.

Naming Hurricanes

In the 1800s only the most violent hurricanes were named, sometimes for a town or an island that was badly damaged. Most of these names were used only locally.

Once it became possible to track tropical storms and hurricanes, weather scientists needed a way to identify them. Starting in 1953, the first tropical storm of the season was given a woman's name starting with A, the second a woman's name starting with B, and so on through the alphabet. In 1979, men's names were added to the list of those used.

Names repeat every six years. But if a storm is particularly violent, its name may be taken off the list. Camille and Hugo, for example, are no longer used. Hurricane Camille means only the storm that swept the Mississippi Delta in 1969, and Hugo the storm that battered the Virgin Islands, Puerto Rico, and Charleston, South Carolina, in 1989.

Different sets of names are used for different parts of the world. Hurricanes that form within 1,000 miles of Hawaii, for example, are given Hawaiian names.

Big Winds and Big Damage

In mid-August of 1992, satellite pictures showed a low-pressure area of wind and rain moving west across the Atlantic. Though the storm did not seem to amount to much, the National Hurricane Center in Miami, Florida, tracked it carefully.

By August 20 the storm was about 400 miles east of Puerto Rico. Here it weakened so much that it almost disappeared. The lower part of the storm was moving northwest, but the upper part was being blown northeast by strong high-altitude winds. For a time, it seemed the storm might be torn apart. Instead, the high-altitude winds began to flow around the storm. It charged ahead, with all its parts moving in the same direction.

By then scientists at the Hurricane Center were working with computer models of storms. They were trying to predict the storm's behavior and decide whether people should be told to leave coastal areas. The scientists fed their computers all the data they had received from satellites, radar, and airplane flights into the storm.

By 4:00 A.M. of August 22, winds within the storm were blowing at more than 75 miles an hour. The storm had become a hurricane. First of the season, it was named Andrew.

As its winds swirled ever faster, Andrew churned across the Bahamas. It was a furious and compact storm, with an eye only eight miles wide and winds that reached out for 60 miles. It was heading for the east coast of Florida.

Hurricane Andrew came ashore in South Florida during the early morning hours of August 24, 1992.

The computer models could not predict exactly where Andrew would come ashore. For 250 miles, from Fort Lauderdale to Key West, people were ordered to evacuate all low-lying areas along the coast.

Sunday, August 23, dawned clear and fair in South Florida. The sky was blue with fleecy clouds. Temperatures rose into the 90s. The air was damp and salty. Herons and frigate birds drifted over blue waters. It could have been any summer day, except that roads were jammed with cars as people fled inland and north.

By evening, wind and sea were rising. Shortly after midnight, in the early hours of August 24, Andrew came ashore south of Miami, with winds gusting to 195 miles an hour.

People woke in terror to dark houses, without electricity. The wind, sometimes shrieking, sometimes growling like a rushing freight train, snatched at shutters and shingles and pounded the sides of houses. Walls bulged in, then out. Howling winds toppled trees, ripped off roofs, blew in windows and doors, and knocked down houses. Where roofs or walls were gone, rain poured in. Inside their houses, people huddled together, held hands, and prayed.

The eye of the storm passed quickly through, bringing only minutes of calm and silence. Then the second half of the storm arrived, with winds howling from the opposite direction.

Andrew tossed a large sailboat into a wooded area and flattened all the trees.

Moving west, Andrew cut a 25-mile-wide path through Everglades National Park, flattening trees, tearing out boardwalks, and leveling the visitors center.

The storm moved out over the Gulf of Mexico and made a second landfall, west of Baton Rouge, Louisiana, where it died out over the swamps and marshes.

The sun rose on a strange landscape. In Miami large boats, hurled ashore, now leaned against lampposts and lay across highways. Wind had stripped the signs off posts and the fronds off palm trees. Fallen trees, telephone poles, and cables blocked streets. Traffic lights had disappeared.

But Miami had been at the edge of the hurricane. The center of the storm had hit to the south, bulldozing the towns of Homestead and Florida City. Twenty miles inland, they had been crushed not by the sea but by the wind. They looked as if they had been bombed, and 15 people had died.

With its front wall stripped away by Andrew, a modern apartment building looked like a doll's house.

The people in this area were not wealthy. Most were fishermen, small farmers, migrant workers, retired couples, people with low-paying jobs in Miami. They had just enough money to buy or rent a small home. Many lived in trailer parks. Some had no insurance. Now their houses were kindling wood. Their trailer homes looked like crushed soda cans. And with their homes had gone everything they owned, from clothes and furniture to toys and family photographs. Of the houses still standing, most had serious damage.

Shopping centers, warehouses, churches, and schools were ripped out of the ground or hammered into piles of twisted steel beams and splintered wood. Trees littered the ground. Lampposts were bent in two. Street signs were gone, and streets were buried under wreckage. Dogs and cats, horses and cows wandered about, lost.

Help was slow to arrive. The armed forces had planned ahead and were ready to move even before Andrew hit. But civilian leaders were slow to realize how great the damage was, slow to ask for help, slow to give orders. Meanwhile, in South Florida some 250,000 people camped out in the ruins as best they could, living with rain and mosquitoes. In all, Andrew had destroyed 20,000 houses and badly damaged another 90,000.

Finally, the troops were given their orders and arrived. Tent cities sprang up. Generators hummed, bringing back electricity. Food and water were supplied. Troops patrolled against looters and directed traffic. Bulldozers and cranes began a giant cleanup. But it would be years before Homestead and Florida City looked like towns again, years before people could put their lives together again.

It would also be years before anyone could tell how plant and animal life had been affected. In the past, many hurricanes have roared across South Florida. Each time, plant and animal life recovered. But in recent years, people have made many changes in the region. Because of these changes, the effects of Andrew's pounding may pose a long-term threat to the ecology of Everglades National Park.

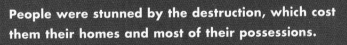

People were stunned by the destruction, which cost them their homes and most of their possessions.

Everglades is home to many kinds of birds, among them the great egret (top) and the roseate spoonbill (bottom). The spoonbill feeds by swinging its bill from side to side and straining tiny organisms out of the water and mud.

Like other national parks, Everglades is a piece of wilderness set aside to be preserved in its natural state. It is a park of birds, mammals, fish, reptiles, and amphibians, and of plants.

Andrew cut through the heart of the park, felling everything in its path. Animals in the park survived well. But the storm left behind a tangled mass of dead and dying plants, lying in torn-up ground.

The last hurricane that seriously damaged Everglades swept through in 1960. That time the park recovered well. Some fallen trees resprouted. Seeds from similar plants blew in on the winds or were carried in by animals.

Since then many changes have taken place in areas around the park. To the north, land has been drained and cleared for towns, ranches, and farms. The natural flow of water through the park has changed, and chemicals seep into the water. Housing developments have gone up right next to the park. And foreign plants have been brought in and planted just outside the park. But they are a problem. Their seeds spread like wildfire, grow fast, and thrive in disturbed soil. Once they take hold, they are nearly impossible to get rid of.

Now park scientists fear that foreign plants will invade the hurricane-damaged areas, take hold, and drive out native plants. This would change the park's plant life. It would also change the animal life, because animals depend on native plants for food and for places to nest and raise their young.

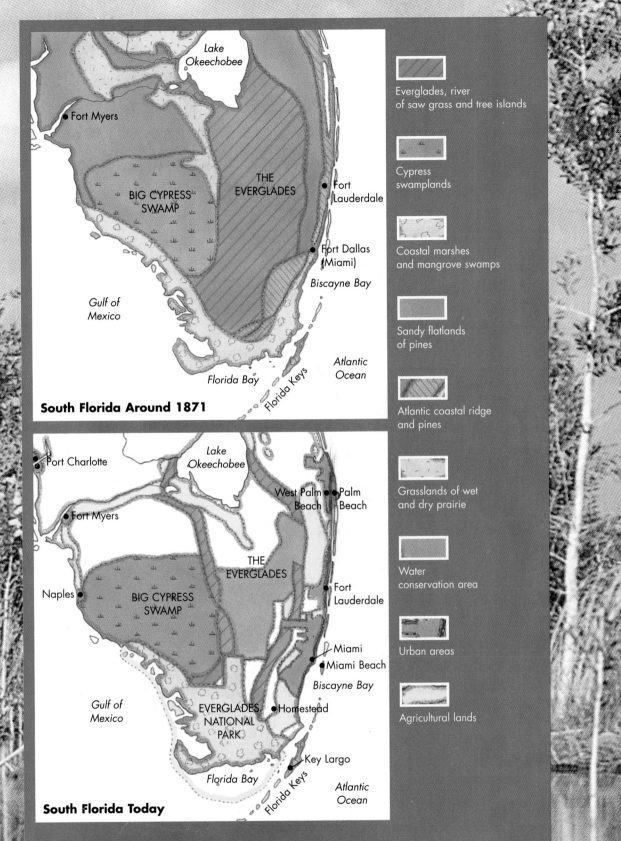

South Florida Around 1871

Lake Okeechobee

Fort Myers

THE EVERGLADES

BIG CYPRESS SWAMP

Fort Lauderdale

Fort Dallas (Miami)

Biscayne Bay

Gulf of Mexico

Atlantic Ocean

Florida Bay

Florida Keys

South Florida Today

Port Charlotte

Lake Okeechobee

West Palm Beach

Palm Beach

Fort Myers

THE EVERGLADES

Naples

BIG CYPRESS SWAMP

Fort Lauderdale

Miami

Miami Beach

Biscayne Bay

Gulf of Mexico

EVERGLADES NATIONAL PARK

Homestead

Key Largo

Florida Bay

Florida Keys

Atlantic Ocean

Everglades, river of saw grass and tree islands

Cypress swamplands

Coastal marshes and mangrove swamps

Sandy flatlands of pines

Atlantic coastal ridge and pines

Grasslands of wet and dry prairie

Water conservation area

Urban areas

Agricultural lands

The Everglades was once a region that stretched from Lake Okeechobee to the mangrove swamps at the tip of Florida. It was a watery land of tall saw grass broken by hammocks, or pieces of higher ground, where hardwood trees grew. Today Everglades National Park preserves a piece of the Everglades and the many kinds of plants and animals that live or nest there.

No one knows how big a change will take place or how it will affect the songbirds and wading birds, the raccoons, bobcats, deer, alligators, snakes, and tree frogs. Park scientists can only wait and see.

Natural scientists are also concerned about damage to mangrove swamps along southern Biscayne Bay, where Andrew came ashore.

The storm surge spent itself on a string of small barrier islands. But the hurricane's winds and waves battered the shore, which was lined with swamps of mangrove trees. The raging winds shredded the mangroves. When mangroves are lost, many food chains and food webs are affected.

A green heron perches on the prop roots of a red mangrove.

It will be years before anyone can tell how badly Andrew damaged the mangrove swamps and the food chains that begin in them. Florida has lost many miles of mangrove swamps in the past thirty years. They have been filled, cleared, and built on. The remaining ones are precious.

Hurricanes are part of nature. They are natural events. And they have been making landfalls for a very long time. In the past, nature always healed itself after a big blow—plant and animal life came back quickly to damaged areas. Today human activities may have changed the ways in which nature can heal itself. Scientists are concerned about these changes.

They are also concerned about another kind of change: the huge number of people who have moved to coastal areas. The years ahead, scientists say, may see more and more of Earth's mightiest storms roaring in from the sea and putting these people at risk.

About the Author

Patricia Lauber

Imagine one hardy green plant with a pink flower pushing up through volcanic ash. Patricia Lauber saw this picture and it inspired her to write a book that tells the story of a volcano and how life returns after an eruption.

To this writer, science is to be told like a story. She says, "I believe that the best science books have a story line: that one thing leads to another, that it is possible to build tension so that the reader really wants to find out what happens next."

How did Ms. Lauber become a writer? She says, "I don't think that I *became* a writer; I think I was born wanting to write. As a very small child, I loved stories and being read to, and soon learned to read myself, because then I could have as many stories as I wanted." This led to the discovery that she could also make up her own stories. Over the years she has made up plenty of them, about anything that interests her.

In addition to her award-winning science books about planets, volcanoes, and hurricanes, Ms. Lauber wrote a series of fictional stories inspired by her dog. The first of these was called *Clarence the TV Dog*. Four more "Clarence" books followed.

Reader Response

Open for Discussion

What do you know about hurricanes now that you did not know before you read this selection? Why might this information be crucial?

Comprehension Check

1. How did Hurricane Andrew affect the people in South Florida? How did it affect the plants and animals in the Everglades? Find details to support your answer.

2. The author says the air flow in a hurricane is like water in a hose. Find another place where hurricanes are compared to something else.

3. Help was slow to arrive after Hurricane Andrew hit Florida. How could this problem have been avoided? Use evidence from the selection to explain.

4. Which **graphic source** shows the birth of a hurricane? Using the diagram, tell how a hurricane starts. (Graphic Sources)

5. If you were going to write a report on the destruction caused by hurricanes over a ten-year period in the United States, which of the following **graphic sources** would you use and why: diagram, chart, map, or schedule? (Graphic Sources)

Test Prep

Look Back and Write

Look back at the diagram on page 163. Read the caption. Inside a hurricane system, where does the sea rise in a bulge? Why?

Test Prep

How to Read a Profile

1. Preview

- This kind of informational article is a profile. It tells about someone's personality and career.

- A display quote is in special type. It's meant to get your attention.

- A separate box, called a sidebar, gives information on a related topic. What does this sidebar describe?

2. Read and Locate Information

- As you read, take notes about why Terry Lynch flies into hurricanes. Use these headings:

Professional Reasons	Personal Reasons

- Read the display quote and the sidebar when you come to them or before or after you read the main text.

3. Think and Connect

Think about "The Fury of a Hurricane." Then look over your notes for "Flying into a Hurricane."

How do you think Terry Lynch might answer people who think he is "nuts" for flying through hurricanes?

FLYING INTO A HURRICANE

BY ROBERT BAHR

"Flying into a hurricane is like 10 hours on the world's best roller coaster," says Terry Lynch, 34. He is the technical crew chief for electronics aboard the *Orion*. He makes sure the weather equipment works right.

"I spend a lot of time in the tail of the plane on the Doppler radar," Lynch says. "That's the roughest place to be. You get whipped up and down like a seesaw."

...FLYING INTO A HURRICANE ISN'T DANGEROUS— JUST EXCITING.

Lynch works for the National Oceanic and Atmospheric Administration (NOAA) in Tampa, Florida. NOAA sends fliers like Lynch into the eye, or center, of the hurricane. There, they get information that can help determine the hurricane's path and strength.

As risky as it sounds, flying into a hurricane isn't dangerous— just exciting. Planes have penetrated hurricanes thousands of times. Only one, in 1955, has ever crashed.

In those days, pilots often had to fly just above the water. Judging the size and movement of ocean waves was the best way to measure the storm's power. Nowadays, with better equipment, planes can stay at 1,500 to 5,000 feet.

"We need to fly into hurricanes," the technical crew chief says, "because we have to know if, when, and where the storm is going to make a landfall— and how much of a wallop it will be packing."

In 1992, Hurricane Andrew devastated parts of Florida and Louisiana. Yet countless lives were saved. People had been warned to leave islands and coastal areas long before the hurricane struck.

Friends were surprised when Lynch went to work for NOAA. "People said, 'You gotta be nuts to fly through hurricanes for a living.'"

But Lynch likes the excitement. "I hate being bored," he says. "With this job, you never know what to expect. Tomorrow I could be off for a week in Australia or Puerto Rico. I could be working on a computer here at my desk.

"Or I might be flying the eye of a hurricane."

HURRICANES AREN'T AS DEADLY ANYMORE

Hurricane Andrew caused an estimated $20 billion in property damage.

But, compared to earlier hurricanes, it cost far fewer lives. A hurricane that struck the Florida Keys in 1935 killed 408. The deadliest of all hit Galveston, Texas, in 1900, killing 6,000. Hurricane Andrew killed 54 in the Bahamas, Florida, and Louisiana.

Modern communications now give people earlier warning.

Thanks to hurricane fliers and other experts, people can get to safe ground long before a hurricane strikes.

Skill Lesson

Fact and Opinion

- A **fact** is something that can be proved true or false. Statements of fact can be proved by checking reference books, observing, measuring, and so on.

- An **opinion** tells a person's ideas or feelings. It cannot be proved true or false, but it can be supported or explained. Some statements of opinion begin with clue words such as *I believe* or *In my opinion*.

- Some paragraphs have both facts and opinions.

Read "A Volunteer's Help" from "Reach Out and Make a Difference" from *Current Health*.

Write About It

1. The author says that young people have a lot of talent and energy. Is this a statement of fact or opinion? How do you know?

2. In the last paragraph, Ellen talks about floods. Find one statement of fact and one statement of opinion in this paragraph.

A Volunteer's Help

from *Current Health*

When Ellen saw the pictures on TV of the huge floods in the Midwest, she decided she wanted to help. She and a couple of friends started a food drive at school. They gathered fifteen cartons of food and toys.

Every Thursday after school, Jim goes to the community center in his neighborhood and reads to the little children there. Jim has been doing this for the past six months.

Three years ago Christy volunteered at the local animal shelter. She has been a valued helper ever since. She helps feed and care for the abandoned dogs and cats that are waiting to be adopted.

Harold has just started going to a six-week program for children with disabilities on Saturday mornings at the recreation center in his town. Most of the time he just plays different games with the other kids. Other times he helps them with craft projects.

All these kids are helping other people in a lot of different ways simply because they want to. There are thousands of kids all across the country who volunteer to help people they know and don't know—adults and other kids. Young people your age have a lot of talent and energy to share with others.

Some kids, such as Ellen and Harold, like to do projects that take a lot of work but don't take a lot of their time. Others, like Jim and Christy, enjoy the chance to help over a longer time period. It gives them a chance to get to know the people better.

"When I saw the pictures of all those homes getting covered with water," says Ellen, "and thought about other kids just like me who now didn't have anything, I felt really sad. Even though we don't live close by, I thought there should be something we could do to help. The teachers at school thought sending things was a good idea, and lots of kids brought stuff in. I felt good about it."

In "Dwaina Brooks," Dwaina also volunteers to help others. Look for facts and opinions as you read about her efforts.

Vocabulary

Words to Know

advised	deliveries	donate
organized	unfortunate	

Words with opposite meanings are called **antonyms**. You can often figure out the meaning of an unknown word by finding a clue in the words around it. Sometimes this clue is an antonym.

Read the paragraph below. Notice how *lucky* helps you understand what *unfortunate* means.

Hoping to Help

It was the holiday season and our class decided to help out at a nursing home. We knew that this season could be a sad time for those <u>unfortunate</u> residents who would spend the holidays alone. Not everyone was lucky enough to have a family or friends nearby. Our teacher <u>advised</u> us to think about what we could do. We decided to make gifts and cards. We <u>organized</u> ourselves into two groups. One group would make gifts and the other group would make cards. The whole class would make the <u>deliveries</u>. All of us were eager to <u>donate</u> time.

Talk About It

Tell about something you volunteered to do that helped others. Use as many vocabulary words as you can.

180

DWAINA BROOKS

by **Phillip Hoose**

On Friday nights, Dwaina Brooks, eleven, and as many as twenty-six of her friends and relatives turn her mother's kitchen into a meal factory for the homeless of Dallas. With the radio set to 100.3—the rap station—and with mayonnaise up to their elbows, they have produced as many as three hundred meals in a night.

Dwaina Brooks, who organized her family and friends to feed homeless people in Dallas

Each morning on her way to school, Dwaina Brooks saw the line of men and women outside a homeless shelter and soup kitchen in Dallas. Many looked cold and sleepy. Sometimes one man stood in the street carrying a sign that said, "I Will Work for Food to Feed My Children." No one ever stopped to talk to him. How could they just pass him by?

At school, her fourth-grade class was doing a unit on homelessness. Once a week, students telephoned a shelter and talked with someone who was staying there. Dwaina would ask the person on the other end of the phone, "How'd you wind up on the streets?" "Do you want to be there?"

"What did you do before?" She listened carefully. Most people's lives had been going along okay, and then something bad had happened. They got fired. The family broke up. They couldn't make a rent payment.

Always she asked, "What do you need?" The answer was always "a home," or "a job." It never seemed as though she could do much more than keep sending her lunch money to the shelter. Then one afternoon, Dwaina talked with a young man who had been without a home for a long time.

"What do you need?" she asked him.

"I need a job and a permanent home," he replied.

"Well, I can't give you that," she answered impatiently. "I don't have a job either. Don't you need anything else?"

"Yeah. I would love a really good meal again."

"Well, now," said Dwaina, brightening. "I can cook."

Why Not?

Dwaina tore into the house that night after school and found her mother, Gail. As usual, she was in the kitchen. "Mama," she said. "I need you to help me fix some stuff to take down to that shelter we call at school. Let's make up as much as we can. Sandwiches and chicken. Let's get everyone to do it. C'mon."

Gail Brooks looked at her daughter. All of her children were generous, but Dwaina had always been a little different. Even when she was a baby, Dwaina couldn't stand to see anyone hurt or left out. If she only took one doll to bed with her, pretty soon she would start wondering if all the others felt bad. The next morning, there would be a bed full of dolls and Dwaina on the floor.

Make food for the homeless? Well, why not? They decided to prepare meals on Friday night. They spent the next three days shopping and preparing. Counting Dwaina's lunch money, which she decided to donate to the cause, they figured they had about sixty dollars to spend. Their challenge was how to make that stretch into as many meals as possible.

Coupons helped cut the prices for sandwich wrapping, cookies, and mayonnaise. Dwaina's uncle got them discount lunch meats from

the store where he used to work. Thursday night was bargain night at the bakery in nearby Lancaster. They drove away with six big loaves of day-old bread for $1.78. "Mama, do you think anyone at the shelter will really eat day-old bread?" Dwaina asked. "We eat it," Gail replied. "If it don't kill us, it won't kill them."

The baker gave them twenty free boxes, too, when he heard how they would be used. Dwaina's aunts and uncles brought over huge sacks of chips and big bottles of salad dressing.

When Dwaina got home from school on Friday, the stage was set. Her mother's table was covered with a plastic cloth. The plastic gloves from the dime store were laid out. Mountains of ham, turkey, and cheese were at one end. Two rows of bread went from one end of the table to the other. They looked like piano keys. A huge jar of mayonnaise was open and ready.

Dwaina's sisters, Stephanie, sixteen, and Crystal, nine, already had aprons tied around their waists. Dwaina turned on the radio, and they all formed an assembly line and dug in. Gail threw chicken into three skillets and got them all going at once. Dwaina slapped meat on open slices of bread and covered them with mayo. Crystal wrapped sandwiches and stuffed sacks. Dwaina looked on proudly as the corner of the kitchen began to fill up with sacks. It looked like a lot of meals.

It was after ten when the last sack was stuffed. The kitchen looked like a tornado had ripped through it. They placed 105 carefully wrapped meals in the bakery boxes, loaded them in the Oldsmobile, and headed downtown.

When they got to the shelter, two men came out to the street and helped carry in the boxes. Dwaina set down her first box and looked around the shelter. It was a big, open room with beds along the walls. It was dark, but some men were up front in a lighted area drinking coffee. She wondered if the man who had said he wanted a good meal was still living there. If he was, she thought with pride, he sure enough would have a treat tomorrow.

"Who'll Be There?"

After that, nearly every Friday night for a year, Dwaina and her mother and whatever sisters were around made food for shelters in Dallas. At first they took the food to the shelters themselves, but then their church volunteered to make the deliveries for them.

Always, Dwaina wanted to make more meals. That shelter had hundreds of people; she and her mom alone probably weren't feeding half of them. One Friday evening, she had an idea: she knew where she could get some extra help, and lots of it too.

The following Monday, she asked her fifth-grade teacher, Mr. Frost, if she could speak to the class while he took roll. Dwaina had been the class leader since the first day of school, when she had told a group of loud boys to shut up so she could hear her teacher. She could be tough or funny or kind. She always seemed to know exactly what would move them.

Now Dwaina smacked both hands on her desk hard to get their attention and stood up. She pushed her glasses up onto her forehead and glared at them for a moment, hands on hips, as if she were about to lecture them.

"Okay, y'all," she began. "We've been reading about the homeless in class, and I can tell you that for some reason it's getting worse and worse." Her eyes swept around the room. "Now, my mama and I been makin' sandwiches this year till we got mayonnaise up to our elbows and we can't make enough. Why should we be up till midnight every Friday night when y'all ain't doin' a thing? Now, listen. I want you to come to my house this Friday night and help. Who'll be there?"

Twenty-three hands went up. When Dwaina excitedly reported this to her mother, Gail Brooks nearly passed out. "Twenty-three kids? Plus *our* family?" "Yeah, Mama, isn't it great! Think how many meals we can make!"

Dwaina and Gail advised each participating family about where to get food cheaply. They made a central list of who would bring what and taped it to the refrigerator. All that week, parents drove boxes of food to the Brooks's small house. At school, the kids made bigger and bigger plans each day. Making food for the shelter was shaping up to be the social event of the year.

"Why don't y'all stay over?" asked Dwaina.

"I'll bring popcorn!" said Claire.

"I got a Hammer tape," said Qiana.

"What about boys?" said Christopher. "Can we sleep over too?"

"Sorry," came a chorus of girls. "Oh, maybe on the kitchen floor."

The next Friday night, twenty-eight people crowded into the Brooks's kitchen. They set up one of the world's longest assembly lines, kicked the radio onto 100.3 FM-JAMZ—the rap station—wrapped towels around their waists, and started in. By midnight, the boxes were filled with more than three hundred sacks.

In a little more than two years, Dwaina Brooks, now in sixth grade, has organized several thousand meals for unfortunate people in the Dallas area. She and her mother and the classmates who sometimes still join in have perfected the art of helping others and having fun at the same time. They do it by doing something they already love to do: cooking and putting meals together.

Dwaina hopes to become a doctor and open her own clinic someday, but she thinks it's crazy to wait till then to start caring for others. "Kids should get going," she says. "There aren't enough jobs out there, especially for people without diplomas. Not even at McDonald's. We should try to help. If we don't act, there will be more and more homeless people. Each of us should have some kind of concern in our hearts for other people. And we owe it too; there isn't a one of us who hasn't been helped by someone."

About the Author
Phillip Hoose

Phillip Hoose is one of those people who wants to make the world a better place. Like Dwaina Brooks and other young people in his book, *It's Our World, Too!*, Mr. Hoose volunteers his time to try to make a difference. As a staff member of the Nature Conservancy, he works to protect the habitats of endangered species. He has organized tenants to improve housing conditions in inner-city neighborhoods. He also helped start the Children's Music Network.

If you like sports, you may enjoy another book that Mr. Hoose has written called *Hoosiers: The Fabulous Basketball Life of Indiana*. This book was named one of the ten best sports books for children by the *Kids' World Almanac of Records and Facts*.

Reader Response

Open for Discussion

If you were to tell someone else about Dwaina's activities, what would you say?

Comprehension Check

1. Do you think that Dwaina would make a good president of a company? Why or why not? Use evidence from the selection to explain.

2. Do you think Dwaina knew how challenging it would be to prepare meals for a shelter? Find examples of how she handled the challenges.

3. The selection describes two times when meals were prepared in Dwaina's family kitchen. How were those occasions similar? How were they different?

4. Go back to page 185. Find three **facts** and one **opinion.** How can you tell the difference between the facts and the opinion? (Fact and Opinion)

5. What was Dwaina's **opinion** about caring for others? What **facts** tell you how much she cared? (Fact and Opinion)

Test Prep
Look Back and Write

Look back at pages 182–184. What caused Dwaina to make her first decision to feed the homeless? Use specific actions or speeches to explain your answer.

Lighting Up Hope

from Zillions magazine

Valorie Darling and Arielle Ring hit it big with their candle-making business. . . . Then they gave away all their profits!

Valorie Darling couldn't believe what she was reading. A pullout in the Spokane, Washington, newspaper said that thousands of Romanian kids were crowded into run-down orphanages. The Eastern European country was so poor that the orphans had little heat, food, or medicine. "I was bawling because of the horrible things these kids were going through," remembers Val.

Val's friend Arielle Ring just happened to read the same article. She immediately thought of helping in some small way.

But the two friends didn't do anything right away. They didn't even talk about the article . . . until about a month later.

A Business Is Born

While making beeswax candles to give as holiday presents, the girls took a break to run an errand at a craft store. They noticed that the store didn't sell beeswax candles.

"Whenever Arielle and I are together we get these big ideas—like starting our own business," says Val. "So, right away, we decided we should sell our candles."

At the same time, Val remembered the Romanian orphans. She mentioned it to Arielle, suggesting that they could do some good with the money they'd make. So the two decided to donate their profits.

Valorie and Arielle hand-roll candles from sheets of beeswax.

Asking for Help

To get started, Val and Arielle pooled the money they'd already earned by babysitting. They used it to buy supplies. And they came up with a name for their new business: The Helping Hearts.

Then Val and Arielle wrote to local businesses, explaining what they were doing and asking the businesses to sell their candles. Within a week, they had several responses!

A restaurant bought 20 pairs. And the owner of a gift shop invited the girls to set up a table in his store. "I told the girls they'd have to do it all themselves," recalls John Ferris, the shop owner. "I knew the candles would sell better if customers heard the girls' story and saw that they were sixth-graders."

When customers came in, Val and Arielle showed off their candles and explained that the profits were going to help orphans in Romania. It took just two hours to sell 200 candles at $5 a pair and earn $500. Even after taking out $120 for the cost of the ribbon, cellophane, gift tags, wax, and wicks, that left $380 for the orphans. "I felt so proud!" remembers Val.

Candle Weather

Later that week, bad weather turned out to be good for the girls' business. "An ice storm hit our area," recalls Arielle. "About 100,000 people were left without power."

"So we went door-to-door selling candles," says Val. "We were a big hit

The girls sold their candles in pairs with tags to explain their cause.

because people needed candles. Plus, they loved the cause."

By Christmas, just a few months after they'd begun, the girls had donated around $3,500 to charities working in Romania. Within a year, they donated about $4,500 more.

A Little Comfort

The charities used the money to buy essential things. "They bought a heater and a generator for an orphanage," Arielle says. "They got new blankets and new mattresses. Things in Romania are a lot cheaper than here. A pair of eyeglasses costs about $5. They got some of those too."

Keeping the business going has been tough, but the benefits have far outweighed the sacrifices. "Hearing stories about how our money helps people feels great," Val says. "You don't think kids can make that much difference in someone's life. But we were able to bring hope to the kids in Romania. And the experience brought Arielle and me a lot closer too."

Author's Viewpoint

- **Author's viewpoint** is the way an author thinks about the subject of his or her writing.

- To learn an author's viewpoint, think about the author's opinion and choice of words. Sometimes you can figure out an author's viewpoint even when it is not stated directly.

- Unbalanced, or biased, writing happens when an author presents only one viewpoint. Balanced writing presents both sides of an issue equally.

Read "Action Against Pollution" from *Kids Who Make a Difference* by Gary Chandler and Kevin Graham.

Talk About It

1. What is the authors' viewpoint on what young people should do to help the environment? How do you know?

2. Do you think the authors present a balanced viewpoint in "Action Against Pollution"? Give your reasons.

Action Against Pollution

by Gary Chandler and Kevin Graham

Young people realize that actions speak louder than words. This is especially true when it comes to threats to the environment. It is helpful to talk about a problem—but just talking about it won't bring about positive change. Doing something about it—acting on a problem—is the key.

Many kids are involved with general efforts to educate and influence others to help the environment. Others are busy designing and working on projects with such specific goals as saving energy, increasing recycling, and reducing pollution. All of them know that their future is dependent on a healthy environment, and they're taking responsibility through a wide variety of actions that will help make the world a better place.

When some fifth-grade students were given a homework assignment on the

First Amendment to the U.S. Constitution, a New Jersey teacher unknowingly sparked an international network of child lobbyists.

In 1987, the teacher in New Jersey asked his students to analyze the news over the weekend. They were to choose an issue that they could use to exercise their freedom of speech—which is protected by the First Amendment. That weekend, the newspapers were full of stories about beach pollution. When the kids returned to class, they decided to do something about the problem. They began writing about their concerns to their state lawmakers. And about twenty of the students decided to form a club called Kids Against Pollution (KAP).

The students began encouraging their classmates to join KAP. Thanks to their hard work and determination, it now has more than 2,500 chapters in twenty countries around the world. KAP members conduct research on pollution, make speeches, and write thousands of letters to lawmakers and the media about their environmental concerns.

LOOK AHEAD

In *Everglades,* think about the author's viewpoint on the Florida Everglades and how they became polluted.

Vocabulary

Words to Know

miraculous	prospered	seeped
pondered	quantities	brim

When you read, you may come across a word you do not know. To figure out its meaning, look for clues in the words and sentences around it. A clue might be found in a description given near the unknown word.

Read the paragraph below. Notice how the description before *brim* helps you understand what it means.

A Wonderful Walk

A group of children walked in the state forest. They learned that melted snow from the mountains flows down, filling the lake to its <u>brim</u>. They spotted deer and raccoon tracks and knew that wildlife <u>prospered</u> there. They saw wildflowers in great <u>quantities</u>, stood beside tree trunks, and touched sap that <u>seeped</u> from the bark. Later, the children <u>pondered</u> what would have happened to that <u>miraculous</u> place if it had not been saved for all to enjoy.

Write About It

Plan a nature story. Then write a sample to show where in the story you might use some or all of the vocabulary words.

Everglades

by Jean Craighead George   paintings by Wendell Minor

*T*he storyteller poled the children under arching trees into a sunny water glade. He sat down and leaned toward them.

"I am going to tell you a story," he said. "It is not a story about a person or a mythical creature. It is not even a story about an animal."

The children looked at each other and waited.

"It's a story about a river." He swung his arms in a wide circle. "This river, the miraculous Everglades of Florida.

"My story will be different from any you have heard, because this river is like no other river on Earth. There is only one Everglades."

The children leaned forward. He began.

Swamp Lily

First there was sunshine on a blue-green sea.

It was the Age of the Seashells.

The seashells formed a rock called limestone on the sea bottom. Over the eons the sea lowered, and the rock became land. The long Florida peninsula took shape in warm, sunny waters.

Purple clouds, flashing with lightning, roiled and boomed above the land. Rain gushed from the storm clouds in summer. Sun bathed the land in winter. Moss grew, then ferns, then grass and trees.

The rain eroded holes in the soft limestone and filled them with water. Florida glistened with green land and blue-green lakes.

One was Lake Okeechobee, round, deep, and as clear as window glass.

Lake Okeechobee filled to its brim and spilled over. The spill became a river that seeped one hundred miles down the peninsula from Lake Okeechobee to the Florida Bay. It was fifty miles wide and only six inches deep in most places.

Lightning Whelk

*T*his river did not chortle and splash. It did not crash over falls and race. It was a slow river that gleamed like quicksilver. We know it today as the Everglades.

Into the shallow, warm river came tiny one-celled animals and plants. They lived and died and made gray-green soil on the bottom of the river. Saw grass took root in the soil.

The grass prospered. When the winds blew, the saw grass clattered like a trillion swords. Each sword was edged with cutting spines. Of the larger animals, only the leathery alligator could walk unharmed among the terrible spears of the saw grass.

Around the stems of the grass scurried the young of insects, and tiny crabs and snails. Little fish found these to be excellent eating. Turtles and alligators found the fish to be excellent eating. Every wild thing ate well, and there was still an enormous abundance.

To the abundance came the birds. Clouds of lacy, white egrets made their home in the Everglades.

Every day a blizzard of wood storks dropped into the grass and dined on the snails, crabs, bugs, and fish.

Great Egret

A profusion of pink flamingos hunted in the shallow mudflats.

Hundreds of miles of roseate spoonbills vacuumed the ponds and shallows with their sievelike bills.

A myriad of little songbirds fluttered through the trees that grew on the islands in the river of saw grass.

Quantities of alligators roamed the grass and dug pools for their young. Into their pools came fish and turtles, herons and anhingas, and billions of frogs, snakes, and snails.

A multitude of panthers, raccoons, deer, and otter came to the river. They made their homes on the beautiful islands.

A plenitude of orchids bloomed and turned the island trees into colorful cathedral windows.

A plethora of lizards and anoles clambered over the orchids, and two thousand kinds of plants, including palms, vines, bushes, grasses, and trees.

When all were in place, the Everglades was a living kaleidoscope of color and beauty. It glittered with orchids, grass, trees, birds, panthers, raccoons, snakes, mosquitoes, fish—all things large and small that make the Earth beautiful.

Florida Chicken Turtle

The storyteller paused. The children looked around and pondered. The storyteller went on:

When the Everglades was perfect, people who called themselves Calusas arrived. They lived gracefully on the fish and game and made tools out of seashells.

The Spanish conquistadors arrived, and the Calusa people disappeared.

The conquistadors were afraid of the flesh-ripping grass and roaring animals of the Everglades, and they moved on.

North of Florida, European men pushed the Creek Indians out of the Carolinas. Some of them walked south until they came to the silvery Everglades. They poled deep into the saw grass and settled on the islands. They are the Seminole (which means *runaway*) Indians. A few of them live here today.

Brown Pelican

*The storyteller paused. The children looked around.
"Where are the clouds of egrets?" a child asked.*

The hunters shot them by the tens of thousands and sold the feathers to decorate women's hats. Only a few survived the slaughter.

"Where are the quantities of alligators?" another child asked.

The hunters shot them by the acres and sold their gleaming hides to make wallets and shoes. Only a few remain.

"Where did the cathedral windows of orchids go?" a third child asked.

The orchid hunters picked gardens and gardens of them and sold them to put on ladies' dresses. Practically none can be found.

Another child looked around. "And where did the mammals and snails and one-celled plants and animals go?"

They vanished when the engineers dug canals in the Everglades and drained the fresh water into the sea to make land. Farmers tilled the land; business people built towns and roads upon it. Pesticides and fertilizers flowed into the river waters and poisoned the one-celled animals and plants. The snails died, the fish died, the mammals and birds died.

"But this is a sad story," said a fifth child. "Please tell us a happy story."

The storyteller picked up his pole and quietly skimmed the dugout canoe across the water and down a trail in the saw grass. Then he sat down and told the children a new story.

Five children and a storyteller poled into the Everglades. Eventually the children grew up and ran the Earth.

The clouds of birds returned to an abundance of fish in the water. The flowers tumbled into bloom. Quantities of alligators bellowed through the saw grass again. A multitude of panthers, deer, raccoons, and otters cavorted on the islands.

"That's a much better story," said the children. "Now pole us home quickly so we can grow up."

Calopogon Orchid

About the Author

Jean Craighead George

The book *Everglades* was probably inspired by Jean Craighead George's lifetime love of nature. As a child, she loved fishing and catching frogs with her older brothers. She learned to observe and appreciate nature from her father, who studied insects and taught his children about the wonders of the Florida Everglades.

To write her books about the great outdoors, Ms. Craighead George gets information firsthand by visiting sites in the wilderness and observing wildlife in their habitats. When Ms. Craighead George wanted to learn about wolves, she and her son, Luke, spent a summer in Alaska. She used what she learned about how these animals live and communicate to write *Julie of the Wolves*, a Newbery award-winning novel.

Reader Response

Open for Discussion

One child says that the storyteller's story is a sad one.
Do you agree? Explain.

Comprehension Check

1. Do you think that the storyteller's story is more interesting for the children than a list of facts would be? Explain why you think so.

2. The storyteller says that the Everglades was perfect at one time. When did the Everglades probably begin to be less than perfect? Find details to support your answer.

3. Compare the description of the animals and plants at the beginning of the story to what the storyteller says about them later.

4. The **author's viewpoint** can be found in the words of the storyteller. What is her viewpoint about hunters in the Everglades? How do you know? (Author's Viewpoint)

5. Think about the **author's viewpoint.** Does she believe that changes in the Everglades are good or bad? What parts of the story make you think so? (Author's Viewpoint)

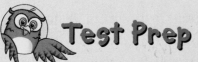 Test Prep

Look Back and Write

Look back at pages 204–207. The storyteller says that the Everglades was perfect. What does he mean by "perfect"? Use specific details to support your answer.

FLORIDA EVERGLADES

from *The World Book Multimedia Encyclopedia*

Everglades, in southern Florida, are one of the most interesting and unusual swamp areas in the world. Everglades National Park, which makes up about one fifth of the Everglades' original area, covers 1,506,499 acres (609,658 hectares). The Everglades extend from Lake Okeechobee to Florida Bay and the Gulf of Mexico.

The northern part of the Everglades consists of a prairie covered by shallow water and by saw grass, a grasslike plant with sharp, jagged edges that grows as high as 12 feet (3.7 meters) in some places. Bustic, gumbo limbo, live oak, mastic, and royal palm trees grow on mounds of higher land called *tree islands*. Near the southern coast, the Everglades become salt marshes and mangrove swamps, where the spreading roots of mangrove trees catch and hold soil. Many animals live in the Everglades.

They include alligators, deer, fish, herons, pelicans, snakes, and the rare Florida panther.

Development of the Everglades. The Everglades were created about 10,000 years ago, after the last major ice sheet of the Pleistocene Ice Age melted. The melting ice raised the level of the sea, which flooded the outlets of Everglades streams and turned the area into a swamp. Various peoples have lived in the Everglades through the centuries. The Seminole Indians fled to the area in the early 1800s during a period of wars against United States troops.

In 1906, the state of Florida began draining parts of the Everglades to make the land suitable for farming. After World War I ended in 1918, farmers moved in and began growing vegetables and sugar cane. Canals were built from Lake Okeechobee southeastward to supply drinking water to the growing communities in and around Miami. By the 1940s, however, the United States government had decided to try to preserve a section of the Everglades. Thus, the southwestern region of the Everglades became the Everglades National Park in 1947.

Environmental problems. In spite of the efforts to protect the Everglades, conditions within the wetlands worsened. The Kissimmee River is the main source of fresh water for Lake Okeechobee and the southern wetlands. During the 1960s, the U.S. Army Corps of Engineers forced the waters of the winding Kissimmee into a straight, concrete canal. These measures sharply reduced the flow of water into the Everglades, with disastrous results for plants and wildlife.

The massive development of southern Florida since 1970 has also damaged the Everglades' water supply. Cities surrounding the Everglades have grown rapidly. These cities reduce the water supply by using huge amounts for drinking, sewage treatment, and other purposes. The growth of agriculture has also contributed to the water problem. Sugar plantations and vegetable farms consume much water, and harmful chemicals used in agriculture run off into the water supply.

Plant species that are not native to the Everglades also pose problems for the area. Seeds from plants, including paperbark trees and Brazilian pepper trees, have been dispersed to the Everglades by high winds. When such seeds take root and develop into plants, they can overpower and replace native Everglades species.

Saving the Everglades. Many groups have joined the fight to save the Everglades. The U.S. Army Corps of Engineers has begun work on a plan to restore the Kissimmee to its original course. In 1989, the U.S. government approved the expansion of the Everglades National Park to gain control of more of the park's water sources. In 1991, the state of Florida agreed to follow a cleanup plan and remove the harmful chemicals that have entered the water supply.

Contributor: Peter O. Muller, Ph.D., Professor and Chairman, Department of Geography, University of Miami.

Preview: Picture

Florida Everglades

| Close | ← | 1 of 1 | → | Show it |

See also LAKE OKEECHOBEE.

215

Drawing Conclusions

- When you form opinions based on facts and details, you are **drawing conclusions.**

- To draw conclusions, think logically. Also use clues from what you've read and your own knowledge and experience.

- To check your conclusion, ask yourself if it makes sense. Are there any other possible conclusions?

Read "Granny's Missing Food" from "The Case of Granny and the Alien Bandit" by Michael Manley from *Ranger Rick.*

Talk About It

1. Why do you think Granny says, "Your friend must think he's some kind of detective or something"?

2. What conclusion can you draw about the looks exchanged between the boys at the end of the story?

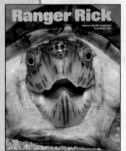

Granny's
MISSING FOOD

by Michael Manley

"Somebody's been stealing my food!"

"Exactly what has been taken?" Clooz asked. His one blue eye and one brown eye sparkled with curiosity. I groaned to myself. I had invited him for a quiet weekend in the country, but I knew that look. He was thinking we had another mystery to solve.

Granny turned to him. "Well, let's see now. There was that chicken I had thawing overnight by the sink, and a bowl of fruit."

"Anything else?"

"I don't think so," she said, scratching her head. "Wait a minute! I was eating cookies while I was watching TV last night. They're gone too."

"Someone stole your cookies?" Clooz asked.

Granny smiled. "Your friend must think he's some kind of detective or something," she said.

"Actually, he *is* a detective, Granny."

Clooz pulled out his business card and handed it to her.

"Clooz Calahan Investigations," she read. "Oh, yes, my grandson here has told me a lot about you. You've solved some pretty tough mysteries, haven't you?"

Clooz smiled and took back his card. (It was the only one he had.)

"Sure could use a detective around here," she said to Clooz.

"Oh, come on, Granny," I said. "It's probably just Farley getting into your food."

"Can't be," Granny snapped. "That old dog up and died last spring. Didn't I tell you?" Then she grabbed Clooz by his shirt sleeve and pulled him off to one side. "Want to know what I think?" she whispered. "It was the *aliens* that did it."

"Aliens?" Clooz asked.

Granny nodded. "It's in all the papers."

"What papers, Granny?" I asked.

"Why, those right there!" She pointed her cane to a pile of newspapers scattered across the coffee table. They were the kind you'd find at the checkout line in the supermarket. Clooz shot me a look. I rolled my eyes.

In "Missing Links," Sherlock and Amanda solve a mystery by using logic and clues. As you read you can draw conclusions by using the same strategies.

Vocabulary

Many words have more than one meaning. To decide which meaning of a word is correct, look for clues in the surrounding sentences or paragraph.

Read the paragraph below. Does *counter* mean "a thing used for counting" or "a display table or cabinet in a store"?

Helping at the Store

My parents work hard at their store. They sell jewelry. Sometimes I help them out when it gets busy. One of my jobs is to make sure everything is neat. I put things away, and if I see a smudge on a counter, I clean it off. Another one of my jobs is to make sure everything is in the right place. Once my parents couldn't find a sapphire ring. Everyone was relieved when I found it mixed in with the watches. Misplaced jewelry indicates just how busy we can get. It also means a successful day at the store.

Write About It

Describe a day you went shopping. Use some or all of the vocabulary words.

Missing Links

by Andrew Bromberg

"**R**emember, Sherlock," Amanda reminded her brother for the tenth time, as they pushed through the doors of the department store, "we came here just to buy Dad a tie, not for you to spend hours playing with all those computer games."

"Okay, okay," he answered, moving quickly down the crowded aisle, only to discover moments later that his sister was no longer in sight. "Amanda," he called in a slightly louder than normal voice, "where are you?"

"Over here. By the jewelry counter."

"Well, really," Sherlock growled after he'd retraced his steps. "I thought you told *me* not to waste time."

"I know, I know," Amanda apologized. "But I just had to stop at the jewelry counter. Look at that man's sapphire ring. I noticed it when I was passing by. Isn't it beautiful?"

Sherlock glanced at the counter, which also held a whole assortment of men's tie pins and cuff links, and had to agree that the ring was beautiful. "But a little too expensive for us." He laughed. "So let's get over to the tie counter."

Finally, they hurried off together to the next aisle, where the ties were kept, while the jewelry salesman stared after them, and then glanced at his watch.

"**F**or Amanda and Sherlock, buying a tie for their father was not as simple as it might sound. Amanda wanted to get one in dark red with narrow blue stripes, while Sherlock favored one with a green background and tiny horses' heads woven into the silk. This happened every time they went to buy a gift together. It seemed to take hours before they could agree on anything.

Sherlock was just bending down to get a better look inside the glass display case, when he suddenly felt something unpleasantly wet on the back of his neck. He straightened up in surprise, only to see that the fire sprinklers all over the main floor of the store had gone off at once.

Alarm bells started ringing, and the entire store was instantly in a state of panic and confusion. Salespeople were racing back and forth, trying to protect their merchandise. Customers were ducking their heads and pulling up their collars, hoping to stay dry. Amanda and Sherlock, once they'd recovered from the shock, began to help the salesman stuff his ties under the glass top of the counter before they were completely soaked. Just as they had the last tie tucked safely away, the bells stopped ringing and the sprinklers stopped as suddenly and mysteriously as they'd started.

"Whew," said Sherlock in the welcome silence, "I'm certainly glad that's over, but we're both soaked."

Amanda was about to suggest that they go right home and come back for the tie the next day, when they both heard frantic cries of "Help! Thief!" coming from the direction of the jewelry counter.

Their wet clothes forgotten, Amanda and Sherlock rushed to see what was going on.

Behind the jewelry counter, the salesman was waving his arms in a state of total distraction. The case that Amanda had been looking into just a few minutes before was now smashed and almost empty. All the cuff links, the tie pins, and the beautiful ring were gone.

"What happened?" Amanda asked the salesman excitedly.

"I don't know, I don't know. I must have been putting some ladies' jewelry away in the next counter . . . there was so much confusion . . . I just didn't see . . . but I haven't been near the case. I know you're not supposed to touch anything. The police will probably want to check for fingerprints."

Sherlock, apparently, was already doing just that. He had his magnifying glass out and was peering intently into the shattered display case.

Amanda thought that the salesman certainly looked upset, and his clothes were in even worse condition than hers and Sherlock's. "Oh, dear, you do look terrible," she couldn't help blurting out. "There's a big white spot on your chin, and a kind of rusty spot on your tie."

"My chin—I don't know—it must be some plaster that fell down when the sprinklers went off. And my tie—I guess I spilled ketchup on it at lunch yesterday. I must not have realized when I put it on this morning. And now this! It's so awful."

Amanda was embarrassed to see that Sherlock now seemed to be using his magnifying glass to study the spot on the salesman's tie. But the poor man was so upset that he didn't even notice.

?

Both Amanda and Sherlock would have loved to be there when the police arrived. Neither one of them could ever resist a good mystery. But this one would just have to be solved without them. They'd promised their mother to be back by noon with two loaves of bread from the bakery department for her luncheon party, and it was already after eleven o'clock.

Finally, by promising him a chocolate éclair to eat on the way home, Amanda managed to lure her brother away from the scene of the crime.

They rushed off to take the escalator down to the lower level where all the food was sold, and as they reached the bottom they both noticed a door marked EMERGENCY EXIT AND SPRINKLER CONTROL ROOM. Seeing the sign reminded Amanda of her soggy blouse, and she shivered slightly as she moved toward the bread counter. Sherlock, of course, headed immediately for the pastries to make his selection.

The warm, fresh-baked bread smelled wonderful, and Amanda wondered how she'd be able to resist breaking off a piece and eating it right then and there. She pointed out what she wanted, and was hardly even paying attention as the baker took the two loaves she'd selected from the counter. He weighed the first one and marked the price on a paper bag, and then he weighed the second. By this time Sherlock had come back, munching on his éclair.

All of a sudden a worried look crossed the baker's face. "I'm so sorry, Miss," he apologized, "but you'll have to make another choice. This loaf doesn't seem to be baked properly and I'm afraid it might have been damaged by the water."

"It looks all right to me," Amanda insisted, and Sherlock nodded energetically.

"No, no, please, your mother would be very angry if I sold you a damaged loaf."

By now she was really worried about the time, and too uncomfortable in her damp clothes to argue, so Amanda hurriedly pointed out another loaf and turned to ask Sherlock for a bite of his éclair. The baker weighed and wrapped the bread and carefully laid the package on the counter with both hands.

He had just said, "That will be two dollars and twenty-five cents, please," when Sherlock and Amanda looked at each other in amazement, realizing that they had just solved the mystery.

The solution to this mystery is on the next page.

The Solution

When Amanda and Sherlock see the missing sapphire ring on the baker's finger, they realize that he and the jewelry salesman must have conspired to steal the jewelry. The baker had set off the sprinklers located near his counter and rushed upstairs in the midst of all the confusion. The jewelry salesman had broken the glass display counter and passed the jewelry to the baker, who went back downstairs, turned off the sprinklers, and hid the jewelry inside the loaf of bread that Amanda later wanted to purchase.

Here are the clues Amanda and Sherlock used to solve the mystery:

Amanda stops at the jewelry counter to admire a man's sapphire ring. The salesman behind the counter is wearing a clean tie.

As Amanda and Sherlock leave the jewelry counter, the salesman glances at his watch because he knows it is getting close to the prearranged time for the baker to set off the sprinklers.

The sprinkler system goes off and throws the store into a state of confusion. While Amanda and Sherlock are busy helping the tie salesman, the baker is at the jewelry counter in the next aisle.

The white smudge on the salesman's chin is not plaster dust, but flour that brushed off on him as he handed the jewelry to the baker. Sherlock, examining the spot on the jewelry salesman's tie with his magnifying glass, suspects that it is blood, not ketchup. In fact, the salesman cut himself when he smashed the jewelry counter.

On the store's lower level, Amanda and Sherlock walk past a door marked EMERGENCY EXIT AND SPRINKLER CONTROL ROOM. It is right next to the bakery counter.

After the baker weighs the second loaf of bread, he refuses to sell it to Amanda. She doesn't know why, but is suspicious when the scale indicates that the bread weighs 15 pounds.

When the baker puts the package on the counter, both Sherlock and Amanda notice that he is wearing the very same sapphire ring Amanda had admired in the jewelry case.

About the Illustrator

Larry Day

Since Larry Day was five years old and growing up in the cornfields of Illinois, he has loved creating pictures. He spent the days of his childhood riding his bicycle or drawing.

When he was in high school, Mr. Day studied art through a correspondence course. This was a good start for his current career as an illustrator in Chicago. To keep his skills fresh, Mr. Day sketches people as he rides the train from his suburban home to the city.

In addition to "Missing Links," Mr. Day has illustrated many other stories, including the classic poem, *Casey at the Bat*. Mr. Day enjoys being an artist. He likes the bond his art has created in his family. "It's nice to support my wife and children who, in turn, strongly support my art."

Reader Response

Open for Discussion

When did you realize that this story is a mystery? Were you able to solve it? Explain.

Comprehension Check

1. Find the parts of the story that tell the reader a robbery has been committed. What are some clues that make Amanda and Sherlock suspicious?

2. Based on evidence in the story, what character traits do you think make Sherlock and Amanda good detectives?

3. Do you think it is necessary for the clues of this story to be explained in "The Solution"? Why or why not?

4. What **conclusions** did you **draw** about the baker before you read "The Solution"? (Drawing Conclusions)

5. Why do you think Amanda and Sherlock **draw** the right **conclusions** about who stole the jewelry? Explain.
(Drawing Conclusions)

Test Prep
Look Back and Write

Look back at pages 220–228. Amanda and Sherlock's trip to the department store does not go as they expect. Explain their *two* reasons for being there. How are their original plans changed by what happens?

Detectives

by Brian Lane

THE TASKS OF INVESTIGATING a crime and identifying the culprit are carried out by detectives. Whether by interviewing witnesses or searching for the tiniest piece of evidence, detectives try to reconstruct a sequence of events until they believe they know what happened. Most detectives are officers in a specialized division of the police, but many others work for private agencies. These detectives, who are often known as private investigators (PI's), can be hired by anybody to investigate anything—for a fee.

SIR ARTHUR CONAN DOYLE
Probably the world's best-known fictional detective is Sherlock Holmes, created in the 1880s by Sir Arthur Conan Doyle (1859–1930), a British writer. Holmes relied on logical deduction and attention to minute detail to solve crimes.

Sherlock Holmes

INTERNATIONAL AGENCY
Police forces around the world are centralized at Interpol (the International Criminal Police Organization), established in 1923. Police detectives can refer to computer files, fingerprints, and criminal records gathered from more than 100 member countries.

RECORDING EVIDENCE
All investigations involve the collection of a wide range of clues. Photographs are vital. They may record a meeting between the individuals under investigation, a crime in progress, or the scene of the crime that has not yet been disturbed by investigators.

A scene-of-crime officer with a magnifying lens can identify small clues, such as hairs or cloth fibers.

MRS. KERNER

Annette Kerner, Britain's most famous private detective, worked from the early 1920s to the 1950s. She became known as "the queen of disguise" and was equally convincing as a waitress in a criminal's café as she was a socialite while thwarting a jewel theft.

PHILLIP MARLOWE

A familiar character in detective fiction is the hard-boiled, tough-talking private eye who lives a lonely life on the city's "mean streets." Phillip Marlowe, created in the 1930s by Raymond Chandler, is perhaps the best-known example of the type, immortalized in novels and films.

PRIVATE EYES THAT NEVER SLEEP

In 1850, U.S. detective Allan Pinkerton established the organization that has become the world's oldest privately owned detective agency—it is still going strong. The term *private eye* came from the Pinkerton Trademark—the words "We never sleep" written under an open eye.

STAKEOUT

A stakeout is an undercover surveillance operation. In this still from the film *Stakeout,* actor Richard Dreyfuss portrays a detective keeping watch. He uses binoculars, wiretaps, and other classic devices to keep crucial witnesses and suspects under surveillance.

AT THE SCENE OF THE CRIME

This officer, dressed in plastic coverall, protective gloves, and shoe covers, is searching for evidence among blades of grass. He is using tools from a scene-of-crime kit to collect evidence. The collection of evidence can be a laborious task at an outdoor crime scene, as there may be a very large area of ground that must be searched for possible clues. The clues may also have been moved or damaged by animals or the weather.

Cap to prevent transfer of hair

Scene-of-crime evidence collecting equipment

Shoe covers to prevent investigators from introducing foreign materials to the scene

Thistles

by Karla Kuskin

Thirty thirsty thistles
Thicketed and green
Growing in a grassy swamp
Purple-topped and lean
Prickily and thistley
Topped by tufts of thorns
Green mean little leaves on them.
And tiny purple horns
Briary and brambley
A spikey, spiney bunch of them.
A troop of bright-red birds came by
And had a lovely lunch of them.

De colores

(Bright with Colors)

A Traditional Spanish Song

De colores,
bright with colors the mountains and valleys
dress up in the springtime.
De colores,
bright with colors all the little birds
fill the skies in the daytime.
De colores,
bright with colors the rainbow brings joy
with the glory of spring.

CHORUS
And a bright love with colors has found us
with peace all around us
that makes our hearts sing. [sing twice]

Hear the rooster,
hear the rooster singing kiri, kiri, kiri, kiri, kiri.
In the morning,
in the morning the hen sings her cara, cara, cara, cara, cara.
All day singing,
baby chicks all day sing pío, pío, pío, pío, pí.

CHORUS
And a bright love . . .

VALUABLES

by X. J. Kennedy

I found a fossil in a rock:
The print of some lost fern
That died a million years or so
Ago. I had to learn

If it was valuable or not —
I rushed right off to show
Aunt Jessie the geologist—
Could it be rare? *She'd* know.

"A beauty of a specimen,"
She said. (Wow! how intense!
I'd struck it rich!) "It's common,
    though,
Worth maybe eighty cents."

But now I keep it on my shelf,
Its stone leaves crisp and nice,
With things that matter to me, not
For sale at any price.

To You

by Langston Hughes

To sit and dream, to sit and read,
To sit and learn about the world
Outside our world of here and now—
    Our problem world—
To dream of vast horizons of the soul
Through dreams made whole,
Unfettered, free—help me!
All you who are dreamers too,
    Help me to make
    Our world anew.
I reach out my dreams to you.

Wrap-Up

How do we show that we care about our surroundings?

Caring for Our Environment

Create a Poster

Each selection you have just read shows someone helping to care for our world.

1. For each selection, **jot down** one or two things people can do to help our environment.

2. **Choose** the help you think is most important. Write it in one sentence.

3. **Create** a poster or wall motto. Use the sentence you have written. Add color or decorations. Display your work.

Be a Storyteller

Retell a Story

In *Everglades,* the storyteller tells a story about a river. Choose a selection from Unit 2 that interests you. Now you be the storyteller and retell that story to listeners.

1. **Decide** which events are the most important. Think about what the characters do and say and what their voices sound like.

2. **Practice** telling the story out loud by yourself.

3. **Tell** the story to your listeners.

Water Travels

Describe in a Letter

What sort of adventure do you imagine when you think about traveling on water? Think about floating in a canoe through the Everglades, watching dolphins from a motorboat, or watching a storm that might turn into a hurricane.

1. **Choose** one of these situations.

2. **Reread** parts that interest you. Imagine being a part of what happens.

3. **Write** a letter to a friend. Tell about your adventure.

Animal Chat

Discuss and Dramatize

With a partner, choose two animal characters from "The Diver and the Dolphins" or *Everglades.*

1. **Talk** about the characters together. Give them names and personalities. Each of you choose one to act.

2. **Discuss** what the characters might say to each other about their world and what kind of shape it is in.

3. **Make** up dialogue for your characters as you **perform** for your classmates. If you like, you can make puppets of your characters and perform with them.

Test Talk

Understand the Question

Find Key Words in the Text

Before you can answer a test question, you have to know where to look for the answer. A test about "Florida Everglades," pages 214–215, might have this question.

Test Question 1

What are the causes of the damage that has been done to the environment in the Florida Everglades? Support your answer with evidence from the selection.

Make sure that you understand the question.
Find the key words. Finish the statement "I need to find out . . ."

Decide where you will look for the answer.

• Some test questions tell you to look in one place for information. The answer is *right there* in the selection.

• Other test questions tell you to look for information that is in different parts of the selection. You have to *think and search*.

• Still other test questions tell you to combine what *you* know with what the *author* tells you. The answer comes from the *author and you*.

See how one student figures out where to look for the answer.

Sitting at the breakfast table on that sunny spring morning, he felt a little dizzy; his heart beat faster, the room looked fuzzy to him. It was now or never, he thought. Would they laugh at him? It didn't matter, this was something he had to do. He had to make a break, and this was how he was going to do it. There was a dream that haunted him, and he had to do something about that dream. He wished he spoke more clearly, but since he couldn't, he asked very slowly.

"I wann tricycle to rrr-ride!"

"How's Jerome gonna ride, when he can't walk yet, Papa?" Liza asked innocently. Jerome picked up his fork and struck her on the arm; when she screamed, he made a face at her.

"Jerome, you stop that!" Mama said. She looked thin and nervous, her fingers tapped on the table.

Round-faced Liza was only five, but already she could ride Tilly's big two-wheeler. She didn't mean to hurt anyone when she reminded the family that eleven-year-old Jerome, who was in the fifth grade, couldn't even walk.

LOOK AHEAD

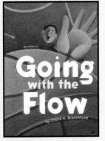

Going with the Flow

In *Going with the Flow*, Mark has to deal with his physical disability when he starts classes at a new school. As you read, get to know the characters by noticing what they say, do, and think.

Vocabulary

Words to Know

| conversation | dribbling | gestured |
| interpreter | volunteers | skied |

Many words have more than one meaning. To decide which meaning of a word is being used, look for clues in the surrounding sentences or the paragraph.

Read the paragraph below. Decide whether *dribbling* means "bouncing a ball" or "trickling slowly."

Snowy Basketball

I'm a sign language interpreter at Reed School. I work with kids who have hearing problems. Today I stopped by the outdoor basketball court to watch some students practice. Although snow covered the court, the team was practicing hard. The kids were dribbling and passing without too much trouble. Cindy, who had skied on icy slopes often, didn't mind the snow at all. But then she slipped and fell. Someone gestured and I hurried over. We had a quick conversation and Cindy said she was fine. We decided practice had to stop until the snow was removed. Cindy signed, "We need volunteers to get rid of this snow!" Someone ran for shovels and we all got to work.

Talk About It

Use vocabulary words to tell about games you have watched or played.

Going
with the
Flow

by Claire H. Blatchford

All the kids were staring at me. All twenty-two of them. I could feel their eyes going over my Nikes, my jeans, my T-shirt, my crew cut, my behind-the-ear hearing aids. It was like I was an alien that had fallen out of the sky and landed in New Jersey.

My face burned. I hate it when people stare at me.

I looked at Mrs. Willcox, the fifth-grade teacher. I caught a couple of the words on her lips, ". . . can't hear . . . speak slowly . . ."

Then she pointed, first at me and then at the door. A woman had entered the classroom. It was my interpreter, Mrs. LaVoie. Why did she have to come on my first day? Nobody would want to talk to me with a grown-up following me around.

"Hi, Mark. How are you?" Mrs. LaVoie signed and mouthed the words silently to me across the room.

The whole fifth grade was watching us.

"This is dumb!" I signed back.

"They've never met a deaf kid before," she replied. "They . . ."

I didn't wait for her to finish. I had to get out of there. I raced down the center aisle, nearly tripped over the leg of some big, long-haired guy with a smirk on his face, and ran out the door.

Mrs. LaVoie found me in the gym under one of the bleachers. She put a hand on my arm.

I pulled away. "I didn't want to come here," I told her. "My sister didn't want to come either. But we had to. Dad got a new job."

"I understand," she said.

How could she understand? She didn't know what I'd left behind in Vermont—the mountains, the ski team, Jamie . . .

By now, Mrs. Willcox and the principal were there too. Mrs. LaVoie touched my arm again.

"I'll help you," she promised.

I didn't move. I wasn't going back to that classroom.

I saw the worry in Mom's eyes when I got off the school bus. I knew from her face that Mrs. LaVoie had called and told her I'd spent the day alone in the gym. You don't have to have ears to hear things like that.

Sarah, home early from school, was in the kitchen. Her rusty red ponytail whipped the air as she turned to face me. "I heard all about it! They say I have a freak of a brother."

"The teacher made me stand in front of the class. They were staring at me."

Sarah rolled her eyes. "You think you're the only one? They stared at me too. What do you expect when you change schools in October?"

"But I'm deaf!" I said.

"Deaf!" Sarah shook her head as she made the sign. "So deaf you won't listen to anyone—not even the interpreter they got for you?"

I went upstairs, two steps at a time. I slammed the door of my room shut, climbed over a mountain of boxes, and flopped facedown on my bed.

All I could think was: *Come on, Sarah! How would you like having to sit with someone Mom's age? How would you feel if the teacher asked for volunteers to take notes and none of the kids put up their hands?* And then I wondered, *Am I a freak?*

I fell asleep. Being deaf is tiring. You have to look, watch, listen, and figure out what's going on all day long. It was like this in Vermont too. But at least there were other deaf kids, kids that knew signs.

Dad's hand woke me, pressing down on my shoulder. I almost didn't open my eyes. I was sure he was mad.

"Supper time," he said. His blue eyes seemed far away behind his thick-rimmed glasses.

I nodded.

"I heard about today," he said.

I shrugged.

"When you make a change, the first few days are always the hardest."

I didn't say anything.

"Did you hear me?" Dad asked.

The words popped out before I could stop them. "Dad, can I go back to Vermont? Maybe I could live with Jamie."

Dad's eyebrows went up. They do that when he doesn't know what to say. He doesn't really know Jamie's parents. They're deaf and they only sign.

"If you did that you'd never talk," Dad said.

"Signing *is* talking."

"I know, but . . ." His eyebrows rose again. "So . . . you're comfortable with Jamie's family?" he asked.

I paused to think about it. Jamie's parents don't think I'm really deaf. I wasn't born deaf, the way they were. I had meningitis when I was three, and everyone in my family but me can hear.

All I knew then was that I wanted to be skiing with Jamie when the snow came. I'm faster than him, but he's sharper on the corners. Real sharp. But there I was in the middle of flat, brown, dull New Jersey.

Dad waved to get my attention. "I tell you what, Mark," he said. "I'll think about it. But you have to promise to try one week of school here."

I put a hand over my mouth to hide my grin. *One week? That's nothing.*

It was cold and gray the next morning. I wondered if it was snowing up north. I'd tried calling Jamie three times on my TDD— that's a telephone device for the deaf—but no one answered. Where was he? Had he forgotten about me already?

At school the big guy I'd nearly tripped over was sitting on my desk. My stomach tightened. What was going on?

When he saw me coming, he hopped down. "I'm . . . eeeth," he said. *Eeeth?* "Teeth?" I asked.

He nearly fell over laughing. The other kids laughed too.

Mrs. LaVoie tapped at my arm. "He's telling you his name." She spelled it out with her fingers. "K-E-I-T-H." My face started burning again. Keith, not teeth. Some words look alike on the lips. Why had I opened my big mouth?

Keith held up a notebook and a pencil. "I'm . . . taking . . . notes . . . for . . . you," he said.

I wanted to sink through the floor and out of sight. I hate it when people mouth everything and talk like I'm two years old. Everyone was watching us. *Only one week of this,* I thought grimly as I reached for the chair to my desk.

Mrs. LaVoie's lips and signs were easy to read. At noon she said she was going home for lunch and would be back after recess.

Keith dropped a couple of tightly folded pages on my desk and ran out.

The only free seat I could find in the cafeteria was near some third graders. I read a book so I didn't have to look at them while I ate. I wasn't very hungry.

When I stepped outside at recess, I saw a bunch of guys playing basketball. They were really into it. Their tongues were almost hanging out of their mouths.

I wanted to watch them, but I didn't want them seeing me. I turned to go and **whack!** Something hit me hard on the neck. There was Keith, his long hair plastered to his sweaty head. I knew from the way he was grinning that he'd thrown the basketball on purpose.

"Come play," he gestured.

I glared at him. He'd called me just like you'd call a dog. I would have gone back inside except for the look on his face. I could hear it as clearly as I hear the thoughts in my own head: *What a wimp! Is he going to run away and hide again?*

I put the book and my lunchbox down and walked onto the court.

"You're . . . on . . . *my* . . . team," Keith said, using preschool language again.

"You don't need to talk so slow," I told him.

"Oh—" The way Keith said it I realized he wasn't sure I could really talk.

One of the guys tossed the ball to me. I caught it and ran off dribbling.

They were fast, but I was faster.

I ran this way and that. Around them, between them, maybe even under them. Anger can give you speed.

I took a wild shot, missed the basket, dove for the ball, got it, and dropped it.

Someone tripped me up from behind. I went flying, hands first, onto the pavement.

It was Keith.

"You—*you* did that?" I yelled.

He waved his fist at me. "Who do you think you are?" he yelled back. He was talking fast now. "*I'm* the captain. You do what I tell you."

We stared at each other. I could have quit, but I didn't want to. It's weird, but I *had* to find a way to stay on that team. I *had* to show him I could do it the way he wanted.

I got up. The palms of my hands were stinging, but I didn't look at them. "What do I do?" I asked.

Keith paused and scratched his arm. "Watch," he replied.

Watch? That's what I do all the time.

"Flow," he added. "Yeah, go with the flow."

I didn't try to call Jamie that night. I was too busy thinking about Keith and basketball. When I skied, it was my speed against Jamie's speed. This was different. I'd never really played *with* other guys on a team before. Would Keith ask me to play again?

For the next three days straight, I played basketball with Keith at recess. Sometimes I could see the others shouting and laughing. I couldn't understand them and felt really out of it. Sometimes Keith and the others shoved me around. Once when that happened I got angry. Keith had tripped me again. I was ready to punch him. But when I saw the look on his face, I suddenly knew he wasn't trying to make me mad. He was just trying to tell me how to flow. Friday, after the last bell, Keith dropped his notes on my desk.

"Thanks, but I don't think I need them," I said.

He frowned. "How come? Aren't they good enough for you?" he asked. He was angry. It was like I'd tripped *him*. Neither of us said anything then because Mrs. Willcox was coming toward us wondering what was going on. We didn't want her in on the conversation.

"I'm not sure I'm coming back," I told him when we were outside. "That's why I said that about the notes."

His mouth fell open. "But you just got here," he said.

I told him about Jamie and the school in Vermont.

"You can't go . . ." Keith was talking a mile a minute now, jumbling the words, gesturing wildly. I had to make him say it over.

He told me that tryouts for the basketball team were coming up soon. "You've gotta try out," Keith said, grabbing my arm. "You're fast, you're smart, and you don't need ears like everybody else to hear what's going on.

"Besides," Keith went on, "if you made the team, we could use sign language."

My bus pulled up then. I had to go. When I looked out the window, Keith put two fingers up in a big V. I read the words on his lips, "We need you."

We need you. No one had ever said that to me before. It felt good.

Well, that was two months ago, and I'm still in New Jersey. And, yes, I'm on the basketball team. I'm teaching the guys some sign language. It comes in handy when we're playing other schools!

Keith still trips me up every now and then when I get going all by myself on the court. He still takes notes for me too. (Some of his notes are really about basketball, but don't tell!)

I'm not saying everything is fine. When you're deaf, you're always deaf. You can't get over it the way you get over a broken leg or a headache. People forget to look at you when they talk. Or they forget to slow down a little or not mouth everything. Or they have trouble understanding what you're saying.

I know there will always be times when I feel left out. But that's okay. I'm learning to go with the flow.

About the Author
Claire H. Blatchford

Like Mark in *Going with the Flow*, Claire H. Blatchford lost her hearing as a child. Her deafness was caused by a severe case of mumps when she was six years old. Unlike Mark, Ms. Blatchford went to a public school at a time when there were no signing interpreters or TTYs (telephone typewriters for the deaf), so it was difficult for her to follow lectures and class discussions. Ms. Blatchford's way of coping and keeping up with her classmates was by reading and writing.

"When I read, and when I wrote, all the hassles of being deaf were instantly removed. I could understand what everyone said without having to ask people to look at me or repeat what they were saying." She remembers how "words took me all over the world, out into space, deep down in the chambers of the heart, high up in the towers of the mind, forward and backward in time."

Among the many other books Ms. Blatchford has written about being deaf are *Many Ways of Hearing* and *Yes, I Wear a Hearing Aid.*

Reader Response

Open for Discussion

Imagine that you are Mark. Tell what you have learned about "going with the flow."

Comprehension Check

1. Mark thinks his new situation in New Jersey is different from what he left in Vermont. What are his reasons?

2. Mark's sister and his father both talk to Mark after his bad day. How are their conversations with Mark different? Which one helps him more? Find details to support your answer.

3. Do you think that Mark would have left his new school if he hadn't been invited to play basketball? Use evidence from the story to explain.

4. How does Mark act on his first day at his new school? Does his **character** change? (Character)

5. What does Mark discover about Keith's **character?** (Character)

 Test Prep

Look Back and Write

Look back at pages 254–258. On page 256, Keith tells Mark to "go with the flow," and at the end of the story Mark says he is learning to do that. What does Keith mean? How does Mark show that he is going "with the flow"? Explain, using details from the selection.

Drive

by Charles R. Smith, Jr.

Drive
draw
and dish.
Can turn
nothing
into
a swish
as I
resist
temptation
to let one
pop
from the top
of the key.
Could be
worth
three,
but only
if I make it.
Fake it
then
take it
strong
to the hOle
with soul
looking to finish
with
a finger roll.

To the left
to the right
earthbound
legs
take flight
ready
to excite
the crowd
into a
frenzy.
Victory—
could be—
if my
finger roll
can clear
the trees.
As I
rise
high
to the sky
I
let fly
my
all
with the
ball
as the
buzzer
sounds
and the
swish

falls.

Graphic Sources

- A **graphic source,** such as a picture, graph, or map, shows information visually.

- Before you read, look for graphic sources of information that could give you an idea of what the article or story is about.

- As you read, compare the written words to the graphic sources for a better understanding of the main ideas.

Read "Train Time" from *The Spectacular Trains* by John Everds.

Talk About It

1. What information does the graphic source in "Train Time" show you?

2. Before you read, what gave you an idea of what the article would be about?

3. Does the map help you understand the paragraphs? Why or why not?

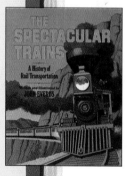

TRAIN TIME
by John Everds

Before 1883 there was no standard time. All the cities and villages throughout the United States were on "sun time." Clocks were set at 12:00 noon when the sun was directly overhead, but this time changed from city to city. When it was 12:00 noon in Washington, it was 12:07 in Philadelphia, 11:53 in Buffalo, 12:12 in New York, and 12:24 in Boston. To make matters worse, each railroad could choose its own time. Trains pulling into the Pittsburgh terminal had their clocks set to six different times. In all, American railroads operated on more than sixty different times.

Railroad companies soon found that to operate efficiently, trains had to arrive and depart on time.

Finally, in 1883, the nation was divided into four time zones. When it was one o'clock in the Eastern Time Zone, it was twelve o'clock in the Central Zone, eleven o'clock in the Mountain Zone and ten o'clock in the Pacific Zone. It now became possible to publish an accurate schedule, and with trains running on standard time, many accidents were avoided.

Standard Time Zones in the United States

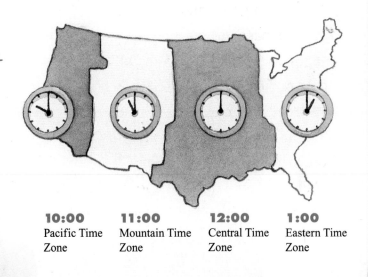

10:00	11:00	12:00	1:00
Pacific Time Zone	Mountain Time Zone	Central Time Zone	Eastern Time Zone

LOOK AHEAD →

In *Kate Shelley: Bound for Legend*, Kate risks her life to warn a train that a bridge has been destroyed. Use the map in the selection to follow her dangerous journey.

Vocabulary

Words to Know

dispatched	downpour	heroic
rescuers	locomotives	rugged
schedules		

When you read, you may come across a word you don't know. To figure out its meaning, look for clues in the words and sentences around it. A clue may be a description near the unfamiliar word.

Read the paragraph below. Notice how the description of *downpour* helps you understand what it means.

Flood!

In the spring of 1995, the Mississippi River flooded parts of Illinois and Missouri when heavy rains fell upon the area. One <u>downpour</u> after another caused the river to rise above its riverbanks and spill over onto the land. Rail lines were swamped with mud and water, and river rocks made paved roads <u>rugged</u>. Cars, trucks, and <u>locomotives</u> couldn't move. Train and bus <u>schedules</u> fell apart. People needing help waited patiently for <u>rescuers</u>, and the National Guard was <u>dispatched</u>. Some <u>heroic</u> people saved lives. Everyone tried to be brave.

Talk About It

Use some or all of the vocabulary words to describe a rescue you know about.

KATE SHELLEY

BOUND FOR LEGEND

by Robert D. San Souci   illustrated by Max Ginsburg

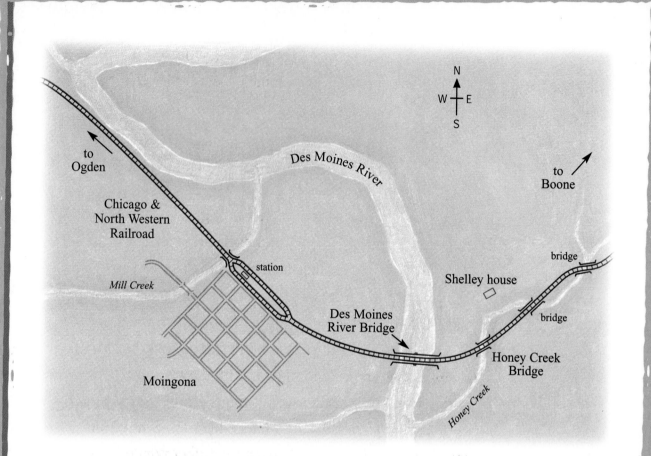

A railroad bridge crossed Honey Creek not far from Kate Shelley's little Iowa farmhouse. Every day trains sped back and forth over the trestle, heading east toward Chicago or west toward the long Des Moines River Bridge on the way to Salt Lake City. As they roared past, the trains brought a touch of excitement to fifteen-year-old Kate's life.

Once the railroad had been the Shelley family's main source of income. Kate's father, who had died three years earlier, had been a section foreman on the Chicago & North Western Railway. Now, in 1881, the farm—a patch of pasture and timber set amid rugged hills in the heart of Iowa—supported the family.

Good-natured, sturdy Kate had taken charge of the family because of her mother's poor health. She helped with the plowing and planting. With her nine-year-old sister Mayme she gathered firewood and tended the vegetable garden. She even taught herself to shoot to keep hawks away from the chickens.

Kate saw the younger children, Margaret, Mayme, and John, off to school in the morning and helped tuck them in at night. She kept them away from the dangerous banks of Honey Creek, because none of them could swim. One brother, James, had drowned shortly after his father's death. Kate was the one who discovered his riderless horse beside the Des Moines River, where the boy had been swept away while wading.

In moments between chores Kate read every book she could lay her hands on, to make up for her lack of schooling. She loved to ride bareback through the forests in autumn or row a skiff along the broad, smooth surface of the river in high summer.

But the railroad was her real love. When errands took her to the little coal mining village of Moingona, a mile away, she would stop by the train station. She would linger in the waiting room with its potbellied stove and high-backed bench. Sometimes she would hear urgent tapping from behind the ticket window as news came over the telegraph wire, or as the stationmaster sent word to distant stations to alert approaching trains of hazards.

Adventure appealed to Kate. "She was absolutely without fear," her sister Mayme would recall later in life. But her adventures were confined to farm and family for the first fifteen years of her life—until one July day in 1881.

When the eastbound freight from Moingona neared the Shelley farm on the afternoon of Wednesday, July 6, 1881, Kate and her mother were taking the wash off the clothesline. It had rained for most of a week, and now black clouds were heaping up on the horizon, threatening another storm. But Kate stopped pulling sheets, shifts, and stockings from the line long enough to watch Engine 230 help a freight train climb the grade up to Honey Creek Bridge on its way to Boone, a town five miles distant.

The freight train was late. Kate knew the schedules by heart, and she could recognize each of the local "pushers" (Number 230 was one) by its whistle. These four locomotives sat on sidetracks until they were needed to help push or pull heavy trains up the steep slope.

As Mrs. Shelley and Kate lifted the full laundry basket, the sky went dark as if a black curtain had been flung across the sun. They barely reached the back door of their two-story clapboard house before the first heavy raindrops began to fall.

Soon the deadly storm broke. "You can only imagine what a fearful thing it is to see the heavens grow black and blacker until the light of day is all shut out," Kate later said, "to see the clouds torn into fragments by the fierce lightnings, and the torrents fall and swallow up the earth."

Thunder rattled loose glass in the window frame, while fierce wind hurled sheets of rain against the house. Kate watched anxiously as Honey Creek's waters rose higher than she had ever seen them.

She soon began to fear for the safety of the animals in the barn on the slope below the house. Putting on an old coat and hat, she hurried to the barn through the ankle-deep water gushing down the hillside.

The water was just as deep inside. The plow horses, cattle, and hogs were splashing nervously in their stalls and pens. Kate led each of them to higher ground in an oat field, then turned them loose.

By the time she returned to the barn for a last look around, the water had grown knee-deep. Hearing a terrified squealing, Kate discovered several piglets that had climbed onto an island of hay. She carried them to the safety of the oat field and tucked them under the sow. Then, drenched and chilled, she ran back to the house.

As she dried off by the kitchen stove, Kate heard the frightening noise of trees being uprooted by the gale. The younger children were fed and put to bed, but the effort didn't take Kate's mind off raging Honey Creek. With every lull in the downpour, Kate saw picket fences, parts of walls, even small trees pile up against the straining supports of the trestle over the brimming stream.

As Kate noted the passing hours, she began to worry about the midnight express. "Surely no trains will be dispatched in this storm," Margaret Shelley said to soothe her daughter.

It was well past eleven o'clock when Kate clearly heard the rumble of a pusher engine climbing the grade to Honey Creek Bridge. She heard its bell clang twice. Then there was a dreadful crash, followed by an awful hiss of steam as hot metal hit cold water.

"Oh, Mother!" cried Kate, clutching Margaret's hand. "It's Number Eleven. They've gone down Honey Creek Bridge!"

For a moment the two stared at each other in horror, while Mayme, awakened by the sound, huddled in the kitchen door. Then Kate reached for her damp coat and soggy straw hat hanging beside the stove. "I must go to help the men," Kate said.

Mrs. Shelley begged her not to go, but Kate insisted. "If that were Father down there," she said, "we'd expect someone to help him." Then, mindful of a graver danger, she added, "And I must stop the midnight train from the west."

Hundreds of passengers bound for Chicago would be aboard the express train headed for the ruined Honey Creek Bridge. Kate told her mother that she would go to Moingona Station and have the stationmaster telegraph a warning down the line. If she couldn't reach the station in time, she would flag down the train herself.

Quickly she took her father's old railroad lantern and filled it with oil. There was no wick, so Kate grabbed an old flannel skirt and tore off a strip. In a moment she had lit the lamp.

"Kate, if you go out there, you'll be lost or hurt," her mother said in a last effort to make her stay.

"I could never forgive myself if I didn't," she replied.

Her mother sighed, "Go, then, in the name of God, and do what you can."

Because the front yard was flooded, Kate followed a path that led up the slope behind the house, then veered toward the shattered trestle. Her mother suddenly ran after Kate, but slipped

in the water streaming down the hillside. Kate helped her to her feet, saw that she was all right, then continued on her way. While Mayme stared from the window, Mrs. Shelley paced back and forth in the mud and water, keeping a frantic watch on Kate.

Kate slogged through the rain until she came to the bluff above Honey Creek. From this twenty-foot drop-off, Honey Creek Bridge had once extended across to the facing bluff. Amid the broken timbers and pilings a small rounded section of the steam engine jutted out of the churning black water. Only a bit of railing marked the sunken "tender," the special car that carried water and coal for the engine. The unfortunate crew had been sent out to check for storm-damaged tracks. Kate would later learn that two men aboard the locomotive had been killed.

Moving along the cliff, Kate waved her lantern. In response two men shouted up to her. She could barely see them as they clung to some willow branches above the raging water. She called

back to them, and they yelled something up to her. But the storm was so fierce that she couldn't make out what they said.

Kate realized that she could do nothing for them by herself, and time was running out for the midnight express. She turned and headed for the Des Moines River Bridge. Moingona Station and its telegraph were on the other side.

Kate struggled on against the pelting rain as bushes and brambles snagged her clothes. The lightning seemed a hundred times more frightening in the open, but it lit the long bridge that was her goal.

Inch by inch, Kate fought her way up the steep approach to the bridge. Though the span was normally a full fifty feet above the water, the angry river seemed only a short distance below her. Before she reached the bridge, the wind extinguished her feeble lamp, and she had no way to relight it.

Fearfully she peered into the dark, afraid that the midnight express might be speeding across the bridge. But no whistle knifed through the howling wind; no engine's headlamp hurtled toward her.

Nearly seven hundred feet long, the Des Moines River Bridge was a ladder of cross ties, each nearly two feet apart. Though Kate had crossed the bridge in good weather, its splintery ties were studded with twisted spikes and nails to discourage such foot traffic.

"Those who cross a railroad bridge on a swiftly moving train can form no conception of the sensation a traveler experiences who attempts to cross on foot," Kate later said. "A misstep would send me down below the ties into the flood that was boiling below. I got down on my hands and knees, carrying yet my useless lantern and guiding myself by the stretch of rail."

Shivering from the wet and cold, Kate crept along, avoiding the worst buffeting of the wind. She would reach her fingers out to locate the next tie, then cross to it with the help of the iron track. Again and again, her skirt or coat sleeve caught on a nail or spike or splinter. Her hands and knees were cut and bleeding. Several times she nearly lost her hold on the rain-slick ties. The hungry river was terrifying to Kate, who was near the spot where her brother James had drowned.

"Halfway over, a piercing flash of lightning showed me the angry flood more closely than ever," Kate would remember, "and swept along upon it a great tree—the earth still hanging to its

roots—was racing for the bridge, and, it seemed, for the very spot I stood upon. Fear brought me upright on my knees, and I clasped my hands in terror, and in prayer, I hope, lest the shock should carry out the bridge."

Kate braced for the crash. But the huge tree swept between the pilings, its branches grabbing and slapping at her through the ties. She was spattered with water and foam from the snapping limbs before the raging waters swept the tree into the darkness downriver.

Without her lantern Kate knew she had no hope of flagging down the midnight express. She had to reach Moingona Station so that a warning could be sent.

So tired that she could only think of reaching the next tie, and then the next, Kate began to crawl the rest of the way across the bridge. The cold numbed the stinging in her hands and knees. Raising her head, she took heart when she saw the lights of the railway station in the distance.

At last she reached solid ground. She paused just long enough to catch her breath. Then, forcing herself to her feet, she ran the half mile remaining to Moingona Station.

She burst into the waiting room, where several men were talking, and blurted out her warning. Kate later admitted that she had no memory of how, exactly, she told her tale. She only remembered someone saying, "The girl is crazy."

But the station agent cried, "That's Kate Shelley! She would know if the bridge was out!"

Then Kate, exhausted by her ordeal, collapsed on the spot.

When she came to a few moments later, she was lying on the hard, cold wooden bench. To her relief she found that the midnight express had not yet come through.

Much later she would learn that the train had been halted forty miles to the west, at the edge of the storm. The passengers were safe, but other lives were still in danger.

"The crew from Number Eleven still need help," Kate said. She quickly agreed to guide the rescue mission to save the men. Though others tried to get her to rest, Kate would not be put off.

Engine 230, sidetracked in the Moingona Station yard, was quickly filled with volunteers carrying ropes and shovels. As it headed for the fallen trestle, the engineer kept sounding the whistle to let the stranded men know that help was on the way.

Riding in the cab, Kate must have held her breath as the train eased across the Des Moines Bridge. But the structure proved solid, and the storm was quieting at last.

Exhausted yet determined, Kate guided the others to where she had seen the two crewmen in Honey Creek. The men, Number Eleven's engineer and brakeman, still clung to branches above the receding water, but there was no way for the rescuers to get down to the stream. Kate had to lead them into the hills behind her home—reversing the path she had traced earlier that evening—to an undamaged railroad bridge beyond the house.

Only now could they follow the track back west to reach the stranded men. By the time they were brought to safety, the rain had almost ceased, and chilly gray dawn had begun to lighten the sky.

Shaking from cold and weariness, Kate was brought home. Her mother hugged her, then put her to bed, mounding the blankets above the shivering girl.

The story of Kate's bravery was telegraphed all over the state and across the nation. She was celebrated in countless newspapers as "the Iowa heroine."

But Kate was too sick to care. Over and over she repeated to Mayme, "I can still feel the cold rain on my face."

At one point her teeth began to chatter so loudly that Mrs. Shelley was forced to send for the doctor; but all he could do was whittle a peg from soft wood. He told Kate's mother, "Put this between her teeth to keep her from breaking them."

Strangers gathered in the yard to look at "Our Kate," as they called her. Some even asked for a bit of her skirt or a lock of her hair. Mrs. Shelley shooed them away.

It was nearly three months before Kate's strength came back. During this time as she lay in bed, she was greeted by the trains that blew their whistles when they passed the Shelley farmhouse.

Finally, one afternoon she announced that she felt well enough to go outside. Escorted by her mother, sisters, and brother, Kate stepped out on the porch, hoping to catch a glimpse of the westbound train. To her surprise, the train stopped in front of the house, and crew and passengers leaned out to cheer her. Red-faced but delighted, she waved back to them.

Later, when she was able to go into town, the trains would stop and carry her to Moingona.

Many honors came to Kate in the days that followed.
She received a medal from the state of Iowa, inscribed:

Presented by the State of Iowa, to Kate Shelley,
with the thanks of the General Assembly
in recognition of the Courage and Devotion
of a child of fifteen years whom neither the fury of the elements,
nor the fear of death could appall in her effort to save human life
during the terrible storm and flood in the Des Moines Valley
on the night of July 6th, 1881.

There were other gifts and awards, but perhaps the most
wonderful for Kate was a lifetime pass on the railroad. In the
years that followed she attended Simpson College, and in 1903
became station agent at Moingona. She held this job until illness
forced her to retire in 1911. She died the following year at the
age of forty-six.

Always modest when asked about her heroic deed, Kate would
say, "I believe that God makes strong the weakest and makes the
poorest of us able to do much for His merciful purposes."

Kate's final train ride came on the day of her funeral.
A special train stopped at the Shelley home to pick up her
coffin and carry her to the Boone depot. Her resting place
was the Sacred Heart Cemetery on the edge of Boone.

About the Author
ROBERT D. SAN SOUCI

Robert D. San Souci always knew that he wanted to be a writer. In fact, before Mr. San Souci could read or write, he would listen carefully while stories were read to him. He then would retell them to others. He says, "But I would add new bits or leave out those I didn't find so interesting—so the storytelling impulse was already at work in me."

The biography, *Kate Shelley: Bound for Legend,* is somewhat different from what Mr. San Souci normally writes. What he is best known for are his retellings of folktales. He likes telling folktales, because "these tales often remind us how alike we are—yet, at the same time, they affirm how wonderful it is that people have so many different, imaginative, and insightful ways of making sense of the world and celebrating its wonders."

About the Illustrator
MAX GINSBURG

Besides illustrating *Kate Shelley: Bound for Legend,* Max Ginsburg has also illustrated the book jackets for many children's books. These include *The Friendship* and *Mississippi Bridge* by Mildred D. Taylor. His artwork has won the Gold Medal from the Society of Illustrators in New York. When he is not illustrating children's books, Mr. Ginsburg often creates paintings that deal with social issues. His paintings have been exhibited in several one-person shows in New York City, where he lives and teaches.

Reader Response

Open for Discussion

Describe what you could have done to help Kate Shelley on that night in 1881.

Comprehension Check

1. Do you think Kate Shelley acted wisely when she went out into the storm to stop the midnight train and to help the people who had been in a crash? Explain, using details from the selection.

2. After reading this biography, what kind of people do you think receive awards and honors like the ones Kate Shelley received? Support your answer with examples.

3. What does the selection tell us about Kate Shelley's activities before the night of July 6, 1881? How did her life change after she got her strength back?

4. Name a type of **graphic source** used in this selection. How does it help you understand the biography? (Graphic Sources)

5. A train schedule is a **graphic source** that is mentioned in the selection but not shown. What kind of information would the train schedule in the biography have? Make up a simple train schedule for those trains. (Graphic Sources)

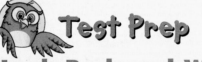

Test Prep

Look Back and Write

With the Honey Creek bridge destroyed, the rescuers couldn't get down to the water to save the engineer and brakeman. Look back at page 276 and at the map on page 266. How did Kate show them another way to reach the men? Explain, using details from the selection.

Test Prep

How to Read a Social Studies Textbook

1. Preview

- Read "Looking Ahead" to find what you need to pay attention to in the article.

- Notice the map. What does it show?

2. Read and Use a Web

- As you read, use a web to help you answer the questions in "Looking Ahead." For example,

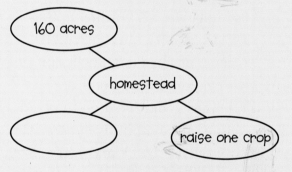

3. Think and Connect

Look over your webs on "The Last Western Frontier." Then look back at *Kate Shelley: Bound for Legend* and answer this question.

What was the difference between the way Kate Shelley and her family made their living and the way the homesteaders lived?

THE LAST
WESTERN FRONTIER

from *America: Yesterday and Today*

LOOKING AHEAD

As you read, look for—

Key words, people, and places:
homestead
transcontinental
Promontory Point

Look for answers to these questions about **main ideas:**

1. What was a homestead, and how did homesteaders live?
2. How was the first transcontinental railroad built?

For hundreds of years, Americans who wanted to make a fresh start in life headed west. To Americans of 1776, the West was land between the Appalachian Mountains and the Mississippi River. To Americans of the 1840s, the West was the land west of the Rocky Mountains, near the Pacific Coast. After the Civil War, Americans settled the last West. The last West was the Great Plains. Find the Great Plains just east of the Rocky Mountains on the map on the next page.

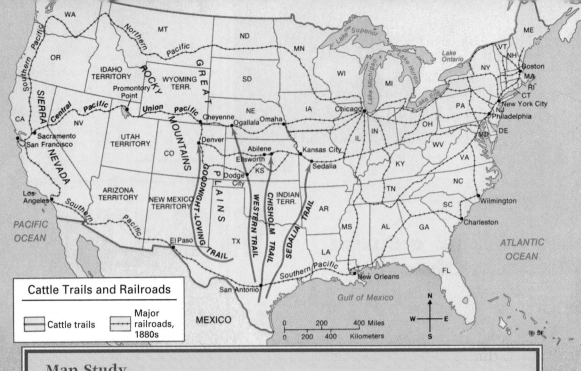

Cattle Trails and Railroads

Cattle trails

Major railroads, 1880s

Map Study

Use your finger to trace the routes of the main railroad lines from east to west. Trace the routes of the main north-south lines. Which city appears to be the major rail center? Name the four cattle trails over which cowboys drove their herds to the railroad for shipment. Which trail is farthest west?

Pioneers traveling west

THE HOMESTEADERS

The pioneers of the 1840s and 1850s had called the Great Plains the "Great American Desert." By the 1860s, however, pioneers looked at this area differently. They saw this land as a promised land.

The United States government was giving this land away. According to the Homestead Act of 1862, anyone could claim 160 acres of this land. Such a piece of land was called a **homestead.** It was free if the homesteader lived on the land and raised one crop within five years. All kinds of Americans—black and white, rich and poor—settled on homesteads. Pioneers came from Europe too. Russians, Norwegians, Swedes, Irish, and Germans all flocked to the Great Plains of the United States.

The Great Plains was a harsh land. In the summer it was baked by one hundred-degree temperatures. In the winter it was frozen at forty degrees below zero. Wooden plows could not cut through the tough sod—dirt held together by tangled grass roots—covering the land. However, pioneers using steel plows found that the soil below the surface was deep and rich. Although they had to battle extremes in weather, hordes of insects, dry spells, and floods, many pioneers succeeded in setting up flourishing farms.

THE GREAT RAILROADS

At the same time pioneers were beginning to settle the Great Plains, Americans were building a **transcontinental** railroad across this region.

In 1862 the Central Pacific Railroad started building its line in Sacramento, California, heading east. Most of the Central Pacific's workers were Chinese. Some of these people were Chinese Americans who had lived in California for years. Others were hired in China and came by ship to California. The Central Pacific's workers laid track through the high Sierra Nevadas. They built bridges across rivers. They blasted tunnels through solid rock. Once across the mountains, they faced the heat of the desert. Use your finger to trace the Central Pacific Railroad on the map on page 284. Through which present-day states did the Central Pacific pass?

Locate the Union Pacific Railroad on the map. Also in 1862 the Union Pacific Railroad line headed west from Omaha, Nebraska. A majority of the Union Pacific's workers were Irish. Black Americans, Swedes, Norwegians, and Mexicans also worked on the railroad. Many of the

Workers laying track in the Sierra Nevadas

workers were Civil War veterans. These workers faced attacks by Indians who lived on the Great Plains. They also had trouble with herds of buffalo that sometimes tore up the track.

After seven years, the two railroad lines met at **Promontory Point,** Utah, on May 10, 1869. The first transcontinental railroad was complete. It stretched from coast to coast, across the entire continent. Later, more transcontinental lines were built. What other transcontinental lines do you see on the map? The railroads helped tie the country together. They also brought more and more people to the West.

from America: Yesterday and Today

285

Plot

- The important events that happen in a story make up the **plot**.

- A plot has a conflict, rising action, climax, and an outcome.

  Conflict is the story's main problem. The conflict can be within a character, between two characters, or between a character and nature.

  During the *rising action,* one event follows another. Each event adds interest or suspense to the conflict.

  The *climax* is the high point when the main character faces the problem directly.

  The *outcome* is the ending of the story.

Read "Anything You Set Your Mind To" from *One-Minute Birthday Stories* **by Shari Lewis and Lan O'Kun.**

Write About It

1. What is the conflict?

2. What events lead up to the climax?

3. Describe the outcome.

Anything You Set Your Mind To

by Shari Lewis and Lan O'Kun

Terry Brink could not learn to swim. He had been trying since he was very little, but the water didn't seem to hold him up. Everybody else floated. Terry sank. It made no sense. He went to the big pool. There, everybody swam except him—or so it seemed.

"What is wrong with me?" he muttered.

"There's nothing wrong with you," the lifeguard replied. "Keep trying." Terry Brink kept trying—and he kept sinking. When his father asked him what he wanted for his birthday, Terry said, "I want to be able to swim."

Terry's dad assured him, "You can do anything you set your mind to."

"I can do anything I set my mind to," Terry Brink repeated to himself.

Early on the morning of Terry's birthday, Terry's mom and dad got the best swimming teacher they could find, and took their birthday boy to the pool. Terry worked and played with the teacher almost all day. Terry blew bubbles. He kicked his feet. He used his arms. First he found that he could stay afloat in one place by using his arms and legs to tread water, and then—suddenly—he was swimming. What had seemed impossible until this particular day suddenly happened! Terry Brink swam across the pool.

"You see," his dad said. "You can do anything you set your mind to."

Terry Brink grinned. "Dad," he said, "for my *next* birthday, I want to fly!"

In "The Marble Champ," Lupe sets her mind to finding a sport she can be good at. Follow the plot of her story to find out if she succeeds.

Vocabulary

Words to Know

championship **opponent** **trophy**
strengthen   **swollen**

Words with opposite meanings are called **antonyms**. You can often figure out the meaning of an unknown word by finding a clue in the words around it. Sometimes this clue is an antonym.

Read the paragraph below. Notice how *teammate* helps you understand what *opponent* means.

A Tennis Triumph

Last night the girls' tennis team brought home a <u>trophy</u>. The team members were very proud because they had won the state <u>championship</u>. To prepare for the tournament, the players spent as many hours hitting tennis balls as they could. Each girl worked on skills she wanted to <u>strengthen</u>. One girl practiced so hard that her elbow became <u>swollen</u>. Luckily, it shrank back to a normal size before the tournament, and she was allowed to play. On the day of the big event, the team was ready. Each teammate faced her <u>opponent</u> with a winning attitude and a great serve.

Write About It

Write about a time when you or your team won or lost. Use as many vocabulary words as you can.

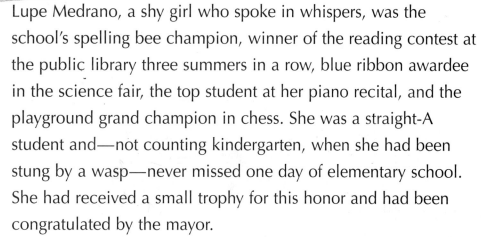

The Marble Champ

by Gary Soto

Lupe Medrano, a shy girl who spoke in whispers, was the school's spelling bee champion, winner of the reading contest at the public library three summers in a row, blue ribbon awardee in the science fair, the top student at her piano recital, and the playground grand champion in chess. She was a straight-A student and—not counting kindergarten, when she had been stung by a wasp—never missed one day of elementary school. She had received a small trophy for this honor and had been congratulated by the mayor.

But though Lupe had a razor-sharp mind, she could not make her body, no matter how much she tried, run as fast as the other girls'. She begged her body to move faster, but could never beat anyone in the fifty-yard dash.

The truth was that Lupe was no good in sports. She could not catch a pop-up or figure out in which direction to kick the soccer ball. One time she kicked the ball at her own goal and scored a point for the other team. She was no good at baseball or basketball either, and even had a hard time making a Hula-Hoop stay on her hips.

It wasn't until last year, when she was eleven years old, that she learned how to ride a bike. And even then she had to use training wheels. She could walk in the swimming pool but couldn't swim, and chanced roller skating only when her father held her hand.

"I'll never be good at sports," she fumed one rainy day as she lay on her bed gazing at the shelf her father had made to hold her awards. "I wish I could win something, anything, even marbles."

At the word *marbles*, she sat up. "That's it. Maybe I could be good at playing marbles." She hopped out of bed and rummaged through the closet until she found a can full of her brother's marbles. She poured the rich glass treasure on her bed and picked five of the most beautiful marbles.

She smoothed her bedspread and practiced shooting, softly at first so that her aim would be accurate. The marble rolled from her thumb and clicked against the targeted marble. But the target wouldn't budge. She tried again and again. Her aim became accurate, but the power from her thumb made the marble move only an inch or two. Then she realized that the bedspread was slowing the marbles. She also had to admit that her thumb was weaker than the neck of a newborn chick.

She looked out the window. The rain was letting up, but the ground was too muddy to play. She sat cross-legged on the bed, rolling her five marbles between her palms. Yes, she thought, I could play marbles, and marbles is a sport. At that moment, she realized that she had only two weeks to practice. The playground championship, the same one her brother had entered the previous year, was coming up. She had a lot to do.

To strengthen her wrists, she decided to do twenty push-ups on her fingertips, five at a time. "One, two, three . . ." she groaned. By the end of the first set she was breathing hard, and her muscles burned from exhaustion. She did one more set and decided that was enough push-ups for the first day.

She squeezed a rubber eraser one hundred times, hoping it would strengthen her thumb. This seemed to work because the next day her thumb was sore. She could hardly hold a marble in her hand, let alone send it flying with power. So Lupe rested that day and listened to her brother, who gave her tips on how to shoot: get low, aim with one eye, and place one knuckle on the ground.

"Think 'eye and thumb'—and let it rip!" he said.

After school the next day she left her homework in her backpack and practiced three hours straight, taking time only to eat a candy bar for energy. With a Popsicle stick, she drew an odd-shaped circle and tossed in four marbles. She used her shooter, a milky agate with hypnotic swirls, to blast them. Her thumb *had* become stronger.

After practice, she squeezed the eraser for an hour. She ate dinner with her left hand to spare her shooting hand and said nothing to her parents about her dreams of athletic glory.

Practice, practice, practice. Squeeze, squeeze, squeeze. Lupe got better and beat her brother and Alfonso, a neighbor kid who was supposed to be a champ.

"Man, she's bad!" Alfonso said. "She can beat the other girls for sure. I think."

The weeks passed quickly. Lupe worked so hard that one day, while she was drying dishes, her mother asked why her thumb was swollen.

"It's muscle," Lupe explained. "I've been practicing for the marble championship."

"You, honey?" Her mother knew Lupe was no good at sports.

"Yeah. I beat Alfonso, and he's pretty good."

That night, over dinner, Mrs. Medrano said, "Honey, you should see Lupe's thumb."

"Huh?" Mr. Medrano said, wiping his mouth and looking at his daughter.

"Show your father."

"Do I have to?" an embarrassed Lupe asked.

"Go on, show your father."

Reluctantly, Lupe raised her hand and flexed her thumb. You could see the muscle.

The father put down his fork and asked, "What happened?"

"Dad, I've been working out. I've been squeezing an eraser."

"Why?"

"I'm going to enter the marbles championship."

Her father looked at her mother and then back at his daughter. "When is it, honey?"

"This Saturday. Can you come?"

The father had been planning to play racquetball with a friend Saturday, but he said he would be there. He knew his daughter thought she was no good at sports and he wanted to encourage her. He even rigged some lights in the backyard so she could practice after dark. He squatted with one knee on the ground, entranced by the sight of his daughter easily beating her brother.

The day of the championship began with a cold blustery sky. The sun was a silvery light behind slate clouds.

"I hope it clears up," her father said, rubbing his hands together as he returned from getting the newspaper. They ate breakfast, paced nervously around the house waiting for 10:00 to arrive, and walked the two blocks to the playground (though Mr. Medrano wanted to drive so Lupe wouldn't get tired). She signed up and was assigned her first match on baseball diamond number three.

Lupe, walking between her brother and her father, shook from the cold, not nerves. She took off her mittens, and everyone stared at her thumb. Someone asked, "How can you play with a broken thumb?" Lupe smiled and said nothing.

She beat her first opponent easily, and felt sorry for the girl because she didn't have anyone to cheer for her. Except for her sack of marbles, she was all alone. Lupe invited the girl, whose name was Rachel, to stay with them. She smiled and said, "OK." The four of them walked to a card table in the middle of the outfield, where Lupe was assigned another opponent.

She also beat this girl, a fifth-grader named Yolanda, and asked her to join their group. They proceeded to more matches and more wins, and soon there was a crowd of people following Lupe to the finals to play a girl in a baseball cap. This girl seemed dead serious. She never even looked at Lupe.

"I don't know, Dad, she looks tough."

Rachel hugged Lupe and said, "Go get her."

"You can do it," her father encouraged. "Just think of the marbles, not the girl, and let your thumb do the work."

The other girl broke first and earned one marble. She missed her next shot, and Lupe, one eye closed, her thumb quivering with energy, blasted two marbles out of the circle but missed her next shot. Her opponent earned two more before missing. She stamped her foot and said, "Shoot!" The score was three to two in favor of Miss Baseball Cap.

The referee stopped the game. "Back up, please, give them room," he shouted. Onlookers had gathered too tightly around the players.

Lupe then earned three marbles and was set to get her fourth when a gust of wind blew dust in her eyes and she missed badly. Her opponent quickly scored two marbles, tying the game, and moved ahead six to five on a lucky shot. Then she missed, and Lupe, whose eyes felt scratchy when she blinked, relied on instinct and thumb muscle to score the tying point. It was now six to six, with only three marbles left. Lupe blew her nose and studied the angles. She dropped to one knee, steadied her hand and shot so hard she cracked two marbles from the circle. She was the winner!

"I did it!" Lupe said under her breath. She rose from her knees, which hurt from bending all day, and hugged her father. He hugged her back and smiled.

Everyone clapped, except Miss Baseball Cap, who made a face and stared at the ground. Lupe told her she was a great player, and they shook hands. A newspaper photographer took pictures of the two girls standing shoulder-to-shoulder, with Lupe holding the bigger trophy.

Lupe then played the winner of the boys' division, and after a poor start beat him eleven to four. She blasted the marbles, shattering one into sparkling slivers of glass. Her opponent looked on glumly as Lupe did what she did best—win!

The head referee and the President of the Fresno Marble Association stood with Lupe as she displayed her trophies for the newspaper photographer. Lupe shook hands with everyone, including a dog who had come over to see what the commotion was all about.

That night, the family went out for pizza and set the two trophies on the table for everyone in the restaurant to see. People came up to congratulate Lupe, and she felt a little embarrassed, but her father said the trophies belonged there.

Back home, in the privacy of her bedroom, she placed the trophies on her shelf and was happy. She had always earned honors because of her brains, but winning in sports was a new experience. She thanked her tired thumb. "You did it, thumb. You made me champion." As its reward, Lupe went to the bathroom, filled the bathroom sink with warm water, and let her thumb swim and splash as it pleased. Then she climbed into bed and drifted into a hard-won sleep.

About the Author
Gary Soto

When Gary Soto was growing up in the barrio, a Mexican American neighborhood in Fresno, California, he had no interest in becoming a writer. It was in college that he began to love reading and started writing stories and poetry of his own. His books for and about young people are based on his own memories of childhood.

Baseball in April and Other Stories, which includes "The Marble Champ," was named a Best Book for Young Adults by the American Library Association.

Reader Response

Open for Discussion

If you were Lupe, what would you say was the best part of becoming a marble champion?

Comprehension Check

1. Do you think Lupe will continue to practice marbles and compete in tournaments? Use evidence from the story to support your answer.

2. Describe how Lupe's father reacts at the dinner table when he finds out about Lupe's new sport. What are some of his other reactions?

3. Are the parts of the story about Lupe's thumb meant to be serious or funny? Explain why you think so.

4. Think about the **plot** of "The Marble Champ." What are the conflict and the rising action in this story? (Plot)

5. Outcome is a **plot** element. What is the outcome of this story? What might the outcome be if Lupe did not win the tournament? (Plot)

Test Prep

Look Back and Write

Look back at pages 289–300. How important an event is the marbles tournament to the people in Fresno, California? Use details from the story to support your answer.

Test Prep

How to Read an Informational Article

1. Preview

- What tells you more about the article—the title or the headings?

- Look at the diagrams and figure out what they show.

2. Read and Use Questions

- Rewrite the headings to form questions. For example,

  What are some warning signs of sports injuries?

  What are some ways to prevent sports injuries?

- Then, as you read, list details that will help you answer each question.

3. Think and Connect

Look over your notes on "The Big Ouchie." Then look back at "The Marble Champ" and answer this question.

Is Lupe's swollen thumb a sports injury? How might she have avoided getting it?

Leah Fish, 12, plays tennis and soccer and loves to ski. One day she noticed a bump on her knee. "I went to a doctor, and he started poking the sore area." The doctor discovered Leah had a knee injury that sometimes happens when kids play sports too much.

Ronnie Strod, 14, has pitched in Little League since he was nine. "Last year, my arm felt sore, but I kept pitching," Ronnie said. "In our fourth game, the pain got so bad, the coach made me sit on the bench." A month later, the elbow still hurt. Ronnie had "Little League elbow," and had to stop pitching for a year. He played third base instead.

Both Leah and Ronnie are among tens of thousands of kids who have "overuse injuries." These injuries to bones, muscles, and tendons (which attach muscles to bones) happen when an athlete puts stress on the same part of the body, over and over.

Ouchie
by Jordan Brown

Now, overuse injuries are on the rise as kids get into soccer, baseball, basketball, gymnastics, and running.

"Years ago, when kids were left to themselves to play sports, overuse injuries were rarely seen," Michelle Glassman says. Her organization works to reduce the number of kids' sports injuries.

"When kids got tired, they just stopped. But now, because of the pressures of organized sports, kids no longer rest as much as they need to." And hard play puts a lot of wear and tear on the same body parts.

Overuse injuries are most common at the start of the season, when many out-of-shape kids suddenly become very active. Injuries also take place during the peak of the season, when kids push themselves to the max.

"When a child does too much, too fast, muscle tissue breaks down and overuse injuries happen," says Jenny Stone of the U.S. Olympic Committee on Sports Medicine.

Kids may also get more overuse injuries because they are growing. So a kid's arms and legs can't stand as much stress as an adult's.

Avoiding Sports Boo-boos

According to the American College of Sports Medicine, half of overuse injuries can be avoided. So, sports lovers, how can YOU avoid getting a big ouchie? Here's what the experts say:

Prepare Your Body

Get in shape before the first day of practice. Soccer players, for example, should start practicing six weeks before the season. Be sure to warm up and cool down.

Take It Slow

Increase your training schedule gradually—by no more than 10 percent from one week to the next.

Get a Pre-season Checkup

Get a physical from a doctor who knows sports medicine.

Listen to Your Body

Stop throwing if your elbow, shoulder, or arm starts to hurt.

Take It Easy

When you feel aches or pain in the same part of the body, take a break. Instead of practicing five days a week, cut back to three.

Don't Hide the Hurt

Tell your coach or parent when you feel pain. If the pain continues, see a doctor.

Obey League Limits

Obey limits set by your sports league. For example, young pitchers should only pitch six innings a week.

Avoid the Same Old Grind

Switch positions every now and then. Instead of catching, play second base.

Use Proper Gear

Use approved equipment for support and to cushion stressful, heavy workouts.

Soccer Injury: Sever Disease

Warning signs:
Heel pain while walking, running, or jumping

Prevention:
1. Gently stretch calf muscles daily and before games.
2. Start an early, gradual running program before the season.
3. Wear soccer shoes with strong arch supports.

"Sever Disease" is an inflammation of the Achilles tendon where it attaches to the foot.

Baseball Injury: Little League Elbow

Warning Signs:
Elbow gets stiff or painful during play and is hard to straighten out.

Prevention:
1. Learn to pitch properly.
2. In pre-season, slowly condition the pitching arm.
3. Limit the amount of throwing. Kids ages 9–12 should pitch no more than four innings a game, and six innings a week.
4. Limit the number of curve balls. (It may be unsafe for kids under 15 to throw curve balls at all: The twisting motion can strain tendons and muscles.)

"Little League Elbow" is an inflammation of the tendon that attaches to the inner elbow.

shortened, lengthened, and moved in all directions. On the sides of the tongue are two jaws. The bee uses its jaws as tools to grasp wax and pollen.

Wings. A bee has two thin wings on each side of its thorax. The two front wings are larger than the hind wings. When the bee flies, the front wings and the smaller hind wings become fastened together by a row of tiny hooks along the edge of the front wings.

The wings can move up and down, and forward and backward. A bee can fly forward, sideways, or backward, and can hover in one place in the air.

Legs. A bee has three legs on each side of its thorax. Each leg has five main joints, plus tiny segments that make up the foot. The worker bee uses its legs for walking, for brushing pollen off its body, and for handling wax.

Wings

Legs

Eyes

Mouth

The Honeybee

In the next selection, "From Bees to Honey," you'll learn how bees live. Notice how the information about beekeeping is organized.

Vocabulary

Words to Know

colony	emerge	producers
condition	nectar	react
storage	venom	

When you read, you may come across a word you don't know. To figure out its meaning, look for clues in an explanation or definition given before or after the unknown word.

Read the paragraph below. Find an explanation or definition for *nectar*. What does *nectar* mean?

Worker Honeybees

Honeybees live in large colonies. The worker honeybees are the busiest in the colony. Some workers collect nectar, a sweet liquid found in flowers. The workers inside the hive are the honey and wax producers. They also clean the hive and keep the honey storage areas in good condition. They take care of the colony's eggs and feed baby bees when they emerge from the eggs. Finally, these workers defend the hive. They react quickly to danger, depending on their stingers, which are filled with venom.

Talk About It

Use vocabulary words to talk about an insect you think is interesting.

From Bees to Honey

from A Beekeeper's Year

by Sylvia A. Johnson

photographs by Nick Von Ohlen

A Beekeeper and His Bees

What do you do when you hear the buzz of a bee? Do you wave your arms, or scream and run? This is what many people do, but not John Wetzler. John is a beekeeper, and he likes to hear that buzzing sound. It tells him that his bees are hard at work.

John and his wife, Mary Ann, make their home in Minnesota, a state that is one of the nation's leading producers of honey. The Wetzlers live in southwestern Minnesota, in a small house on the banks of the Des Moines River. In the yard next to the house are stacks of white boxes, some more than six feet high. These are beehives. John has twenty-four hives in all, ten at his place and the rest on a farm nearby.

John and Mary Ann don't make a living keeping bees. John is a retired high school teacher. For the Wetzlers, as for many other people in rural areas, beekeeping is a hobby. About two hundred thousand American beekeepers are *hobbyists,* who own fewer than twenty-five hives.

Like many hobbyists, John Wetzler is a beekeeper for only one reason: he likes working with bees. "Keeping bees is different from owning cows or chickens," he says. "That's because honeybees are not really domesticated animals." Bees in a hive behave in just the same way as bees in the wild. Like wild bees, they collect flower *nectar* to make honey for food. And they make as much honey as they possibly can. "There's no such thing as too much honey for a colony of bees!" says John. Since the beekeeper also wants a lot of honey, his main job is to assist his bees in doing what comes naturally.

The relationship between humans and honeybees goes back thousands of years. In prehistoric times, people took honey from the hives of wild bees in hollow trees. About four thousand years ago, the Egyptians kept bees in cigar-shaped hives made of clay. During the Middle Ages, beekeepers used dome-shaped hives called *skeps*, which were woven of straw.

John Wetzler, like most modern beekeepers, uses hives made of wood. A hive consists of several boxes, or *hive bodies*, which are open at the top and bottom. Hanging inside each hive body are ten movable wooden *frames*. The frames hold sheets of wax called *foundation*, on which bees build the six-sided cells of their combs.

A frame holds a sheet of foundation on which bees build their wax cells.

The inner cover of a hive

The *colony* of bees that lives in one of John Wetzler's hives is just like a colony in the wild. It is made up of thousands of bees, as many as sixty thousand in a large colony. Most are *worker bees* (all females), which do different jobs around the hive. There is one *queen bee.* She is the mother of the colony and the only one that lays eggs. Each colony also has a small number of male bees, called *drones,* which serve as mates for queens.

Whether a colony of bees lives in a wooden hive or in a hollow tree, its activities are determined by the seasons. The cold winter is a quiet time for bees. But with the first breath of spring, the hive starts buzzing and the beekeeper's year begins.

A Beekeeper's Tools

In Minnesota, a beekeeper's outdoor work doesn't really get started until April. By then, most of the snow has melted, and the air is filled with the rich smell of wet earth. Maple trees have burst into bloom, their tiny flowers clustered high on the branches. On a bright morning in early April, John Wetzler finishes his bowl of oatmeal sweetened with honey and gets ready to check his hives.

First John puts on his bee suit, a kind of coverall that fastens tight at the wrists and ankles. He also gets out his hat with its heavy veil. The zipper at the bottom of the veil connects with a zipper around the neck of the suit. This outfit is designed to keep out angry bees that might sting someone disturbing their hive.

Despite this protection, beekeepers do get stung. Most eventually develop a kind of immunity to bee venom, so that stings don't really bother them. John Wetzler says he is glad that bees sting. "If they didn't, a lot more people would probably take up beekeeping."

A beekeeper's equipment includes a veiled hat, a hive tool, and a smoker.

After he is dressed, John collects his beekeeping tools. His most important piece of equipment is his *smoker*. A smoker does just what its name suggests: it produces smoke from material burned inside it. John burns old twine, which smolders a long time and makes plenty of thick, cool smoke.

When John opens a hive, he puffs smoke on the bees, using the bellows attached to the smoker. Smoke makes bees react as if their hive is on fire. Preparing for escape, they hurry to the honey stores and load up on honey. A bee carrying honey isn't able to sting very well. Smoking bees makes it safer and easier for the beekeeper to do his work.

The other piece of equipment that John takes to the bee yard is his *hive tool*. This small metal tool is used to open hives and loosen frames. Bees seal up cracks in their hive with a sticky substance called *bee glue*. The beekeeper has to break these seals to look inside.

Before he can open his hives this April morning, John must first remove the black plastic wrapping that has protected them during the long winter. With that job done, he carefully takes the cover off each hive and puffs smoke inside. Then he peers in to see what the bees are doing.

Looking for Brood

As part of his spring check, John removes a few frames from each hive to look for *brood:* eggs and developing young bees. Queen bees usually start laying eggs in February. By April, the hive should be brimming with new life. The first hive John opens today has plenty of brood. But when he takes a frame from the second hive, he sees a lot of empty cells. Something has definitely gone wrong here.

Maybe the bees have run out of food. Hungry bees need to be fed with sugar syrup, a mixture of water and granulated sugar. John gives them syrup in a bucket with small holes in the lid. He turns the bucket upside down on top of the opening in the hive's inner cover. The bees come to the opening to get the syrup oozing from the bucket.

If a hive has a shortage of brood, the problem may be a queen who is not laying enough eggs. This hive will need a new queen, and quickly too. If young bees are not produced in spring, then the colony will not have enough workers in the busy summer season. John has ordered some new queens from a bee supplier in Georgia. When they arrive, he will install them in the hives.

After checking each hive, John makes a record of its condition. "It's not easy writing notes while wearing heavy gloves," John explains, "so I've developed my own record-keeping system." He puts a brick on top of each hive. The position of the brick tells him at a glance what the condition of the hive is.

John's Brick Code

Brick Lengthwise
flat: everything OK
edge: inspection needed

Brick Across
flat: hive being fed
edge: needs feeding

Brick Diagonal
flat: colony requeened
edge: colony needs queen

Bees at Work

While the beekeeper is busy with his spring chores, the bees are hard at work too. Each day, more young bees emerge from their cells and join the hive work force.

During the first twenty days of their lives, workers do indoor jobs. As "house bees," they clean and repair cells and feed developing young bees. They may spend some time as guards, protecting the hive from intruders such as wasps. House bees also receive nectar and *pollen* from *foragers* returning to the hive. As the nectar is passed along, enzymes in the bees' bodies start the process that turns it into honey.

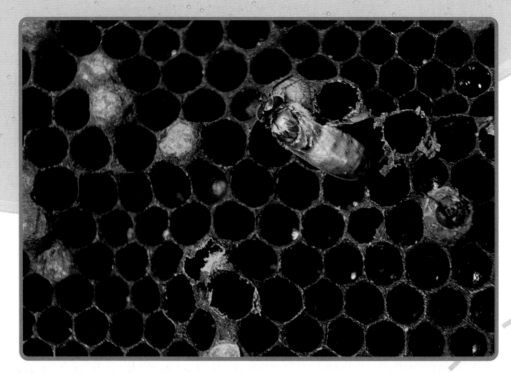

This young worker bee has just hatched.

This forager bee collects nectar.

When a worker is about twenty days old, she is ready to become a forager, or field bee. To prepare for this job, she makes short flights around the hive. After the bee has learned to recognize the hive and find her way home, she starts on her foraging trips.

On a warm summer day, a forager may make as many as ten trips. During each one, she collects nectar or pollen from around one hundred flowers. Despite this hard work, a forager produces only one-twelfth of a teaspoon of honey during the six short weeks that she lives!

Supering Up

In southwestern Minnesota, the early part of July, with its long sunny days, is the peak of the honey season. The beekeeper's main job at this time of year is to give the bees someplace to store all the honey they are producing. He does this by putting *supers* on his hives.

Supers are small boxes containing frames and wax combs. They are stacked on top of the hive bodies, where the bees live and raise their young. When the bees find these extra storage places, they begin putting honey in them. As long as the nectar flow lasts, the bees will fill super after super. How many supers does John put on a hive? "Usually four or five, but I've had as many as nine," the beekeeper says with quiet satisfaction. When the supers start piling up, John has to use a stepladder to reach the ones on top.

John wants to have only honey in his supers. But if the queen gets into this part of the hive, she will lay eggs there. To prevent this, John uses a *queen excluder*. He places this sheet of plastic between the upper hive body and the first honey super. The openings in the excluder are too small for the large queen to pass through. But they are just the right size for the worker bees. The workers can store honey in the cells of the supers, while the queen is busy down below laying eggs in the hive bodies.

Taking Honey

In Minnesota, summer begins winding down in August. The weather is still hot, and corn plants are heavy with ears of yellow corn. But many of the summer flowers are gone. In fields and road ditches, tall spikes of goldenrod begin to appear. At night, the loud, shrill chorus of insects sends a message that autumn is just around the corner.

In the bee yard, the supers are full of mild, light-colored honey made from a combination of clover and alfalfa nectars. It is time for the beekeeper to start taking his share. John Wetzler removes a frame of honey when at least three-quarters of the cells have wax caps on them. Bees make these caps to protect the honey from moisture. Beekeepers know that capped honey is ripe and ready to extract.

John puts a super on a hive.

A frame of honey is ready to be removed when most of its cells are capped.

An electric knife makes decapping easy.

The decapped frames go into the extractor.

In the Honey House

John Wetzler's honey house is a small building not far from the bee yard. It has large glass windows and a concrete floor that is usually a little sticky. Along the walls are stacks of supers. The air is warm and heavy with the sweet smell of honey.

In the honey house, honey is taken from the frames and put into glass jars. The extracting process is simple, but it has several steps. John often has people helping him with it. Today his wife, Mary Ann, and some neighborhood children are lending a hand.

The first step in the extracting process is cutting the wax caps off the honey-filled cells. John uses a large knife that is heated electrically. Propping a frame up over the *decapping tank*, he carefully slices off the caps, first on one side and then on the other. The wax caps fall down into the tank, along with some trickles of honey. But most of the honey stays in the cells because the clever bees have built them to slant upward.

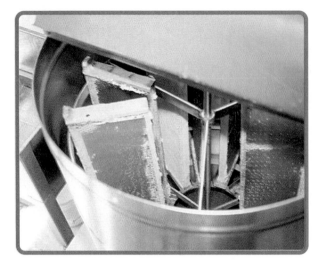

Frames in the extractor

After the honey is extracted from the cells, it is drained into buckets.

Once a frame is uncapped, John and his helpers place it in the *honey extractor*. This barrel-shaped machine has a rack that holds twelve frames. When the extractor is full, John turns on the motor and the machine spins like a washing-machine tub. The rapid spinning pulls the honey from the cells and throws it against the walls of the extractor. It runs down and collects at the bottom, where it is drawn out through a spigot.

While John uncaps more frames, his helpers drain the honey from the extractor and put it into buckets. Filters over the tops of the buckets catch bits of wax and other impurities. The bucketfuls of honey are then poured into bottling pails. Mary Ann is in charge of the bottling. Turning the spigot on and off, on and off, she and her assistants fill jar after jar with pale golden honey.

Putting labels on the jars is the final step. Now the honey is ready to be loaded into boxes and taken to farmers' markets in nearby towns. John and Mary Ann spend many sunny late-summer afternoons at the markets, selling honey and answering questions about beekeeping. Sometimes Mary Ann tells people about the delicious cookies, muffins, and breads that can be made using honey. "Let's get an extra jar so we can make some!" says a young customer.

Chores in Autumn

When the leaves of the oak trees around John Wetzler's place turn gold and clumps of purple asters dot the fields, it is time for autumn chores in the bee yard.

During September, the bees continue to gather the last nectar of the year from late-blooming flowers such as goldenrod and asters. After the first frost, usually in late September, the flowers are gone, and the honey season is over.

On a crisp day in early October, John goes from hive to hive, gently lifting up the hive bodies. He can tell from their weight about how much honey each hive contains. In Minnesota, a colony of bees needs at least a hundred pounds of honey to get through the winter. Those without enough honey have to be fed with sugar syrup.

John's last autumn chore is wrapping the hives. Only beekeepers who live in cold climates provide this winter protection for their bees. John Wetzler wraps his hives in sheets of black plastic and roofing paper. The material will shelter the bees from harsh winds. And its black color will absorb the weak winter sun, helping to warm the hives during the cold months to come.

John wrapping his hives for the winter

About the Author
Sylvia A. Johnson

Sylvia A. Johnson is fascinated by all areas of science. Her books have covered a wide range of topics, from what is inside an egg to coral reefs to bees.

Ms. Johnson has contributed more than twenty-four books to the "Natural Science Books" series. This series originated in Japan. In the United States, the series won an award from the New York Academy of Sciences for its scientific information, beautiful photography, and clear and informative language. Ms. Johnson has also won awards from the National Council of Social Studies for Outstanding Trade Books for Children.

If you liked reading about how humans and wildlife help each other as they do in "From Bees to Honey," try the book *Raptor Rescue!: An Eagle Flies Free* by Ms. Johnson. This book is about the Raptor Center at the University of Minnesota. Injured raptors, or birds of prey, are sent there for medical attention and then, when they are well, set free in the wild. Many birds have been saved by the dedicated volunteers at the center.

Reader Response

Open for Discussion

What did you know about honeybees before you read "From Bees to Honey"? What did you learn about them when you read the selection?

Comprehension Check

1. After reading "From Bees to Honey," do you think beekeeping is difficult to do? Why or why not? Find details to support your answer.

2. How is the work of bees and beekeepers similar? Explain their relationship, using details from the selection.

3. Why do you think beekeeping is a hobby rather than a full-time job for John Wetzler and many other American beekeepers?

4. Think about the **text structure** of "From Bees to Honey." How is the selection organized—chronological order, cause and effect, problem and solution, or compare and contrast? How do you know? (Text Structure)

5. If you were going to write a report on the situations described in "Looking for Brood" on page 314, what kind of **text structure** would you use? Give examples that support your answer. (Text Structure)

Test Prep
Look Back and Write

Look back at "John's Brick Code" on page 315. Read the code and study the photograph. What is the condition of the hive shown? Explain how you can tell.

People and Animals

Approximate time scale of the domestication of some animals

Dog   Sheep/Goat   Pig/Cow   Llama

10,000 BC   9000 BC   7000 BC   5000 BC

SINCE THE EARLIEST TIMES, people have hunted wild animals for their meat, skins, and fur. Then, in about 10,000 BC, the first farmers began to tame and breed wild animals to feed the growing populations. This process, called domestication, played a vital role in the development of human civilization. Since then, people have continued to rear animals for food and clothing, as well as train them to work and breed them as pets.

DOMESTICATED ANIMALS

When people selected animals to domesticate, they looked for certain desirable characteristics. Camels, for example, can travel without water and also provide milk and wool. Geese and ducks will supply meat and eggs as well as feathers for warm bedding.

ANIMALS FOR FOOD

From the vast cattle ranches of South America to the cramped cages sometimes used for chickens, rearing animals for food today is big business. In the western world, technology makes the land highly productive, producing plenty of cheap food.

Cattle ranches take up a lot of space. In some places, such as South America, large areas of land have been cleared to make way for cattle ranches.

Beekeepers wear thick clothes and hats with veils to protect them from bee stings.

BEEKEEPING

Although honeybees normally build nests in the wild, people also construct hives to attract bees so they can harvest the honey and beeswax— used for candles, lipsticks, polishes, and other products.

KEEPING PETS

Many adults and children keep animals as pets. The most popular pets are cats, dogs, fish, and budgerigars, although some people have more unusual pets, such as spiders. Pets provide their owners with companionship and affection in return for food and shelter.

Some pets need a lot of exercise and have to be looked after for many years.

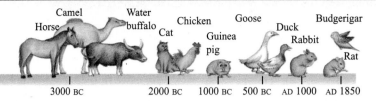

Horse	Camel	Water buffalo		Cat	Chicken	Guinea pig	Goose	Duck Rabbit	Budgerigar	Rat
3000 BC			2000 BC		1000 BC	500 BC		AD 1000	AD 1850	

Leeches feed by attaching themselves to the bodies of animals, piercing their skin and drinking their blood. The medicinal leech gives out a chemical substance that thins the blood and prevents it from clotting (an anticoagulant). Doctors are interested in finding out more about this anticoagulant.

Anterior sucker

Scientific name: *Hirudo medicinalis*
Size: Swells up to 5 in (12 cm) in length after feeding
Habitat: Small, muddy ponds edged with plants
Distribution: Found wild in Europe and parts of Asia, introduced in North America
Diet: Blood of other animals

WORKING ANIMALS

Many animals are trained to work because of their strength or special skills. Elephants and llamas are used to carry heavy loads over long distances, while oxen, water buffalo, and horses can be used where a farmer has no tractor. Dogs are particularly intelligent animals and can be taught to guide blind people, control herds of sheep, and help police to track down criminals.

This farmer in Asia is using a water buffalo to pull his plow through the mud of a flooded paddy field.

ANIMALS IN ZOOS

Zoos allow people to see animals from all over the world and to learn about their behavior. In a good modern zoo or wildlife park, the emphasis is placed on educating the public about wild animals and helping to conserve them.

At a zoo, visitors can see wild animals up close.

Merino sheep can survive the heat in Australia and still produce a fleece of good wool.

ANIMAL PRODUCTS

Animal furs were important for the survival of early peoples, but have now become fashion items in many countries. Other traditional animal products include wool from sheep, goats, and alpacas. Australia is the world's chief wool-producing country, where most of the sheep are Merinos that were introduced there in the 18th century.

Some people think that game shooting helps preserve habitats and the wildlife that lives there.

ANIMALS AND SPORTS

From horseracing and game shooting to circuses and bullfighting, many sports and leisure activities involve animals. However, these animals are not always kept in the best conditions. Many modern circuses now have no animal acts because they do not want to keep wild animals in cramped cages.

Sheep-shearers work quickly—some can clip a lamb in less than a minute.

325

Skill Lesson

Summarizing

- **Summarizing** means telling just the main ideas of an article or the plot of a story.

- A good summary is brief. It does not include unnecessary details, repeated words or thoughts, or unimportant ideas.

Read "What Do Animals Say?" from *The Christian Science Monitor*.

Talk About It

1. Which of these summary statements is better? Explain.

   a. Throughout the world, animals have different sounds because they are imitated in different languages.

   b. English has many echoic words.

2. Shorten this sentence to make it a better summary: *People throughout the world have different words to imitate sounds of pigs, dogs, poodles, roosters, St. Bernards, and French pigs.*

What Do Animals Say?

No one knows how language began, but one interesting idea is the "bow-wow" theory. It says that people first spoke by imitating the sounds they heard. A tribe would all use the same barking sound to talk about a dog.

These are called "echoic" words, because they echo the sound they describe. English has more echoic words than any other language. (Examples: buzz, caw.)

We know that not all dogs have the same bark. St. Bernards "woof woof!" but poodles tend to "arf arf!" Other languages use different words.

Here are some animal sounds from languages around the world. Try them! Do you think any of the foreign words sound more like what the animals say?

Pig: Pigs "oink" in the United States, but they make very different sounds elsewhere. Russian pigs "khru-khru," and Rumanian ones "guits-guits." In Greece, big pigs "gru" and little ones "koi." In France, pigs say "oui-oui" (also the French word for "yes"). Perhaps French pigs are more agreeable than American ones!

Dog: In French, a dog's "bow-wow" is "oua-oua" (pronounced "wah-wah"). In Italian, it's "bu-bu," and in Rumanian, "ham-ham." Vietnamese dogs "gau-gau," and Turkish ones "hov-hov."

Rooster: In America, they "cock-a-doodle-doo!" In France, they "cocorico!" Spanish ones "quiquiriquí!" In Arabic, it's "kko!" and in Russian, "kukareku!"

LOOK AHEAD

In "Babe to the Rescue," you can summarize what happens to Babe, the new piglet on the farm, as he talks to the other animals and figures out the best way to herd sheep.

Vocabulary

Words to Know

chaos   confusion   raid

sensible   instinct   civil

unexpected

Words with similar meanings are called **synonyms**. Sometimes a synonym can be the clue that helps you figure out the meaning of an unknown word.

Read the paragraph below. Notice how *disorder* helps you understand what *chaos* means.

Farmer Emmett's Farm

Life on Farmer Emmett's farm was one of <u>chaos</u> for the animals. What disorder! It was all because Rooster had gotten angry at Hen when she said she didn't like his crowing. And although it was his <u>instinct</u> to crow loudly each day, he stopped. When he stopped, Farmer Emmett didn't wake up on time. The animals were fed, put to bed, and taken to pasture at <u>unexpected</u> times. Rat wanted to plan a <u>raid</u> on Hen's coop, but the other animals didn't think this was <u>sensible</u>. Instead they asked Hen to be <u>civil</u> to Rooster and to apologize. Hen agreed, Rooster began crowing again, and the <u>confusion</u> stopped.

Write About It

Use vocabulary words to describe a farm you have visited or read about.

BABE
to the Rescue

from *Babe: The Gallant Pig*
by Dick King-Smith

*Farmer Hogget, a sheep farmer, wins a piglet named
Babe at a fair. When he brings Babe home, the sheepdog Fly
adopts him and begins teaching Babe about herding sheep.
Mrs. Hogget, however, wants to fatten Babe up for a holiday
dinner. What does the future hold for Babe?*

After the last of the puppies had left, the ducks heaved a general sigh of relief. They looked forward to a peaceful day and paid no attention when, the following morning, Fly and Babe came down to the pond and sat and watched them as they squattered and splattered in its soupy green depths. They knew that the old dog would not bother them, and they took no notice of the strange creature at her side.

"They'll come out and walk up the yard in a minute," said Fly. "Then you can have a go at fetching them back, if you like."

"Oh yes, please!" said Babe excitedly.

The collie looked fondly at her foster child. Sheep-pig indeed, she thought, the idea of it! The mere sight of him would probably send the flock into the next county. Anyway, he'd never get near them on those little short legs. Let him play with the ducks for a day or two and he'd forget all about it.

When the ducks did come up out of the water and marched noisily past the piglet, she half expected him to chase after them, as the puppies usually did at first; but he sat very still, his ears cocked, watching her.

"All right," said Fly. "Let's see how you get on. Now then, first thing is, you've got to get behind them, just like I have to with the sheep. If the boss wants me to go round the right side of them (that's the side by the stables there), he says 'Away to me.' If he wants me to go round the left (that's the side by the Dutch barn), he says 'Come by.' O.K.?"

"Yes, Mum."

"Right then. Away to me, Babe!" said Fly sharply.

At first, not surprisingly, Babe's efforts met with little success. There was no problem with getting around the ducks—even with his curious little seesawing canter he was much faster than they—but the business of bringing the whole flock back to Fly was not, he found, at all easy. Either he pressed them too hard and they broke up and fluttered all over the place, or he was too gentle and held back, and they waddled away in twos and threes.

"Come and have a rest, dear," called Fly after a while. "Leave the silly things alone, they're not worth upsetting yourself about."

"I'm not upset, Mum," said Babe. "Just puzzled. I mean, I told them what I wanted them to do but they didn't take any notice of me. Why not?"

Because you weren't born to it, thought Fly. You haven't got the instinct to dominate them, to make them do what you want.

"It's early days yet, Babe dear," she said.

"Do you suppose," said Babe, "that if I asked them politely . . ."

"Asked them politely! What an idea! Just imagine me doing that with the sheep—'please will you go through that gateway,' 'would you kindly walk into that pen?' Oh no, dear, you'd never get anywhere that way. You've got to tell 'em what to do, doesn't matter whether it's ducks or sheep. They're stupid and dogs are intelligent, that's what you have to remember."

"But I'm a pig."

"Pigs are intelligent too," said Fly firmly. Ask them politely, she thought. Whatever next!

What happened next, later that morning in fact, was that Babe met his first sheep.

Farmer Hogget and Fly had been out around the flock, and when they returned Fly was driving before her an old lame ewe, which they penned in the loose box where the piglet had originally been shut. Then they went away up the hill again.

Babe made his way into the stables, curious to meet this, the first of the animals that he planned one day to work with, but he could not see into the box. He snuffled under the bottom of the door, and from inside there came a cough and the sharp stamp of a foot, and then the sound of a hoarse complaining voice. "Wolves! Wolves!" it said. "They never do leave a body alone. Nag, nag, nag all day long, go here, go there, do this, do that. What d'you want now? Can't you give us a bit of peace, wolf?"

"I'm not a wolf," said Babe under the door.

"Oh, I knows all that," said the sheep sourly. "Calls yourself a sheepdog, I knows that, but you don't fool none of us. You're a wolf like the rest of 'em, given half a chance. You looks at us, and you sees lamb chops. Go away, wolf."

"But I'm not a sheepdog either," said Babe, and he scrambled up the stack of straw bales and looked over the bars.

"You see?" he said.

"Well I'll be dipped," said the old sheep, peering up at him. "No more you ain't. What are you?"

"Pig," said Babe. "Large White. What are you?"

"Ewe," said the sheep.

"No, not me, you—what are you?"

"I'm a ewe."

Mum was right, thought Babe, they certainly are stupid. But if I'm going to learn how to be a sheep-pig I must try to understand them, and this might be a good chance. Perhaps I could make a friend of this one.

"My name's Babe," he said in a jolly voice. "What's yours?"

"Maaaaa," said the sheep.

"That's a nice name," said Babe. "What's the matter with you, Ma?"

"Foot rot," said the sheep, holding up a foreleg. "And I've got a nasty cough." She coughed. "And I'm not as young as I was."

"You don't look very old to me," said Babe politely.

A look of pleasure came over the sheep's mournful face, and she lay down in the straw.

"Very civil of you to say so," she said. "First kind word I've had since I were a little lamb," and she belched loudly and began to chew a mouthful of cud.

Though he did not quite know why, Babe said nothing to Fly of his conversation with Ma. Farmer Hogget had treated the sheep's foot and tipped a potion down its protesting throat, and now, as darkness fell, dog and pig lay side by side, their rest only occasionally disturbed by a rustling from the box next door. Having at last set eyes on a sheep, Babe's dreams were immediately filled with the creatures, all lame, all coughing, all, like the ducks, scattering wildly before his attempts to round them up.

"Go here, go there, do this, do that!" he squeaked furiously at them, but they took not a bit of notice, until at last the dream turned to a nightmare, and they all came hopping and hacking and maa-ing after him with hatred gleaming in their mad yellow eyes.

"Mum! Mum!" shouted Babe in terror.

"Maaaaa!" said a voice next door.

"It's all right dear," said Fly, "it's all right. Was it a nasty dream?"

"Yes, yes."

"What were you dreaming about?"

"Sheep, Mum."

"I expect it was because of that stupid old thing in there," said Fly. "Shut up!" she barked. "Noisy old fool!" And to Babe she said, "Now cuddle up, dear, and go to sleep. There's nothing to be frightened of."

She licked his snout until it began to give out a series of regular snores. Sheep-pig indeed, she thought, why the silly boy's frightened of the things, and she put her nose on her paws and went to sleep. Babe slept soundly the rest of the night, and woke more determined than ever to learn all that he could from their new neighbor. As soon as Fly had gone out on her rounds, he climbed the straw stack.

"Good morning, Ma," he said. "I do hope you're feeling better today?"

The old ewe looked up. Her eyes, Babe was glad to see, looked neither mad nor hateful.

"I must say," she said, "you'm a polite young chap. Not like that wolf, shouting at me in the middle of the night. Never get no respect from them, treat you like dirt they do, bite you soon as look at you."

"Do they really?"

"Oh ar. Nip your hocks if you'm a bit slow. And worse, some of them."

"Worse?"

"Oh ar. Ain't you never heard of worrying?"

"I don't worry much."

"No no, young un. I'm talking about sheep-worrying. You get some wolves as'll chase sheep and kill 'em."

"Oh!" said Babe, horrified. "I'm sure Fly would never do that."

"Who's Fly?"

"She's my m . . . she's our dog here, the one that brought you in yesterday."

"Is that what she's called? No, she bain't a worrier, just rude. All wolves is rude to us sheep, see, always have been. Bark and run and nip and call us stupid. We bain't all that stupid, we do just get confused. If only they'd just show a bit of common politeness, just treat us a bit decent. Now if you was to come out into the field, a nice well-mannered young chap like you, and ask me to go somewhere or do something, politely, like you would, why, I'd be only too delighted."

6

Mrs. Hogget shook her head at least a dozen times.

"For the life of me I can't see why you do let that pig run all over the place like you do, round and round the yard he do go, chasing my ducks about, shoving his nose into everything, shouldn't wonder but what he'll be out with you and Fly moving the sheep about afore long, why don't you shut him up, he's running all his flesh off, he won't never be fit for Christmas, Easter more like, what d'you call him?"

"Just Pig," said Farmer Hogget.

A month had gone by since the Village Fair, a month in which a lot of interesting things had happened to Babe. The fact that perhaps most concerned his future, though he did not know it, was that Farmer Hogget had become fond of him. He liked to see the piglet pottering happily about the yard with Fly, keeping out of mischief, as far as he could tell, if you didn't count moving the ducks around. He did this now with a good deal of skill, the farmer noticed, even to the extent of being able, once, to separate the white ducks from the brown, though that must just have been a fluke. The more he thought of it, the less Farmer Hogget liked the idea of butchering Pig.

The other developments were in Babe's education. Despite herself, Fly found that she took pleasure and pride in teaching him the ways of the sheepdog, though she knew that of course he would never be fast enough to work sheep. Anyway the boss would never let him try.

As for Ma, she was back with the flock, her foot healed, her cough better. But all the time that she had been shut in the box, Babe had spent every moment that Fly was out of the stables chatting to the old ewe. Already he understood, in a way that Fly never could, the sheep's point of view. He longed to meet the flock, to be introduced. He thought it would be extremely interesting.

"D'you think I could, Ma?" he had said.

"Could what, young un?"

"Well, come and visit you, when you go back to your friends?"

"Oh ar. You could do, easy enough. You only got to go through the bottom gate and up the hill to the big field by the lane. Don't know what the farmer'd say though. Or that wolf."

Once Fly had slipped quietly in and found him perched on the straw stack.

"Babe!" she had said sharply. "You're not talking to that stupid thing, are you?"

"Well, yes, Mum, I was."

"Save your breath, dear. It won't understand a word you say."

"Bah!" said Ma.

For a moment Babe was tempted to tell his foster mother what he had in mind, but something told him to keep quiet. Instead he made a plan. He would wait for two things to happen. First, for Ma to rejoin the flock. And, after that, for market day, when both the boss and his mum would be out of the way. Then he would go up the hill.

Towards the end of the very next week the two things had happened. Ma had been turned out, and a couple of days after that Babe watched as Fly jumped into the back of the Land Rover, and it drove out of the yard and away.

Babe's were not the only eyes that watched its departure. At the top of the hill a cattle truck stood half-hidden under a clump of trees at the side of the lane. As soon as the Land Rover had disappeared from sight along the road to the market town, a man jumped hurriedly out and opened the gate into the field. Another backed the truck into the gateway.

Babe meanwhile was trotting excitedly up the hill to pay his visit to the flock. He came to the gate at the bottom of the field and squeezed under it. The field was steep and curved, and at first he could not see a single sheep. But then he heard a distant drumming of hooves and suddenly the whole flock came galloping over the brow of the hill and down toward him. Around them ran two strange collies, lean silent dogs that seemed to flow effortlessly over the grass. From high above came the sound of a thin whistle, and in easy partnership the dogs swept around the sheep, and began to drive them back up the slope.

Despite himself, Babe was caught up in the press of jostling bleating animals and carried along with them. Around him rose a chorus of panting protesting voices, some shrill, some hoarse, some deep and guttural, but all saying the same thing.

"Wolf! Wolf!" cried the flock in dazed confusion.

Small by comparison and short in the leg, Babe soon fell behind the main body, and as they reached the top of the hill he found himself right at the back in company with an old sheep who cried "Wolf!" more loudly than any.

"Ma!" he cried breathlessly. "It's you!"

Behind them one dog lay down at a whistle, and in front the flock checked as the other dog steadied them. In the corner of the field the tailgate and wings of the cattle truck filled the gateway, and the two men waited, sticks and arms outspread.

"Oh hullo, young un," puffed the old sheep. "Fine day you chose to come, I'll say."

"What is it? What's happening? Who are these men?" asked Babe.

"Rustlers," said Ma. "They'm sheep rustlers."

"What d'you mean?"

"Thieves, young un, that's what I do mean. Sheep stealers. We'll all be in that truck afore you can blink your eye."

"What can we do?"

"Do? Ain't nothing we can do, unless we can slip past this here wolf."

She made as if to escape, but the dog behind darted in, and she turned back.

Again, one of the men whistled, and the dog pressed. Gradually, held against the headland of the field by the second dog and the men, the flock began to move forward. Already the leaders were nearing the tailgate of the truck.

"We'm beat," said Ma mournfully. "You run for it, young un." I will, thought Babe, but not the way you mean. Little as he was, he felt suddenly not fear but anger, furious anger that the boss's sheep were being stolen. My mum's not here to protect them so I must, he said to himself bravely, and he ran quickly around the hedge side of the flock, and jumping onto the bottom of the tailgate, turned to face them.

"Please!" he cried. "I beg you! Please don't come any closer. If you would be so kind, dear sensible sheep!"

His unexpected appearance had a number of immediate effects. The shock of being so politely addressed stopped the flock in its tracks, and the cries of "Wolf!" changed to murmurs of "In't he lovely!" and "Proper little gennulman!" Ma had told them something of her new friend, and now to see him in the flesh and to hear his well-chosen words released them from the dominance of the dogs. They began to fidget and look about for an escape route. This was opened for them when the men (cursing quietly, for above all things they were anxious to avoid too much noise) sent the flanking dog to drive the pig away, and some of the sheep began to slip past them.

Next moment all was chaos. Angrily the dog ran at Babe, who scuttled away squealing at the top of his voice in a mixture of fright and fury. The men closed on him, sticks raised. Desperately he shot between the legs of one, who fell with a crash, while the other, striking out madly, hit the rearguard dog as it came to help, and sent it yowling. In half a minute the carefully planned raid was ruined, as the sheep scattered everywhere.

"Keep yelling, young un!" bawled Ma, as she ran beside Babe. "They won't never stay here with that row going on!"

And suddenly all sorts of things began to happen as those deafening squeals rang out over the quiet countryside. Birds flew startled from the trees, cows in nearby fields began to gallop about, dogs in distant farms to bark, passing motorists to stop and stare. In the farmhouse below Mrs. Hogget heard the noise as she had on the day of the Fair. She stuck her head out the window and saw the rustlers, their truck, galloping sheep, and Babe. She dialed 999 but then talked for so long that by the time a patrol car drove up the lane, the rustlers had long gone. Snarling at each other and their dogs, they had driven hurriedly away with not one single sheep to show for their pains.

"You won't never believe it!" cried Mrs. Hogget when her husband returned from market. "But we've had rustlers, just after you'd gone it were, come with a huge cattle truck they did, the police said, they seen the tire marks in the gateway, and a chap in a car seen the truck go by in a hurry, and there's been a lot of it about, and he give the alarm, he did, kept screaming and shrieking enough to bust your eardrums, we should have lost every sheep on the place if 'tweren't for him, 'tis him we've got to thank."

"Who?" said Farmer Hogget.

"Him!" said his wife, pointing at Babe who was telling Fly all about it. "Don't ask me how he got there or why he done it, all I knows is he saved our bacon and now I'm going to save his, he's staying with us just like another dog, don't care if he gets as big as a house, because if you think I'm going to stand by and see him butchered after what he done for us today, you've got another think coming, what d'you say to that?"

A slow smile spread over Farmer Hogget's long face.

About the Author
Dick King-Smith

One reason Dick King-Smith can write about farm animals so well is that he was a farmer for twenty years before he started writing children's books. When his farm in England stopped making enough income to provide a living for his family, Mr. King-Smith went back to school and became a teacher. While teaching elementary school, he started developing ideas for children's books. Most of them had to do with farm animals.

Mr. King-Smith's first book, *The Fox Busters,* dealt with chickens who work to get a group of foxes out of their henhouse. Many stories have followed and many awards came after them. *Babe: The Gallant Pig* was named a *Boston Globe-Horn Honor* Book and a Notable Book by the American Library Association. *Babe* was also made into a successful movie.

Even though Mr. King-Smith has written poetry for his own enjoyment most of his life, it wasn't until he was near retirement age that he started writing for an audience. He is enjoying his retirement and writing lots of books, to "make up for lost time."

Reader Response

Open for Discussion

From beginning to end, Babe is an unusual pig. What surprising things did you find out about him along the way?

Comprehension Check

1. Even though Babe is not a sheepdog, the sheep do what he says. What is it about Babe that makes the sheep obey him? Explain, using details from the story.

2. Why do you think Ma calls Fly a wolf instead of a dog?

3. Farmer and Mrs. Hogget do not feel the same about Babe at first. How are their thoughts different? Why do Mrs. Hogget's feelings change? Use evidence from the story to explain.

4. **Summarize** what happens when Babe comes upon the sheep rustlers. (Summarizing)

5. If you were to **summarize** the story, would you include Babe's conversation with Fly about rounding up the ducks? Why or why not? (Summarizing)

Test Prep

Look Back and Write

Look back at pages 339–341. Describe the rustlers' plan to steal the sheep. Use details from the story to explain the steps they take.

CRY WOLF

a fable by Aesop
retold by Naomi Lewis

A shepherd boy saw a movement in the bushes. "A wolf!" he thought. He rushed to a little hill and called for help— "A wolf! A wolf!" At once a crowd of villagers left their work and ran to save the flock. This made the boy laugh, and a few days later he again called "Wolf!" just to see the villagers come running. He played the trick a third time and a fourth. But the people had grown tired of being made to look like fools and paid no more attention to his shouts. So when a wolf really did appear the boy cried "Wolf!" in vain.

Nobody came to help; sheep were lost, and so was the shepherd's job.

——— MORAL ———

Don't play with truth, I tell you true,
or truth in turn will play with you.

Stars

by Gary Soto

I got a gold star for reading a book
And a blue star for math.

I got a bronze star
For remembering six of the nine planets circling above.
I peeled it off my test
And wore it home on my knee.

I got stars for my handwriting,
And a star for spelling *hippopotamus*
With my eyes closed.

I like the light these foil stars give off,
Shiny as spoons.

My homework piles up, a galaxy of stars.
I'm good at school.
I bet I could even get a star for eating my lunch—
My sandwich sticking to the roof of my mouth.

Where do stars come from?
From a blast of light in outer space?
From billions of years of heavenly flight?
No, they come from the store,
Or so I learned.

Now I have my own box of stars.
Every time I feel bad, I can lick a star
And just press it to my bedroom wall.

When I forget to pick up my socks, I get a star.
When I spill my milk, I get a star.
When someone calls me a name,
I get a star where it hurts, right on my heart.

Stars for kickball and the times I feel good.
Stars for when I jump from the chicken coop.
Stars when I clap my hands and my cat meows from the roof.
Stars when my kite swings its moon face in the air.

I'm my own teacher, my own student.
I can speak in Spanish.
I can say, *Las estrellas danzan en mis paredes*.

This happens when I turn off the lights.
At night, I blink my flashlight,
And a hocus-pocus of stars comes alive on the walls,
All shiny, all floating, all orbiting my sleep.

Remember

by Nikki Grimes

I remember that time
I stood on stage
at the Countee Cullen Library
and recited my poem
and hardly noticed
how loudly my knees
were knocking
'cause you were there
smiling from the front row
to let me know
that I was doing
just fine.

Limericks

A tutor who tooted the flute
Tried to teach two young tooters to toot,
    Said the two to the tutor,
    "Is it harder to toot or
To tutor two tooters to toot?"

                    Carolyn Wells

A bugler named Dougal MacDougal
Found ingenious ways to be frugal.
    He learned how to sneeze
    In various keys,
Thus saving the price of a bugle.

                    Ogden Nash

A bridge engineer, Mister Crumpett,
Built a bridge for the good River Bumpett.
    A mistake in the plan
    Left a gap in the span,
But he said, "Well, they'll just have to jump it."

                    Anonymous

What do we learn from our experiences?

A Worker's Day

Write a Journal

Imagine yourself as one of the people or characters in Unit 3. What was your day like? Write about it in your journal.

1. **Choose** one of the selections in this unit. Who is the main person or character?

2. **Reread** parts that interest you. Imagine how that person or character thinks and feels about what happens.

3. **Write** a journal entry. Write it in the first person (use the pronouns *I* and *me*). Tell about your day, the obstacles you faced, and the work you accomplished. Did you learn anything?

A "Best Job" Award

Nominate a Character

Each main person or character in the selections you have just read has done a job well. Think about which one you would nominate as having done his or her job best of all.

1. **Evaluate** how your chosen person or character did his or her job.

2. **Persuade** others that yours is the best choice. Create an advertisement, a billboard, or write a letter to the editor.

Honor a Hero

Design a Statue

Both Kate, in *Kate Shelley: Bound for Glory*, and Babe, in "Babe to the Rescue," save others' lives by their brave acts. Often we honor heroes by erecting statues to them.

1. **Design** a statue of either Kate or Babe. Put it on a pedestal. Often, statues show heroes in action. What brave act will you show Kate or Babe doing?

2. On the pedestal, **write** a legend that tells who is being honored and why.

Story Theater

Dramatize a Scene

With two or three classmates, choose a selection from Unit 3 that you think would work well on stage. Choose one scene that is dramatic, exciting, or full of action.

1. **Plan** how you will stage it. One way is to have one or more narrators read from the text, while others take parts and act.

2. **Rehearse** your presentation at least once from beginning to end.

3. **Perform** your dramatic scene for your classmates.

Test Talk

Answer the Question

Make the Right Choice

Before you can answer a multiple-choice test question, you have to decide on the best answer. A test about "The Marble Champ," pages 289–300, might have this question.

Test Question 1

How does Lupe's father feel about her playing marbles?

Ⓐ He is irritated that he has to attend the marbles championship instead of playing racquetball.

Ⓑ He feels that marbles is not a sport that girls should play.

Ⓒ He is happy and proud that his daughter has found a sport she can do well in.

Ⓓ He is not interested in sports and can't understand why she is.

Understand the question.
Find the key words. Finish the statement "I need to find out . . ."

Narrow the answer choices.
Read each answer choice carefully. Eliminate any choice that you know is wrong.

Find the answer in the text.
Is the answer *right there* in one place in the text, or do you have to *think and search*? Does the answer depend on the *author and you*?

Choose the best answer.
Mark the answer. Check it by comparing it with the text.

See how one student makes the right choice.

Lupe's father never says anything about girls in sports, so it's not **B**. And I know it's not **D** because he plays racquetball. He gives up racquetball to come to the tournament, but I don't think he's irritated about it. I'd better go back to the story and check.

No, the story says he wanted to encourage her, so it's not **A**. That leaves **C**. He takes the family out to celebrate, and he wants Lupe to put her trophies on the table. That sounds proud to me. The answer must be **C**.

Try it!

Now decide on the best answer to these test questions about "The Marble Champ."

Test Question 2

Why is Lupe so determined to win the marble championship?

Ⓐ She has never won a sports contest.

Ⓑ She wants to get even with Alfonso for his insults.

Ⓒ She has never won anything in her life.

Ⓓ Her brother is unable to play this year.

Test Question 3

How does Lupe win her second trophy?

Ⓕ She returns to the marble championship the following year.

Ⓖ She is awarded the trophy for good sportsmanship.

Ⓗ She is given the trophy when her opponent doesn't show up.

Ⓘ She beats the winner of the boys' division.

Time and Time Again

What things are worth repeating over time?

Skill Lesson

Compare and Contrast

- **Comparing** is telling how two or more things are alike. **Contrasting** is telling how two or more things are different.

- Authors sometimes use clue words such as *similar to*, *like*, or *as* to compare things. They may use clue words such as *different from*, *but*, or *unlike* to contrast things.

- When there are no clue words, compare and contrast by asking "What does this remind me of?"

Read "A Visitor from Japan" from *Lucky Charms & Birthday Wishes* by Christine McDonnell.

Write About It

1. Compare Japan and the United States according to what Mr. Uchida points out. What clue words help you compare?

2. Contrast Japan and the United States. What clue words help you see the contrast?

A Visitor from Japan

by Christine McDonnell

One day at the beginning of October Mrs. Higgenbottom told the class, "We're having a visitor with us for a few weeks, a teacher from another country. His name is Mr. Uchida, and he's from Japan."

Everyone began to talk at once.

"Can he speak English?"

"What does he look like?"

"What do they eat in Japan?"

"When's he coming?"

The questions blurred together in a hubbub.

"Class, simmer down. I'll answer your questions one at a time."

Mrs. Higgenbottom showed them where Japan was on the globe, and she propped a big map of Japan against the board. The class spent the rest of the afternoon making lists of questions to ask Mr. Uchida.

He arrived on Monday. He had gray hair and a very soft voice. He showed them slides of his town and of the children at the school where he taught.

Every day the class learned something new about Japan. Sometimes they pushed all the desks away and sat on straw mats. They practiced eating with chopsticks, and they learned Japanese words.

Emily was disappointed by some of the things that Mr. Uchida told them. Japanese cities looked a lot like American cities—big, modern, and crowded. People wore the same kinds of clothes as they did in America—suits and dresses and even blue jeans.

"But there are some things that are very different," Mr. Uchida assured them, and he showed them colorful kimonos and wooden clogs. He taught them how to draw with black sumi ink and brushes and how to write short poems called haiku. You had to count the syllables, five in the first line, then seven, then five in the last line. Each poem was like a puzzle; you had to search for the right-size words.

LOOK AHEAD

In "The Yangs' First Thanksgiving," a Chinese family, the Yangs, have their first Thanksgiving with an American family. As you read, compare and contrast the families and their cultures.

Vocabulary

Words to Know

dismayed	insult	winced
impression	records	sprouts

Many words have more than one meaning. To decide which meaning of a word is being used, look for clues in the sentence or the paragraph.

Read the paragraph below. Does *records* mean "vinyl disks used to play music on a phonograph" or "the written facts about a person or group"?

A Celebration for Grandma

When I asked my parents about plans for celebrating Grandma's birthday, I was dismayed to learn that we had none. I got to work immediately! First I sent out fifty invitations. Mom winced at this news, but I explained that I invited everyone in the records department at City Hall where Grandma works. If we didn't invite everyone, we might insult someone. I also planted seeds in a flowerpot to put in front of our building. The tiny sprouts poking up through the soil would be beautiful flowers by the time of the party. I really wanted to make a good impression. After all, it was a celebration for Grandma.

Talk About It

Describe a celebration you'd like to plan. Use some or all of the vocabulary words.

The Yangs' First Thanksgiving

from Yang the Third and Her Impossible Family by Lensey Namioka

"The Conners are inviting us for Thanksgiving dinner!" yelled Fourth Brother as he hung up the phone.

The Conners are our neighbors here in Seattle, and Matthew Conner is Fourth Brother's best friend. He takes violin lessons from Father, and he also plays in our family string quartet.

Eldest Brother plays first violin, and Second Sister plays viola. I'm the third sister in the Yang family, and I play cello. Fourth Brother plays baseball. He has a terrible ear, and he was relieved when Matthew took his place as the second violin.

We were all happy about the invitation. For weeks, we had been hearing about the American holiday called Thanksgiving. Since coming to this country, we have tried our best to do everything properly, but when Mother heard that preparing a Thanksgiving dinner involved roasting a turkey, she was horrified.

"I can't even roast a pigeon," she cried. "If I tried to wrestle with a turkey, I'd lose!"

We didn't have an oven in China. Almost nobody does. If you want a roast duck or chicken, you buy it already cooked in the store—sometimes chopped into bite-size pieces. When Mother saw the big box under the stove in our Seattle kitchen, she didn't know what it was at first. Even now, months later, she was still nervous about the black cavity and thought of it as a chamber of horrors.

Now we'd learn how real Americans celebrate Thanksgiving. We'd get a delicious meal, like the ones I had seen illustrated in all the papers and magazines.

What excited me most was hearing that Holly Hanson and her mother were invited too. Holly was in the school orchestra with me. She played in the viola section, so I didn't get a chance to talk to her much. But I really wanted to.

When I was little, we had a tin candy box, and on the lid was the picture of a princess with curly blond hair. Holly Hanson looked just like the princess in that picture. She was in a couple of my classes in school, and she always spoke in a soft, unhurried way. I thought that if the princess on the candy box spoke, she would sound just like that.

At the Conners' I would finally get a chance to get acquainted with Holly. But I was nervous, too, because I wanted so much to have my family make a good impression.

When Thanksgiving Day came, the whole Yang family showed up at the Conners' exactly at two o'clock. We'd thought two was a strange time for a dinner party, but Matthew explained that since people stuff themselves at Thanksgiving, eating early gives everybody a chance to digest.

We all tried to look our best for the dinner. Father had on the dark suit he wore for playing in public. Instead of her usual cotton slacks and shirt, Mother wore a dress she had bought at the Goodwill store for three dollars. It was a very nice dress, but on her slender figure, the huge shoulder pads made her look like a stranger—an aggressive stranger.

Eldest Brother wore a suit too. Second Sister and I wore skirts, and Fourth Brother had on his clean blue jeans. I hoped we'd all look presentable when we met Holly and her mother.

Mrs. Hanson and Holly arrived a few minutes after we did, and we were introduced. My parents had told us we should all shake hands with the Hansons. Mrs. Hanson looked a little startled when six Yang hands were extended toward her.

Although our etiquette book clearly said shaking hands is the polite thing to do, I decided that in America, children don't usually do it.

Except for that, things seemed to be going pretty well. The dining table looked beautiful, with china plates and tall glasses—even for the young people, who drank juice. I carefully studied the way the knives, forks, and spoons were set.

I was delighted when Mrs. Conner seated me next to Holly, but the only thing I could think to say was "I've seen you in the orchestra."

It sounded stupid as soon as I'd said it, but Holly just nodded and murmured something.

The dinner began with Mr. Conner saying some words of thanks for his family's good fortune. It was like a toast at a Chinese banquet, and I thought he sounded very dignified.

Mrs. Conner carried the whole roast turkey into the dining room on a platter, and we all exclaimed at the size of the turkey. It was the largest bird I had ever seen, dead or alive.

Mr. Conner began sharpening a wicked-looking knife. Then he took up the knife and a big fork, and began to cut thin slices of meat from the bird.

We Yangs looked at one another in wonder. Instead of complaining about being made to do the slicing, Mr. Conner looked pleased and proud.

After slicing a pile of turkey meat, Mr. Conner started to scoop from the stomach of the bird. I was horrified. Had Mrs. Conner forgotten to dress the turkey and left all the guts behind?

Chicken is an expensive treat in China. When Mother wanted to boil or stir-fry a chicken, she had to buy the bird live to make sure it was fresh. Killing, plucking, and dressing the chicken was a gruesome job, and Mother hated it. The worst part was pulling all the guts out of the stomach. Sometimes, when the bird was a hen, she would even find a cluster of eggs inside.

Watching Mr. Conner scooping away, I was embarrassed for him. I exchanged glances with the rest of my family, and I could see that they were dismayed too.

To my astonishment—and relief—what Mr. Conner scooped out was not the messy intestines. Mrs. Conner had not forgotten to dress the bird after all. She had stuffed the stomach of the bird with a savory mixture of bread and onions!

We gasped with admiration, and Mrs. Conner looked pleased. "I hope you like the stuffing. I'm trying out a new recipe."

Mr. Conner placed some slices of turkey meat on each plate, then added a spoonful of the stuffing mixture. Next he ladled a brown sauce over everything. He passed the first plate to Mother.

"Oh, I couldn't take this," Mother said politely. She passed the plate on to Mrs. Hanson.

Mrs. Hanson was jammed up against Mother's shoulder pad at the crowded table. She passed the plate back to Mother. "Oh, no, it's meant for you, Mrs. Yang."

Mother handed the plate back again. "You're so much older, Mrs. Hanson, so you should be served first."

Mrs. Hanson froze. In the silence, I could hear the sauce going *drip, drip* from Mr. Conner's ladle.

"What makes you think so?" asked Mrs. Hanson stiffly. "Just what makes you think I'm older?"

"Mom, let's skip it," Holly whispered.

I had already learned that in America it isn't considered an honor to be old. Instead of respecting older people, as we do, Americans think it is pitiful to be old. Mrs. Hanson must have thought that Mother was trying to insult her. Would Mother say something else embarrassing?

She didn't disappoint me. "Well, how old are you, then?" Mother asked Mrs. Hanson.

I winced. In school, I had once asked a friend how old our teacher was. We do this a lot. When we meet a stranger, we often ask him how old he is. My friend told me, however, that in America it's rude to ask people's ages. I was really grateful to her for the warning.

After Mother's question, Mrs. Hanson sat completely still. "I am thirty-six," she replied finally, each syllable falling like a chunk of ice.

"Oh, really!" said Mother brightly. "You look much older!"

A whuffling sound came from Matthew and his brother, Eric. Unable to look at the Hansons, I stole a glance at Mr. Conner. His face was bright red, and he seemed to be having trouble breathing. Mrs. Conner was bent over, as if in pain. I looked down at my plate and wished I could disappear.

Somehow, the dinner went on. Mrs. Hanson finally unclenched her jaw and told Mrs. Conner how delicious the cranberry sauce was. I figured she was referring to the red sticky mound of poisonous-looking berries. I put a berry in my mouth and almost gagged at its sour taste. Next to me, Fourth Brother quietly spat his cranberries into his paper napkin. When he caught my eye, he looked guilty. He wadded up the napkin and stuffed it into his pocket. I hoped he wouldn't forget about it later.

The rest of the food was delicious, though. I thought the stuffing tasted even better than the turkey meat. The good food seemed to relax everybody, and people began to chat. Eldest Brother, who liked to do carpentry, was asking Mr. Conner's advice about various kinds of saws. Mrs. Hanson and Mrs. Conner talked about what kind of cake they were planning to make for the bake sale at the next PTA meeting.

I took a deep breath and turned to Holly. "How do you like the piece we're playing for the winter concert? The violas have a pretty good part."

Holly picked at her cranberries. "I may have to pass up the concert. My viola teacher wants me to play in a recital, and I have to spend all my time practicing for that."

Holly spoke in her usual pleasant voice, but she didn't sound enthusiastic about the recital.

"Do you like your viola teacher?" I asked. "My father teaches viola, as well as violin, you know."

Mrs. Hanson turned her head. "Holly takes lessons from the first violist of the Seattle Symphony!"

I flushed. She sounded as if she thought I was drumming up lessons for my father.

Father looked interested. "Does Holly take lessons from Silverman? He's a marvelous musician! It must be wonderful to be accepted as his pupil!"

Mrs. Hanson's expression softened. "Holly works awfully hard. She can be a regular whirlwind at times!"

I stopped worrying. Apparently Mrs. Hanson had got over her anger at being called old, and we Yangs were not disgracing ourselves. We all used our knives and forks correctly and waited for permission before helping ourselves from the serving dishes in the middle of the table.

I asked Holly about herself. "Do you have any brothers or sisters?"

"No, there's just Mom and me at home." She added softly, "My parents were divorced three years ago."

I tried to find something sympathetic to say but couldn't think of anything. Holly's expression didn't tell me much. "Do you spend much time with your father?" I finally asked.

"I stay with him during the summer," said Holly. "He has a boat and takes me sailing."

I was impressed. "A boat? Your father must be rich!"

As soon as the words left my mouth, I wished I could take them back. I had forgotten that in America it isn't polite to discuss money. However hard I tried, I just couldn't remember everything.

Holly was silent for a moment. Finally she said, "My mom supports the two of us. She works in the records department in a hospital. But Dad pays for my music lessons." She looked curiously at me. "Does your mother work?"

"No, she spends all her time shopping and cooking," I admitted. Suddenly my mother, with her ridiculous shoulder pads, looked dumpy sitting next to the elegant Mrs. Hanson, who worked with records in a hospital. Were they LP records, cassette tapes, or CDs? I wondered. It sounded like a glamorous job.

"I wish my mother had a job," I said wistfully. Mother had been a professional pianist, but in Seattle she hadn't been able to find work.

At least Second Sister and I earned some money baby-sitting, which is something girls don't do in China. If Chinese parents have to go out, they usually try to get the grandparents to look after the children.

"Do you do any baby-sitting?" I asked.

"I do a little," said Holly. Suddenly she smiled. "What I like best is to baby-sit dogs."

"Baby-sit dogs," I repeated slowly. "You mean dog-sit?"

Holly laughed. I could see *this* was something she really enjoyed talking about. "When my neighbors are busy, I take their dogs for walks," she explained. "I just love animals."

"If Holly had her way, our house would be overflowing with pets," said Mrs. Hanson.

"Did you keep pets in China?" Holly asked me.

I shook my head. "We didn't have room."

"We could barely squeeze our family into our Shanghai apartment," said Father, "much less have room for pets."

"Until recently, it was actually illegal to keep a dog in many cities," added Mother. "If a dog was heard barking, the police would come to investigate."

Holly looked shocked. "How about cats, then? Are you allowed to keep cats?"

"Cats are allowed," said Father. "They don't take up much room, and they don't create a sanitation problem in the streets. But keeping them is still a luxury most people can't afford."

"Well, it's different here," said Mrs. Hanson. "Holly and I have a cat and six kittens at the moment."

"If you have a house with a yard, you'd have room enough for a cat," Holly said to me. "Do you live in a house?"

I wondered why she sounded so eager as she asked the question. Before I could say anything, Father answered. "We're renting half of a house, but it would be quite impossible for us to keep a cat. We have so many instruments and piles of sheet music lying around that any kind of pet would be a disaster."

The excitement faded from Holly's face, and I knew our family had disappointed her in some way. I wondered why.

Mrs. Conner began to clear the dinner plates. Matthew and his brother, Eric, jumped up to help her. Fourth Brother also got up, but Mrs. Conner told him to sit down again. "Two helpers are all I need, Sprout. The kitchen isn't big enough for more than that."

"Sprout?" said Father. I knew he loved stir-fried bean sprouts. He looked eagerly around the table and was disappointed when he didn't see any.

I laughed. "Sprout is what everybody calls Fourth Brother, Father."

My American friends call me Mary, the name I picked for myself, since my Chinese name, Yingmei, is too hard for them to remember. In fact I had trouble remembering *American* names when I first came. I still keep a list of new words and phrases for memorizing, and a lot of the entries are names.

My family could never remember my new American name, though. When people mentioned Mary, the Yangs would say, "Who is Mary?" So it was good to see Father puzzled by Sprout for a change.

Mr. Conner nodded. "Yeah, Sprout is a good name for the little guy." He added quickly, "The little guy with the big bat." Mr. Conner was proud of Fourth Brother's success with baseball, because he was the one who had coached him.

Mr. Conner was right. Sprouts look small and weedy, but they push up from the earth with a lot of determination. Fourth Brother is like that.

After the plates were cleared, Mrs. Conner brought in dessert: ice cream and three different kinds of pies. From the way their eyes were shining, I guessed that Eric and Matthew thought this was the best part of the meal. Personally, I enjoyed the turkey and the stuffing so much that I didn't feel like eating anything more, especially something sweet.

Again, the first slice of pie went to Mother. This time she didn't try to pass it to Mrs. Hanson. She had learned her lesson.

Mrs. Hanson looked at the piece of pie served to her. "Oh, I couldn't eat all this. I've already put on two pounds this month, and I can't afford to gain another ounce."

"Of course you can afford it!" Mrs. Conner said heartily. "You're so skinny, you could put on ten pounds and still look terrific."

Mother was staring at Mrs. Hanson and Mrs. Conner during this exchange. We Chinese think that being fat is good. It's a sign of good fortune. Thin people are considered unfortunate and miserable.

But I knew that here, being thin is supposed to be attractive. A lot of the girls in school are worried about their weight, and some of them even go on diets.

I saw Mother open her mouth. Don't say it, Mother, I wanted to shout. Don't say it!

But she did. Radiating good will, Mother said, "Why, you're not skinny at all, Mrs. Hanson. You're actually quite fat!"

We had been living in America for almost a year, and I had finally learned the names of all the American holidays. But ever since that dinner with the Conners, I'll always think of Thanksgiving Day as Memorial Day, because I'll remember it for a long, long time. So will Mrs. Hanson.

About the Author
Lensey Namioka

You probably thought this story about the Yangs was funny. The author, Lensey Namioka, has a way of seeing the humor in things. Ms. Namioka's positive outlook on life comes from realizing that being different shouldn't make a person unhappy. She didn't always feel this way though. Like the character Mary Yang, Ms. Namioka was an immigrant who had to learn American ways when she was a young schoolgirl. Her family moved to the United States when she was eight. When discussing her move to America, she said, "At first it made me unhappy always to be an outsider. Gradually I began to accept the fact. We enjoyed our social lives, and what did it matter if we looked or sounded different from our friends and neighbors?" Ms. Namioka's book *Yang the Third and Her Impossible Family* was given Parents' Choice recognition in 1995. She wrote another book about the musical Yang family entitled *Yang the Youngest and His Terrible Ear*.

Reader Response

Open for Discussion

Do you think this story is funny or serious or both? Why?

Comprehension Check

1. Why will Mary remember her family's first Thanksgiving dinner for a long, long time? Give examples from the story.

2. Find examples that show that Mary knows more about American customs than her family does. Does Mary's knowledge make it easier for her? Explain.

3. What might happen if the Conners and the Hansons were to visit the Yangs? Explain, using evidence from the story.

4. **Compare** and **contrast** Mrs. Yang with Mrs. Hanson. How are they alike? How are they different? (Compare and Contrast)

5. **Compare** a turkey and a chicken. Now **contrast** the way the Conners' turkey was prepared with the way Mrs. Yang would prepare a chicken in China. (Compare and Contrast)

 Test Prep

Look Back and Write

Look back at pages 361–364. Why is Mary both happy and nervous about her family's invitation to the Conners' for Thanksgiving? Support your answer with details from the story.

The HARVEST MOON Festival

by Hoong Yee Lee Krakauer

Author's Note

At the end of each summer, we celebrated our favorite holiday, the Harvest Moon Festival. On this Chinese version of Thanksgiving, under the fullest and brightest moon of the year, my entire family would gather to eat sweet golden harvest mooncakes, sing Chinese poem songs, and make our annual toasts to the lucky Harvest Moon. On one particular Harvest Moon Festival, in the year of the Rabbit, I came to believe that this special Chinese holiday would always bring good luck to me and my family, throughout the year.

In the kitchen, tall stalks of bamboo steamers full of *hao gao* (HA-oh GA-oh)—small, plump shrimp dumplings—rattled merrily on the stove. Mama was busy stirring big iron woks filled with shredded meat and vegetables.

"Look, girls!" said Popo, our grandmother, taking a tray out of the oven. *"Yue bing* (yoo-EH bing)*!"*

"Mooncakes!" cried Hoong Yee.

"*Rabbit* Mooncakes!" cried Hoong Wei.

Oh, Mama's mooncakes were beautiful! The little honey-colored cakes were shaped like rabbits in honor of the Year of the Rabbit. Each one was carefully wrapped in a thin golden crust with curled edges, and each was filled with a rich, dark sweetness.

"Hoong Yee, Hoong Wei! *Fai di lai* (fay di lay)*!* Hurry!" called Mama. "The guests are here."

Mama handed the girls a dish of preserved plums and a *cha hu* (cha hoo)—a woven bamboo container filled with hot tea—to serve the arriving guests.

"*Nin hao* (nin ha-oh)*?* How are you?" said Hoong Yee and Hoong Wei together as they bowed respectfully to their elder relatives.

What a wonderful feast Mama had prepared! Platters of Hoong Wei's favorite dishes filled the center of the large table—paper-thin scallion pancakes, mustard greens laced with oyster sauce, and *zong zi* (zong zi), balls of sticky rice wrapped in dark green lotus leaves.

Everything looks so delicious, thought Hoong Wei, and the best part—the rabbit mooncakes—is yet to come!

Hoong Wei made her way to the piano and sat down next to her sister.

The room fell quiet. All eyes were on Hoong Yee and Hoong Wei in their bright silk jackets with the round golden buttons. Softly they began to play. Mama joined in, singing in her clear, sweet voice:

By my bed, the moon shines bright
And appears like icy foam.
I raise my head in moonbeams' light;
My head in hand, I long for home.

At the end of the final refrain, Hoong Wei looked up.

"*Hao ji le* (HA-oh ji lee)*! How wonderful!" she cried happily. "Look what Popo is bringing us!"

Into the living room came Popo, carrying a dessert tray.

After the relatives were served their mooncakes, Baba, our father, lifted his glass and made the first good luck toast to the Harvest Moon. "May the Harvest Moon bless us with good fortune and bring our family together on this night each year."

Hoong Wei whispered her own toast. "*Xie xie nin* (shi-EH shi-EH nin). Thank you, bright moon."

Main Idea and Supporting Details

- The topic is what a paragraph, article, or story is about.

- The **main idea** is the most important idea about the topic.

- Sometimes the main idea is stated. When it is not, you have to decide what is most important and put it into your own words.

- **Supporting details** tell more about the main idea.

- Knowing the main idea will help you better understand and remember what you read.

Read "Saving Nome" from "Husky Express: The First Great Race" by Norma Lewis from *Cricket*.

Write About It

1. Is the following sentence a main idea or supporting detail? *A dogsled relay carrying serum could save Nome's citizens from diphtheria.* How do you know?

2. Find two details that support the main idea.

Saving Nome

by Norma Lewis

It happened in Nome, Alaska, January 1925. Children were dying of diphtheria (diphtheria is a contagious disease common in the 1800s and early 1900s. Say it: dif-theer-ee-uh). The city council quarantined (to quarantine means to isolate) the town. Schools and shops closed, and everyone stayed indoors to avoid catching the deadly disease. Dr. Curtis Welch faced an epidemic, and he was running out of serum.

Nome, on the Bering Sea, was easily reached by ships during the summer, but it became isolated when the sea and rivers froze. The nearest serum supplier was in Seattle, two thousand miles away, and the next ship couldn't sail to Nome until spring. Dr. Welch couldn't wait

Cricket

that long. The lives of Nome's fifteen hundred citizens were in danger.

Someone suggested he find a doctor in Alaska who could send extra serum to Nome by dogsled.

"That would take two weeks, maybe three," he said. "Then it'll be too late."

But the suggestion gave him an idea. Dr. Welch went to the Army Signal Corps station and sent a radio appeal for help. An Anchorage doctor heard it and offered to send serum north by train to Nenana. The Alaska Railroad ran a special train as soon as the serum was packed and ready.

But Nenana was still 674 miles east of Nome. A dogsled relay was Dr. Welch's only hope. Nineteen mushers, including Indians, Eskimos, and white pioneers, volunteered. They decided that no team would travel farther than the next village, so no time would be lost sleeping or feeding and resting the dogs. It just might work.

As you read "The Jr. Iditarod Race," use the main idea and supporting details to better understand how Dusty and his sled dogs get through the ups and downs of the Jr. Iditarod Race.

Vocabulary

Words to Know

cargo	obstacles	injuries
skids	overtakes	delays
wilderness	announcer	

When you read, you may come across a word you don't know. To figure out its meaning, look for clues in the words and sentences around it. A clue might be found in specific details or examples.

Read the paragraph below. Notice *obstacles* and the specific details or examples. What does *obstacles* mean?

Bobsledding

Bobsledding is an exciting winter sport. Teams ride down a steep, icy track in a sled. This isn't a race where one sled <u>overtakes</u> another. Instead the winner is the team with the fastest time after four runs. The run might be in the <u>wilderness</u>, but the path itself is smooth with no <u>obstacles</u>, such as trees or rocks. However, when a bobsled <u>skids</u> and crashes, <u>injuries</u> result. First-aid teams with their <u>cargo</u> of medical supplies help quickly. Accidents cause long <u>delays</u>, so everyone is happy when the <u>announcer</u> states that the race can continue.

Write About It

Use vocabulary words to write sentences about a winter adventure.

THE JR.
IDITAROD
RACE

from *Iditarod Dream*
photographs and text
by Ted Wood

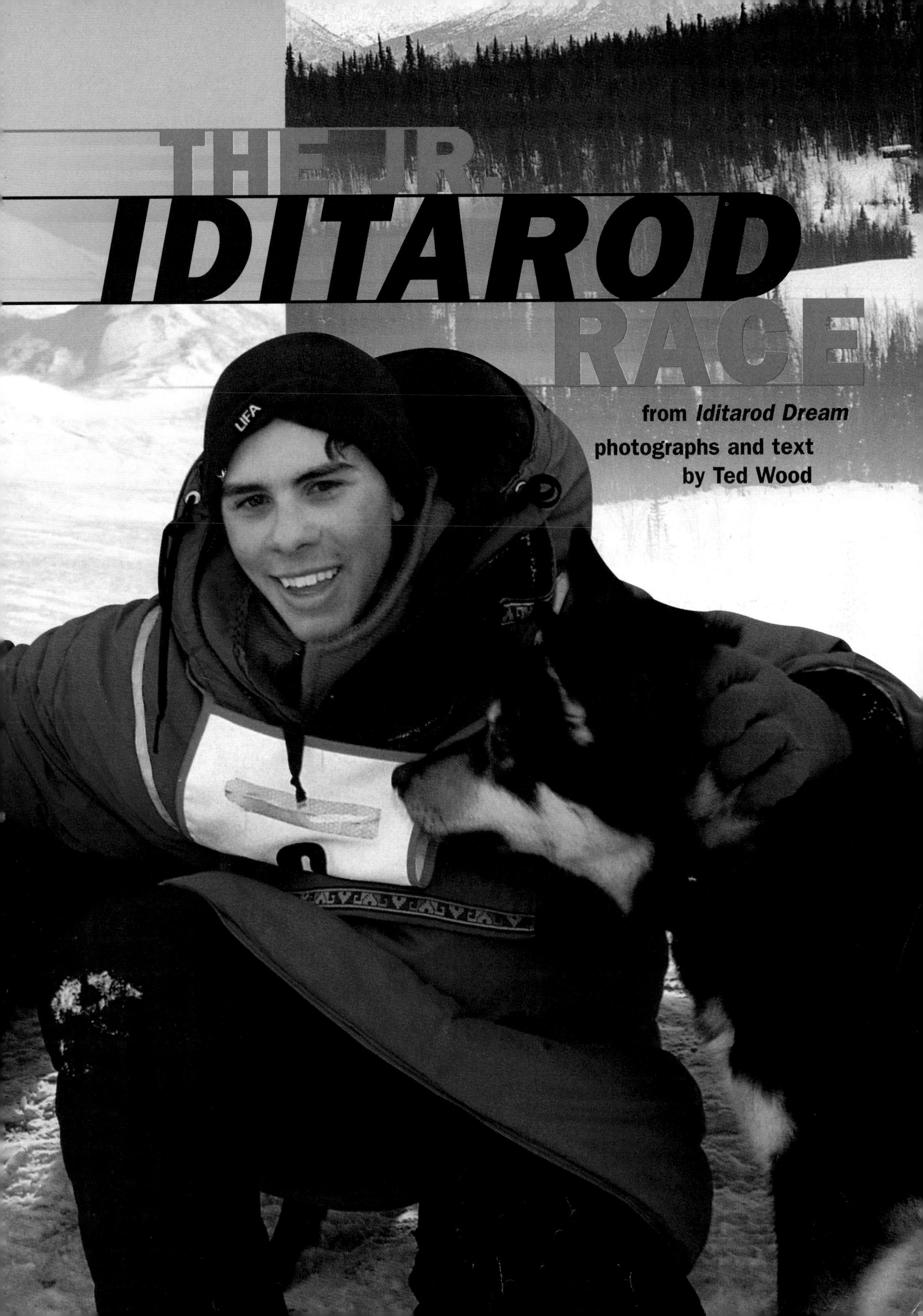

INTRODUCTION

Each March, as the darkness of winter begins to fade, an excitement spreads across Alaska. With the daylight comes Alaska's most famous event—the Iditarod Trail Sled-Dog Race. Known as the last great race, the Iditarod pits musher and dog against nature's most severe conditions. Starting in Anchorage, the racers drive their teams over mountain passes, through bitter Arctic winds, and across frozen seas to Nome, 1,180 miles away.

But dog mushing wasn't always a sport in Alaska. Eskimos in the Far North used their huskies for work, pulling their hunting sleds across the ice in search of seals. In winter, towns like Nome were cut off from the rest of Alaska as sea ice blocked the ports. Mail and supplies had to come from Anchorage by sled, pulled by the same Eskimo huskies.

In the winter of 1925, Nome was hit with a horrible epidemic: diphtheria. There was no medicine in town—

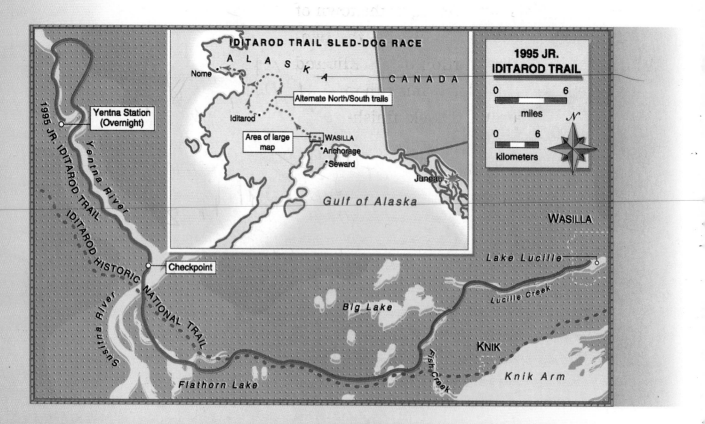

and without medicine, everyone might die. A train could bring medicine from Anchorage to Nenana, but no farther. The race was on to save the town. A dog team sped from Nenana, carrying the life-saving medicine, which was relayed team to team all the way to Nome. The brave mushers and dogs succeeded. The medicine stopped the epidemic and saved Nome.

Dog teams no longer supply Nome. Snowmobiles and airplanes now connect the town to southern Alaska. But the heroism of the dog teams was not to be forgotten, and in 1973 a famous Alaskan musher named Joe Redington decided to honor their bravery with a race that followed the same trail as the medicine relay to Nome. The trail was the Iditarod, and the race was named for the trail.

Because the race was so difficult and dangerous, only adults could enter. There was no event for young mushers dreaming of an Iditarod championship. So in 1977, race organizers started the Jr. Iditarod for kids fourteen to seventeen years old. Starting in the town of Wasilla, just north of Anchorage, the two-day race follows a portion of the Iditarod National Trail. The dog teams run to an overnight camp and back, finishing in Wasilla 158 miles later. This is the story of the Jr. Iditarod and of a young musher whose winning spirit leads him to victory.

DUSTY...
A MUSHER IN THE JR. IDITAROD

LOADING UP AND ON THE ROAD— ALMOST RACE DAY

It's the night before Dusty leaves for the Jr. Iditarod Trail Race. The fifteen-year-old has worked hard to train his dogs for this big event. Ozone is injured, so his lead dogs will have to be Annie and QT.

Early the next morning, Dusty and his father load his sled onto the truck and put the dogs into their traveling pens. Ozone, unable to race, watches the truck leave the yard, wishing she were going.

The day is clear and cold. Mount McKinley, the highest peak in North America, stands like a giant before the truck. The trip south to race headquarters in Wasilla takes four hours.

Dusty's thoughts return to last year's Jr. Iditarod, his first. He remembers the thirty-below-zero temperatures and how his glasses were so coated with ice he couldn't see the trail. And how on the return—when perhaps he'd been headed for victory—he got lost, wandering for four hours before he found the right trail. He finished fourth. But this year his glasses are gone, replaced with contact lenses, and his dog team is the best he's ever had. He can only hope the huskies take him down the right trail.

That evening they reach Iditarod headquarters, where all the racers are gathered for the pre-race meeting. He sees familiar faces from last year—Andy Willis, the favorite to win this year, and Noah Burmeister, who came all the way from Nome. One at a time the fifteen racers pick numbers from a hat to set their starting positions in tomorrow's race. (There is no number 1 position competing in the race; instead the slot is reserved to honor a dedicated supporter of that year's Jr. Iditarod race.) The racers start two minutes apart. Dusty picks number 6, a good position and the same he had last year. Andy will start fourteenth and Noah ninth. Dusty leaves with his father for his final night's sleep before the race.

The next morning Dusty and his dad arrive two hours before the race. It's zero degrees, which is perfect for the dogs. Any warmer, and they would overheat. The race begins on frozen Lake Lucille and runs seventy-nine miles north through forests, over windswept swamps, and up the ice-covered Yentna River to a cabin called Yentna Station, the halfway point.

Last year the race started ten miles farther up the trail. Dusty is worried about starting here. The lake ice is barely covered with snow and is so hard that if he loses control at the start, he could get dragged across the lake. His safety hook, used to stop and hold the sled, won't be able to grab

DUSTY'S STARTING POSITION—
NUMBER 6

R. IDITAROD TRAIL RACE
START ▽ FINISH

GO!

the ice. Dusty checks the brakes on his sled and begins to pack the required supplies. Every racer must carry two pounds of food per dog in case of emergency, and must finish with the same amount. (The four pounds each dog will eat for dinner has been flown to Yentna Station the day before.)

Ten minutes before his start, Dusty, his father, and three friends working as handlers hook the dogs up to the sled. Each dog looks small but is tremendously powerful. Dusty has to walk each dog from the truck, lifting its front legs off the snow. With all four legs down, a sled dog would pull Dusty off his feet. Even hooked up, the dogs are so excited by the other teams it takes every hand to hold them in place.

Dusty's team moves to the starting line, straining against the handlers. His mother rides the sled with him, stepping on the brakes to help control the sled. She's nervous, remembering how Dusty got lost last time. But she's also very proud, and she kisses him good-bye before hopping off the sled.

The dogs are pulling so hard now that five people can barely hold them back. Then the announcer yells, "Go!" The handlers step away and Dusty flies from the start.

They cross the lake safely, following the red plastic cones marking the route. But as they enter the woods Dusty is on edge. He's never done this part of the trail, and it's crowded with obstacles. Snowmobiles roar along the same trail, and within ten miles he has to cross four roads. Sometimes the roads are so slick the dogs fall, or they get confused by the cars and spectators. Dusty knows he just needs to survive this part until he hits the main Iditarod Trail.

At the first road, the team roars over the pavement and around a sharp turn coming off the road. But they're going too fast, and the sled skids sideways, crashing into a tree. Dusty stops dead and can't believe he didn't break the sled. *I'm out of control*, he says to himself. *I'd better slow the team down.*

OVERCOMING OBSTACLES ON THE TRAIL

Back on the trail, he uses his track brake to slow the dogs. He gets them into a strong, steady pace and is able to pass two racers only five miles from the start. He crosses the next road and quickly overtakes another racer. Right before the final road crossing, ten miles out, Dusty passes the last racer. He knows he's in the lead now, that his team is running well, but he can't think about that. He just wants to get through this part and onto the main Iditarod Trail, which he knows from last year's race.

Finally, eleven miles out, Dusty hits the familiar trail leading into the thick Alaskan forest. The team is running perfectly now, strong and fast, as they head into the hilly section of the race. Dusty is in a rhythm too. He runs beside the sled up hills to lighten the load for his team. Around tight corners he jumps from left runner to right runner, digging in the edges to steer the sled through the curves.

STEERING THROUGH THE CURVES

The trail is only a few feet wide in the woods, and coming around a blind corner the dogs run smack into two snowmobiles stopped in the path. Unable to pass, the dogs spin and run in circles, tangling their lines before Dusty can get to them. It takes him five minutes to straighten them out and get under way. As he goes around the next curve and down a hill, he spots another snowmobile roaring full speed toward him. The machine almost hits Annie and QT in the lead, but it flies off the trail to avoid the collision. The two lead dogs stop dead, but the others can't. They pile into each other, making a huge tangle of dogs and line.

Dusty can't believe it. Two tangles in less than five minutes. He frantically unknots his team, sure that another racer will catch up to him because of the delays. A tangle is a musher's second-worst nightmare. The dogs can injure their feet in the lines, or strangle when they wrap around each other.

Finally under way, Dusty and the dogs are on edge and can't settle into a pace. *Please don't see another snowmobile*, he says to himself. Then he spots moose tracks on the trail, and his fears mushroom. Running into a moose is a musher's worst nightmare. Because dogs look like wolves to a moose, a moose may attack a team and can kill several dogs before a musher can frighten it off. There's no going around a moose. If Dusty sees one, all he can do is wait for it to move and hope it doesn't charge.

But the team carries him safely out of the forest and onto a wide, open meadow. Dusty passes a small wooden sign that says "Nome 1,049 miles" and knows from the year before that he can relax for a while through these barren flats. The flats lead to frozen Flathorn Lake, three and a half hours from the start. Here, on the edge of the lake, Dusty takes his first break. He tosses all the dogs fish snacks, big chunks of frozen salmon that will keep their energy up. He says hi to each as well, checking their feet for injuries. QT and Blacky have splits in the webs between their toes, so Dusty puts booties on their feet to protect them as they run.

He takes only five minutes, still expecting to see another racer coming close behind. Trails cross in every direction at the lake, and it's here that Dusty got lost last year. Today, he chooses the right path and speeds out onto the huge snowy lake. It's like running on an ocean of white; Dusty feels relaxed and at home. Out on the lake he suddenly realizes how big his lead is. He can see five miles behind him and there's not one racer in sight. He can't believe it. *Where are Andy and Noah?* he asks himself.

RUNNING ON AN OCEAN OF WHITE

NOME 1049 Miles

From the lake Dusty turns on to the Susitna River. It looks like a winding snow highway disappearing into the wilderness. Here, he stops at the one checkpoint in the race, and while an official examines his sled and required cargo, Dusty checks the dogs. He decides to take Annie off the lead. She's been looking back while running and seems nervous. She must not have recovered from the encounter with the snowmobile, Dusty thinks.

Dusty moves young Jazz to lead with QT. But Jazz proves too inexperienced, and three miles from the checkpoint Dusty switches Jazz for Bettie. Now the team is running well again, and they move quickly, silently, up a tributary of the Susitna called the Yentna River. There's no need to yell orders here. They know the way to Yentna Station, but Dusty still calls their names to keep them happy.

Just after five P.M.—seven hours after he started— Dusty arrives at Yentna Station, the halfway point and overnight stop. The station is a little log house that can only be reached by plane, snowmobile, or dog sled. Visitors can stay in the house, but racers can't. By the rules, they have to stay with the dogs.

Dusty feels great. He knows he's had a fast race—but, more important, the dogs look fresh and are still eager to run. He smiles to himself, knowing that his training has paid off.

But there's no time to relax. He has hours of dog chores to do. Each racer gets one bale of straw for bedding; after Dusty ties the sled off to a small tree, he spreads the straw around the dogs. It will protect them from the cold snow as they sleep.

Next, he fires up his stove to melt snow for water. While it heats, he fills a cooler with twenty pounds of hamburger and dry food. He pours the heated water into the cooler, letting the frozen meat soak up the warm liquid. Twenty hungry eyes watch as Dusty finally dishes up the warm meal.

After dinner, Dusty checks the dogs' feet for web cracks, putting on ointment where needed. Then he hears other dogs and looks up. He'd forgotten about the other racers. It's Noah, the second racer to arrive at Yentna—thirty-eight minutes behind Dusty. Andy arrives next, eight minutes after Noah. Over the next four hours the remaining racers straggle in. Everyone is required to stay at Yentna ten hours. Dusty arrived so early that his departure time is three-thirty the next morning. He decides not to sleep and helps the other racers build a big fire in the snow. They all help each other; that's the rule of the wilderness.

Before his three-thirty start, Dusty melts more water for the dogs, feeds everyone, packs his sled, and finally makes sure his head-lamp batteries work for the trip back.

It's snowing lightly as he leaves Yentna, and there's no moon. The only light comes from Dusty's head lamp. The dogs are excited to run, but Dusty doesn't like the night. He can't see the trail markers or nearby moose. The dogs are his only eyes, so he chooses Bettie and QT to lead him out. They did the trail once, Dusty figures, so they can do it again.

Once again the dogs are gobbling up the miles. They run the Yentna River and Flathorn Lake in the dark; at first light, Dusty stops at the Nome sign. As he gives the dogs fish snacks, he finally lets himself believe that if nothing bad happens he can expect to win. Dusty and his team move through the hills easily and take all four road crossings smoothly.

Finally, the lake appears, like a welcome mat, and Dusty begins to smile as he heads for the finish. He's running so fast that the spectators and most of the racers' families haven't arrived yet. But he spots his mother and father cheering him on, and when he crosses the finish line his mother showers him with hugs and kisses. His father's proud smile is so big it almost looks frozen with happiness.

TV and radio announcers swarm Dusty. "How does it feel to win, Dusty?" they ask.

AT THE FINISH

THE WINNER

"I would have had a big smile even if I'd come in last," he says. "But it feels great to win."

Because he ran so fast, rumors are flying that Dusty has mistreated his dogs, pushing them too hard. But now, looking at them, everyone knows this isn't true. The dogs are still strong, barking, jumping, and eager to run farther. Dusty has treated them just right. He knows they are his trusted partners—and they're champions.

About the Author and Photographer

TED WOOD

Ted Wood is a writer and photographer who has traveled the world for his work. For his book about Dusty's Jr. Iditarod race, he journeyed to the Alaskan wilderness. His photographs, taken in places as distant as southern India and Vietnam, have been published in many children's books and magazines for adults. Mr. Wood makes his home in Wyoming.

Reader Response

Open for Discussion

What is the main focus of the selection—the race or the racer? Explain your answer.

Comprehension Check

1. Why is the Iditarod championship such a great tradition for Alaskans? Use details from the selection to explain.

2. What were some of Dusty's problems in his previous Jr. Iditarod Race? What challenges did he face in the race described in this selection? Which race was probably more difficult?

3. For a while, there were rumors that Dusty had mistreated his dogs. Do you agree with the rumors? Give evidence from the selection to support your answer.

4. Which is the **main idea** of the last two paragraphs on page 390? **a.** Each dog looked small but was very powerful. **b.** Dusty's mother rode on the sled with him for a short distance. **c.** Dusty and his dogs eagerly started the race. Find two **supporting details** for the main idea. (Main Idea and Supporting Details)

5. What is the **main idea** of the paragraphs on page 396? Name three **supporting details** for the main idea. (Main Idea and Supporting Details)

 **Test Prep**

Look Back and Write

Look back at the map on page 386. Study the routes of the Iditarod National Trail and the Jr. Iditarod Trail. How does the Jr. trail follow a part of the National Trail? How does it differ?

Dogs in Sports

by Juliet Clutton-Brock

OVER THE AGES, people have used dogs as entertainment in a great variety of sports. Dogs like to compete with each other. A sight hound is a dog that hunts by sight, rather than smell. The large number of different breeds of sight hounds have all been developed for coursing, or chasing after, fast-running prey such as hares. They were often used—together with birds of prey—in the sport of falconry. In northern Africa and Asia, both the saluki and the Afghan hound were bred for chasing gazelles. Today, in greyhound racing, dogs are bred for speed, and run after a mechanical "hare."

Keen sight of the borzoi will help it to win a race—or, as in former times, to hunt well.

MUZZLED
Dogs get very excited when they are racing, so usually they wear muzzles to keep them from biting other dogs during a race.

GOING TO THE DOGS
Greyhounds and whippets are the number-one choice around the world as racing dogs. Here, though, the greyhound is used for advertising Camembert cheese.

BORZOI

Deep chest and freely swinging shoulders enable the dog to take long strides.

Long, muscular lower legs

SALUKI

Well-feathered tail is long, set low, and gently curved.

Well-muscled legs make the saluki a powerful runner.

Dense, curly ruff on neck

THE ROYAL SALUKI
The saluki is one of the oldest breeds of sight hound in the world. Dogs of this type can be seen in the tomb paintings of ancient Egyptian pharaohs. For thousands of years salukis have been bred by Arab peoples and used, together with falcons, for hunting.

THE HARE AND THE DOG
The use of greyhounds for hare coursing is probably one of the most ancient of all sports. To course is to chase game by sight, not scent.

AWAY TO THE RACES
Dogs have been used in the Arctic for hundreds of years to draw sleds. Today they have been mostly replaced by mechanical snowmobiles. However, the sport of sled racing over long distances with huskies has become very popular—especially in Alaska.

Long, wavy, silky hair is usually white with splotchy dark markings.

BEAUTIFUL BOUNDER
The borzoi comes from Russia. It used to be called the Russian wolfhound because it was used by the aristocracy for hunting and chasing wolves. The borzoi may have been developed from long-legged sight hounds such as the saluki. They were bred to look as aristocratic and beautiful as possible to match the noble aspirations of the Russian emperors.

Ankle joint, or hock, is high on the leg, which makes the leg very long and powerful.

Predicting

- **Predicting** is giving a statement about what you think might happen next in a story or come next in an article. The statement you give is a **prediction.**

- You can make predictions based on what you already know and what has already happened in the story or article.

- After you predict something, continue reading to check your prediction. As you learn new information, you might need to change your prediction.

Read "Why Bears Have Short Tails" by Sandra Begay from *And It Is Still That Way: Legends Told by Arizona Indian Children* collected by Byrd Baylor.

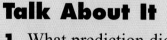

AND IT IS
STILL
THAT WAY

Legends told by
Arizona Indian Children

collected by
BYRD BAYLOR

Talk About It

1. What prediction did you make about Bear?

2. What information did you use to make your prediction?

3. How close was your prediction to what really happened?

Why Bears Have Short Tails

by Sandra Begay

Fox was fishing in the river. When he had ten fish, he put them on his back and walked off into the woods.

Bear came along and saw Fox with the fish on his back.

"How come you have so many fishes on your back? How are you fishing those fishes out of the water?"

Fox said, "It's easy. You sit on the ice and put your tail in the river. The fishes catch onto your tail and when you get up, there will be all of those fishes just hanging on."

"Thanks," said Bear as he ran off toward the river.

Predict what Bear is going to do.

He didn't know Fox was laughing as he went along through the woods with his ten fish.

Bear sat on the ice. He sat there a long time, waiting and waiting. He didn't notice any fish jumping onto his tail. All he noticed was that his tail was freezing. It hurt.

After a long time, Bear said, "I can't feel my tail."

He got up and looked. It was true. His long tail had frozen off. All he had left was a very short tail.

Bear was angry. He gave up fishing and ran into the woods looking for Fox.

Fox was cooking his ten fish when Bear grabbed him.

Bear said, "You tricked me, and my beautiful long tail froze off. So now I'm taking you back to that river. I'll throw you in and let you freeze."

"No," Fox said. "Don't do that. If you let me go, I'll give you all my fish."

So Bear let Fox go and ate all the fish himself and warmed his short tail by Fox's fire.

Now all bears have short tails. This is how it happened.

LOOK AHEAD

In "The Night Alone," Ohkwa'ri remembers a tale about a bear as he spends his first night away from his family. As you read, predict what might happen.

Vocabulary

Words to Know

| bruised | reckless | lodge |
| pouch | possession | |

Words with opposite meanings are called **antonyms.** You can often figure out the meaning of an unknown word by finding a clue in the words around it. Sometimes this clue is an antonym.

Read the paragraph below. Notice how *careful* helps you understand what *reckless* means.

Camping with Dad

Once when Dad and I went camping, we built a lodge in the woods. First, I had to convince him not to put up our tent. Then I went looking for branches and twigs. Soon my arms were filled. I was so excited about the lodge, I began running and tripped on a rock. Dad rushed over with his pouch of first-aid supplies and tended to my bruised head and arms. Hurrying was a reckless thing to do, and I promised to be more careful. By nightfall, the lodge was ready. I crawled in, arranged my sleeping bag, and put my favorite possession, an old telescope in a leather case, beside me.

Write About It

Tell about a time you weren't careful. Use some or all of the vocabulary words.

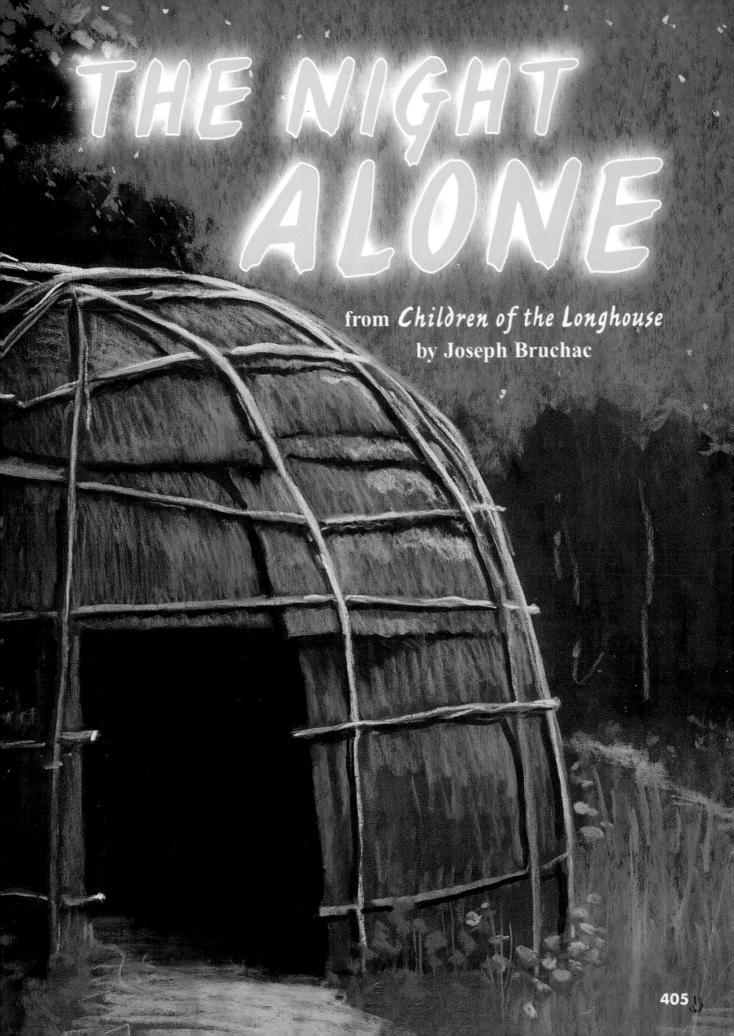

THE NIGHT ALONE

from *Children of the Longhouse*
by Joseph Bruchac

Fifty Mohawk Indian families live in the big longhouse. Ohkwa'ri has lived there all of his eleven years but now wants his own small lodge to stay in sometimes. He discusses this idea with his uncle, Big Tree. Big Tree reminds Ohkwa'ri that he has made enemies of Grabber and his friends, who might attack him in his own little lodge. After listening to Ohkwa'ri's response, Big Tree agrees to his nephew's idea. This is what happens the first night Ohkwa'ri sleeps in his own lodge away from the village.

The first two times during the night when Ohkwa'ri woke up, he tried to reach under what he thought was his usual bed to find the elm bark box in which he kept his stone. That stone had in it two big, beautiful crystals, each as big as a man's thumb. It was his favorite possession, and he sometimes took it out in the night to hold it above him and watch the light from their central fire flicker and reflect from its facets. He realized now that reaching for that elm bark box was probably something that he did every night.

"I will not wake up again," he said to himself after that second time. But he was wrong.

He had hardly drifted off to sleep when the sound of scratching against his little lodge made him sit bolt upright. There was still some light from the flicker of his small fire, and when he leaned his head close enough to his door to look through the cracks, he saw two little shadows poking about. One of them made a chirring sound and the other one chirped and growled in reply. Raccoons. He should have known that they would come. Of all the animals in the forest none were more curious.

One of the raccoons poked its nose right against the side of the lodge and began to climb up on it.

"*Hooo!*" Ohkwa'ri cried, making the sound of the horned owl.

The raccoon jumped down and disappeared as fast as a deerskin ball scooped up by a *Tekwaarathon* stick. Its companion scooted away almost as quickly.

Ohkwa'ri laughed silently as he listened to the sound of the two raccoons scurrying away through the dry oak leaves.

The next time he woke was when he had heard a strange sound. It was like the sound of regular footsteps. He listened and listened. An owl had been calling earlier, but now that sound was gone. From the other side of the great hills the lonely, unanswered call of a wolf had drifted to him once during the night, but that wolf had called only once. Even the wind, which had whispered its familiar song through the maple and oak leaves, was now holding its breath. Everything was completely silent.

Ohkwa'ri listened and listened. He began to realize that he was listening for things he could not hear. The small fire he had made in front of his new lodge had burned out long ago and so he could not hear the sound of it burning. Back in the big longhouse there was always the sound at night of the fires. Their hissing and crackling and popping noises were as familiar and reassuring as the nearby sounds of breathing from his family.

At night in the big longhouse he could always hear the sounds other humans make. He heard their yawns and their sighs. He heard the creaking of sleeping benches and the thump of hands or feet against the sides of the lodge when someone rolled over.

He heard the sound of people when they woke and whispered to each other and laughed in a soft, knowing way. He heard the ones who woke and got up to place more wood on the fire in the winter when it grew quite cold before the dawn. He heard those others who woke when it was so warm in the summer that they would take a deerskin robe with them and go sleep outside near the longhouse wall. He heard the coughing that was so common in the late winter, especially on moist days when the smoke from the fires did not rise through the smoke holes but flowed around within the longhouse like a dry gray river. Those sounds filled every night, and the night was strangely quiet without them.

But there had still been that sound. Ohkwa'ri listened and listened. He could hear his own breathing. But that was not it. He listened further. *Blum-blump . . . blum-blump . . . blum-blump . . . blum-blump.* It was like the two-step beat of the water drum. Then he knew what it was. He was hearing the sound of his own heart beating.

The last time he woke, just before the dawn light, was when the light from outside his lodge grew so bright that he thought surely it was dawn. It was so bright that he pushed open the woven door he had propped in place and crawled out. There, looking down from the sky, was Grandmother Moon. Her full round face seemed as warm and caring as the face of his own grandmother. Her silver light made the river below him shimmer and gleam like a string of pale wampum beads. It was so bright that he could make out the shapes of the big longhouse and the other, smaller buildings of his own village on the far side of the river.

Ohkwa'ri stood and lifted his hands toward the moon.

"Grandmother," he said, "thank you for coming to visit me when I was feeling so lonely. You have reminded me what my mother taught me. Wherever I go, I will never be truly alone."

The light from the bright face of Elder Brother, the Sun, shone between the woven branches of the rough lodge door. Ohkwa'ri opened his eyes as those first rays of dawn touched his face. He felt cold and stiff. He had missed being able to stretch out to his full length, for his small round lodge was only big enough for him to lie curled up on the earth like a sleeping chipmunk. He lay there, breathing slowly, thinking about the night he had just passed.

As Ohkwa'ri walked down the hill toward the river, it seemed to him he could hear and see things better this morning than ever before. He was just a little tired from his wakeful night, but that night alone and going without a meal had sharpened his senses.

"It is just as my uncle Big Tree told me," Ohkwa'ri said to himself as he stopped to look at a beech leaf, seeing as if for the first time how its notched edges glittered in the sun, feeling with a finger the toughness of the leaf. "You are able to see better and hear better when you go without food for a time."

He remembered the story Big Tree told of the two young men who were always competing with each other. They both belonged to the Turtle Clan and so they were very stubborn. After they had both fasted for some days, each one tried to outdo the other with what he could see and hear.

"I can see the farthest hill," said the first man. "Can you see it?"

"Yes. I can also see the tallest pine tree on top of that farthest hill," said the second. "Can you see that?"

"Indeed I can," answered the first, "and I can see the highest branch on top of that tree."

"Ah," said the second man, "then can you see the butterfly resting on top of the smallest twig on that highest branch?"

"Of course," said the first man.

"I am now counting how many spots there are on its wings," said the second.

"There are six on each wing," said the second man.

"But listen! I can hear that butterfly's wings as they flap," said the first.

"Ah," said the second man, "I hear that too, but I also hear the butterfly breathing. Can you . . . ?"

But the two young men never finished their discussion. For at that moment their two mothers, who had walked up unheard behind them, each poured a cup of water onto the heads of their sons.

Now, as Ohkwa'ri walked, he began to hear a noise. It was a sound like an animal growling. He stopped and listened more closely, trying to figure out from where that sound came. It did not take him long, for the sound came from his own stomach. It was growling with hunger.

Ohkwa'ri patted his stomach.

"I am sorry," he said. "You are complaining because I have neglected you, my stomach. I left home without bringing any food with me. Now we will have to wait until I have crossed the river. But try to be quiet, my friend. A bear may hear you and think that you are another bear calling to him."

Ohkwa'ri smiled as he remembered how his father, Two Ideas, had explained to him the way bears talk to each other. They had been walking in the woods for a long time and Ohkwa'ri's stomach had also been reminding him that it was past the time to eat.

"They growl like your stomach does, my son," he said to Ohkwa'ri.

His father was not always available to do things with Ohkwa'ri, for the younger sister of Two Ideas had several children, a son and two daughters. As a good uncle, Two Ideas had as much responsibility for helping with the upbringing of his sister's children as with the children of his wife. Thus, Two Ideas spent a good part of almost every day in the small Turtle Clan longhouse built just a spear's throw to the north of the great longhouse of the Bear Clan.

Ohkwa'ri did not mind. It was the way things were supposed to be. After all, his father and he were of two different clans. And it was that way with every father and son among the Longhouse People. You always had to marry someone of a different clan. That happened, as was right and proper, when a man's mother agreed with the mother of that man's future wife that the two young people should be allowed to marry. After the marriage the man would go and move into the longhouse of his wife's clan. And all children would belong to the clan of their mother.

Ohkwa'ri liked his father very much, and so he was glad that the longhouse where his father's nephew and two nieces lived was right next to their own. After all, his father would have been away much more often, going to teach things to his nephew. And his father had much to teach. For one, Ohkwa'ri's father was among the best hunters in their village. It was sometimes said that no one knew more about the ways of the animals than did Two Ideas.

As they walked that day in the forest, Two Ideas had talked to Ohkwa'ri about the bears. "You must always show them respect," he said. "Especially a mother bear who has cubs. Remember what happened to Grabber."

It was hard for Ohkwa'ri not to laugh out loud when he thought of how Grabber got his nickname. As a young man Grabber had thought very highly of himself. He wanted everyone to call him by a different name than the one he had been given by the midwife when he was born. He wanted to be known as Walks with the Bears. He had even taken the time and trouble to make a tattoo on his thigh that would stand for his name. He took a long time pricking his leg with a bone awl and then rubbing in wood ashes to make his tattoo. Most of the people had tattoos of one kind or another. Rubbing in the wood ash made the tattoos a beautiful blue color. But most people either had simple tattoos—lines, circles, curves like the shape of an uncoiling fern leaf—or asked the help of an older man or woman who was very good at drawing things to help them. This young man, though, was too proud of himself to ask for help. But he was not a very good artist. As a result the tattoo he made looked not like a man walking with a bear but like a very ugly porcupine leaning against a dead tree.

One day (before he became known as Grabber) that young man had decided that he would do something which no one else in the village had ever done. He would have a bear cub as a pet. So one fine spring day he set out from the village toward the place where the bears live to catch a bear cub. People shook their heads as they watched him go, but no one tried to stop him. It was widely accepted that one could never tell another person what they should or should not do. If they attempted to do something that they shouldn't, then they would learn soon enough why it was not a good thing to do.

It was not unusual for people in their village to have one of the animals of the forest living with them in their lodge. It was so commonly done that such animals would even be tolerated by the people's dogs. Usually those were orphan animals whose mothers had been killed in an accident or by a hunter. Such pets as raccoons and beaver were common and were regarded no longer as wild animals but as members of the family. Troublesome members of the family, at times.

A bear, though, was a different story, and stealing a young cub from its mother was not something that was advisable to try. So when that young man who wanted to be known as Walks with the Bears set out to catch a bear cub one spring, everyone in the village watched him go, and waited. They did not wait long. Elder Brother, the Sun, had traveled only the width of two hands across the sky when that young man came running as fast as he could back into the village, his eyes wide with fright, his hands holding onto his backside. He was shouting as he ran.

"The bear grabbed me! The bear grabbed me!"

He did not stop when he reached the village but ran right through it, right through the fields by the river, and right to the river itself. Perhaps he intended to run across the river too, but the water did not hold him up. Several people who had followed him pulled him out of the water before he could drown. The back of his loincloth had been torn by the swipe of a bear's claws and there were some deep scratches on his backside, but he was not badly hurt. From that day on, though, that young man became known to everyone not as Walks with the Bears but as Grabber.

"I am a hungry, hungry bear," Ohkwa'ri said as he listened to his stomach growling. As he walked down the rocky trail toward his canoe, which he had drawn up into the alders at the edge of the river, he wondered what food might be ready so early in the morning. His thoughts were divided between his hunger and his memory of Grabber's story. He began to walk faster as he thought of food. He no longer considered the possibility of danger. By the time Ohkwa'ri reached the place where the trail curved around a great stone to cross a rocky ledge, he was no longer watching where he put his feet.

Suddenly he heard a sound like pebbles being shaken in a hollow gourd. His heart leaped into his throat as he threw himself to one side to keep from stepping on the huge rattlesnake that was coiled in the middle of the trail. He landed hard on his shoulder. The rattlesnake was no more than an arm's length away from him. Its tail a blur of motion, it lifted up its head and looked at him.

Ohkwa'ri did not move. The rattlesnake's eyes were bright as crystals as it moved its head back and forth, flicking out its tongue. Then, deciding this reckless young human was no real threat, it uncoiled itself and crawled off the trail, disappearing into the rocks.

Ohkwa'ri sat up slowly. My sister is right, he thought. I forget to think sometimes. I will try not to be so reckless from now on. He stood up and began to walk again down the trail. This time he watched where he stepped. As he walked, he rubbed his bruised shoulder. I have learned a lesson, he thought. Then he shook his head and sighed. By now, he thought, the pot of food in our lodge will be empty. I will have to wait until later in the day to eat.

But when Ohkwa'ri reached over his canoe, he saw two things. The first was a small basket made of birch bark filled with ripe strawberries.

Otsi:stia, he told himself, remembering that she had gone to pick berries at the same time he had left to build his new lodge. She must have crossed the river and placed these here for him before it grew dark last night. Thank you, my sister, he thought.

He lifted up the berry basket and picked up the second thing in his canoe. It was a pouch that looked just like the one his uncle Hand Talker had worn on his waist. He sat down, placing the basket of berries at his side. Then he opened the drawstring of the pouch and shook out its contents onto his lap. It was pemmican, smoked deer meat with maple sugar and dried blueberries pounded into it. Preserved by the maple sugar, food such as this would keep for a long, long time. And it was very good to eat.

Thank you, my junior uncle, Ohkwa'ri thought.

Plucking a trembling leaf from a nearby alder, he took a few of the biggest berries and a pinch of the pemmican and placed them onto the leaf.

"Little People," Ohkwa'ri said, "I am happy to share this good food with you."

He leaned over to place the leaf on the other side of the small alder's trunk so that the Little People could come for their meal without being seen.

He unhooked the bear-head drinking cup from his belt and went down on one knee next to the wide river. He leaned over where the rocks made a small pool at the river's edge and dipped his cup deep under the surface to get the cold, clean water near the bottom. Then, feeling happy inside despite his bruised shoulder, Ohkwa'ri sat back to enjoy his morning meal.

Joseph Bruchac

Joseph Bruchac was raised by his grandparents in the foothills of the Adirondack Mountains of New York. Even though his family heritage is a mixture of English and Native American, the Native American part was seldom mentioned. "Everybody in the county knew he was Indian," Mr. Bruchac has said of his grandfather. "It was taken for granted—but he would not talk about it." Mr. Bruchac believes it is important that people of any culture have a sense of self worth. "Have pride in what you are and recognize that we as human beings make ourselves," he advises. Because of those feelings, Mr. Bruchac has spent much of his life trying to create understanding between people of different cultures.

Mr. Bruchac started becoming interested in his heritage when he was a teenager. He often met with other Native Americans to discuss his Abenaki culture and language. The more he learned, the more interested he became. Before long he was writing poems, folk tales, picture books, and novels about his Native American roots. Mr. Bruchac's books have won many awards, including the Parents' Choice Honor Award and a Nonfiction Honor Award from *Boston Globe-Horn Book.*

Mr. Bruchac lives in the same house in New York where he was raised.

Reader Response

If you were trying to sleep in a small lodge alone in the woods, as Ohkwa'ri did, what would you be thinking about?

Comprehension Check

1. Look back at the story. At which times is Ohkwa'ri concerned about being alone? At which times does he feel comforted?

2. Why do you think Ohkwa'ri feels happy at the end of the story despite his bruised shoulder? Do you think he will want to spend another night alone in his lodge? Support your answer with evidence from the story.

3. What story is Ohkwa'ri reminded of when he thinks of his uncle's statement that people who go without food for a time can see and hear better? What do you think the point of the story is?

4. What did you **predict** about Ohkwa'ri's night alone at the beginning of the story? After checking your prediction, did you find that you were correct? Explain. (Predicting)

5. Grabber wanted a bear cub for a pet. What did you **predict** would happen? What clues helped you? (Predicting)

Test Prep

Look Back and Write

Look back at pages 407–418. How do the people of Ohkwa'ri's longhouse show that they care for each other? Use details from the story to explain your answer.

HOW THE SUN CAME

by Jack Frederick Kilpatrick
and
Anna Gritts Kilpatrick

Test Prep

How to Read a Myth

1. Preview

- Read the title. Myths were usually told to explain something in nature. The title often will tell you what part of nature the myth explains.

- Read the first paragraph. Then predict what the animals will do to solve their problem of stumbling around in darkness.

2. Read and Understand

- Look for explanations of nature. How does the myth explain why something happened, such as why an opossum's tail is bare? Take notes in a cause-effect chart. For example,

Cause	Effect
There was no light.	The animals called a meeting.

3. Think and Connect

Think about "The Night Alone." Then look over the causes and effects you have charted for "How the Sun Came."

In his night alone, Ohkwa'ri thinks about events in his life and about explanations for those events. Why might he recall this myth or a similar myth?

There was no light anywhere, and the animal people stumbled around in the darkness. Whenever one bumped into another, he would say, "What we need in the world is light." And the other would reply, "Yes, indeed, light is what we badly need."

At last, the animals called a meeting and gathered together as well as they could in the dark. The red-headed woodpecker said, "I have heard that over on the other side of the world there are people who have light."

"Good, good!" said everyone.

"Perhaps if we go over there, they will give us some light," the woodpecker suggested.

421

"If they have all the light there is," the fox said, "they must be greedy people, who would not want to give any of it up. Maybe we should just go over there and take the light from them."

"Who shall go?" cried everyone, and the animals all began talking at once, arguing about who was strongest and ran fastest, who was best able to go and get the light.

Finally the 'possum said, "I can try. I have a fine big bushy tail, and I can hide the light inside my fur."

"Good! Good!" said all the others, and the 'possum set out.

As he traveled eastward, the light began to grow and grow, until it dazzled his eyes, and the 'possum screwed his eyes up to keep out the bright light. Even today, if you notice, you will see that the 'possum's eyes are almost shut, and that he comes out of his house only at night.

All the same, the 'possum kept going, clear to the other side of the world, and there he found the sun. He snatched a little piece of it and hid it in the fur of his fine bushy tail, but the sun was so hot it burned off all the fur, and by the time the 'possum got home his tail was as bare as it is today.

"Oh, dear!" everyone said. "Our brother has lost his fine bushy tail, and still we have no light."

"I'll go," said the buzzard. "I have better sense than to put the sun on my tail. I'll put it on my head."

So the buzzard traveled eastward till he came to the place where the sun was. And because the buzzard flies so high, the sun-keeping people did not see him, although now they were watching out for thieves. The buzzard dived straight down out of the sky, the way he does today, and caught a piece of the sun in his claws. He set the sun on his head and started for home, but the sun was so hot that it burned off all his head feathers, and that is why the buzzard's head is bald today.

Now the people were in despair. "What shall we do? What shall we do?" they cried. "Our brothers have tried hard; they have done their best, everything a man can do. What else shall we do so we can have light?"

"They have done the best a man can do," said a little voice from the grass, "but perhaps this is something a woman can do better than a man."

"Who are you?" everyone asked. "Who is that speaking in a tiny voice and hiding in the grass?"

"I am your Grandmother Spider," she replied. "Perhaps I was put in the world to bring you light. Who knows? At least I can try, and if I am burned up it will still not be as if you had lost one of your great warriors."

Then Grandmother Spider felt around her in the darkness until she found some damp clay. She rolled it in her hands, and molded a little clay bowl. She started eastward, carrying her bowl, and spinning a thread behind her so she could find her way back.

When Grandmother Spider came to the place of the sun people, she was so little and so quiet no one noticed her.

She reached out gently, gently, and took a tiny bit of the sun, and placed it in her clay bowl. Then she went back along the thread that she had spun, with the sun's light growing and spreading before her, as she moved from east to west. And if you will notice, even today a spider's web is shaped like the sun's disk and its rays, and the spider will always spin her web in the morning, very early, before the sun is fully up.

"Thank you, Grandmother," the people said when she returned. "We will always honor you, and we will always remember you."

And from then on pottery making became woman's work, and all pottery must be dried slowly in the shade before it is put in the heat of the firing oven, just as Grandmother Spider's bowl dried in her hand, slowly, in the darkness, as she traveled toward the land of the sun.

Context Clues

- **Context clues** are words that can help you figure out a word that is unfamiliar to you.

- When you come to an unfamiliar word, decide if it is important to the meaning of the sentence or paragraph. If it is, use context clues to understand it.

- Look for specific clues by asking yourself questions like, "Does the sentence give a definition or explanation of the word?"

Read "Physical Fitness" from _Health for Life_, a Scott Foresman textbook.

Talk About It

1. What context clues help you figure out the meaning of *agility?* How do the clues help?

2. Using context clues, tell what *physical fitness* means.

Health for Life   Scott Foresman

Physical Fitness

· ·

from *Health for Life*

Have you ever noticed how healthy you feel after a long bicycle ride or a hard game of basketball? Many young people enjoy being active. They can play for hours without getting tired. These people have good physical fitness.

Physical fitness helps you have fun. You can take part in sports and games with your friends. Being active regularly can also give you energy to stay alert and study. Exercise and fresh air help you look and feel healthy.

Physical fitness involves health fitness and skills fitness. Health fitness helps you stay healthy and look your best. Regular exercise helps keep your heart and lungs healthy. Certain exercises build strong, flexible muscles that can work for a long time without tiring. Exercise also helps you keep the amount of body fat that is right for you.

Skills fitness helps you perform well in activities that require special skills. Building skills fitness can help you do better in the sports and games you enjoy. How could you use the parts of skills fitness listed below?

The Parts of Skills Fitness

- Agility is the ability to change body positions quickly and to control body movements.
- Balance is the ability to keep upright while standing still or moving.
- Coordination is the ability to use the senses with body parts and to use two or more body parts together.
- Power is the ability to combine strength and speed.
- Reaction time is the amount of time it takes to start moving once a signal is heard or seen.
- Speed is the ability to perform a movement or cover a distance quickly.

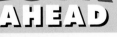

AHEAD

In "The Heart of a Runner," Ebonee Rose works at being physically fit. Use context clues as you read about how she prepares for and runs a relay race.

425

Vocabulary

Words to Know

overcame	athlete	ankle
confident	relay	sprint
responsible		

When you read, you may come across a word you don't know. To figure out its meaning, look for clues. A clue might be an explanation or definition given before or after the unknown word.

Read the paragraph below. Notice how the explanation of *relay* helps you understand what it means.

Relay Race

Do you know what a relay is? It's a race made up of teams. Each person on a team is responsible for running a certain part of the distance. To prepare for a relay, each athlete on the team trains hard. As the runners practice, they encourage each other to sprint as fast as they can. It is important that these runners feel confident about each other's abilities. Such intense training can sometimes cause foot, knee, or ankle injuries. The runners are happy when they can say that they overcame their injuries and went on to win the race.

Write About It

Use vocabulary words to describe a time when teamwork helped you meet a goal.

The Heart of a Runner

from Running Girl: The Diary of Ebonee Rose

by Sharon Bell Mathis

Eleven-year-old Ebonee Rose, nicknamed E.R., is a runner. She has been training with her team, the Gazelles, for the All-City Track Meet. Queenie, the new girl on the team, is E.R.'s pacer. This means that at practice Queenie runs beside E.R. to help her keep up a certain running speed. Queenie is a fast runner, but how will she do at All-City? At practice, she keeps dropping the baton, which is to be passed from runner to runner. E.R. writes her thoughts, hopes, and fears about the meet in a diary she has named Dee.

Tuesday, June 10

Dee,

"I was hysterical when my ankle twisted. At first I fell down, and then I jumped up, and then I just sat down and held my whole leg. Coach Teena was trying to get me to at least stop moving, but I couldn't. It hurt too much. How could I <u>hurt</u> myself when All-City is only 11 days away? The buzzing around in my head was—I'm sorry, Coach Teena, I'm sorry, I'm sorry.

Coach Teena wrapped a blue ice pack around my ankle and took me to the hospital. My mother left school and met us in the emergency room.

My ankle was not broken. I had a slight sprain. I worried about All-City. Coach Teena worried about me. Momma said, "What is more important—a track meet or <u>you</u>, Ebonee Rose?"

I wanted to say All-City, but I didn't.

Later Momma said, "We've got a pool at home. It knows what to do with a sore ankle."

E.R.

Dee,

My ankle is doing OK. Daddy heated the pool to what Momma called the boiling point. All I know is that the warm water felt good against my ankle. Sometimes I sat on the edge of the pool—my foot in the water—and read my track books.

At practice Coach Teena said, "Great!" But she wouldn't let me run my laps (especially with Queenie pacing me). Queenie's the best pacer I've ever had at Main Track. Too bad she's so mean!

Momma said, "Her mother's dead, E.R., and she doesn't have a family. Try and be a friend to Queenie."

I thought about that for a long time.

Coach Teena is trying to help Queenie not to exaggerate her stride, just run naturally, plain—to conserve her energy, not explode at the very beginning of the 400 meters. Queenie uses a long stride and then she does this strange-looking short stride. I'm not sure which one of us will anchor the relays, but at practice Queenie dropped the baton three times.

Ms. Dotty, Queenie's foster mother, has the biggest yard in the whole neighborhood—and the biggest pool too. But I found out that Queenie can't tread water.

E.R.

Queenie

She runs
like me
fast/faster
<u>fastest</u>

We are rabbits
for each other

23 laps/I want
to stop/fall
"Keep going," she says.
"They think we can't."

Lap 31/we run slow
cool down/talk

Queenie,
maybe someday
we will be
friends

Thursday, June 12

Dee,

All-City Track Meet is 9 days away.

My ankle is doing great now, but it was still wrapped when I went to school the other day. The kids were saying, "E.R., what's wrong with your foot? You can't race at All-City?" They were scared for me.

Last night Momma and I ran for an hour. Daddy followed us in the car. When we came back, I swam in our pool for a while, exercising my ankle. Then I took my bath and went to bed.

But this running girl can't sleep. If only you were real, Dee, and not just my diary.

E.R.

11:30 p.m.

Dee,

Me again. I still can't sleep. Oh, DEE! I forgot to tell you my pictures of Flo Jo came in the mail. Her real name is Florence Delorez Griffith Joyner. The sportswriters call her Flo Jo, and that's what I call her too.

She's one of the fastest women in the world, and I was so sad when she chose not to compete in the 1996 Olympics in Atlanta. Momma said, "Be thankful for what she's already given."

Florence Griffith Joyner ("Flo Jo")

In the 1984 Olympics in Los Angeles, Flo Jo won a silver medal in the 200 meters. In the 1988 Olympics in Seoul, Korea, she won a gold medal for the 100 meters, a gold medal for the 200 meters, a gold medal for the 4 × 100-meter relay, and a silver medal for the 4 × 400-meter relay. She ran anchor for the 4 × 400-meter relay.

Can you believe it! Can you <u>believe</u> it!

Dee, her fingernails are long and pretty and all different colors. She cuts off one of the legs from her tights and runs barelegged. Or she'll wear white lace tights. All kinds of tights mixed together. Sharp! Sharp! (Oh, Gail Devers painted her long fingernails <u>gold</u> for the 1996 Games.)

When Flo Jo was a little girl, she used to race jackrabbits in the Mohave Desert. That's why when Queenie paces me, I call her a rabbit. Flo Jo started running when she was 7 years old, 4 years younger than I am now. When she was 14, she won the annual Jesse Owens Youth Games in Los Angeles. She won again at 15. Guess what kind of pet she had when she was in high school? A boa constrictor!

Flo Jo is married to Jackie Joyner-Kersee's brother, Alfrederick (Al) Joyner. He's her coach. He won a gold medal in the 1984 Olympics in Los Angeles. Isn't that cool? The <u>Jo</u> in Flo Jo means <u>Joyner</u>.

I have to tell you what an anchor is. An anchor is the final leg of a relay, the fastest runner. The anchor has to overcome any slowness of the other three runners and power on to the end. The lead runner, or lead-off, is the first leg of a relay team. That runner has to be superfast, and confident too.

The runners in a relay depend on one another to be fast and not make mistakes. Like dropping one of the batons. I'm not mentioning any names, but you know who I mean!

Baton passing is really scary. At the Olympics in Seoul, Korea, in 1988, the women's 4 × 100-meter race had a shaky baton-passing moment—from Flo Jo to Evelyn Ashford! But Evelyn Ashford was the anchor and she overcame it. The team won a gold medal.

E.R.

P.S. I traced my hand on this page. Then I used my markers to make all the fingernails different colors.

Dee,

At the end of practice, Coach Teena came over to me. This is what she said: "Queenie's going to be lead runner in the 4 × 100 meters. You'll anchor, E.R."

<u>I'm glad Queenie didn't drop the baton today</u>, I thought. So, now I know—it's me. The anchor. I have to supply the final power. I will have to overcome the other runners' mistakes, if they make any. I am the last one—and the main one—responsible for winning.

The flower petals in my stomach have begun to flutter, Dee. To shift and drift. I've tried to make them fall back down, to lie flat, but the petals are swirling faster and faster. Can I do it? Can I win? Can I bring the team the victory we want so badly?

"How's that ankle, still OK? Be honest, E.R."

"No problem, Coach Teena," I said truthfully.

"OK, I got you in the 100 meters, 200 meters, 4 × 100-meter relay, and long jump."

LONG JUMP? <u>NO!</u>

"Do I <u>have</u> to long-jump?" I asked her.

"You have to have a field event," she said.

"Yuck! I only want to sprint." The long jump means flying!

"E.R., you have to do a field event, that's the rule," Coach Teena said. "This is a track-and-<u>field</u> meet, remember? Your long jump is pretty good, but we need to work on your takeoff. Also, your heels. Keep your legs together when you land."

E.R.

Dee.

Queenie was sick today at our last practice. She spit up twice. She felt dizzy. She said she didn't want to run tomorrow. The whole team yelled at her. Except me.

I sat down on the bench beside her. Queenie kept holding her stomach and looking at me. "I'm not playing, Rosie. I'm really sick!"

"You might feel better tomorrow," I said.

"I hate tomorrow," she said. "Everybody thinks I'm going to drop the baton. I know that's what they think. You think it too!"

I didn't answer Queenie; I sat closer and put my arm around her. She said, "Go with me to the rest room again."

I did. Queenie spit up again. She was leaning against the wall. I leaned against the wall too. "Talk to me, Rosie," she said.

"It's OK to be nervous," I said.

Wyomia Tyus

"I'm tense, not <u>nervous</u>."

I told her, "Willye White said if there were no butterflies in her stomach, she didn't feel right. She ran in five Olympics (1956, 1960, 1964, 1968, and 1972). She was lead runner—just like you."

"I don't want to have to run and win and do all this stuff," Queenie insisted, pulling away from me. "I just want to have fun."

"Like Wyomia Tyus," I told her.

Queenie just sat still.

I moved closer and held Queenie tight. She did not pull away. "Just have fun, Queenie," I whispered. "Maybe we'll win the relay."

"I <u>have</u> to win," she said.

"Well, we'll win then," I answered. "There will be golden apples at the feet of our competition." I told Queenie the story of the ancient Greek myth of Atalanta—the hunter who agreed to marry the man who could beat her running. She was tricked by Hippomenes, who dropped golden apples that she paused to pick up. Hippomenes won the race. "Hippomenes might drop golden apples to stop the other runners tomorrow," I said.

"I hope he brings lots of apples," Queenie said.

E.R.

Saturday, June 21

Dear Dee,

All-City Track Meet at Poage Park is over. This is what happened.

Early this morning I thought of Wyomia Tyus. Twice she won gold medals for the 100 meters at the Olympics, back to back: in 1964, in Tokyo, Japan, and in 1968, in Mexico City, Mexico. She was the first athlete _ever_ to do that!

Also, Wyomia Tyus did something else I had to do today— ran anchor for the 4 × 100 relay. In 1968 she won a gold medal for that too.

I took my bath before Momma and Daddy got up. I pulled on my burgundy-and-gold team shorts, my tank top, and my burgundy socks with the gold letters: GAZELLES. I slipped my feet into old raggle-taggle sneakers, then used a key to attach steel spikes to my black track shoes. I tied the track shoes together by their burgundy-and-gold laces; I hung them around my neck. I painted each of my fingernails a different color: red, pink, green, yellow, orange, blue, purple, turquoise, gold, and burgundy stripes. I took off my socks and sneakers, and painted my toes to match. But I am not Flo Jo. I am Ebonee Rose, Running Girl. I tied my ponytail with burgundy and gold ribbons.

Today I was the fastest runner in the world. I ran for myself. I ran for the Gazelles.

Before we went to Poage Park, Momma and Daddy sat at the breakfast table. They talked about the morning news, but I knew they were thinking about All-City. I sat there and ate a plate of fruit: sliced cantaloupe, honeydew, kiwi, peaches, and whole green grapes. It was 6:30 A.M. I thought about my first race, the 100 meters. I would run it at 10:30 A.M.

Momma and Daddy wore their matching sweatsuits in burgundy and gold. On the back of Daddy's shirt was: EBONEE ROSE'S DADDY. On the back of Momma's shirt was: EBONEE ROSE'S MOMMA. I didn't have my track number then. Coach Teena pinned it on my shirt, front and back, as soon as I got to Poage Park. Coach Teena kissed my cheek when she pinned on my number, 8146. She said, "Run like the cheetah, be graceful as the gazelle" to all the girls on the team, and hugged each of us.

Aunt Zenzele grinned and said, "You go, girl!"

I was ready. The petals within me began to flutter.

E.R.

Momma

Momma sat close to me in the car. She said, "When you were born, your tiny legs were moving so fast—running, I think."

"Suppose we don't win," I said.

"Suppose you don't lose," she said.

"What if I can't run fast enough?" I fussed.

"What if you run too fast?" she fussed back.

I stopped talking, leaned on her.

She stopped talking, leaned on me.

Daddy

Daddy tied the laces of my track shoes too tight, adjusted my number three times. He poured bottled springwater onto his handkerchief and wiped my face. Said, "Don't be nervous, baby." Rubbed the left side of my face twice.

He pulled my socks up straighter, recentered my
number, front and back. Retied my shoelaces. He tied the bow
on the left bigger than the bow on the right.

Daddy hugged me, patted my back, smiled with a frown on his
face. Said this was just another track meet.

Again.

Coach Teena

"This is your race, E.R.!"

"I know."

"How you feel?"

"I like 100 meters."

"Uh-huh."

"I _love_ this dash!"

"That's more like it! You gonna run over the rest of 'em."

"I saw some good—"

"E.R., they're not as fast as you. I told you that before. Showed
you on film."

"I know."

"Act like it! Get on your blocks, teach somebody how to
run today!"

Starting Blocks

I adjust my wooden blocks. I stretch my legs and look at them, see other legs in my own: Robin Campbell's legs. I remember the words of Robin Campbell's I read in a book: "You've got to believe you're good . . . but other people are good too." (Robin Campbell was in the fourth grade when she joined her school track team. At 14 she beat the Russians in her first international competition, in 1973, in Richmond, Virginia.)

How fast can I run today? I must be both cheetah and gazelle.

My race is about to begin. I straddle my blocks, wait for the command.

"ON YOUR MARK!"

My left leg is in front.

My power leg is in back, ready.

"SET."

I raise my hips, shift my weight over my hands.

"GO!"

200 Meters

I look down the track. See Tidye Pickett. See Louise Stokes. Audrey Patterson. Alice Coachman. See Mae Faggs. Mildred McDaniel. Wilma Rudolph. Wyomia Tyus. Willye White. I see Nell Jackson, the first African American head coach of an American Olympic team, in Melbourne, Australia, 1956. I run toward them all.

Relay

Our relay is next. We are holding hands: Queenie, Bunky, Marti, and me. The four of us stand closer, hold tighter. We do not let go. Coach Teena has her arms stretched across our backs.

We start our ritual. First we call out our own names—then say, "Here!" Since this is a relay, we also call out the names of relay gold medalists from the Olympics in Atlanta, in 1996: "Gail Devers!" "Chryste Gaines!" "Kim Graham!" "Carlette Guidry!" "Maicel Malone!" "Jearl Miles!" "Inger Miller!" "Rochelle Stevens!" "Gwen Torrence!" "Linetta Wilson!"

We answer "Here!" for all of them.

Coach Teena called the names of Tidye Pickett and Louise Stokes, the first African American women who took part in the Olympic trials. "Trailblazers!" she said. We answered, "Los Angeles, 1932!" "Berlin, 1936!" Then Coach Teena said, "Nell Jackson!"

Seventeen athletes present. Four could be seen. This is what happened.

Queenie

Queenie is out there—leading. Our crowd is pumped up, screaming. Queenie runs faster than ever, to the passing zone.

She does not drop the baton. She passes it perfectly! Our fans in the bleachers are going crazy. I hear them while I wait in my zone.

Bunky passes the baton to Marti, whose bowlegs are not as long as mine. She runs with power toward me—her bowlegs are like

Gail Devers

piston rods. Marti hands the heavy wooden tube to me. Anchor. I've got to secure this race, dig in, keep it steady, grip the prize, not let it get away. Anchor.

I take off! This race is mine. Blue track beneath my winged feet. I run through heaven and outrace angels. Wings clap for me. I lean forward, break the tape.

We win.

Queenie and the others ran to meet me. We kept on running around the track. The officials let us. Our spikes danced on sky blue turf.

THE PRIZE WAS OURS!

We won first place at All-City. My long jump didn't help much. I wanted to be an eagle but couldn't soar high enough. Still, I got a third-place ribbon. I thought I would finish in seventh place.

On the Main Track team bus, we made up all kinds of songs about winning. We got noisier and noisier. None of the grown-ups stopped us—they were singing too. The loudest song of all, on the bus, was "Happy Birthday," to Jay-Jay. I sang it solo in a silly-willy-nilly way. Definitely off-key. It was fun, fun, fun.

Audrey Patterson

Coach Teena was presented with the huge city trophy. The name MAIN TRACK CLUB will be inscribed on the brass plate beneath the golden track shoe. We get to keep the trophy for one year.

"At last, at last," Coach Teena said. She held the trophy high and reminded us that Audrey Patterson, a great sprinter and coach, believed that being a good athlete isn't only about winning—it means being prepared "physically, mentally and spiritually."

E.R.

From the Author
Sharon Bell Mathis

In my imagination, Ebonee Rose did not start out as a runner. She began as the only girl on a championship peewee football team. She was a star running back who wrote poetry. Then my editor suggested that more girls ran track than played football. What if Ebonee Rose became a sprinter?

Oh, no! I panicked. Could I start all over again and write an entirely different story? What about my two years of football notes and research? I reminded myself that I had trusted my editor's guidance for over twenty years. She was challenging me to go in a new direction, to write a better book. It was scary!

For three days, I worked crossword puzzles, reorganized closets, and stayed away from my computer. I didn't want to think about writing.

On the morning of the fourth day, I was ready.

I began by tearing up everything I'd written about football. I looked through the manuscript and picked out a few poems that could be switched from football to track. I copied those poems onto a new disk and shredded the manuscript. When my mind was finally free of football, I discovered that I knew nothing about track-and-field, other than the names of a few famous champions. Scary! Scary!

I began the march toward a new story by visiting the Sojourner Truth Room of the Oxon Hill Maryland Library where I began to read about the glorious accomplishments of African American athletes who had excelled in track. There were junior champions, state champions, national champions, college and university champions, Olympians, Special Olympians. Indoor track! Outdoor track!

After months and months of writing notes, reading books, magazines, and newspapers, watching videotapes, interviewing athletes and coaches, observing sprinters, visiting the World Wide Web, watching the 1996 Olympics, sending and receiving faxes, I had the information I needed. I could not have done it alone. Thirty-eight wonderful people are acknowledged in *Running Girl.* Each one helped in my quest for information.

It was time to write the new manuscript—a mixture of poetry, prose, and quotations. I looked for historic and modern photographs to include in the book.

Early on a Sunday morning, the new Ebonee Rose was born. She was so cute that I gave her a nickname. I called her E.R. and she liked it! She loved track so much that at the library she borrowed mostly track books. If she dreamed, she wanted to dream only about running!

Ebonee Rose would know everything about African American female track champions. I saw her as a kind of human encyclopedia, a living database. But E.R. wouldn't brag; she simply recorded what she knew into her diary—along with her feelings about the newest runner on the team—a girl named Queenie. Queenie was fast and friendly, but she kept dropping the relay baton. Would the team come in second, again, at the All-City Track Meet? Would Queenie care?

While I was writing *Running Girl* I found myself among elementary school children racing against one another in a schoolyard in Washington, D.C. The children ran, testing their skills, girls against girls, boys against boys, girls against boys. They created makeshift relay teams, using scattered twigs and sticks as batons, winning and losing, falling down, getting up—all the while laughing. So much laughter! Such fun! I felt privileged to be in the midst of their joy. Unknowingly, they handed me fabulous gifts. They gave me a chance to share a moment in their lives, the opportunity to watch their laughing faces press against the wind, and a time to hear the rhythmic beat of young feet on patchy grass.

There was an historic moment, too, when I phoned Alice Coachman—a real superstar. Alice Coachman was the first African American woman to win the Olympic gold medal. It happened at the 1948 Olympiad in London, England. She had the winning high jump. Guess who placed the gold medal around her neck? King George VI! Ms. Coachman was so gracious. It was a thrill to speak to her.

Finally, after a year, the writing was over. I had created my E.R., my Ebonee Rose. Ebonee Rose taught me how to run and she taught me how to meet challenges, no matter how scary. She taught me how to be brave.

Most of all, Ebonee Rose trusted me. She traded her football pads and her helmet for a T-shirt and baggy shorts. Without fear, she pulled off her old football cleats and picked up her new track shoes. Reaching down, she pushed her feet into the new shoes and tied the laces. When she walked to her blocks and placed her feet on them with confidence—I cheered for her, clapped my hands, and yelled excitedly: GO! GO! GO! Ebonee Rose, my E.R., turned to me and smiled. Then she lifted her arms and waved.

Our book was finished. She was saying good-bye.

Reader Response

Open for Discussion

Imagine that you are writing an advertisement for "The Heart of a Runner." Would you say that everyone or just people who are interested in sports should read it? Give reasons for your answer.

Comprehension Check

1. Why do you think that Ebonee Rose writes in her diary as if her diary were a real person?

2. Look back at the story. You are a new member of Ebonee Rose's track team. What advice would Ebonee Rose give you about running a relay race? Use evidence from the story to support your answer.

3. Look back at the story. Why do you think Ebonee Rose writes so much about past successes of women runners such as Flo Jo and Robin Campbell?

4. Which **context clues** on page 435 give you an idea of what a *field event* is? Give a definition of a field event based on the context clues. (Context Clues)

5. Using the **context clues** on page 445, what do you think *secure* in the phrase *secure this race* means? How did the clues help? (Context Clues)

Test Prep

Look Back and Write

Look back at page 444. Before the relay race, Ebonee says that there are seventeen athletes present, but only four could be seen. What does she mean? Explain, using details from the story.

Finding a Way to Win

by Daniel Lee

Test Prep

How to Read an Informational Article

1. Preview

- What does the title mean? Do the pictures help you understand what the article is about?

- What will you learn from the sidebars (extra information in boxes)?

2. Read and Take Notes

- Find unfamiliar words that are in boldface or italic type. Write a question about each one. For example,

What is orienteering?

- Then, as you read, take notes that will help you answer each question.

3. Think and Connect

Think about "The Heart of a Runner." Then look over your notes for "Finding a Way to Win."

What skills does Carlie in "Finding a Way to Win" have that she could use in Ebonee's sport in "The Heart of a Runner"? What skills does Ebonee have that she could use to orienteer?

Could you win a race if you didn't know where the track was?

Carlie Huberman can. She can find her way through a course of checkpoints in the woods using just a map and a compass to tell her which way to go.

It's a sport called *orienteering*, and Carlie is good at it. An orienteering course is made of several goal points, called *controls*, scattered around a wooded area and marked on a map. The idea is to use your map to find and visit each control as fast as possible.

"At the last national meet I went to, there were some teenagers on the white course, and I had the lowest time," says Carlie, who lives in North Carolina.

Carlie has been orienteering ever since she can remember. Her father, mother, and older sister, Lori, all orienteer too.

"I learned to use a compass and a map over time since I was two, so I don't really know when or how I learned," she says.

That doesn't mean learning the sport is easy. At a meet, the first time you see a map of the course and the controls is right at the starting line.

"I look at my map and orient it and start walking or running down the trail," says Carlie, "depending on how far it is to the next control, so I'm not tired and can do my best."

As she nears the first checkpoint, "I start looking from side to side for the control and the feature that it is supposed to be on, such as a pile of

In the "O" Know

Orienteering, or "O," uses two main tools.

Compass: A housing with a magnetic needle that always points north, so you can find every other direction too

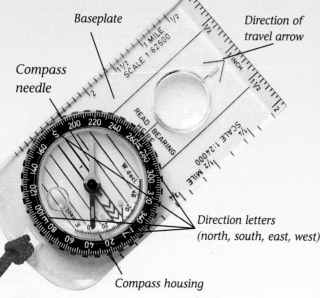

Baseplate

Direction of travel arrow

Compass needle

Direction letters (north, south, east, west)

Compass housing

Lines close together mean a steep slope.

Lines forming a circle show a hill or valley.

Contour Map: A map using curving lines to show bumps, holes, and hills on the ground, also called a *topographical* (top-o-GRAF-i-kal) map

rocks, a fallen-down tree, or a stream or path junction," she says.

"When I find the control, I run as fast as I can and punch my punch card in the right spot," she says. That proves she actually found the control.

Ribbons usually mark the trail from the last control to the finish line. Most people run, to get the best time possible.

"Everyone cheers you on," says Carlie. "Your time does not stop until you run past the finish line."

Orienteering isn't an easy sport, but Carlie thinks it is definitely worth doing. "It's better not to always do the easy thing, because you get to think and you get to learn. Orienteering really makes you think."

Watch Your Directions

Don't have a compass? Any watch or clock with a dial can help.

1. Hold watch up so small hand points to the sun. (Use this method only between 6 A.M. and 6 P.M.)

2. Imagine a line halfway between the small hand and the twelve. That line points south.

3. North is behind you, east is on your left, west is on your right.

You can use a digital watch too; just draw a picture of a clock face showing the correct time and follow the steps above. Note: You'll need to draw a new correct clock face to repeat this later.

Skill Lesson

Author's Purpose

- **Author's purpose** is the reason or reasons an author has for writing.

- Authors don't usually state a purpose, so it helps to remember that the four common purposes are to persuade, inform, entertain, and express.

- If you know an author's purpose, you may change how you read to match what you read. For example, if an author wants to explain a difficult idea, you may decide to read slowly to make sure you understand the information. But when an author's purpose is to entertain, you may want to read quickly.

Read "Your Life Remembered" from _Do People Grow on Family Trees?_ by Ira Wolfman.

Write About It

1. What do you think the author's reasons were for writing this article?

2. Did you read the article quickly or slowly? Why?

Your Life
REMEMBERED

BY IRA WOLFMAN

One of the best ways to practice putting together the story of your ancestors is by telling your own story. You may not think you have much to tell, but you do. Think of someone 100 years from now, wondering about your life. Imagine the questions he or she will have: Who were you? Where did you come from? What was your life like? What did you do with your days? What kind of home did you live in? Who else was in your family? What contact did you have with the other members of your family? Where had you traveled? What mattered most to you? What did you hope to accomplish?

You don't have to answer those particular questions. There may be others that are more important to you, that give more of a sense of who you are. You choose. Then sit down and try to write about yourself—something that will tell your descendants 100 years from now what it felt like, and was like, to be you.

You can use more than just words in this life history. Photographs are very helpful. So are relevant documents. There are dozens of possibilities here, in fact: your birth certificate; a report card; an award for athletic or academic achievement; your medical or dental records; a map you draw of your neighborhood; letters you wrote, or letters someone wrote to you; a list of your favorite books, sports teams, movies, or records.

Be sure to include stories about yourself. Don't just tell what *you* remember; think about things you've heard about yourself from members of your family. Talk about things you're proud of and things you've done that you're not so proud of. A little bit of the less-than-perfect side of your life will make your history much more honest and realistic.

LOOK AHEAD

In *The Memory Box*, Zach and his grandparents find a clever way to share and preserve memories of their lives. As you read, think about the author's purpose for writing the story.

Vocabulary

| recall | traditions | sheath |
| souvenirs | squished | reel |

Words that are spelled and pronounced the same but have different origins and meanings are called **homonyms.** *Bat,* meaning the wooden club you hit a ball with, and *bat,* meaning an animal, are homonyms.

Read the paragraph below. Decide whether *reel* means "to wind on a fishing spool" or "to suddenly sway from shock."

A Fishing Tradition

My family has many <u>traditions</u>. One of my favorites is what happens every summer. For as long as I can <u>recall</u>, we have rented a cabin on a lake and gone fishing. The first time I was allowed to <u>reel</u> in a fish, I stood a few feet from shore. I can still feel how that fish tugged on my line and how the mud <u>squished</u> through my toes. Soon after that, I got my own fishing knife with a blue <u>sheath</u> to cover it. It is one of my treasured <u>souvenirs</u> from our summer outings, because it reminds me of how proud I felt when I caught my first fish.

Talk About It

Use vocabulary words to tell about one of your family's traditions.

The Memory Box

by Mary Bahr
illustrated by David Cunningham

When I woke up this morning, I knew it was going to
be a great vacation. Gramps was standing by my bed,
holding the tackle box.

"Already too hot for catching walleye," he said.

"I bet Zach would like to throw out a line anyway, this
being his first day," Gram argued from the doorway. She was
holding a plateful of butter-dripping cinnamon rolls. As I said,
it was going to be a great vacation. Three weeks of fishing
Gramps's lake and eating Gram's cooking.

Now, from the boat, I could see Gram waving at us
fishermen from the dock on the sky blue lake. Behind her on
the hillside sat their berry red house in the middle of the dark
green northern woods. The colors reminded me of a painting
I saw once.

Gramps and I rested our bamboo poles on the side of the boat. Our bobbers rode the glittery waves.

"It's a Memory Box day," Gramps said as we waited for the perch to decide if they were hungry.

"What's a Memory Box?" I asked, dangling my hands in the cool water. I wondered if fish ever nibbled fingers.

"Remind me to tell you after the fish fry we're gonna have tonight. Now let's get quiet and catch 'em."

And we did. We got so quiet I could hear the fish circling our night crawlers. But it still took three hours of sweaty, itchy stillness before we hauled in enough to fill Gram's skillet.

"It's a Memory Box day."

"Don't forget the Cook's Rule," Gram said as we unloaded our catch. We always cleaned ourselves and the fish in the lakeside shed. But every summer Gram reminded us, anyway! "Nothing but good smells at my dinner table," she'd say, pushing us back out if we tried to sneak in without washing first.

In the shed, for the first time ever, Gramps handed me the long filet knife, the knife that's about a hundred years old. The one I hope will be mine someday.

"I think you're old enough to handle the blade," he said, "and to hear the true tale of the Cook's Rule." He guided my fingers as I gutted my fish. "That first time I caught fish for Gram to cook, I brought them into the kitchen to clean. I don't think she was prepared for fish eyes staring back at her out of the sink. She screamed so loud I dropped the frypan and broke my toe. After that, the fish and I went to the shed."

We laughed. Everybody knew Gramps usually made up most of his "true tales."

After dinner, we dragged our fish-full bellies to the porch to watch the sun slip into the lake. Crickets fiddled and owls hoo-ooted, but the rest of the world was quiet. All except Gram and Gramps and me in our rickety rockers on the wooden porch.

"Hmm-mmmm-m." Gramps was settling in, getting ready for another true tale. He's a great storyteller. Gram thinks so, I know, because she always puts down her cross-stitch when he begins.

"It was your Great-Gram who told me about the Memory Box," Gramps said, staring at the sunset sky. "It's a special box that stores family tales and traditions. An old person and a young person fill the box together. Then they store it in a place of honor. No matter what happens to the old person, the memories are saved forever."

"It's a special box that stores family tales and traditions."

"What do you mean, 'no matter what happens'?" I asked Gramps. I didn't like his story much.

The sun practically disappeared before Gramps answered. "Do you know this old body just flunked a physical exam for the first time?"

Gram stopped rocking.

"This old person must make his Memory Box," Gramps said after a long silence. He stopped rocking, too, and looked me square in the eye. "Is this young person ready?"

"I guess. Sure." The words stuck in my mouth like caramel from a Halloween apple.

Gram disappeared into the house and made a pot-and-pan racket.

"Zach? The door, please?" she called through the screen. "I emptied an old recipe box so we can start *our* Memory Box," she said, handing me a treasure chest a pirate would love. "Now I'll leave my men alone."

My fingers traced the designs carved in the smooth, shiny wood.

"I gave that to your grandmother on our wedding day," was all Gramps said. Then we sat in the dark and watched the fireflies dart past the porch. Maybe Gramps was already searching his mind for memories to put in the box. He never said.

But for the rest of my vacation, we remembered, Gramps and Gram and me. We especially remembered when we were fishing. "Thoughts come faster when bobbers are jumping," Gram said as she wrote our memories on paper scraps.

"How about the time I climbed the water tower?" I asked Gramps. "Mom said no, but you turned your back so I could make it to the top."

"You nearly fell off, as I recall." He scratched the whiskers that appeared on his face for the first summer ever. I wondered about those whiskers. Didn't Gramps tell me once how much Gram hated it when he didn't shave?

"How about the time I laid my freshly picked blueberries on the porch to sun-dry?" Gram remembered. "Zach came in from his swim and squished a path right through those juicy berries."

"Looked like an old blue rug to me," I said, remembering how Gram's face had turned red and my feet had turned blue at the same time.

It was Gramps's job to add photos and souvenirs to the Memory Box. He found a picture of my second birthday party when I had taken a bite off the top of the cake. There was a shot of Gram in her wedding dress with flowers in her hair and one of Dad in his football uniform when he still *had* hair. Another was of Gramps and Mom the day he had taught her to ride a bike. She had ridden it too. Right over his foot!

We added other important stuff, like my first soccer medal and Gram's chocolate-chip cookie recipe.

"We especially remembered when we were fishing."

We added new memories too.

We wrote about the morning the three of us rolled green apples down the hill for a herd of deer that rested in the long grass.

And the time we watched a raccoon bandit watch *us* as she ate a trayful of cookies that Gram had set to cool on the picnic table.

And a picture of the trophy walleye I caught the morning we put the boat on the lake before the sun even got up.

As the days passed, I noticed something different about Gramps. A major small change, if you know what I mean. One afternoon I saw him sitting in the swing that hung between two giant pines. I headed on over. But I stopped

when I heard him talking to somebody else. Gramps was telling Francie how to reel in a northern pike that was fighting her hook. He was talking to her as if she were right there. But nobody was. Especially not *Francie*—she's my mom.

And one afternoon we hiked to find nature stuff I could take back to school. Gramps wandered off the trail into a poison ivy patch as if he didn't even see it. I yelled until he stopped, but he wouldn't come back. I had to go get him and take him by the hand. That day it seemed like his body walked with me, but his thoughts strolled somewhere else.

None of it made sense until the morning Gram shook me awake.

"Get dressed, Zach. Help me find Gramps. He's been gone too long."

"Probably just fishing." I stared at Gram as if she were a crazy lady.

"But he forgot his shoes." She looked back at me as if *I* were the crazy one. "Check the shed. Whistle if you find him first."

I ran toward the lake, even faster when I saw the shed door swinging. But Gramps wasn't inside.

Outside again, I stopped to listen, the way hunters do. I thought I heard noises out back, so I circled the woods around the shed. When I found Gramps, I whistled loud. He was sitting on the ground like a scout in front of a campfire. His feet were bare, and one was bleeding.

"Forgot my shoes." He tried to hide his face. It was shiny with tears.

Gram moved the fastest I'd ever seen. She sat on the ground beside Gramps while I ran back for his slippers. We helped him back to the house. Led him, if you want to know the truth. While we bandaged his foot and made him lie down on his bed, Gramps was quiet. We waited until the snoring began before Gram and I tiptoed out of the room.

"Remember that first Memory Box night?" Gram asked. She sat in the kitchen. "Gramps was trying to tell you about Alzheimer's disease . . . when the body stays but the mind leaves."

She stared off, and I just waited until she looked at me again.

"The mind doesn't go all at once, or all the time, but it never comes back quite the same way. When Dr. Johnson suggested Gramps might have Alzheimer's, it explained so many things about this past year—Gramps forgetting to shave, his talking to me like we were kids again, his getting lost on trails he'd hiked for years."

I thought about the poison ivy and Francie's fishing lesson.

"It scares Gramps, knowing he'll forget. That's why the Memory Box is so important."

When Gramps woke up, he called me. I stood at his bedroom door. He sat on the bed.

"Did Gram tell you about this useless old man? And how he needs to find a home for special things like this?" He handed me the old fishing knife from the shed. "I forgot the sheath, so I went back . . . and got lost."

"Thanks," I whispered, holding the knife the way Gramps had taught me. My own, very first knife. I'd always wanted one. *This* one. But now it didn't seem so important.

"Your mom's going to hurt," Gramps said. "When it gets bad, bring out our Memory Box. Show her what I remember."

I hugged Gramps. We both felt better.

The rest of my vacation bolted like a fawn when you try to sneak too close. The day Dad and Mom came to take me back for school, we had such a great barbecue that we decided it should be part of the Memory Box. I could tell Dad already knew about Gramps because he shot a zillion photos of Gramps and Gram.

"… we decided it should be part of the Memory Box"

When it was time to leave, Gramps squeezed me hard.

Gram squeezed me soft. "Add things to the Memory Box you want Gramps to remember," she whispered as she handed it to me. "And bring it with you next summer. We'll need it, you and I."

I waved as our car drove away—away from the best and worst summer ever. This time Gramps and Gram had taken care of me. Next summer, Gram and I would take care of Gramps. And the summers after that . . . well, we'd figure out something.

As the car hit the top of the hill, I watched Gramps slowly disappear into the horizon.

And I hugged my Memory Box.

About the Author
Mary Bahr

Mary Bahr believes that each person is unique. "There's a specialness about each and every one of us no matter what we're labeled . . . gifted, average, or learning disabled," she said. "Our life's journey is discovering that specialness, cultivating it like a hothouse plant and sharing it somehow with the rest of the world." Ms. Bahr hopes that this positive message comes through in her writing.

Ms. Bahr has had two careers—writing and working in libraries. She has written columns, stories, articles, and poems that were published in many magazines, including *Living with Children, Highlights for Children,* and *Purpose.* Ms. Bahr was born in Minnesota. She now lives in Colorado with her husband and four children.

About the Illustrator
David Cunningham

Besides *The Memory Box,* David Cunningham has illustrated many other children's books, as well as educational texts. He wrote and illustrated the well-received book *Nightfall, Country Lake,* a book about the natural world. Mr. Cunningham lives near Chicago, where he operates his own business as an artist.

Reader Response

Open for Discussion

If you were Zach, how would you define the word *memory?*

Comprehension Check

1. Do you think that Zach will continue to treasure the Memory Box for years to come? Use evidence from the story to explain.

2. Look back at the story. What kinds of memories are important to Gramps, Gram, and Zach? Why are those memories important to them?

3. Gramps has Alzheimer's disease. What changes does Zach begin to notice about Gramps? What changes has Gram seen over the past year? What changes does Gramps tell the others about himself? Find details to support your answer.

4. Of the following purposes, which do you think was the **author's** main **purpose** for writing *The Memory Box?*
   a. to persuade; **b.** to inform; **c.** to express; **d.** to entertain. Explain your answer. (Author's Purpose)

5. Find sentences in the story that support the **author's purpose** you chose in Question 4. (Author's Purpose)

Test Prep

Look Back and Write

Look back at pages 458–469. What is the setting of this story? Use details from the story to describe the time and place in which the story is set.

 **Test Prep**

How to Read an Informational Article

1. Preview

- How do the title and headings help you understand what the article is about?

- Look at the picture. Notice the labels, called callouts, that are connected by lines to parts of the picture.

2. Read and Take Notes

- Rewrite each heading to form a question. For example,

How are memories stored?

- Then, as you read, take notes that will help you answer each question.

3. Think and Connect

Think about *The Memory Box.* Then review your notes on "The Brain and Memory."

Would the information in this article help Zach understand what is happening to his grandfather in *The Memory Box?* Use details to explain why it would or would not help.

The BRAIN and Memory

by Seymour Simon

The Parts of the Brain

The brain has three main sections: the cerebrum, the cerebellum, and the brain stem. The cerebrum fills the whole upper part of the skull, about nine-tenths of a person's whole brain. *Cerebrum* comes from the Latin word that means "brain." The cerebrum is divided into four parts, called lobes. This is the "thinking brain," in which language, memory, sensations, and decision making are located.

The deeply wrinkled gray surface of the cerebrum is called the cerebral cortex. The cortex is about as thick as a piece of cardboard, and if it was flattened out, it would take up as much space as the top of a kitchen table. The cortex is made up of ten to fourteen *billion* neurons. That's many more neurons than there are people in the entire world.

The cerebral cortex is working every time you listen to music, taste an apple, play with a computer, or make some part of your body move.

Short- and Long-Term Memory

Can you remember what you had for breakfast this morning? That's called short-term memory. Short-term memory has a very limited time span. You probably can't remember what you had for breakfast two weeks ago. But you can remember some things that happened to you months or even years ago, such as your first day at school. That's called long-term memory.

An area in the front of the cortex seems to deal with short-term memory, while the rest of the cortex deals with both long- and short-term memories. Two narrow motor strips on either side of the cortex control muscles all over your body, such as those in your lips, eyes, neck, thumbs, and so on. Other areas of the cortex receive information from the skin, eyes, ears, nose, and taste buds. Still other areas are related to speech, learning, and thinking.

How Memories Are Stored

The actual memories seem to be stored in the chemicals found in nerve cells. One theory is that a change happens in the chemicals that relay nerve impulses. Another idea is that there is a change in the cells' internal chemistry, called RNA. Scientists are just beginning to find out how and where the brain stores memories and where thinking occurs. New discoveries about the brain are constantly being made, but many mysteries still remain.

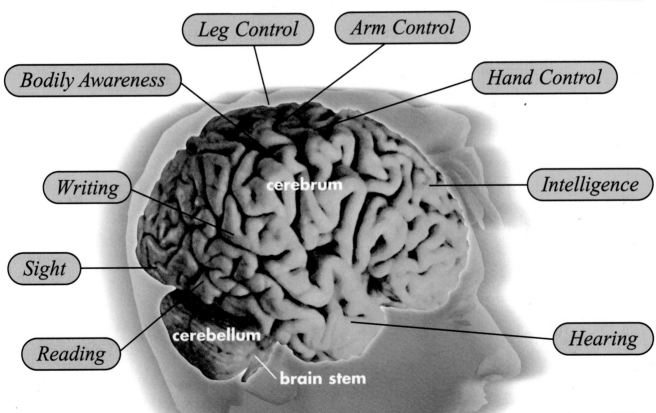

Leg Control
Arm Control
Bodily Awareness
Hand Control
Writing
cerebrum
Intelligence
Sight
cerebellum
Reading
brain stem
Hearing

Poetry

The Turkey Shot Out of the Oven

by Jack Prelutsky

The turkey shot out of the oven
and rocketed into the air,
it knocked every plate off the table
and partly demolished a chair.

It ricocheted into a corner
and burst with a deafening boom,
then splattered all over the kitchen,
completely obscuring the room.

It stuck to the walls and the windows,
it totally coated the floor,
there was turkey attached to the ceiling,
where there'd never been turkey before.

It blanketed every appliance,
it smeared every saucer and bowl,
there wasn't a way I could stop it,
that turkey was out of control.

I scraped and I scrubbed with displeasure,
and thought with chagrin as I mopped,
that I'd never again stuff a turkey
with popcorn that hadn't been popped.

CAMPFIRE

by Janet S. Wong

Just think—
when Mother was my age,
she could build a fire
with sparks from rocks,
catch a bunch of
grasshoppers and
roast them whole
for a summer
night's snack!

"Get me a good stick,"
she says, "thin but strong,"
and I bring her one
from the woods
behind our tent.
On the way back
I see a brown bag
by her feet—
could it be?

When the fire is spitting ready,
she reaches
in the bag, rustling,
and hands me
one big, fat, luscious
marshmallow.

A Song of Greatness

**A Chippewa Indian Song
translated by Mary Austin**

When I hear the old men
Telling of heroes,
Telling of great deeds
Of ancient days,
When I hear them telling,
Then I think within me
I too am one of these.

When I hear the people
Praising great ones,
Then I know that I too
Shall be esteemed,
I too when my time comes
Shall do mightily.

Lemon Tree

by Jennifer Clement
translated by Consuelo de Aerenlund

If you climb a lemon tree
feel the bark
under your knees and feet,
smell the white flowers,
rub the leaves
in your hands.
Remember,
the tree is older than you are
and you might find stories
in its branches.

WRAP-UP

What things are worth repeating over time?

SHARE A TRADITION

Write a Letter

Each main character or person in the selections you have just read experiences tradition. In a tradition, people do things a certain way because they have done them that way before—perhaps for many years. For example, some people follow tradition to celebrate birthdays or national holidays.

1. **Choose** a main character or person. Think about a tradition that he or she experiences.

2. **Imagine** taking part in the tradition. Reread parts of the selection that describe the tradition.

3. **Write** a letter to the character or person. Tell why you would like to share the tradition with him or her. Tell about your own tradition.

BE A SPORTS ANNOUNCER

Retell a Scene

Both Dusty in "The Jr. Iditarod Race" and Ebonee in "The Heart of a Runner" are involved in sports events. What if these races had sports announcers? Choose a race that either Dusty or Ebonee is involved in.

1. **Reread** the parts you need for detailed information.

2. **Listen** to an exciting TV or radio sports announcer. Then write a script for your own commentary.

3. **Deliver** your commentary for an audience.

HOW TO FACE NEW EXPERIENCES

Create a Poster

The Yang family in "The Yangs' First Thanksgiving" and Ohkwa'ri in "The Night Alone" experience something for the first time.

1. With a partner, **discuss** how these characters react to their new experiences. Then talk about how you face new experiences. Jot down all your ideas.

2. **Choose** your three best ideas.

3. **Write** them on a poster with the title "How to Face New Experiences." Color or decorate the poster and display it.

MEMORIES TO LIVE BY

Compare and Explain

Ohkwa'ri in "The Night Alone" and Zach in *The Memory Box* learn how memories can help them get through difficult situations.

1. **Reread** parts of the stories to find a memory that Ohkwa'ri and Zach each have.

2. Think about how each character uses that memory to get through something difficult. **Compare** their experiences.

3. **Explain** to a classmate what you have learned about memories to live by. Use Ohkwa'ri and Zach as examples.

Test Talk

Answer the Question

Use Information from the Text

Some test questions tell you to support your answer with details from the text. To answer such questions correctly, you must include information from the text.

A test about "How the Sun Came," pages 421–423, might have this question.

Test Question 1

According to the myth, did animals always look and act as they do now? Explain your answer, using details from the myth.

Understand the question.
Read the question carefully to find the key words. Finish the statement "I need to find out . . ."

Decide where you will look for the answer.

The answer may be *right there* in one place, or you may have to *think and search* for it. The answer may depend on the *author and you.*

Make notes about details that answer the question.

Check your notes.
Reread the question and your notes. Ask yourself, "Do I have enough information?" If details are missing, go back to the selection.

See how one student uses information from the text to answer the question.

I need to find out if animals always looked and acted the same. I'd say no, but I'll search different parts. Here's the 'possum, who used to have a "fine, bushy tail" but burned it off with a piece of the sun. The buzzard burned off all his head feathers too and is still bald today. Now I wonder about actions.

Grandmother Spider seems to have changed too. Today her web is "shaped like the sun's disk and its rays." So I guess it wasn't like that before she stole the sun. Then my answer is that some animals did change their looks or their behavior, and this myth tells why.

Try it!

Now use what you have learned to find text information to answer these test questions about "How the Sun Came," pages 421–423.

Test Question 2

Why do the animals think they must steal a piece of the sun in order to get light? Find details to support your answer.

Test Question 3

Why is pottery making woman's work, according to this myth? Support your answer with details from the myth.

Traveling On

Where do people's journeys take them?

Setting

- The **setting** is the time and place in which a story happens.

- In some stories, the author tells you exactly when and where the story takes place. In other stories, the author tells about the setting through details, and you have to figure out the time and place.

- Sometimes the author tells only one part of the setting, either the time or the place.

- In some stories, the setting is very important. It affects what happens in the story and why. In other stories, it isn't important.

Read "The Year of Mother Jones" from *Three Cheers for Mother Jones!* **by Jean Bethell.**

THREE CHEERS for MOTHER JONES!
by Jean Bethell

Talk About It

1. What do you know about the setting in "The Year of Mother Jones"?

2. Does the setting affect how the characters act? How?

3. Is the setting important to the story? Why or why not?

The Year of Mother Jones

by Jean Bethell

Philadelphia, PA, November 1903
My name is James. This is my sister, Emmy. She's only seven years old. We work here in this dirty old mill. It's the worst job in the world. We work twelve hours a day. We don't go to school. We never get out in the sun. We're tired all the time. Sometimes we have accidents and get hurt. They pay us two dollars a week.

That's father over there. He gets thirteen dollars a week. Our family can't live on that. That's why Emmy and I have to work. We hate it. Everybody who works here hates it.

Last summer we tried to do something about it. We went to see the owner. "Please raise our pay," said Father, "so our kids won't have to work."

"We want to go to school," I said. But he wouldn't listen.

"Get back to work or I'll fire you!"

That made us mad. So we walked out. We all went on strike! We walked around the front of the mill. We waited for the owner to offer us more money.

Then a lady called Mother Jones came to the mill. She was old—as old as my grandma. But she had a lot of spunk. She shook her fist at the mill owner. "Shame on you!" she said. "Hiring babies to do men's work."

"Hooray for Mother Jones!" we shouted.

"Set these children free!" she cried. "Give their parents enough to live on!"

"Never!" said the mill owner.

"Then we'll go see the President!" said Mother Jones.

"What can he do?" asked Father. "Can he raise our pay? Can he keep our children out of the mills?"

"Let's find out," said Mother Jones. "Let's ask him for help. That's what presidents are for—to help people."

Mother Jones was seventy-three when she led the Children's Crusade to see President Theodore Roosevelt. Although he was against child labor, he could not persuade Congress to pass a federal law making it illegal. Another thirty-five years went by before such a law was finally enacted.

LOOK AHEAD

In "I Want to Vote," Lila learns about another important human right—the right to vote. As you read, think about how the setting affects the story.

Vocabulary

Words to Know

banners   stockings   trolley
headlines   splattered   parlor
pavement

Words with similar meanings are
called **synonyms.** You can often
figure out the meaning of an
unknown word by finding a clue
in the words around it. Sometimes
this clue is a synonym.

Read the paragraph below. Notice
how *splashed* helps you understand
splattered.

The Exciting City

When she was young, Grandmother loved going to
the city. She saw bands play during parades and
watched people carrying colorful banners. She
heard newsboys shouting the headlines as they ran
along the pavement. Riding the trolley was fun, but
when she got off she would get splashed by passing
vehicles if there were puddles in the road. Her
white stockings would be splattered with mud, but
she didn't mind. The excitement of the city was
better than sitting at home in the parlor.

Write About It

Imagine riding a trolley in the 1900s.
Use vocabulary words to tell about
your experience.

486

I WANT TO VOTE!

from A Long Way to Go   by Zibby Oneal

It was 1917 in America—a time when men and women were not considered equal. Lila was learning about women's rights from her grandmother, who was fighting for their right to vote. Lila, like Grandmama, couldn't understand why boys had more freedom than girls. When Katie Rose, the family nursemaid, invited Lila to her home, Lila had an unforgettable afternoon. She met Mike, Katie Rose's brother, and persuaded him to let her, a girl, go with him to sell newspapers. It was an experience that changed Lila's life.

Lila counted more than thirty newsboys waiting to pick up their papers outside the office building where she and Mike stopped. A man was dumping great rope-bound bundles onto the sidewalk. "You wait here," Mike said and hurried into the crowd. In his cloth cap and knickers he looked just like every other boy waiting there. Lila soon lost sight of him.

She stood on the sidewalk, feeling out of place in her Sunday coat and white hair bow—the only girl on the street. Maybe this is a mistake, she thought.

In a few minutes, Mike was back, carrying a canvas bag on his shoulder. "Go ahead, take some," he said, "since you're so strong." He handed Lila the bag, half full.

Her shoulder sagged under the weight. "Heavy, aren't they?" Mike asked.

Lila shrugged. "Not very."

She didn't think that he believed her. "Come on, then. I sell on the corner of Tenth Street," he said.

Lila tried to hurry. The strap of the bag cut into her shoulder, and the weight of it bumped against her hip, but she didn't intend to let that slow her down. She walked as fast as she could.

"The headlines aren't much good today," Mike said. "All we got today is some speech about Liberty Bonds and a fire in a warehouse in Brooklyn." He shrugged. "So I'll have to use my imagination. That's what you do when the headlines aren't much. It's like advertising. Nobody's going to want to read the bond speech, of course, so I guess I'll have to work on the fire."

Lila didn't see how he could talk so much carrying papers. She could hardly breathe. Her shoulder ached and her arm was going numb. But of course she didn't say so. She wouldn't say so if she had to walk another five miles. She bit her lip and kept going.

Then, just when she thought she couldn't carry the papers much longer, when her arm felt dead as a stick of wood, they stopped.

"This is it," said Mike. "My corner." He dropped most of his papers onto the sidewalk. Gratefully Lila dropped hers.

"Now let's see you sell," Mike said, but he didn't wait to watch. Instead he began running after customers, waving papers, shouting, "Read all about the big fire in Brooklyn! Read about the flames forty feet high!"

Lila pulled a paper from the bag and looked at it. She couldn't see where he was getting all that. The paper didn't say a thing about flames. It didn't really say much about the fire. That was what he meant by imagination, she guessed, but it didn't seem quite fair to fool people that way.

She ran her eyes down the front page. The bond speech. The fire. But then she saw, down at the bottom of the page, not taking much space, a small article headed, SUFFRAGISTS REFUSE TO EAT. Lila read as fast as she could. There were suffragists in jail in Washington who wouldn't eat a bite. They said they'd rather starve than do without the vote. The paper called it a hunger strike.

Lila's eyes widened. This was news. This was something interesting. And, besides, it was true. She pulled a few more papers from her bag and stood herself right in the middle of the sidewalk. "Suffragists starving to death!" she yelled. "Read all about it!"

To her amazement, someone stopped to buy a paper. She tried again. "Read all about the ladies starving to death in Washington!" And, again, someone stopped.

"Crazy women," the man said, but he paid her and didn't seem to think it was strange at all to see a girl selling papers.

Lila felt encouraged. Over and over she waved her papers at people walking past. She shouted her headline until she was hoarse, but it felt good to be hoarse, to be shouting and running.

People bought papers. Maybe they would have bought them anyway, thought Lila. She didn't know, but she didn't care. She was too busy selling. In no time, her bag was empty.

She hadn't had time to think about Mike, but now, bag empty, she turned around to look for him. He was leaning against a lamppost, watching her. "I sold them all," she said breathlessly.

"Yeah. Well." Mike kicked the lamppost with the toe of his shoe. "I guess you showed me."

There were things that Lila felt like saying, but she decided not to say them. Instead she picked up the empty canvas bag and slung it over her shoulder. Together they started back the way they had come.

So now it was really over—the wonderful afternoon. Now she would go home with Katie Rose and turn into a proper little girl again. It was like the end of a fairy tale, Lila thought. Except it was sad.

On the trolley she leaned against Katie Rose and closed her eyes. It was over, Lila thought, but she would remember, and a memory, like a jawbreaker, lasted a long, long time.

"And then," said Lila on Sunday morning, bouncing on Grandmama's bed. "And then—"

"Lila, you've told me all about it three times."

"Oh, I liked it all so much, but I'm not going to tell anyone else about it. Just you." Lila looked out the window at the sunlight on the fence around the park. "I wish girls could sell papers," she said a little sadly. "I mean all the time."

"There are more and more things that girls can do. Think of all the jobs women have now that there's a war on. When I was your age we didn't dream of working in offices and factories."

"That's women. I mean girls." And then, "Do you think that if women could vote, they'd let girls sell papers?"

Grandmama laughed. "I don't know. I suppose there'd be a better chance of that happening."

"Then I'm a suffragist," Lila said. "I *thought* I was, but now I'm sure."

"That's fine."

Lila frowned. "But what can I do?"

"Believe that women have rights the same as men."

That wasn't what Lila had in mind. She wanted action. She wanted to shout headlines, run around yelling. "I could give speeches," she said. She imagined herself standing on a wooden box speaking to crowds in the street. It would be a lot like selling papers.

But Grandmama only laughed again. "You're still too young to make speeches."

"But I want to do *something*. It's no use just sitting around believing things."

Grandmama looked thoughtful. "Well, there's a suffragist parade a week or so before the state election. We're going to march up Fifth Avenue all the way from Washington Square to Fifty-ninth Street."

"With signs?" said Lila. "And banners?"

"Oh, yes, and music too. We're going to make people notice us."

"Would you take me?"

"Well, I was thinking—"

Lila sat up straight. "I'm coming."

"But not without permission you aren't. Not unless your mama and papa agree."

"I'll make them agree," said Lila, though she had no idea how she'd do that.

"Well, I'll try to help you," Grandmama said. "At least I'll mention the parade."

While they were waiting for dessert, Grandmama brought up the parade. She did it in a kind of offhanded way, as if it were something she'd only just remembered. "And I think Lila would like to march too," she said. Lila looked down at her napkin and crossed her fingers. But Papa said no.

It was such a small word, no, but it seemed to Lila that it was the biggest word in her life. So many nos. She felt tears of disappointment prickling in her eyes. She couldn't look up.

When, after lunch, Papa said, "Come on, Lila, it's time for our Sunday walk," Lila felt like saying, "No!" She didn't want to go for a walk with her father. She felt too mad and disappointed. All the same, she went to get her coat, because a little girl didn't say no to her father.

"Which way shall we walk?" he asked her when they were standing on the pavement.

"I don't care." And she didn't. She didn't care at all.

"What about Fifth Avenue then?"

Lila had known he'd choose that. Papa liked walking along Fifth Avenue, looking at the new motorcars pass by. One day, he said, he thought he might buy one.

"Has the cat got your tongue?" Papa said.

"No. I'm thinking."

"About important things?"

"I was thinking about the parade. It's going to come right up this street."

"Lila, you must forget the parade."

They waited to cross the street while a car passed. "That's a Pierce Arrow," Papa said. "It's really something, isn't it?"

Lila nodded. She supposed so.

"Maybe when George is older we'll buy one like that. He can learn to drive it."

"What about me?"

"Oh, you'll be a beautiful grown lady by then. You can ride in the back and tell George where to take you. You'll have all kinds of pretty clothes to wear. We'll go shopping for things like the dress in that window."

"I'd rather learn how to drive a motorcar," she said. "I'd rather be *doing* something."

Papa didn't understand. "There'll be plenty for you to do. Tea dances and parties and all that sort of thing."

"Those aren't the things I want to do."

"No? What then?"

"Oh!" Lists of things came tumbling into Lila's head. She wanted to march in the parade, turn cartwheels, walk on her hands, roll her stockings down. She wanted to run and yell, sell papers—but that was not what Papa meant. He meant later, when she was grown-up. What did she want to do *then*? Lila closed her eyes and squeezed them tight. "I want to vote," she said.

The words were out before she knew she was going to say them, but suddenly they seemed just right. "I want to be able to vote same as George."

When she opened her eyes, Papa was looking at her. "That's what you want more than anything?"

Lila nodded. She dug her fists into her pockets and looked up at Papa bravely. "It's what Grandmama says. Girls are people too. They have rights. It isn't fair the way it is. Billy Ash says he's smarter than me just because he's a boy. But I'm the one who gets all A's, not him. So why should he be allowed to vote and not me? Why should George if I can't? It's not fair, Papa. It's not fair to girls."

Lila paused for breath, but she couldn't stop talking. "When I grow up, I want to be just like Grandmama. I want to make things fair for everyone. That's why I want to march in the parade—to show people that's what I think. And if they put me in jail for marching, then I just won't eat, like the ladies in Washington."

Then Lila stopped. She didn't have anything else to say.

"Well," said Papa, "that was quite a speech."

When they reached the corner of Twenty-first Street and were almost home, Papa said, "How did you happen to know about those women in Washington, the ones who aren't eating? Did Grandmama tell you?"

Lila shook her head, still counting cracks. "No," she said. "I read it in the paper."

"Did you really? For heaven's sake." If she hadn't known better, Lila thought that he sounded proud of her.

After supper, she had her bath and watched Katie Rose laying out her clothes for school the next day. The same old stockings. The same old dress. Lila sighed. Everything was the same old thing again.

And that was when Grandmama came in. She had a funny, puzzled sort of expression. "It looks as if we'll be going to the parade together," she said.

Lila paused. The damp ends of her hair swung against her shoulders. "What?"

"Your father says you may go."

"With you? To the parade?" Lila felt as if she couldn't take it all in so fast.

"That's what he says."

"But why?"

Grandmama shrugged. "I don't know what you said to him on that walk, but you must have said something."

Lila swallowed. He had called it a speech. She had made a speech and he'd listened! A bubble of happiness began to rise inside her. He had listened and it was all right.

There were weeks of waiting before the parade. October crawled by like a snail. Lila imagined marching a hundred times before, at last, the day arrived, the special Saturday.

Grandmama was in the parlor, reading the paper. "I'm ready!" Lila cried.

Grandmama looked up. "That's fine, but you'll have a bit of a wait. The parade won't begin for several hours."

Lila twirled on the piano stool. She practiced marching between the parlor windows. Grandmama rattled the paper. "President Wilson has come to his senses, I see. He says he wishes our cause godspeed."

"What does that mean?" asked Lila.

"It means he wishes us luck. He's changing his spots, I think, just like your papa."

"What does *that* mean?"

"He's changing his mind. It says here he's leaning toward a constitutional amendment."

"So maybe there won't *be* a parade?"

"Of course there'll be a parade. We haven't *got* the amendment yet."

When at last they set out for the parade, Mama stood in the parlor window, waving. Lila skipped and whirled up the sidewalk. They were going to catch a cab at the corner.

The cab dropped them a block from Washington Square. Lila could hear snatches of music as they walked toward it. "Those are the bands warming up," Grandmama said. "There's going to be a lot of music."

Lila trotted along beside her. The music grew louder and louder. And then they were in Washington Square, and Lila's eyes opened round as saucers.

There were women everywhere, hundreds and hundreds of them. Some carried flags, some were unrolling banners with words printed on them. There were women dressed in nurses' uniforms, women in Red Cross costumes, women wearing yellow chrysanthemums in their hats. So many women! There were old women, young women, white women, black women. There was even a woman standing in line propped on crutches.

"How can she march on crutches?" Lila whispered.

"She can if she makes her mind up to do it," Grandmama said. "That's what this is all about."

"Line up! Line up!" someone was shouting. A bass drum boomed. Grandmama took Lila's hand and they slipped quickly into line.

And then the music began. All at once, all the bands were playing and the columns of women began to move. Left, left. Lila was marching. Above her, the yellow banners streamed.

Out of Washington Square they marched and onto Fifth Avenue. Before and behind came the sound of the drums, and the flags snapped in the breeze. Left, left. On they went up the street, marching in time to the music.

From the curbs came the sound of whistles and cheers. Yellow streamers flew from the shop doors. White-gloved policemen held back the crowds as the bands and the marchers passed.

499

Lila felt she could march forever, her feet in step with the drums. Back straight, chin up. Left, left, left.

Just as they were crossing Tenth Street, it happened. The bands were playing, "Over There." People on the sidewalk were shouting. Lila was looking into the crowd when something splashed at her feet.

It splashed and then it splattered red pulp and yellow seeds all over her stockings, all over the hem of her coat. "Someone threw a tomato!" she cried. "Someone threw it right at me!" She tugged Grandmama's hand. There were tears in her eyes.

Grandmama looked down. "Never mind. Just keep marching."

"But, Grandmama, a tomato! It's all over my legs!"

"These things happen sometimes, Lila. It is part of doing what we're doing. There are lots of people who don't want us to vote, lots who don't like this parade. Now be a brave girl. Show them they can't stop you. Keep marching."

Lila thought she was going to cry. Her feet kept moving, but she had lost step. She looked down at the red juice all over her white stockings. And then she got mad. She stuck out her chin and looked straight ahead, and her feet began to move in time with the music.

Left, left. A tomato couldn't stop her. She thought about the woman on crutches. She thought of the women who were still in jail in Washington and about the ones who weren't eating. She thought of all the speeches that Grandmama had made. She thought of her own speech to Papa. A tomato wasn't much, she thought. A tomato was nothing.

Head up, looking straight ahead, Lila marched on, her feet keeping time with the music.

By the time the parade reached Twenty-first Street, Lila's stockings were dry. The bands were playing "Tipperary." Lila knew the words to that song. She knew they talked about a long way to go. She began to sing to herself as she marched along.

And then Grandmama began singing. And soon women all around them had taken up the song. They sang about what a long way there was to go, and it seemed to Lila that those words meant a lot to them.

It was twilight by the time the parade broke up and Grandmama said, "Let's go home in a cab." Lila was glad to hear that. She didn't feel like walking.

While they waited for a taxi, Lila looked down at her tomato-splattered stockings. She felt proud of them. They were like a badge. She didn't even think of rolling them down.

ZIBBY ONEAL

"I don't recall when I didn't want to be a writer," states author Zibby Oneal. Mrs. Oneal's family thought that books were "as necessary to life as food. There were toppling stacks of books on every flat surface in the house."

Mrs. Oneal originally wrote stories specifically for her two children, Elizabeth and Michael. Her books grew from those stories.

In talking about her book *A Long Way to Go*, from which "I Want to Vote!" comes, Mrs. Oneal remembers, "Women had had the right to vote for only fourteen years when I was born. My grandmother had been denied the right for most of her life. When I think of the suffrage movement in this way, it seems like history that has only just finished happening."

Some other books that Mrs. Oneal has written specifically for young adults include *War Work*, *The Language of Goldfish*, *A Formal Feeling*, and *In Summer Light*. She has also written a picture book collection of stories, *Maude and Walter*, which is a biography of American painter Grandma Moses.

Mrs. Oneal has received many writing honors including the American Library Association Notable Book and Best Book for Young Adults awards.

Reader Response

Open for Discussion

If you had the opportunity, would you have marched with Lila and the suffragists in the parade? Why or why not?

Comprehension Check

1. Mike doesn't think that Lila will succeed at selling newspapers. Why do you think Mike has these doubts? Find details to support your answer.

2. The suffragists in jail in Washington, D.C., say "they'd rather starve than do without the vote." Do you think they are right or wrong to stage the hunger strike? Explain.

3. When the tomato splatters on Lila's stockings, she feels like crying. Then she holds her head up and keeps marching in time with the music. Use evidence from the story to explain this change in Lila.

4. What is the story's **setting?** How do you know about the time in history when the story takes place? (Setting)

5. Think about where this story takes place. How does this part of the **setting** add to the story's excitement? Explain. (Setting)

Test Prep

Look Back and Write

Look back at pages 493–496. What causes Lila's father to change his mind about letting her attend the suffragist parade? Use evidence from the selection to support your answer.

Technology Connection

 **Test Prep**

How to Read a Web Site

1. Preview

- The first page is the home page. It works like a book's table of contents.

- Look at the list of links to other pages. This Web site's pages are listed at the left. Words and phrases in the text that are underlined or in color may also be links.

2. Read and Locate Information

- Visitors to a Web site usually don't read from beginning to end. They browse to find interesting information. Sometimes they follow link after link through the Web site.

- As you read, jot down your own questions or comments. What can kids do to get involved in voting?

3. Think and Connect

Think about "I Want to Vote." Then review what you have learned about "Kids Voting USA Online."

The message center for this Web site is called "Wish Tree." What wish for your country would you leave there? What wish do you think Lila might leave?

Kids Voting USA is a nonprofit, nonpartisan, grassroots organization dedicated to securing democracy for the future by involving youth in the election process today.

Overview   How It Works   Campaign 2000   Testimonials

Overview How It Works Campaign 2000 Testimonials

Overview:

Kids Voting USA.
Kids Voting USA is a nonprofit, nonpartisan, grassroots organization working with schools and communities to enhance civics education and provide youth a voting experience at official polls on election day.

How It Began.
In 1988, three businessmen from Arizona traveled to Costa Rica on a fishing trip and caught much more than fish! These three founders of Kids Voting learned that voter turnout is about 80 percent in Costa Rica. Why? How? Voting is mandated by law in Costa Rica; however, this is not enforced. *Instead, Costa Ricans attribute this high voter turnout to their tradition of children accompanying Mom and Dad to the polls.* Youths learn early the importance of voting in a democracy. As a result, Costa Ricans believe their form of government is well preserved for the future.

Kids Voting USA.
Today, Kids Voting USA is the *only* program of its kind that enables students to visit <u>official</u> polling sites on election day, accompanied by parent or guardian, to cast a ballot similar in content to the official ballot. Kids Voting USA teaches youth—through a special curriculum, family participation, and community involvement—the importance of being informed and the responsibilties of voting.

Kids Voting USA Scope.
The Kids Voting USA Network of state organizations is growing fast, presently reaching 5 million students, 200,000 teachers, 6,000 schools, 80,000 volunteers, and 20,000 voter precincts.

Summary:

Mission.
Kids Voting USA is securing the future of democracy by educating and involving youth in the election process today.

It's Unique.
No other program offers the comprehensive Kids Voting USA curriculum, invites students into the official polling sites on election day, and gives students the opportunity to experience voting just as adults do.

Community, School, & Family.
Kids Voting USA is a program that elicits the best from the community, the classroom, and the household to deliver a valuable experience to youth and family that strengthens democracy now and for the future.

KIDS VOTING USA

ONLINE

Introduction

Sponsors

KVUSA News

Education

Teachers

Students

USA Network

It Works

Site Map

505

KIDS VOTING USA

ONLINE

Introduction

Sponsors

KVUSA News

Education

Teachers

Students

USA Network

It Works

Site Map

Overview How It Works Campaign 2000 Testimonials

How It Works:

Election Day. Students K–12 go to official polls, with parents and guardians, and cast their own ballots in their own polling booth on the same issues and candidates as adults do. High school students go to polls independently.

Kids Voting USA is not only building youth involvement in democracy, but participating communities see adult voter turnout increase between 5 percent and 10 percent.

Before Election Day in the Classroom. In Kids Voting, there is active preparation in the classroom. The Kids Voting USA curriculum stimulates active creativity in the classroom. It's an educator-acclaimed series of activities that is upbeat, thought-provoking, and action-packed—students learn by doing. The curriculum develops information-gathering and critical thinking skills in students.

Before Election Day in the Community. In Kids Voting, community participation is key. Excitement for the political process is rediscovered among adults because of the youth involvement. A community Kids Voting organization raises funds, prints the curriculum and ballots, and recruits poll volunteers to greet and assist students on election day. The entire community joins together, regardless of political perspective, to enable this important experience for local youth.

Not politics as usual, but the refreshing realization that all have a vested interest in the process.

VOTE

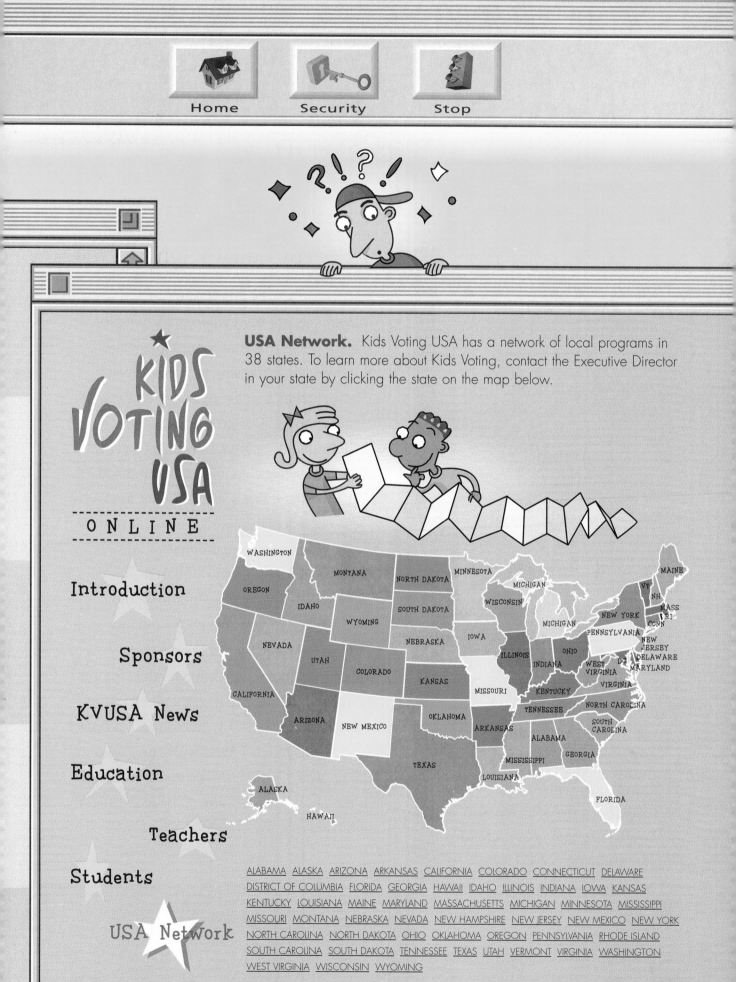

Home   **Security**   **Stop**

USA Network. Kids Voting USA has a network of local programs in 38 states. To learn more about Kids Voting, contact the Executive Director in your state by clicking the state on the map below.

KIDS VOTING USA
ONLINE

Introduction

Sponsors

KVUSA News

Education

Teachers

Students

USA Network

ALABAMA ALASKA ARIZONA ARKANSAS CALIFORNIA COLORADO CONNECTICUT DELAWARE DISTRICT OF COLUMBIA FLORIDA GEORGIA HAWAII IDAHO ILLINOIS INDIANA IOWA KANSAS KENTUCKY LOUISIANA MAINE MARYLAND MASSACHUSETTS MICHIGAN MINNESOTA MISSISSIPPI MISSOURI MONTANA NEBRASKA NEVADA NEW HAMPSHIRE NEW JERSEY NEW MEXICO NEW YORK NORTH CAROLINA NORTH DAKOTA OHIO OKLAHOMA OREGON PENNSYLVANIA RHODE ISLAND SOUTH CAROLINA SOUTH DAKOTA TENNESSEE TEXAS UTAH VERMONT VIRGINIA WASHINGTON WEST VIRGINIA WISCONSIN WYOMING

Paraphrasing

- **Paraphrasing** is explaining something in your own words.

- After you read a sentence or paragraph, put it into your own words. Don't change the author's meaning or add your own opinion.

- Paraphrasing can help you study for tests because you will remember ideas better when you put them into your own words.

Read "A Dream of Equal Rights" from *Martin Luther King, Jr., and the March Toward Freedom* by Rita Hakim.

Write About It

1. Paraphrase the first paragraph. Did you use your own words and include all of the author's thoughts?

2. Paraphrase what you read about the "I Have a Dream" speech. How could paraphrasing help if you had a test on this speech?

A Dream
of Equal Rights

by Rita Hakim

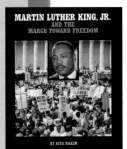

Movements are born when many people share a belief that things must change. But every great movement needs a leader. Often, it takes a single person to shape a clear vision of how the world can be.

In the 1960s, a great movement swept the United States. People around the nation realized that society did not treat all of its citizens fairly. They got together to demand equal rights for all.

The basic rights of citizens are called civil rights. In the 1960s, black Americans led the fight for civil rights. Many people had different ideas about how to win these rights. But one man came forward to lead them. His name was Martin Luther King, Jr. His most famous speech was titled "I Have a Dream." His dream was the dream of everyone involved in the civil rights movement: peace, justice, and equality.

On August 28, 1963, Martin Luther King, Jr., gave one of the great speeches in American history. Nearly 250,000 people had gathered at the Lincoln Memorial in Washington, D.C. They had come together to demand equal rights for all.

Martin Luther King, Jr., spoke to them and to millions of other people watching on TV. He began reading his prepared speech, but then he stopped and put away his notes. He did not need to read. What he wanted to say was in his heart. All his life he had witnessed racism. Now was his chance to present his vision of equality to the nation and the world.

"I have a dream!" he cried. "I have a dream that one day on the red hills of Georgia, sons of former slaves and sons of former slave owners will be able to sit down together at the table of brotherhood. . . . I have a dream that my four little children will one day live in a nation where they will not be judged by the color of their skin but by the content of their character."

LOOK AHEAD

In "The Long Path to Freedom," Harriet Tubman also has a dream of a better world. As you read about her escape from slavery, paraphrase the story of her hard journey.

Vocabulary

Words to Know

liberty	plantation	unconscious
vow	quickened	runaway
slavery		

When you read, you may come across a word that you don't know. To figure out its meaning, look for clues, such as an explanation or definition, in the surrounding sentences or paragraph.

Notice how *vow* is used in the paragraph below. What explanation or definition helps you figure out what it means?

Frederick Douglass

Frederick Douglass was born into slavery in 1817. In 1838 he escaped from his master and headed north. As Douglass reached the Massachusetts border, he quickened his pace. Suddenly he was free, and he made a vow, a solemn promise, to help other runaway slaves. Douglass told the world about slavery. He spoke about slaves who were beaten unconscious in the fields of the plantation and about children who were taken from their mothers at the auction block. For over fifty years, he fought for liberty and justice for all Americans.

Talk About It

Use vocabulary words to tell what it might have been like to live on a plantation.

The Long Path to Freedom

From *The Story of Harriet Tubman*
by Kate McMullan

Harriet, the daughter of Ben and Rit, was born a slave. She married John Tubman, who was born free. She brought to his house a beautiful quilt and her thoughts about escaping. John told his wife that he would inform Dr. Thompson, the master, if she tried to run away. It was years earlier that Harriet Tubman had been hit in the head with a two-pound weight when aiding an escaping slave. This left her with a large scar on her forehead, sudden sleeping spells, and the desire for freedom.

Go Free or Die!

Freedom. The word was always on Harriet's mind now. She'd often heard her mother complain that she was supposed to be free. Now Harriet decided to find out if this was true. With the money she made hiring out her time, she paid a lawyer five dollars, a large sum in those days. He looked in the record books. He discovered that Rit's first owner had died. In his will he left Rit to a woman named Mary Patterson. Rit was to serve Mary until she was forty-five. But Mary died young. Since there was no word about Rit in her will, Rit legally became free when Mary died.

Rit should have been free! But no one had told her. She had been tricked! Another owner had snatched her up, and she remained a slave. Harriet realized that papers and contracts were white men's tools. She couldn't trust them to make her free. She would have to try another way.

Early one morning Harriet was working in a field that was close to a road. A neighboring white woman drove up in a buggy. She wore the plain dress of a Quaker. Seeing that no one was around, the woman stopped and spoke to Harriet. She asked her name and how she had gotten the scar on her head. Harriet told the woman her story. She knew that Quakers didn't believe in slavery and could be trusted. After this the woman made a habit of talking to Harriet when no one was watching. Once she whispered that if Harriet ever needed help, she could come to her farm near Bucktown. Bucktown, Maryland, was a tiny town near Dr. Thompson's plantation.

Harriet was grateful to the white woman. Yet she knew that escape would be especially dangerous for her. She

might have one of her spells and be caught while sleeping on the road. With the big scar on her forehead, she would be easy to recognize. So, for the time being, Harriet kept the Quaker woman's words a secret in her heart.

News soon came to the plantation that a slave trader from the South had arrived. Someone whispered to Harriet that she and three of her brothers were to be sold to him. Sold South! Harriet ran to find her brothers. She told them what she had learned. They must run away!

That night Harriet waited until her husband, John, fell asleep. Then she slid silently out of their cabin. She met her brothers, and they started off through the woods. Harriet took the lead. She knew the woods. They did not. Every owl that hooted, every frog that croaked startled them. They did not move very fast. And to Harriet they seemed to stomp and crash like a herd of cattle!

Harriet kept encouraging them on. But at last her brothers stopped. They were frightened. They were going back.

Harriet began to protest. They must go on!

But her brothers were firm. It was too risky.

At last Harriet said that she was going North alone. But her brothers didn't think she should. They grabbed her. She fought them tooth and nail, but three men were too many for her. They forced her to walk back to the plantation.

Only two days passed before a little water boy whispered more news to Harriet as she worked in the field. She and her brothers had been sold. The slave trader was coming for them that same night!

What was she to do? If she stayed, she would be put in the chain gang. She knew she would die on the

long walk South. But if she ran, who would go with her? Not her three brothers. Not her husband. John might even help the men with guns and bloodhounds who were sure to come after her! If Harriet ran, she would be all alone.

"There's one of two things I've got a *right* to, liberty or death," Harriet explained years later. "If I could not have one, I would have the other. No man will take me back alive."

Harriet straightened up and walked away from the field. She must let someone know that she was leaving. Otherwise, her family might think she was headed South with the dreaded chain gang.

Harriet saw Rit walking toward her on her way to milk a cow. But she knew she couldn't tell her mother. Rit would make a great fuss.

As Rit drew near, Harriet told her to go back to the cabin. Harriet said that she would do the milking that night. This was Harriet's good-bye to her mother.

After she milked the cow, Harriet went to the Big House. She planned to find her sister Mary, who worked there. She could trust Mary with her secret.

Mary was in the kitchen, but several other slaves were too. Harriet needed to tell Mary in private, so she pretended to wrestle with her sister. She pulled her outside, away from the others.

Harriet was about to tell Mary that she was running away. But before she could, Dr. Thompson rode up to the house on his horse. He would not be happy to see two slaves chatting during working hours. Mary made a dash for the kitchen. As she hurried away, Harriet did the only thing she could think of. She began to sing:

I'm sorry, friends, to leave you,
Farewell! Oh, farewell!
But I'll meet you in the morning,
Farewell! Oh, farewell!

I'll meet you in the morning,
When you reach the Promised Land:
On the other side of Jordan,
For I'm bound for the Promised Land!

That evening Harriet did nothing to call attention to
herself. She went to bed as usual and waited until she was
sure John was sleeping soundly. Then she got up. She
packed a little corn bread and salt pork in a bandanna.
Then she folded up the beautiful quilt she had made.
She was taking it with her.

Silently Harriet made her way through the dark
woods. She remembered how Ben had told her that even
bloodhounds couldn't follow a scent through water, so
Harriet waded in streams whenever possible. Her long
skirt heavy with mud, she came to the farmhouse of the
Quaker woman. Trembling, she knocked on the door.

When the Quaker woman saw that it was Harriet,
she quickly let her in. But the woman told Harriet that
it wasn't safe for her to stay at the farmhouse. Harriet
must travel on that very night.

The Quaker woman explained to Harriet that she had
more than ninety miles to go before she would cross the
Mason-Dixon Line to freedom. First, she must follow the

Choptank River north for forty miles. The river would become narrower as it reached its source. When the river ended, Harriet should follow the road to Camden, Delaware. Just outside of the town she should look for a white house with green shutters. On a small slip of paper the woman wrote down a message for the Hunns, the people who lived in the white house. When she got there, Harriet should give the paper to them. They would tell her what to do next. The Hunns' house would be Harriet's first stop on the Underground Railroad.

As Harriet was leaving the farmhouse, she felt very grateful to the Quaker woman for helping her. She wanted to repay her kindness. She had no money, but she had one thing she valued. Harriet gave the woman her beautiful quilt.

Crossing the Line

Harriet started off again through the woods. All night she walked north, wading in the Choptank whenever possible. As the sun began to rise, Harriet dug a hole in the underbrush. She climbed in and pulled some grass and weeds over her head. There, she rested as best she could through the day.

In the evening Harriet began following the river again. By now she knew she must be missed. Dr. Thompson would have slave hunters and dogs out looking for her. She quickened her step, alert for any unfamiliar sound in the woods.

At times Harriet's path north led her to a road. Then she would watch and listen for some time. Not until she was sure the coast was clear would she race across.

Finally the river narrowed, just as the Quaker woman had said it would. At last it was just a trickle, and beyond it Harriet saw a dirt road. Taking a last drink from the Choptank and pulling her bandanna down to hide her scar, Harriet walked swiftly along the side of the dark road. And then, without warning, a sleeping spell came on. Harriet sank to the ground, unconscious.

When she woke up, it was still pitch dark. But she heard men's voices and horses snuffling and stomping on the road. She dared not move a muscle. The men were slave hunters! She could hear them talking about a runaway girl!

Then one of the men told the others that they should turn back. They would start hunting again early in the morning. And they would bring their dogs with them too.

Harriet's heart pounded as she listened to the men ride off. When she was sure that they were far away, she got up and began running toward Camden again. Now she must find the Hunns' house before morning!

But the sun rose before Harriet reached the white house with green shutters. She saw a woman in the yard feeding chickens. Harriet began to panic. What if this wasn't the right white house? What if this woman wasn't Mrs. Hunn? Fearfully Harriet approached the house.

The woman looked up and saw the tired, dusty runaway walking toward her.

Without speaking, Harriet held out the slip of paper to her. The woman read it and then smiled.

"Welcome, Harriet," she said. "I am Eliza Hunn. I am glad to see thee."

Harriet knew from the way Eliza Hunn said *thee* instead of *you* that she was a Quaker. She led Harriet inside her house and fixed her breakfast.

Harriet stayed for three days with Eliza Hunn and her husband, Ezekiel. She ate her meals with them, and they talked. Most of the time Harriet stayed hidden inside the house. But when she wanted some fresh air, she took a broom and swept the Hunn's yard. No one passing the house would think that the black girl sweeping the yard could be a runaway slave. And for the first time Harriet slept in a real bed at night.

The fourth night Eliza gave Harriet freshly washed clothes and packed up a parcel of food. Then Ezekiel helped her climb into the back of his wagon. He covered her with a blanket.

Ezekiel drove the wagon through the little town of Camden. On the far side he stopped the wagon beside some woods. Making sure no one was on the road, he told Harriet to climb out. He explained that it wasn't safe for him to drive her any farther. Slave hunters were everywhere in these parts. The best thing for her to do was walk north through the woods to Wilmington, Delaware. Just before Wilmington she would see a cemetery. That was where she should wait for the next conductor. Ezekiel told her it would take two nights of walking.

After thanking Ezekiel, Harriet turned and disappeared into the woods. Once again she walked all night, following the North Star. She thanked God for bringing her this far. At dawn Harriet hid in a hollow tree and waited for sundown.

After another long night's walk Harriet reached a graveyard. There she saw a man. He was muttering to himself. Harriet wondered if he was crazy. But as she drew closer, she made out the words he was saying over and over. "I have a ticket for the railroad. I have a ticket for the railroad." Joyfully Harriet walked up to him.

The man introduced himself to Harriet as Mr. Trent. He handed her men's work clothes and explained that she was to disguise herself as his workman. Quickly Harriet put on the clothes, laced up a pair of work boots, and pulled a man's hat down to hide her scar. With a shovel over her shoulder, Harriet followed Mr. Trent into Wilmington.

In the busy city no one looked twice at the black man with the shovel. Mr. Trent led Harriet to a house next to a small shoe shop and knocked.

"I have a shipment for you," Mr. Trent told the man who opened the door. "One bale of cotton."

The man nodded. Thanking Mr. Trent, Harriet slipped inside the house.

Harriet stayed in Thomas Garrett's house all day. He was another Quaker, well known for helping slaves. Because he owned a shoe factory, he always supplied runaways with a new pair of much-needed shoes for their journey.

The next evening, a Sunday night, Mr. Garrett gave Harriet fancy women's clothes to wear. He gave her gloves and a hat with a thick veil. When she was dressed, Harriet sat right up beside Mr. Garrett as he drove his buggy through town. In her elegant clothes, no one would guess that Mr. Garrett's companion was a runaway.

Just north of Wilmington Mr. Garrett stopped the buggy. He gave Harriet a piece of paper with the word *Pennsylvania* printed on it. He knew that Harriet couldn't read. But he whispered to her that she would come to a signpost farther down the road. He told her to check the sign for the word that was printed on the piece of paper. When she crossed that road, she would be in a free state. Then she should walk the short distance from the sign to the city of Philadelphia.

Mr. Garrett told her that this was the most dangerous part of the journey, even though it wasn't far to Pennsylvania. Slave hunters watched the Pennsylvania border like hawks.

In the dark Harriet started up the road. She was close to freedom! But all of a sudden her sixth sense sent her a warning. Harriet dashed into the woods and hid. A few minutes later she heard horses galloping along the road. She stayed hidden until all was quiet. Then she ran through the woods, not stopping until she came to the road.

The sun was just coming up as she held the slip of paper up to the signpost. The words were the same! In another minute Harriet crossed the magical Mason-Dixon Line!

Later Harriet told how it felt. "I looked at my hands to see if I was the same person now that I was free. There was such a glory over everything, the sun came like gold through the trees, and over the fields, and I felt like I was in Heaven."

Harriet was no longer a slave. She was free! Yet the wonder faded when Harriet realized just where her long, dangerous journey had brought her. Years afterward she said, "I had crossed the line of which I had so long been dreaming. I was free, but there was no one to welcome me to the land of freedom. I was a stranger in a strange land, and my home, after all, was down in the old cabin quarter, and the old folks and my brothers and my sisters and friends were there. But I was free. And they should be free also!" Harriet made a vow at that moment. Someday she would return to Maryland. She would gather her family around her. And she would lead them to freedom.

About the Author
Kate McMullan

Ms. McMullan writes both historical fiction and realistic fiction. For a historical piece based on actual events, like the one about Harriet Tubman, Ms. McMullan does very careful research. It is important to her that everything in the story be accurate.

Ms. McMullan's husband is an illustrator who works with her on many books. When their daughter was young, she became the inspiration for several picture books, which the McMullans created together. One of these books, *Nutcracker Noel,* came about after years of attending her daughter's ballet recitals. This book was named one of the Ten Best Picture Books of the Year by the *New York Times.*

Some books that Ms. McMullan has written for elementary school students are *The Great Eggspectations of Lila Fenwick, The Great Ideas of Lila Fenwick,* and *Great Advice from Lila Fenwick.* The main character is a sixth grader who has lots of adventures and a few misadventures.

Reader Response

Open for Discussion

The word *freedom* was always on Harriet Tubman's mind. Do you think freedom means as much to you as it did to her? Explain.

Comprehension Check

1. Harriet Tubman was concerned about her sleeping spells and the big scar on her forehead. How did those two things affect her journey to freedom?

2. Make a list of the people who helped Harriet Tubman along the way. Next to each person in the list, write how he or she helped Harriet Tubman.

3. After crossing the Mason-Dixon Line, why did Harriet Tubman compare herself to a stranger in a strange land? How did she plan to change that feeling? Use evidence from the selection to explain.

4. The first time that Harriet Tubman tried to escape is described on page 514. **Paraphrase** the passage. (Paraphrasing)

5. Now **paraphrase** the section of the selection that begins with Harriet Tubman falling to the ground unconscious and ends with her arrival at the Hunns' house. (Paraphrasing)

FCAT **Short Response**

Look Back and Write

Look back at pages 514–516. Why does Harriet Tubman decide to run away from the plantation? Explain, using details from the selection.

FCAT

How to Read an Informational Article

1. Preview

- Read the title. Think about what you already know about the Underground Railroad. What more do you expect to learn from this article?

- Look at the map. What does the key tell you about why the states have different colors?

2. Read and Interpret Information

- Read the article to find out how the Underground Railroad operated.

- Read the map to find out where the escaping slaves went. Jot down the free states the slaves passed through on their way north.

3. Think and Connect

Think about "The Long Path to Freedom." Look at your notes for "How the Underground Railroad Got Its Name."

On the map, trace the main escape route closest to the one Harriet Tubman might have used. Which states did she actually travel through?

How the UNDERGROUND RAILROAD Got Its Name

by James Haskins

There is a story in Underground Railroad lore that in 1831 a slave named Tice Davids ran away from his master in Kentucky. With the master in hot pursuit, Davids made his way to the Ohio River, which formed the border between the slave state of Kentucky and the free state of Ohio. The master saw Davids plunge into the river and, as he searched frantically for a boat, kept his eyes on his slave. When he set off after his slave in a boat, he went directly toward him. When Davids reached the opposite shore near the town of Ripley, Ohio, his master was just minutes behind him. But then Tice Davids vanished from sight.

529

The owner combed the countryside. He searched through Ripley, which was known as an antislavery town. But he could find no trace of his runaway slave. He finally gave up, concluding that Davids had escaped on "an underground road."

The story spread about the slave who had gained his freedom on an "underground road." As it spread, it was added to, as stories often are. Steam-engine railroad trains had just come into use.

The *Tom Thumb,* a steam-powered locomotive built by Peter Cooper, had its first successful run in 1830. The changeover from horse-drawn engines to steam-powered ones inaugurated the great age of the railroad that still excites people's imaginations. Pretty soon the story was that Tice Davids had escaped on an *underground railroad.*

There never was an actual railroad that ran underground and carried escaped slaves to freedom. But the term fit the way many slaves in the South made their way to the free states of the North and even to Canada, for they always traveled in secret, or "underground." The term *underground railroad* first appeared in print in the 1840s, and soon other railroad terms were being used. The fugitive slaves were referred to as "parcels" and "passengers." Those who helped them in one way or another along the way were called "conductors." People who offered their homes as "depots" or "stations" were called "stationmasters."

No one knows who helped the slave named Tice Davids—if indeed there ever was a real Tice Davids. His story may be a myth, for there is at least one other version of the origin of the term *underground railroad* that places its beginning in Chester County, Pennsylvania. No one knows whether Tice Davids, if he was a real person, succeeded in reaching a place where he could live in freedom. No one knows how many slaves tried to escape, or how many people tried to help them during the two-and-a-half centuries of slavery in the United States.

Especially in the early days, the Underground Railroad was a secret activity, and few written records were kept. The names of most of the slaves who escaped, and the names of many people—black and white—who aided them, are lost to history. But hundreds of stories have survived, and altogether they make a thrilling chapter in the long history of slavery and the attempts to fight it.

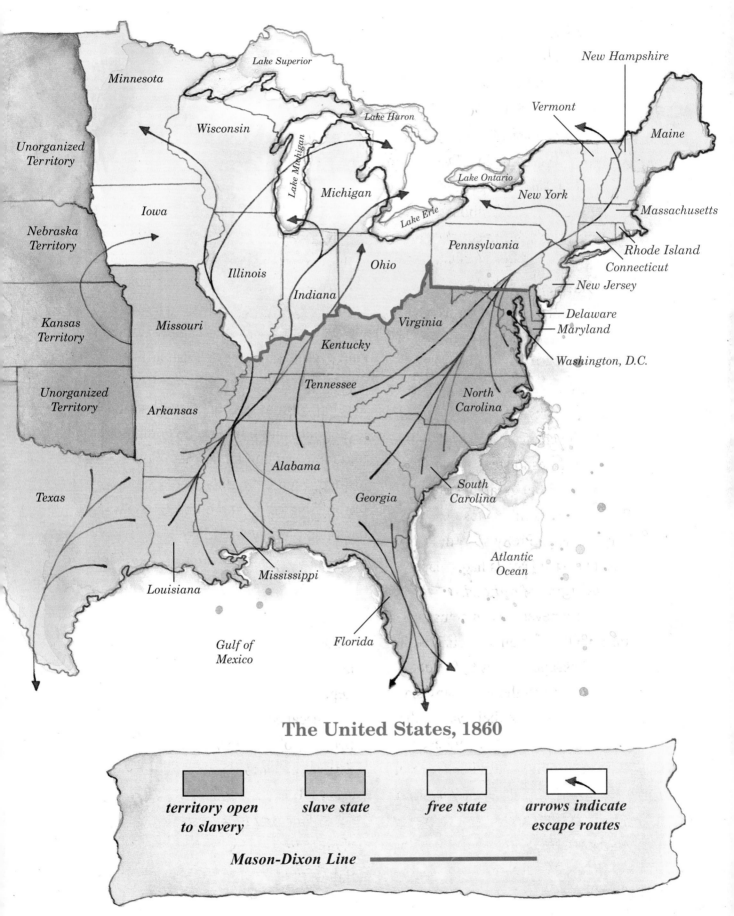

The United States, 1860

territory open to slavery

slave state

free state

arrows indicate escape routes

Mason-Dixon Line

Visualizing

- **Visualizing** is creating a picture in your mind as you read.

- An author may help you visualize by using imagery. This happens when an author uses words that give you a strong mental picture, or image. *Enormous billowing clouds* is an example of imagery.

- Another way an author may help you feel a part of what you are reading is through sensory details. Authors use words that describe how something looks, sounds, smells, tastes, or feels. *Pale golden light* is a sensory detail that helps you imagine how something looks.

Read "Little Billy's Swan Rides" from "The Minpins" by Roald Dahl.

Talk About It

1. What words helped you visualize what happened in the story?

2. If you were an illustrator, what part of the story would you illustrate? What would you show?

Little Billy's Swan Rides

by Roald Dahl

From then on, Swan came every night to Little Billy's bedroom window. He came after Billy's mother and father had gone to sleep and the whole house was quiet. But Little Billy was never asleep. He was always wide awake and eagerly waiting. And every night, before Swan arrived, he saw to it that the curtains were drawn back and the window was open wide so that the great white bird could come gliding right into the room and land on the floor beside his bed. Then Little Billy would slip into his dressing gown and climb on to Swan's back and off they would go.

Oh, it was a wondrous secret life that Little Billy lived up there in the sky at night on Swan's back! They flew in a magical world of silence, swooping and gliding over the dark world below where all the earthly people were fast asleep in their beds.

Once, Swan flew higher than ever before and they came to an enormous

billowing cloud that was shining in a pale golden light, and in the folds of this cloud Little Billy could make out creatures of some sort moving around.

Who were they?

He wanted so badly to ask Swan this question, but he couldn't speak a word of bird-language. Swan seemed unwilling to fly very close to these creatures from another world, and this made it impossible for Little Billy to see them clearly.

Another time, Swan flew through the night for what seemed liked hours and hours until they came at last to a gigantic opening in the earth's surface, a sort of huge gaping hole in the ground, and Swan glided slowly round and round above this massive crater and then right down into it. Deeper and deeper they went into the dark hole. Suddenly there was a brightness like sunlight below them, and Little Billy could see a vast lake of water, gloriously blue, and on the surface of the lake thousands of swans were swimming slowly about. The pure white of the swans against the blue of the water was very beautiful.

LOOK AHEAD

In *Chester Cricket's Pigeon Ride*, Chester also has a high-flying adventure— through New York City. As you read, visualize what happens on his very first pigeon ride.

Vocabulary

Words to Know

excursions	clinging	gale
thrill	feelers	

Many words have more than one meaning. To decide which meaning of a word is being used, look for clues in the surrounding sentences or the paragraph.

Notice *gale* in the paragraph below. Does it mean "a very strong wind" or "a noisy outburst"?

Butterflies and Roller Coasters

To me, a roller-coaster ride is a <u>thrill</u>. For Uncle Pete, it's his butterfly collection. Sometimes Uncle Pete takes me on <u>excursions</u>, looking for new specimens. Once when we were in a meadow, I noticed a butterfly <u>clinging</u> to my shirt. That close, I could see its long <u>feelers</u> and fragile legs. I took a deep breath and blew it away. It must have felt like a <u>gale</u> to the delicate butterfly. After it flew away, I decided that even though butterflies were not as exciting as roller-coaster rides, they were interesting.

Talk About It

Using vocabulary words, tell a partner about an excursion you have had.

from

Chester Cricket's Pigeon Ride

by George Selden   illustrated by Garth Williams

*Although Chester Cricket enjoys his
new life in New York, he misses his country
home in Connecticut. One night he decides to
explore the city, hoping to find a tree, a leaf, or
anything that reminds him of the country. Instead
he finds a great adventure when he meets Lulu Pigeon.*

"Now what is your *story*, Chester C.? How come you're singing down here in the city instead of out in the sticks somewhere?"

Chester told Lulu all about himself: being trapped in the picnic basket, and then found by Mario in the subway station, and then being "adopted," as you might say, by Tucker Mouse and Harry Cat.

"Dooo all the crickets in Connecticut sound like that?" asked Lulu, bobbing her head in disbelief.

"Oh, I don't know," answered Chester bashfully. As a matter of fact, he'd been told by a well-traveled robin named John that he was the finest musician in the state, but that wasn't the kind of thing you would tell a complete stranger.

"Now, what about *you?*" he asked, when he'd finished his own strange tale.

"Oh, me!" Lulu chortled delightfully. "I'm what yooo'd call a pecuoooliar pigeon. Or maybe even a kookoo bird."

Then Lulu told Chester *her* story. It seems that she came from a very old and aristocratic family of pigeons. In fact, her great-great-great—she couldn't remember how many greats—grandmother and grandfather, the Hynrik Stuyvesant Pigeons, claimed to have crossed the Atlantic clinging to one of the yardarms of a vessel sailing to New Amsterdam. Lulu explained that that was what New York was called when it was still a Dutch city, before the English took over.

"They claimed they were 'bored' with the Old World and wanted tooo explore the New Frontiers," Lulu squawked derisively. "But I just think they couldn't make a living in Holland any more."

Anyway, the Hynrik Stuyvesant Pigeons and all their descendants prospered greatly in the great New World. They became probably the most famous and respected pigeon family on the island of Manhattan—so famous and respected, indeed, that now they refused to eat any bread crumbs except those that were thrown out on Park Avenue.

"But about a year ago," said Lulu, "I had a beakful of all that ritzy jazz, so I told my snooooty relatives bye-bye and just flapped out. I decided that I'd rather, like, fly with the times. That's why I moved down here tooo Bryant Park. It's nearer where the action is. Yooo get what I mean?"

"I guess so," said Chester—although he didn't understand her completely. Lulu had a strange New York way of talking that was sort of hard to understand. But Chester meant to try, because he was beginning to like this pigeon very much. Even if there might be some kookoo bird in her.

"But don't you *ever* see any of your family now?" he asked.

"Oh, shoooor." Lulu scratched the earth with one claw. "Every once in a while I fly up to Central Park. There's an elm tree up there reserved solely for the Stuyvesant Pigeon clan, if yooo please!"

"Where's Central Park?" asked the cricket.

"You don't know where Central *Park* is?" said Lulu. "Big beautiful Central Park!—the best place in the city—"

"I guess I don't," Chester apologized. He explained that Mario had taken him on several excursions, but not, as yet, to Central Park.

"Say!" exclaimed Lulu. "How would you like a real tooor of Nooo York? One that only a pigeon could give."

"Well, I'd love one," said Chester, "but—"

"Hop on my back, just behind my neck. Nope—" Lulu bobbed her head jerkily, trying to think. "—Yooo couldn't see down through my wings too well." Then she gave a big scratch and exclaimed, "I got it! You sit on my claw—take the left one there—and wrap a couple of feelers around." Chester hesitated a minute or two. He was quite sure no cricket had ever done *this* before.

"Go on! Get on!" Lulu ordered. "You're in for a thrill."

"All right—" Chester mounted the pigeon's claw, with a feeling that was partly excitement, part fear, and held on tight.

"First I gotta rev up."

Lulu flapped her wings a few times. And then—before Chester could gasp with delight—*they were flying!*

To fly!—oh, be flying!

"Sorry for the bumpy takeoff," said Lulu.

But it hadn't seemed bumpy to Chester at all.

"It'll be better when I gain altitooode."

Back in Connecticut, in the Old Meadow, when Chester made one of his mightiest leaps—usually showing off in front of a friend like Joe Skunk—he sometimes reached as high as six feet. But in seconds Lulu had passed that height, and in less than a minute she was gliding along at the level of the tops of the sycamore trees.

"Okay down there?" she called into the rush of air they sped through.

"Oh—oh, sure—I mean, I guess—" There are times when you don't know whether you feel terror or pleasure—or perhaps you feel both all at once, all jumbled together wonderfully! "I'm fine!" the cricket decided, and held on to Lulu's leg even tighter. Because now they were far above even the tops of the trees, and Chester could see whole blocks of buildings below him. He suddenly felt all giddy and free.

"How about a spin up to Central Park first?"

"Great, Lulu! I want to see *everything*!"

The pigeon flew east, to Fifth Avenue, and then due north. High though they were flying, Chester could see how beautiful the store windows were in the street beneath. The finest shops in all the world are on Fifth Avenue, and the cricket would have liked to fly a bit lower, to get a closer look. But he thought better of it and decided to leave all the navigating to Lulu. Besides, there was something strange up ahead. A huge rectangle of dark was sliding toward them—close, then closer, then under them.

"Here's Central Park," Lulu screeched against the wind.

And now Chester had another thrill. For there weren't only sycamore trees in the park. The cricket could smell birches, beeches, and maples—elms, oaks—almost as many kinds of trees as Connecticut itself had to offer. And there was the moon!—the crescent moon—reflected in a little lake. Sounds, too, rose up to him: the shooshing of leaves, the nighttime countryside whispering of insects and little animals, and—best of all—a brook that was arguing with itself, as it splashed over rocks. The miracle of Central Park, a sheltered wilderness in the midst of the city, pierced Chester Cricket's heart with joy.

"Oh, can we go down?" he shouted up. "Lulu?—please!"

"'Course, Chester C." The pigeon slowed and tilted her wings. "Anything you want. But let's not call on my relatives. They're a drag, and they're all asleep by now anyway."

"I don't want to *visit* anybody!" said Chester, as Lulu Pigeon coasted down through the air, as swiftly and neatly and accurately as a little boy's paper airplane, and landed beside the lake. "All I want is—is—" He didn't know how to say it exactly, but all Chester wanted was to sit beside that shimmering lake—a breeze ruffled its surface—and look at the jiggling reflection of the moon, and enjoy the sweet moisture and the tree-smelling night all around him.

And chirp. Above all, Chester wanted to chirp. Which he did, to his heart's content. And to Lulu Pigeon's heart's content too.

But even the loveliest intervals end.

Song done—one moment more of silent delight—and then Lulu said, "Come on, Chester C., let me show you some more of my town"—by which she meant New York.

"Okay," said Chester, and climbed on her claw again.

"I want you to see it *all* now!" said Lulu. Her wings were beating strongly, rhythmically. "And the best place for that is the Empire State Building."

They rose higher and higher. And the higher they went, the more scared Chester got. Flying up Fifth Avenue had been fun as well as frightening, but now they were heading straight for the top of one of the tallest buildings in all the world.

Chester looked down—the world swirled beneath him—and felt as if his stomach turned over. Or maybe his brain turned around. But something in him felt queasy and dizzy. "Lulu—" he began anxiously, "—I think—"

"Just hold on tight!" Lulu shouted down. "And trust in your feathered friend!"

What Chester had meant to say was that he was afraid he was suffering from a touch of acrophobia—fear of heights. (And perched on a pigeon's claw, on your way to the top of the Empire State, is not the best place to find that you are afraid of great heights.) But even if Lulu hadn't interrupted, the cricket couldn't have finished his sentence. His words were forced back into his throat. For the wind, which had been just a breeze beside the lake, was turning into a raging gale as they spiraled upward, around the building, floor past floor, and approached their final destination: the television antenna tower on the very top.

And they made it! Lulu gripped the pinnacle of the TV antenna with both her claws, accidentally pinching one of Chester's legs as she did so. The whole of New York glowed and sparkled below them.

Now it is strange, but it is true, that although there are many mountains higher than even the tallest buildings, and airplanes can fly much higher than mountains, *nothing* ever seems quite so high as a big building that's been built by men. It suggests our own height to ourselves, I guess.

Chester felt as if not only a city but the entire world was down there where he could look at it. He almost couldn't see the people. 'My gosh!' he thought. 'They look just like bugs.' And he had to laugh at that: like bugs—perhaps crickets—moving up and down the sidewalks. And the cars, the buses, the yellow taxis, all jittered along like miniatures. He felt that kind of spinning sensation inside his head that had made him dizzy on the way up. But he refused to close his eyes. It was too much of an adventure for that.

"Lulu, my foot," said Chester, "you're stepping on it. Could you please—"

"Ooo, I'm sorry," the pigeon apologized. She lifted her claw.

And just at that moment two bad things happened. The first was, Chester caught sight of an airplane swooping low to land at LaGuardia Airport across the East River. The dip of it made his dizziness worse. And the second—worse yet—a sudden gust of wind sprang up, as if a hand gave them both a push. Lulu almost fell off the Empire State.

Lulu *almost* fell off—but Chester *did!* In an instant his legs and feelers were torn away from the pigeon's leg, and before he could say, 'Old Meadow, farewell!' he was tumbling down through the air. One moment the city appeared above him—that meant that he was upside down; then under him—he was right side up; then everything slid from side to side.

He worked his wings, tried to hold them stiff to steady himself—no use, no use! The gleeful wind was playing with

him. It was rolling him, throwing him back and forth, up and down, as a cork is tossed in the surf of a storm. And minute by minute, when he faced that way, the cricket caught glimpses of the floors of the Empire State Building plunging upward as he plunged down.

Despite his panic, his mind took a wink of time off to think: "Well, *this* is something that can't have happened to many crickets before!" (He was right too—it hadn't. And just at that moment Chester wished that it wasn't happening to *him*.)

He guessed, when New York was in the right place again, that he was almost halfway down. The people were looking more and more like people—he heard the cars' engines—and the street and the sidewalk looked *awfully* hard! Then—

Whump! He landed on something both hard and soft. It was hard inside, all muscles and bones, but soft on the surface—feathers!

"Grab on!" a familiar voice shouted. "Tight! Tighter! That's it."

Chester gladly did as he was told.

"*Whooooey!*" Lulu breathed a sigh of relief. "Thought I'd never find you. Been around this darn building at least ten times."

Chester wanted to say, "Thank you, Lulu," but he was so thankful he couldn't get one word out till they'd reached a level where the air was friendly and gently buoyed them up.

But before he could even open his mouth, the pigeon—all ready for another adventure—asked eagerly, "Where now, Chester C.?"

"I guess I better go back to the drainpipe, Lulu. I'm kind of tired."

"Aw, no—!" complained Lulu, who'd been having fun.

"You know, I'm really not all that used to getting blown off the Empire State Building—"

"Oh, all right," said the pigeon. "But first there's one thing you *gotta* see!"

Flying just below the level of turbulent air—good pilot that she was—Lulu headed south, with Chester clinging to the back of her neck. He felt much safer up there, and her wings didn't block out as much of the view as they'd thought. He wanted to ask where they were going, but he sensed from the strength and regularity of her wingbeats that it was to be a rather long flight. And the wind was against them too, which made flying more difficult. Chester held his peace, and watched the city slip beneath them.

They reached the Battery, which is that part of lower New York where a cluster of skyscrapers rise up like a grove of steel trees. But Lulu didn't stop there.

With a gasp and an even tighter hold on her feathers, Chester realized that they'd flown right over the end of Manhattan. There was dark churning water below them. And this was no tame little lake, like the one in Central Park. It was the great deep wide bay that made New York such a mighty harbor. But Lulu showed no sign whatsoever of slowing. Her wings, like beautiful trustworthy machines, pumped on and on and on and on.

At last, Chester saw where the pigeon was heading. On a little island, off to the right, Chester made out the form of a very big lady. Her right hand was holding something up. Of course it was the Statue of Liberty, but Chester had no way of knowing that. In the Old Meadow in Connecticut he never had gone to school—at least not to a school where the pupils use books. His teacher back there had been Nature herself.

Lulu landed at the base of the statue, puffing and panting to get back her breath. She told him a little bit about the lady—a gift from the country of France, it was, and very precious to America—but she hadn't flown him all that way just to give him a history lesson.

"Hop on again, Chester C.!" she commanded—and up they flew to the torch that the lady was holding. Lulu found a perch on the north side of it, so the wind from the south wouldn't bother them.

"Now, just look around!" said Lulu proudly, as if all of New York belonged to her. "And don't anybody ever tell *this* pigeon that there's a more beautiful sight in the world."

Chester did as he was told. He first peered behind. There was Staten Island. And off to the left, New Jersey. To the right, quite a long way away, was Brooklyn. And back across the black water, with a dome of light glowing over it, the heart of the city—Manhattan.

About the Author
George Selden

One night in the Times Square subway station George Selden heard an unexpected sound—the chirp of a cricket. It reminded him of his Connecticut home in the country. It also gave him a great story idea—a country cricket lost in the big, busy city of New York. Mr. Selden invented friends such as a cat, mouse, and pigeon to help Chester Cricket. In all six books that he wrote about Chester Cricket, the theme of friendship is always important.

As a young man, Mr. Selden never guessed he would write books for young people. He was interested in nature, archaeology, and music. But he also loved to read children's literature, even as an adult. His love of literature helped him write great books and win many awards.

About the Illustrator
Garth Williams

Garth Williams was inspired by his parents, who were both artists. He recalls one of his first artistic experiences: "One day my father left his studio door open. I entered and found a pile of drawings he had ready to send to New York. I spent a long time looking at them and adding my art to them. I was not punished. 'I'm afraid he's going to be an artist,' my father said, and removed my additions."

Mr. Williams did become an artist. He has illustrated many books, including several about Chester Cricket.

Reader Response

Open for Discussion

You are Chester Cricket telling your friends back home about the high points of your trip. What are they?

Comprehension Check

1. What parts of the city does Chester see when Lulu takes him on a tour? How are parts of the city different? Use details from the story to support your answer.

2. What do Lulu's and Chester's words and actions tell you about their characters? Make a list of traits for each character.

3. This story is a fantasy, yet Chester's and Lulu's thoughts and conversations seem realistic. Find parts of the story when either Chester or Lulu react as you or your classmates might.

4. **Visualize** Chester's ride as he and Lulu approach Central Park. Describe what he sees. Use as many details from the story as you can. (Visualizing)

5. Look back at page 548. What can you **visualize** about Chester's view of New York City from the top of the Empire State Building? Which words help you picture what the city looks like? (Visualizing)

 Test Prep

Look Back and Write

Look back at pages 538–541. Why do Chester and Lulu set off on their "ride"? Explain your answer by telling what they say and do.

Easy RIDERS

by Howard Robinson

HEY MOM, WHERE WE OFF TO NOW?

By riding piggyback, this baby lemur goes everywhere Mom goes, quickly and safely. Here are some other cool and "easy" ways that other animals get a ride.

NECK TREK

When you were a baby, your parents carried you in their arms or in a backpack. Many kinds of animal babies get carried too. Have you ever seen a mother cat carry her kittens by the scruff of the neck? Lions and other wild cats carry their babies in the same way.

Carried Along by Mom or Dad

HOP ONTO POP

Some dads get into the act too. Both Mom and Pop poison frogs of Central and South America may carry their tadpoles on their backs. After the eggs have hatched, the tadpoles climb on for a ride, and the parent heads to a pool of water. There, the tadpoles slip off and swim away.

Larger animals also do a lot of piggybacking. Water birds, baboons, chimpanzees, opossums, koalas, and lemurs are just a few of the animals that carry their babies piggyback.

GATORS ON THE GO

Even baby alligators and crocodiles may get a lift. Mom builds her nest on land and lays her eggs in it. After the babies hatch, she sometimes picks them up in her mouth (very gently!) and carries them to the safety of nearby water. See the baby crocs peeking out of their mom's mouth?

557

HANG ON AND GO!

The most famous hitchhiker of all might be the remora (re-MORE-uh). Eight species (kinds) of these fish live in warm oceans all around the world. And even though they are good swimmers, they catch a ride whenever they can—on sharks, rays, whales, barracudas, and even sea turtles.

How does a remora hold on? With a plate on top of its head that works like a suction cup. The remora swims up to a large animal and presses this plate against it. The plate grabs hold and sticks tight. Now all the remora has to do is relax and go along for the ride—no matter how fast the animal may swim. (A blue shark may shoot ahead at 40 miles [64km] per hour, but a remora attached to it easily hangs on.)

The remora not only gets a free ride, but it may also get free food. While a shark attacks its prey, for example, food scraps float around in the water. The remora unsticks itself, darts out, and grabs a quick bite. It may also nibble pests from the shark's skin.

A Little Help from a Friend

RIDE A CRAB-MOBILE

You probably wouldn't think of sea anemones (uh-NEM-uh-neez) as hitchhikers because they usually stick to one place. There they wait for tiny fish and other food to come close enough. Then they grab it with their poisonous tentacles.

But some kinds of anemones stick to the snail shells that hermit crabs live in. As the anemones sit there, they get carried wherever the crabs may crawl. When the crabs tear apart their meals, bits of food float close enough for the anemones to get a share.

SEAGOING SNAIL

A violet snail rides the waves on a raft of silvery bubbles. After making the raft, the snail hangs beneath it and floats wherever the wind and waves may take it. When the snail bumps into a jellyfish, it reaches out with its snout and scrapes off bits of flesh for dinner.

Did you check out those white things hanging on to the snail's shell? They're barnacles (BAR-nuh-kulz), and they're waving their feathery brown feet in the water, trying to catch something to eat. The barnacles glued themselves to the snail, and now they're riding the rider!

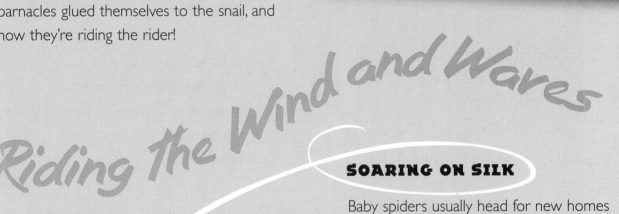

Riding the Wind and Waves

SOARING ON SILK

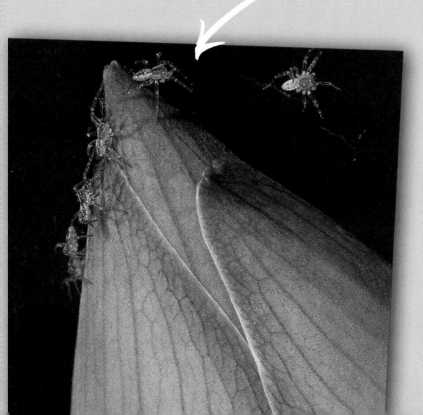

Baby spiders usually head for new homes soon after they hatch. Some kinds sail away by "ballooning." Here's how: First they climb up a tall plant or to any high place, as these spiders are doing. Then they let out long strands of silk from their back ends. The strands catch a breeze and carry the spiders away. A spider may sail for only a few feet. But others may travel hundreds of miles.

These are just a few of the animals that have "easy" ways of getting free rides. There are lots of others, like baby wolf spiders that ride on Mom's back and hawks that get a lift on rising currents of air and . . . Well, why not just go out and try to discover some for yourself?

559

Context Clues

- **Context clues** are words that help explain an unfamiliar word.

- Context clues can appear just before or after an unfamiliar word. But sometimes they are in a different part of the story or article, far from the unfamiliar word.

- Look for specific context clues such as definitions, explanations, examples, and descriptions.

- Using context clues will help you read and understand information more quickly.

Read "Butterfly Memorial" from "A Million Butterflies" from *Time for Kids*.

Write About It

1. Using context clues, tell what *ghetto* and *the Holocaust* mean.

2. What does *remembrance* mean? What context clues helped you figure out its meaning? Where did you find these clues?

Butterfly Memorial
from *Time for Kids*

When Pavel Friedmann was about eleven years old, his family was forced to leave their home in Poland. The Friedmanns and other Jewish families were moved into a walled-off, isolated area called a ghetto. While he was living in the ghetto, Pavel wrote a poem called "The Butterfly." Part of the poem reads,

> Such, such a yellow
> Is carried lightly way up high
> It went away I'm sure because it wished to
> kiss the world
> goodbye.

It was the last butterfly Pavel would ever see. He was one of six million Jewish people who were killed during World War II. The murder of Jews by members of Germany's Nazi Party from 1938 to 1945 is known as the Holocaust. It is considered to be one of the most evil acts in history.

Of the six million Jewish people who died in the Holocaust, 1.2 million were children. Eleanor Schiller, a teacher in Myrtle Beach, South Carolina, was looking for a way to help her students understand the huge number of young lives lost in the Holocaust. After she read Pavel's poem, an idea took flight. She decided to invite students everywhere to create 1,200,000 paper butterflies to display for Holocaust Remembrance Day on April 23. Says Schiller: "I wanted kids to realize that this is a world where we can all work together."

The students at Schiller's religious school, Chabad Academy, have been cutting out butterflies for weeks. They've made about 125,000 butterflies.

Student Becky Hemmo, thirteen, says the project is special to her. "Butterflies are just like children—colorful and free. Butterflies don't live long, and these kids didn't live long. We should remember what happened, to stop it from ever happening again."

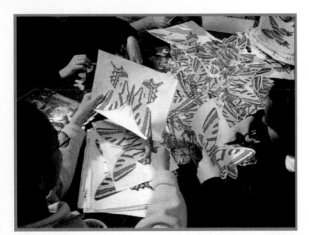

LOOK AHEAD

In *Passage to Freedom,* a Japanese diplomat and his family save hundreds of lives during the Holocaust. As you read, use context clues to figure out words that are unfamiliar to you.

Vocabulary

Words to Know

agreement	superiors	disobey
translated	permission	issue
cable	representatives	

Words with opposite meanings are called **antonyms.** To figure out an unknown word, look at the words nearby. A clue to the meaning could be an antonym.

Read the paragraph below. Notice how *obey* helps you understand *disobey.*

Time to Vote

As town clerk, Juan had ideas about how to improve voter turnout. His superiors were glad to grant him permission to make changes. First he wired his office with cable so he could access the Internet. He created a Web site and posted news about town representatives and translated the news for Spanish-speaking citizens. He also listed some laws people seemed to disobey. If people knew about these laws certainly they would obey them! He suggested that a voting booth be put in the town square. The mayor came to an agreement with Juan and promised to issue a permit for the booth. On election day Juan put up signs that said "Vote Today!"

Write About It

Use vocabulary words to tell how you would improve where you live.

by Ken Mochizuki

Passage to Freedom
The Sugihara Story

illustrated by Dom Lee

There is a saying that the eyes tell everything about a person.

At a store, my father saw a young Jewish boy who didn't have enough money to buy what he wanted. So my father gave the boy some of his. That boy looked into my father's eyes and, to thank him, invited my father to his home.

That is when my family and I went to a Hanukkah celebration for the first time. I was five years old.

In 1940, my father was a diplomat, representing the country of Japan. Our family lived in a small town in the small country called Lithuania. There was my father and mother, my Auntie Setsuko, my younger brother Chiaki, and my three-month-old baby brother, Haruki. My father worked in his office downstairs.

In the mornings, birds sang in the trees. We played with girls and boys from the neighborhood at a huge park near our home. Houses and churches around us were hundreds of years old. In our room, Chiaki and I played with toy German soldiers, tanks, and planes. Little did we know that the real soldiers were coming our way.

Then one early morning in late July, my life changed forever.

My mother and Auntie Setsuko woke Chiaki and me up, telling us to get dressed quickly. My father ran upstairs from his office.

"There are a lot of people outside," my mother said. "We don't know what is going to happen."

In the living room, my parents told my brother and me not to let anybody see us looking through the window. So, I parted the curtains a tiny bit. Outside, I saw hundreds of people crowded around the gate in front of our house.

The grown-ups shouted in Polish, a language I did not understand. Then I saw the children. They stared at our house through the iron bars of the gate. Some of them were my age. Like the grown-ups, their eyes were red from not having slept for days. They wore heavy winter coats—some wore more than one coat, even though it was warm outside. These children looked as though they had dressed in a hurry. But if they came from somewhere else, where were their suitcases?

"What do they want?" I asked my mother.

"They have come to ask for your father's help," she replied. "Unless we help, they may be killed or taken away by some bad men."

Some of the children held on tightly to the hands of their fathers, some clung to their mothers. One little girl sat on the ground, crying.

I felt like crying too. "Father," I said, "please help them."

My father stood quietly next to me, but I knew he saw the children. Then some of the men in the crowd began climbing over the fence. Borislav and Gudje, two young men who worked for my father, tried to keep the crowd calm.

My father walked outside. Peering through the curtains, I saw him standing on the steps. Borislav translated what my father said: He asked the crowd to choose five people to come inside and talk.

My father met downstairs with the five men. My father could speak Japanese, Chinese, Russian, German, French, and English. At this meeting, everyone spoke Russian.

I couldn't help but stare out the window and watch the crowd, while downstairs, for two hours, my father listened to frightening stories. These people were refugees—people who ran away from their homes because, if they stayed, they would be killed. They were Jews from Poland, escaping from the Nazi soldiers who had taken over their country.

The five men had heard my father could give them visas— official written permission to travel through another country. The hundreds of Jewish refugees outside hoped to travel east through the Soviet Union and end up in Japan. Once in Japan, they could go to another country. Was it true? the men asked. Could my father issue these visas? If he did not, the Nazis would soon catch up with them.

My father answered that he could issue a few, but not hundreds. To do that, he would have to ask for permission from his government in Japan.

That night, the crowd stayed outside our house. Exhausted from the day's excitement, I slept soundly. But it was one of the worst nights of my father's life. He had to make a decision. If he helped these people, would he put our family in danger? If the Nazis found out, what would they do?

But if he did not help these people, they could all die.

My mother listened to the bed squeak as my father tossed and turned all night.

The next day, my father said he was going to ask his government about the visas. My mother agreed it was the right thing to do. My father sent his message by cable. Gudje took my father's written message down to the telegraph office.

I watched the crowd as they waited for the Japanese government's reply. The five representatives came into our house several times that day to ask if an answer had been received. Any time the gate opened, the crowd tried to charge inside.

Finally, the answer came from the Japanese government. It was "no." My father could not issue that many visas to Japan. For the next two days, he thought about what to do.

Hundreds more Jewish refugees joined the crowd. My father sent a second message to his government, and again the answer was "no." We still couldn't go outside. My little brother Haruki cried often because we were running out of milk.

I grew tired of staying indoors. I asked my father constantly, "Why are these people here? What do they want? Why do they have to be here? Who are they?"

My father always took the time to explain everything to me. He said the refugees needed his help, that they needed permission from him to go to another part of the world where they would be safe.

"I cannot help these people yet," he calmly told me. "But when the time comes, I will help them all that I can."

My father cabled his superiors yet a third time, and I knew the answer by the look in his eyes. That night, he said to my mother, "I have to do something. I may have to disobey my government, but if I don't, I will be disobeying my conscience."

The next morning, he brought the family together and asked what he should do. This was the first time he ever asked all of us to help him with anything.

My mother and Auntie Setsuko had already made up their minds. They said we had to think about the people outside before we thought about ourselves. And that is what my parents had always told me—that I must think as if I were in someone else's place. If I were one of those children out there, what would I want someone to do for me?

I said to my father, "If we don't help them, won't they die?"

With the entire family in agreement, I could tell a huge weight was lifted off my father's shoulders. His voice was firm as he told us, "I will start helping these people."

Outside, the crowd went quiet as my father spoke, with Borislav translating.

"I will issue visas to each and every one of you to the last. So, please wait patiently."

The crowd stood frozen for a second. Then the refugees burst into cheers. Grown-ups embraced each other, and some reached to the sky. Fathers and mothers hugged their children. I was especially glad for the children.

My father opened the garage door and the crowd tried to rush in. To keep order, Borislav handed out cards with numbers. My father wrote out each visa by hand. After he finished each one, he looked into the eyes of the person receiving the visa and said, "Good luck."

Refugees camped out at our favorite park, waiting to see my father. I was finally able to go outside.

Chiaki and I played with the other children in our toy car. They pushed as we rode, and they rode as we pushed. We chased each other around the big trees. We did not speak the same language, but that didn't stop us.

For about a month, there was always a line leading to the garage. Every day, from early in the morning till late at night, my father tried to write three hundred visas. He watered down the ink to make it last. Gudje and a young Jewish man helped out by stamping my father's name on the visas.

My mother offered to help write the visas, but my father insisted he be the only one, so no one else could get into trouble. So my mother watched the crowd and told my father how many were still in line.

One day, my father pressed down so hard on his fountain pen, the tip broke off. During that month, I only saw him late at night. His eyes were always red and he could hardly talk. While he slept, my mother massaged his arm, stiff and cramped from writing all day.

Soon my father grew so tired, he wanted to quit writing the visas. But my mother encouraged him to continue. "Many people are still waiting," she said. "Let's issue some more visas and save as many lives as we can."

While the Germans approached from the west, the Soviets came from the east and took over Lithuania. They ordered my father to leave. So did the Japanese government, which reassigned him to Germany. Still, my father wrote the visas until we absolutely had to move out of our home. We stayed at a hotel for two days, where my father still wrote visas for the many refugees who followed him there.

Then it was time to leave Lithuania. Refugees who had slept at the train station crowded around my father. Some refugee men surrounded my father to protect him. He now just issued permission papers—blank pieces of paper with his signature.

As the train pulled away, refugees ran alongside. My father still handed permission papers out the window. As the train picked up speed, he threw them out to waiting hands. The people in the front of the crowd looked into my father's eyes and cried, "We will never forget you! We will see you again!"

I gazed out the train window, watching Lithuania and the crowd of refugees fade away. I wondered if we would ever see them again.

"Where are we going?" I asked my father.

"We are going to Berlin," he replied.

Chiaki and I became very excited about going to the big city. I had so many questions for my father. But he fell asleep as soon as he settled into his seat. My mother and Auntie Setsuko looked really tired too.

Back then, I did not fully understand what the three of them had done, or why it was so important.

I do now.

Afterword

Each time that I think about what my father did at Kaunas, Lithuania, in 1940, my appreciation and understanding of the incident continues to grow. In fact, it makes me very emotional to realize that his deed saved thousands of lives, and that I had the opportunity to be a part of it.

I am proud that my father had the courage to do the right thing. Yet, his superiors in the Japanese government did not agree. The years after my family left Kaunas were difficult ones. We were imprisoned for eighteen months in a Soviet internment camp; and when we finally returned to Japan, my father was asked to resign from diplomatic service. After holding several different jobs, my father joined an export company, where he worked until his retirement in 1976.

My father remained concerned about the fate of the refugees, and at one point left his address at the Israeli Embassy in Japan. Finally, in the 1960s, he started hearing from "Sugihara survivors," many of whom had kept their visas, and considered the worn pieces of paper to be family treasures.

In 1969, my father was invited to Israel, where he was taken to the famous Holocaust memorial, Yad Vashem. In 1985, he was chosen to receive the "Righteous Among Nations" Award from Yad Vashem. He was the first and only Asian to have been given this great honor.

In 1992, six years after his death, a monument to my father was dedicated in his birthplace of Yaotsu, Japan, on a hill that is now known as the Hill of Humanity. In 1994, a group of Sugihara survivors traveled to Japan to re-dedicate the monument in a ceremony that was attended by several high officials of the Japanese government.

The story of what my father and my family experienced in 1940 is an important one for young people today. It is a story that I believe will inspire you to care for all people and to respect life. It is a story that proves that one person can make a difference.

Thank you.
Hiroki Sugihara

About the Author
Ken Mochizuki

Ken Mochizuki, who wrote Hiroki Sugihara's story in *Passage to Freedom,* is an American—an Asian American. Because of his Asian features, though, some people incorrectly assume that he is from an Asian country. Sometimes people even ask him if he speaks English! Because of these experiences, Mr. Mochizuki wants "to show that people of Asian and Pacific Islander descent in this country are Americans who are a part of everyday American life, and they have been Americans for a long time."

The message in his books applies to people of all backgrounds. "I hope to convey to young readers that they should actually get to know others, rather than to assume things about them," he says.

Baseball Saved Us was Mr. Mochizuki's first book. It is the story of how Americans of Japanese descent were imprisoned in internment camps during World War II. It was given the Parents' Choice Award.

About the Illustrator
Dom Lee

Passage to Freedom is the third book that Dom Lee has illustrated for Ken Mochizuki. He also created the illustrations for Mr. Mochizuki's books *Baseball Saved Us* and *Heroes.*

Mr. Lee moved to the United States from Seoul, Korea, when he decided that he wanted to be a book illustrator. After arriving in the U.S. and earning a master's degree in fine art, Mr. Lee won his first chance to illustrate a book after an editor saw his work at an art exhibition.

Reader Response

Open for Discussion

If you were Hiroki's father, what would be going on in your mind before you made the decision to write the visas?

Comprehension Check

1. Do you think that Hiroki's mother showed courage? Give examples from the selection to support your answer.

2. At the end of the selection, Hiroki says that back then, he did not fully understand what his family had done. Find sentences to show what Hiroki *did* understand and feel.

3. Do you think that Hiroki's memory of his family's first Hanukkah celebration is a good way to begin the selection? Why or why not?

4. What **context clues** helped you figure out the meaning of *refugees* on page 567? (Context Clues)

5. What do you think *reassigned* means on page 572? Where did you find **context clues** to help you figure out the meaning? (Context Clues)

Test Prep
Look Back and Write

Look back at pages 568–570. How did Mr. Sugihara's family help him make his decision to assist the Jewish refugees? Find details to support your answer.

1939 1940 1950 1960

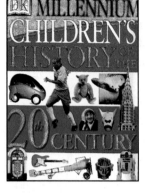

Jazz king is "In the Mood"

AUGUST 1

The rich saxophone sound of the Glenn Miller Band has scored a huge hit in the United States with its latest recording, the swinging riff tune "In the Mood." Thirty-five-year-old Miller is now established as one of the country's most popular band leaders. The Glenn Miller Band is famous for its popular orchestrated dance music. Its leader achieves the band's distinctive sound by blending the playing of a clarinet with a quartet of saxophones.

17-year-old Judy goes to Oz

AUGUST 17

Tonight is the Hollywood premiere of a new film, *The Wizard of Oz*, a magical $3 million Technicolor musical fantasy starring a bright new actress, 17-year-old Judy Garland. The story follows the dream adventures of Dorothy, who is carried away by a twister to the magical land of the Munchkins, where she meets a scarecrow, a tin man, and a cowardly lion.

Dorothy meets the scarecrow on the yellow brick road.

Young evacuees arrive in the countryside.

British children evacuate cities

AUGUST 31

As the prospect of war with Germany draws nearer, one-and-a-half million British children are being evacuated out of large cities and into safer areas in the countryside or small towns that are less likely to be targets of air raids. The children, who are being accompanied by their schoolteachers, are only allowed to carry one spare set of clothes and a gas mask. Buses have been taken off their usual routes to carry the children to train stations. Billeting officers are receiving the "townie" children and introducing them to their new host families.

JULY – SEPTEMBER

JUL UK prime minister Winston Churchill urges the UK to make a military alliance with the Soviet Union.

AUG The Soviet Union shocks the rest of Europe by signing a nonaggression pact with Germany.

Nazi-Soviet Pact

SEP US president Franklin D. Roosevelt announces that the US will remain neutral in the European war.

SEP Stained-glass windows are removed from Notre Dame Cathedral for fear of air raids in Paris, France.

SEP The first football game is televised by NBC-TV from Randall's Island, New York.

SEP In the US, Birds Eye introduces the first precooked frozen meals, chicken fricassée and steak.

North Rose Window

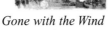

German tanks advance into Poland.

Poland is invaded

SEPTEMBER 1

Hitler has invaded Poland. The invasion began when the Luftwaffe, the German air force, led by state-of-the-art dive-bombers, launched a massive attack on Polish air-fields, communication centers, and the entire railroad system. Columns of fast-moving German tanks raced ahead of the Polish infantry, cutting supply lines and spreading mass panic and terror. It is the first time the Germans have used their revolutionary "Blitzkrieg," or "lightning war," tactics, which are aimed at taking the enemy by surprise.

War is declared

SEPTEMBER 3

At 11:15 this morning, the British prime minister Neville Chamberlain informed an anxious nation that Britain is at war with Germany. Yesterday the British government had issued Adolf Hitler with an ultimatum demanding he withdraw all German forces from Poland. Hitler failed to reply, and conse-quently Britain declared war. Some hours later, the French ultimatum ran out, and at 5 P.M. France, too, declared war. The World War I Allies of 1914 find themselves once again united in a war against oppression.

Winter war in Finland

NOVEMBER 30

The Soviet Union has invaded Finland after the Finns refused to surrender Karelia, an area of land bordering the outskirts of the Soviet city of Leningrad. Over a million soldiers of the Red Army have launched a massive attack across the frozen waters that divide Finland from Russia. The Finns have only a handful of tanks and aircraft, but their ski patrols are very well trained for conducting warfare in the snow.

DISPATCH
SPECIAL LATE NEWS
WAR
OFFICIAL

OCTOBER – DECEMBER

NOV In Munich, Germany, Adolf Hitler narrowly escapes a bomb explosion that kills seven high-ranking Nazis.

NOV Magnetic mines laid by German submarines sink 60,000 tons of British shipping off the east coast of England.

DEC *Gone with the Wind,* the most eagerly awaited film of the year, is released in the US.

DEC In the US, General Electric launches the first refrigerator with a freezer compartment.

Gone with the Wind

DEC In London, UK, the Royal Opera House is turned into a dance-hall to entertain the public during blackouts.

DEC In the US, nylon stockings go on sale for the first time, at a price of $1.15 a pair.

Nylon Stockings

Paraphrasing

- **Paraphrasing** is explaining something in your own words.

- When you paraphrase, include only the author's ideas and opinions.

- Check your paraphrasing by asking yourself, "Did I use my own words? Did I keep the author's meaning?"

- Use paraphrasing as a strategy when you study for tests and when you need to give information in oral and written reports.

Read "Samuel Adams" from *Why Don't You Get a Horse, Sam Adams?* by Jean Fritz.

Talk About It

1. Tell a friend what this article is about.

2. Reread the article and think about what you told your friend. Did you use your own words? Did you accidentally change the authors meaning?

3. If you had to write a report about Samual Adams, how could you use paraphrasing?

Samuel Adams

by Jean Fritz

Samuel Adams didn't want the British soldiers, or redcoats, to control the colonies in America. He became one of the leaders of the revolution against England.

By 1775 Samuel was talking openly of independence. He was fifty-three years old now and at the top of the king's "most wanted" list of American traitors. John Hancock was on the list too.

On April 18 the redcoats marched out of Boston, looking for an American cannon that was hidden in Concord and looking (so it was said) for Samuel Adams and John Hancock, who were hidden in a friend's house in Lexington. Samuel wasn't afraid of trouble. The more trouble there was with the redcoats, the sooner Americans would be willing to declare their independence and the better he'd like it. But of course, he preferred not to be caught.

Fortunately for Samuel and John, the Americans had discovered what the English were up to. Ahead of the redcoats rode Paul Revere. He galloped up to the house where Samuel Adams and John Hancock were staying.

"The redcoats are coming!" he cried.

Samuel jumped out of bed, ready to fly for his life. (He was in such a hurry that he left his watch under his pillow.) John also jumped out of bed, but he was more eager to fight than to fly. He grabbed his sword and began to polish it.

Samuel told him to put his sword away. "We aren't meant to be soldiers," he said. "We are the brains behind the Revolution. It is our duty to escape."

Reluctantly John put his sword away and made ready to escape. Now, of course, as everyone knows, the way to escape from an enemy is on the back of a horse. You lean forward and with hooves thundering behind, you streak into the night. But Samuel Adams couldn't ride a horse.

LOOK AHEAD

Samuel Adams escaped from the British because of Paul Revere's warning cries. "Paul Revere's Ride" is a poem that describes the night Paul Revere made those warnings. Think about how you would paraphrase the story the poem tells.

Vocabulary

Words to Know

fate	glimmer	magnified
fearless	lingers	somber
tread	steed	

When you read, you may come across a word you don't know. To figure out its meaning, look for clues, such as an explanation, near the unknown word.

Read the paragraph below. Notice how the explanation of *glimmer* helps you understand what it means.

"The Star-Spangled Banner"

It is September of 1814. Francis Scott Key is on a British ship, which fires at Fort McHenry. What will be the fort's <u>fate</u>? Key imagines hearing the gallop of a <u>steed</u> and the <u>tread</u> of <u>fearless</u> American soldiers on the move. At dawn, a <u>glimmer</u> of light appears in the sky. Key <u>lingers</u> on the <u>somber</u> deck, watching the faint, unsteady light. Suddenly he sees the huge U.S. flag flying above Fort McHenry. The size of the flag is <u>magnified</u> even more by the dawn's light. This glorious sight inspires Key to write the poem that Americans now know as their national anthem.

Write About It

Use vocabulary words to tell how your national anthem makes you feel.

Paul Revere's Ride

by Henry Wadsworth Longfellow
illustrated by Ted Rand

Listen, my children, and you shall hear
Of the midnight ride of Paul Revere,
On the eighteenth of April, in Seventy-five;
Hardly a man is now alive
Who remembers that famous day and year.

He said to his friend, "If the British march
By land or sea from the town tonight,
Hang a lantern aloft in the belfry arch
Of the North Church tower as a signal light —

One, if by land, and two, if by sea;
And I on the opposite shore will be,
Ready to ride and spread the alarm
Through every Middlesex village and farm,
For the country folk to be up and to arm."

Then he said, "Good night!" and with muffled oar
Silently rowed to the Charlestown shore,
Just as the moon rose over the bay,
Where swinging wide at her moorings lay
The *Somerset*, British man-of-war;
A phantom ship, with each mast and spar
Across the moon like a prison bar,
And a huge black hulk, that was magnified
By its own reflection in the tide.

Meanwhile, his friend, through alley and street,
Wanders and watches, with eager ears,
Till in the silence around him he hears
The muster of men at the barrack door,
And the measured tread of the grenadiers,
Marching down to their boats on the shore.

Then he climbed to the tower of the Old North Church,
By the wooden stairs, with stealthy tread,
To the belfry-chamber overhead,
And startled the pigeons from their perch
On the somber rafters, that round him made
Masses and moving shapes of shade —

By the trembling ladder, steep and tall,
To the highest window in the wall,
Where he paused to listen and look down
A moment on the roofs of the town,
And the moonlight flowing over all.

Beneath in the churchyard, lay the dead,
In their night-encampment on the hill,
Wrapped in silence so deep and still
That he could hear, like a sentinel's tread,
The watchful night-wind, as it went
Creeping along from tent to tent,
And seeming to whisper, "All is well!"

A moment only he feels the spell
Of the place and the hour, and the secret dread
Of the lonely belfry and the dead;
For suddenly all his thoughts are bent
On a shadowy something far away,
Where the river widens to meet the bay —
A line of black that bends and floats
On the rising tide, like a bridge of boats.

Meanwhile, impatient to mount and ride,
Booted and spurred, with a heavy stride
On the opposite shore walked Paul Revere.

Now he patted his horse's side,
Now gazed at the landscape far and near,
Then, impetuous, stamped the earth,
And turned and tightened his saddle girth;

But mostly he watched with eager search
The belfry tower of the Old North Church,
As it rose above the graves on the hill,
Lonely and spectral and somber and still.

And lo! as he looks, on the belfry's height
A glimmer, and then a gleam of light!
He springs to the saddle, the bridle he turns,
But lingers and gazes, till full on his sight
A second lamp in the belfry burns!

A hurry of hoofs in a village street,
A shape in the moonlight, a bulk in the dark,
And beneath, from the pebbles, in passing, a spark
Struck out by a steed flying fearless and fleet:

That was all! And yet, through the gloom and the light,
The fate of a nation was riding that night;
And the spark struck out by that steed, in his flight,
Kindled the land into flame with its heat.

He has left the village and mounted the steep,
And beneath him, tranquil and broad and deep,
Is the Mystic, meeting the ocean tides;
And under the alders that skirt its edge,
Now soft on the sand, now loud on the ledge,
Is heard the tramp of his steed as he rides.

It was twelve by the village clock,
When he crossed the bridge into Medford town.
He heard the crowing of the cock,
And the barking of the farmer's dog,
And felt the damp of the river fog,
That rises after the sun goes down.

It was one by the village clock,
When he galloped into Lexington.
He saw the gilded weathercock
Swim in the moonlight as he passed,
And the meeting-house windows, blank and bare,
Gaze at him with a spectral glare,
As if they already stood aghast
At the bloody work they would look upon.

It was two by the village clock,
When he came to the bridge in Concord town.
He heard the bleating of the flock,
And the twitter of birds among the trees,
And felt the breath of the morning breeze
Blowing over the meadows brown.

And one was safe and asleep in his bed
Who at the bridge would be first to fall,
Who that day would be lying dead,
Pierced by a British musket-ball.

You know the rest. In the books you have read
How the British Regulars fired and fled —
How the farmers gave them ball for ball,
From behind each fence and farmyard wall,
Chasing the redcoats down the lane,
Then crossing the fields to emerge again
Under the trees at the turn of the road,
And only pausing to fire and load.

So through the night rode Paul Revere;
And so through the night went his cry of alarm
To every Middlesex village and farm —
A cry of defiance and not of fear,
A voice in the darkness, a knock at the door,
And a word that shall echo for evermore!

For, borne on the night-wind of the Past,
Through all our history, to the last,
In the hour of darkness and peril and need,
The people will awaken and listen to hear
The hurrying hoof-beats of that steed,
And the midnight message of Paul Revere.

About the Author
Henry Wadsworth Longfellow

During his lifetime (1807–1882), Henry Wadsworth Longfellow was probably the best-loved American poet. Of the hundreds of poems that he wrote, *Paul Revere's Ride* is the one for which he is most remembered. Mr. Longfellow also wrote about other well-known figures in American history including Miles Standish, John and Priscilla Alden, and Hiawatha.

Mr. Longfellow was born in Portland, Maine. As a boy, he did very well in school. In fact, he entered college at the age of fourteen. By the time Mr. Longfellow was forty-seven, he decided that the only thing he wanted to do was write. In 1868, he became the first American poet to be honored in England with a statue in the Poet's Corner at Westminster Abbey in London.

About the Illustrator
Ted Rand

Besides illustrating children's books, Ted Rand has worked as a teacher and a portrait and landscape painter. His paintings have been exhibited in art shows in New York, Honolulu, San Francisco, and Seattle.

Except for his four years in the U.S. Navy, Mr. Rand has lived in the state of Washington his whole life. He currently lives on Mercer Island with his wife, who is a children's book author. The Rands have collaborated on several books, including *Prince William* and *The Cabin Key*.

Reader Response

Open for Discussion
What is your favorite stanza from the poem? Read it aloud.

Comprehension Check

1. Paul Revere appears to be following a schedule. Make a time line that shows all of the places Paul Revere went. If possible, include the time of day he arrived.

2. Why does the poet say that the meeting-house windows in Lexington looked "as if they already stood aghast at the bloody work they would look upon"?

3. Paul Revere was a real person. Why do you think a poem was written about his ride on a horse? Use the text and illustrations to support your answer.

4. **Paraphrase** the text on the first page of *Paul Revere's Ride*, beginning after the words "He said to his friend." How are the words you use different from the words in the poem? (Paraphrasing)

5. Now **paraphrase** the text on page 589 and page 591. What are some of the words you used in place of the poem's words? (Paraphrasing)

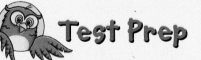 **Test Prep**

Look Back and Write

Look back at pages 584–595. What does Paul Revere mean by "One, if by land, and two, if by sea"? Explain what this message means and why it is so important to the people in the villages and farms.

Sybil
Sounds the Alarm

by Drollene P. Brown

☆☆☆

A red sky at night does not usually cause wonder. But on the evening of April 26, 1777, the residents of Ludingtons' Mills were concerned. The crimson glow was in the east, not from the west where the sun was setting.

The Ludington family sat at supper, each one glancing now and again toward the eastern window. Sybil, at sixteen the oldest of eight children, could read the question in her mother's worried eyes. Would Henry Ludington have to go away again? As commander of the only colonial army regiment between Danbury, Connecticut, and Peekskill, New York, Sybil's father did not have much time to be with his family.

Thudding hooves in the yard abruptly ended their meal. The colonel pushed back his chair and strode to the door. Although Sybil followed him

☆☆☆☆☆☆☆☆☆☆☆☆☆☆☆☆☆☆☆☆☆☆☆☆☆☆☆☆☆☆☆☆☆☆☆

with her eyes, she dutifully began to help her sister Rebecca clear the table.

The girls were washing dishes when their father burst back into the room with a courier at his side.

"Here, Seth," said the colonel, "sit you down and have some supper. Rebecca, see to our weary friend."

Sybil, glancing over her shoulder, saw that the stranger was no older than she. A familiar flame of indignation burned her cheeks. Being a girl kept her from being a soldier!

Across the room, her parents were talking together in low tones. Her father's voice rose.

"Sybil, leave the dishes and come here," he said.

Obeying quickly, she overheard her father as he again spoke to her mother.

"Abigail, she is a skilled rider. It is Sybil who has trained Star, and the horse will obey her like no other.

"That red glow in the sky," Colonel Ludington said, turning now to his daughter, "is from Danbury. It's been burned by British raiders. There are about two thousand Redcoats, and they're heading for Ridgefield. Someone must tell our men that the lull in the fighting is over; they will have to leave their families and crops again."

"I'll go! Star and I can do it!" Sybil exclaimed. She faced her mother. "Star is sure of foot, and will carry me safely."

"There are dangers other than slippery paths," her mother said, softly. "Outlaws or deserters or Tories or even British soldiers may be met. You must be wary in a way that Star cannot."

A lump rose in Sybil's throat. "I can do it," she declared.

Without another word, Abigail Ludington turned to fetch a woolen cape to protect her daughter from the wind and rain. One of the boys was sent to saddle Star, and Sybil was soon ready. When she had swung up on her sturdy horse, the colonel placed a stick in her hand.

As though reciting an oath, she repeated her father's directions: "Go south by the river, then along Horse Pound Road to Mahopac Pond. From there, turn right to Red Mills, then go north to Stormville." The colonel stood back and saluted. She was off!

At the first few isolated houses, windows or doors flew open as she approached. She shouted her message and rode on. By the time she reached the first hamlet, all was dark. There were many small houses there at the edge of Shaw's Road, but everyone was in bed. Lights had not flared up at the sound of Star's hoofbeats. Sybil had not anticipated this. Biting her lower lip, she pulled Star to a halt. After considering for a moment, she nudged the horse forward, and riding up to one cottage after another, beat on each door with her stick.

"Look at the sky!" she shouted. "Danbury's burning! All men muster at Ludingtons'!"

At each village or cluster of houses, she repeated the cry.

When lights began to shine and people were yelling and moving about, she would spur her horse onward. Before she and Star melted into the night, the village bells would be pealing out the alarm.

Paths were slippery with mud and wet stones, and the terrain was often hilly and wooded. Sybil's ears strained for sounds of other riders who might try to steal her horse or stop her mission. Twice she pulled Star off the path while unknown riders passed within a few feet. Both times, her fright dried her mouth and made her hands tremble.

By the time they reached Stormville, Star had stumbled several times, and Sybil's voice was almost gone. The town's call to arms was sounding as they turned homeward. Covered with mud, tired beyond belief, Sybil could barely stay on Star's back when they rode into their yard. She had ridden more than thirty miles that night.

In a daze, she saw the red sky in the east. It was the dawn. Several hundred men were milling about. She had roused them in time, and Ludington's regiment marched out to join the Connecticut militia in routing the British at Ridgefield, driving them back to their ships on Long Island Sound.

Afterward, General George Washington made a personal visit to Ludingtons' Mills to thank Sybil for her courageous deed. Statesman Alexander Hamilton wrote her a letter of praise.

Two centuries later, visitors to the area of Patterson, New York, can still follow Sybil's route. A statue of Sybil on horseback stands at Lake Gleneida in Carmel, New York, and people in that area know well the heroism of Sybil Ludington. In 1978, a commemorative postage stamp was issued in her honor, bringing national attention to the heroic young girl who rode for independence.

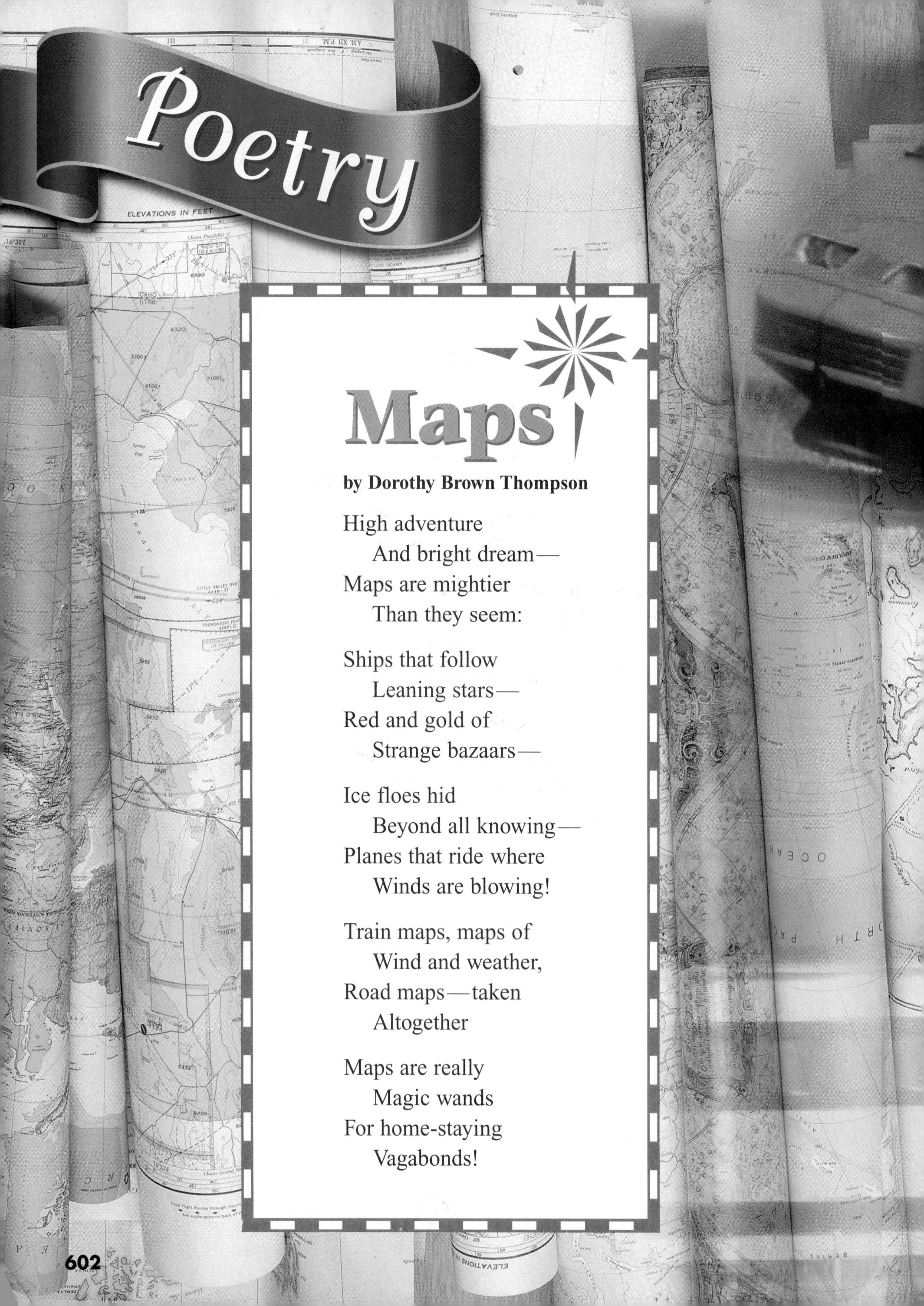

Maps

by Dorothy Brown Thompson

High adventure
    And bright dream—
Maps are mightier
    Than they seem:

Ships that follow
    Leaning stars—
Red and gold of
    Strange bazaars—

Ice floes hid
    Beyond all knowing—
Planes that ride where
    Winds are blowing!

Train maps, maps of
    Wind and weather,
Road maps—taken
    Altogether

Maps are really
    Magic wands
For home-staying
    Vagabonds!

Travel

by Edna St. Vincent Millay

The railroad track is miles away,
    And the day is loud with voices speaking,
Yet there isn't a train goes by all day
    But I hear its whistles shrieking.

All night there isn't a train goes by,
    Though the night is still for sleep and dreaming
But I see its cinders red on the sky
    And hear its engine steaming.

My heart is warm with the friends I make,
    And better friends I'll not be knowing,
Yet there isn't a train I wouldn't take,
    No matter where it's going.

Miss Pearl

by Angela Johnson

She told immigrant stories,
and talked about growing up in
Jamaica when she got sad.
She stayed clear of heavy traffic,
and walked down the dirt back roads
after the sun went down.
Miss Pearl would cook all day long,
and stay up all night
feeding me and Walter jerk chicken.
She says leaving Shorter is
like leaving Jamaica
and her family again.
She says she'll move to Atlanta
to live with her grandniece.
But she'll miss the dirt roads.
And when I tell her
she might like the city,
she asks me if I do.
But instead I tell her about growing
up in Shorter.

Mountain Mist

by Francisco X. Alarcón

tender
breath
of mountains

playful
steam
clouding

the windows
of the village
bakery

the golden
eyeglasses
of my father

the windshield
of my family's
station wagon

as we cross
Mexico's western
mountain range

Wrap-Up

Where do people's journeys take them?

Who's Who

Write a Biographical Entry

A journey may be a trip from one place to another, or it may be an experience that changes someone's life. Think about the people and main characters in the selections in this unit. How are their lives changed by the journeys they take?

1. **Choose** the person or character that interests you most.

2. **Reread** to get the highlights of her or his story.

3. **Write** a brief entry for a biographical encyclopedia. In 3–4 sentences tell who your person or character is and what changed her or his life.

Travels

Compare Rides

Chester in *Chester Cricket's Pigeon Ride* and Paul Revere in *Paul Revere's Ride* both go for a ride.

1. **Make** a chart with these headings: *Character, Where he went, Why he went, Results of his ride.*

2. Fill in the chart. **Reread** the selections for more details.

3. Use the chart to **explain** how Chester Cricket's and Paul Revere's rides are different.

Message to the World

Create a Rights Poster

Lila in "I Want to Vote," Harriet Tubman in "The Long Path to Freedom," and Mr. Sugihara in *Passage to Freedom* all work to win basic rights for themselves or others. Which one do you admire most? What rights does he or she try to win?

1. **Write** one sentence that might be that person's "message to the world."

2. **Create** a poster with that sentence as its main message. Add a picture that will catch people's attention. Display your work.

"All Together Now . . ."

Present a Choral Reading

With 3–4 of your classmates, choose an exciting part of a selection to read aloud.

1. **Plan** who will read what lines. Some lines should be read solo—with one reader narrating or playing a person or character. Some lines should be read by two people, and some should be read by the whole group.

2. **Rehearse** your presentation at least one time all the way through.

3. **Perform** your reading for an audience.

Test Talk

Answer the Question

Write the Answer

Tests often tell you to write an answer. A test about "How the Underground Railroad Got Its Name," pages 529–531, might have this question.

Test Question 1

How does the term *underground railroad* describe the way many slaves in the South made their way to the free states of the North? Explain, using details from the article.

Get ready to answer.

- Read the question to find key words.

- Finish the statement "I need to find out . . ."

- Decide where to look for the answer.

- Make notes on details for your answer and check them.

Write your answer.

- Begin your answer with words from the question. Include details from your notes.

- Check your answer. Ask yourself:

  ✓ **Is my answer correct?** Are some details incorrect?

  ✓ **Is my answer complete?** Do I need to add more details?

  ✓ **Is my answer focused?** Do all my details come from the selection? Do they all help answer the question?

See how one student writes a correct, complete, and focused response.

I'll start my answer with words from the question. "The term **underground railroad** describes the way . . ." I remember that railroads were just getting started, but I need to explain why the slaves' escapes made people think of a railroad—and why it was "underground."

The term <u>underground railroad</u> describes the way many slaves made their way to the free states of the North because the escaping slaves traveled in secret, or "underground." They followed established paths like rails, they stopped off at safety houses like stations or depots, and they were helped by people who showed them the way like railroad conductors. . . .

Try it!

Write correct, complete, and focused answers to these test questions about "How the Underground Railroad Got Its Name," pages 529–531.

Test Question 2

Why are the stories of many slaves who escaped and many people who helped them lost to history? Use details from the article to support your answer.

Test Question 3

Look back at the map on page 531. Did the United States have more slave states or more free states in 1860? How can you tell?

Think of It!

How do we find

a new way?

Theme

- **Theme** is an underlying meaning or message of a story. A story can have more than one theme.

- Themes can be statements, lessons, or generalizations that stand on their own such as: *Life is what you make of it*.

- Sometimes the author states a theme directly. Sometimes readers have to figure out a theme on their own by asking, "What did I learn by reading this story?"

- Look for evidence in the story to support the theme or themes.

Read "King Midas" from *Favorite Greek Myths* retold by Mary Pope Osborne.

Write About It

1. What do you think is the theme of this story?

2. What evidence in the story supports this theme?

King Midas

retold by Mary Pope Osborne

"King Midas," Bacchus said, "because you have been so hospitable to me—ask for anything you wish, and I will grant it to you."

"What an idea!" said Midas. "Anything I wish?"

"Indeed, anything," said Bacchus.

"Ah, well," said the king, chuckling. "Of course, there's only one thing: I wish that everything I touch would turn to gold!" Midas looked sideways at Bacchus, for he couldn't believe such a gift could really be his.

"My friend, you already have all the gold you could possibly want," said Bacchus, looking disappointed.

"Oh, no! I don't!" said Midas. "One never has enough gold!"

"Well, if that's what you wish for, I suppose I will have to grant it," said Bacchus.

Bacchus soon took his leave. As Midas waved good-bye to him, his hand brushed

an oak twig hanging from a tree—and the twig turned to gold!

Midas looked around excitedly. He leaned over and picked a stone up from the ground—and the stone turned into a golden nugget! He kicked the sand—and the sand turned to golden grains!

King Midas threw back his head and shouted, "I'm the richest man in the world!" Then he rushed about his grounds, touching everything. And everything, *everything* turned to gold: ears of corn in his fields! Apples plucked from the trees! The pillars of his mansion!

Finally, exhausted but overjoyed, King Midas called for his dinner. His servants placed a huge banquet meal before him on his lawn. "Oh, I'm so hungry!" he said as he speared a piece of meat and brought it to his mouth.

But suddenly King Midas realized his wish may not have been as wonderful as he thought—for the moment he bit down on the meat, it too, turned to gold.

LOOK AHEAD

In "The Baker's Neighbor," two neighbors have different ideas about wealth and happiness. As you read, think about the theme or themes.

Vocabulary

Words to Know

fragrance inspects pastries
pleasures privilege scowling
trial

Words with similar meanings are called **synonyms.** You can often figure out the meaning of an unknown word by finding a clue in the words around it. Sometimes this clue is a synonym.

Read the paragraph below. Notice how *smell* helps you understand what *fragrance* means.

A Tasty Decision

One of the pleasures of Judge Lee's day was going to Pete's Bakery. He loved the fragrance of bread and pastries baking. That wonderful smell made his mouth water. One day on the way to a trial, the judge stopped at the bakery. A customer was scowling at Pete, "Who inspects this bread? It's stale!" Pete insisted that the bread was fresh. The judge asked, "May I have the privilege of tasting it?" The judge decided that the bread was delicious, but the customer must have a free loaf. "The customer is always right," he declared.

Talk About It

Discuss the job of a baker. Use as many vocabulary words as you can.

THE BAKER'S NEIGHBOR

adapted by Adele Thane

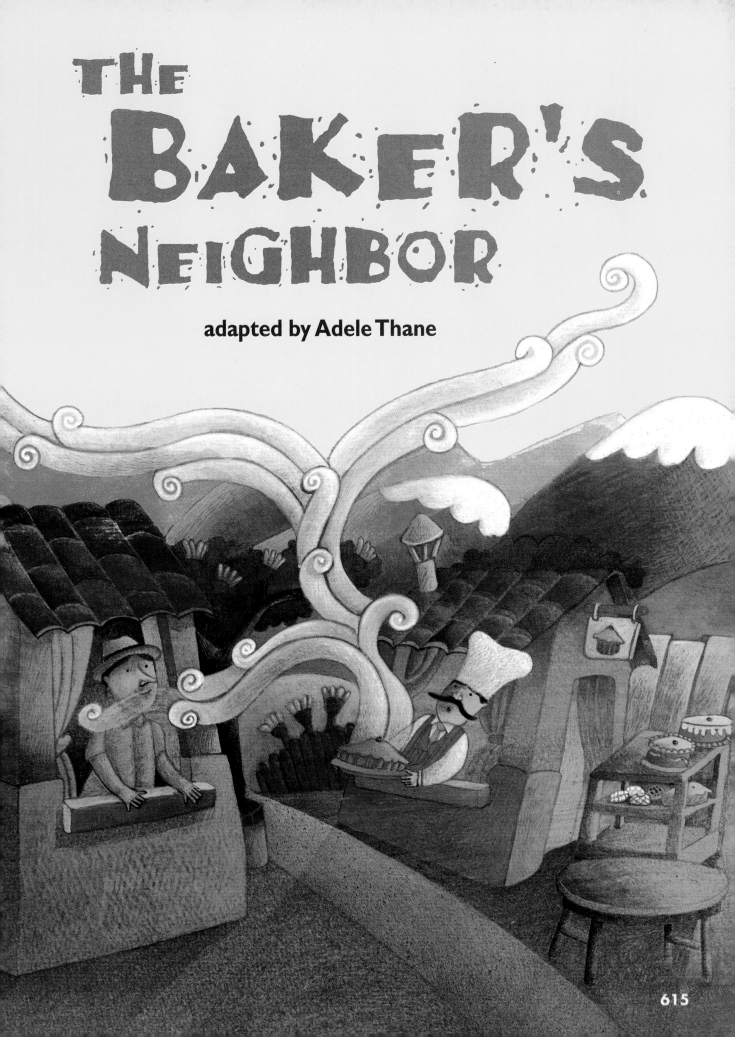

CHARACTERS:

MANUEL GONZALES, a baker

PABLO PEREZ, his neighbor

CARLOS, a boy

RAMONA
INEZ } his sisters
ISABEL

JUDGE

THREE WOMEN

VILLAGERS

SETTING: A street in an old town in Peru. Manuel's Bakery is at right. There is an outdoor counter with shelves for the display of pastries in front of the bakery, and a wooden table and stool near the counter. Across the street, at left, is the patio of Pablo's house, with a bench and chairs on it. At the rear of the stage, there is a flowering tree with a circular seat around the trunk.

AT RISE: It is early morning. MANUEL comes out of the bakery with a tray of pies, which he carries to the counter. As he is putting the pies on a shelf, PABLO steps out onto his patio, sniffs the air and smiles with delight.

PABLO: Good morning, Baker Manuel. Your pies smell especially delicious this morning. How many did you bake last night?

MANUEL (*sullenly*): What's it to you, Pablo? You never buy any; you just smell them. Every day you stand there and fill your nostrils with the fragrance of my pastries. It's a miracle there's any flavor left in them when my customers come to buy.

PABLO: But it makes me happy to smell your pastries. You are the best baker in Peru. Everyone says so.

MANUEL: Well, why don't you buy a pie or a cake and take it home? Then you could smell it all you want.

PABLO: Oh, but if I bought it and ate it, I couldn't smell it any more.

MANUEL (*snorting in disgust*): Bah! (*When he finishes setting out the pies he goes into the bakery with the empty tray.* PABLO *crosses to the counter and inhales deeply, closing his eyes in delight.* MANUEL *returns with tray of cakes and cash box. He pushes* PABLO *away from counter.*) Hey! Take your big nose away from there! I can't sell those pies if you sniff them all over! (PABLO *saunters back to his patio.* MANUEL *places tray of cakes on counter, then carries cash box to table and sits down.*)

PABLO: Are you going to count your money, Manuel? (MANUEL *ignores* PABLO *but empties coins from cash box onto table.* PABLO *then sits in a chair and watches* MANUEL *with an amused smile.*) How much did you take in yesterday?

MANUEL: None of your business! (*He inspects each coin carefully, then writes in a small notebook, adds figures, scowling and mumbling to himself.* CARLOS *and his sisters enter left. They stop when they see* MANUEL *counting his money and talk quietly together.*)

RAMONA: Gracious, what a lot of money!

CARLOS: Papa says the bakery has made Manuel the richest man in town.

INEZ: If he's that rich, why doesn't he smile? He looks so cross and unfriendly.

CARLOS: That's because he's a miser. A miser doesn't like people— only money. The more money he has, the more he wants. And he keeps it all to himself—he never shares it with anyone.

ISABEL (*catching sight of* PABLO): There's Pablo!

CARLOS and **GIRLS** (*enthusiastically, ad lib*): Hello, Pablo! How are you? Good to see you! (*etc.*)

PABLO (*beaming at them as he gets up*): Hello, my young friends, hello! You're up bright and early.

ISABEL: We're going to the bakery.

RAMONA: Carlos is going to treat us.

CARLOS: I helped Papa pick beans and he gave me this.

    (*He holds up a silver coin.*)

PABLO: You're a good boy, Carlos.

INEZ (*starting across to the bakery*): Come on! Let's see what

    there is. (*Children crowd around the counter.*)

RAMONA: Look at those coconut patties!

ISABEL: And the jelly roll! Yummy!

INEZ: Carlos, why don't you buy a pie and cut it into quarters?

    Then we'd each have a piece.

CARLOS: I don't know. I'd sort of like a cake.

MANUEL (*impatiently*): Well, young fellow, what do you want?

    (*to* INEZ) Keep your fingers off that pie!

INEZ (*indignantly*): I didn't touch it!

MANUEL: Come now, hurry up and decide. This isn't a waiting room.

    I have to make a living. What with rent and taxes, it's as much

    as I can do.

CARLOS: How much is that cake with the pink frosting?

MANUEL: You can't afford that. How much money do you have? (CARLOS *holds out his hand to show him.*) Not enough. That cake costs three times what you can pay.

CARLOS: What *can* I buy with my money? I want something for all of us.

MANUEL: You can have four tapioca tarts—and I'm giving them away at that price. (*He hands tarts to* CARLOS.) Here you are. Now take your tarts over to Pablo and let him smell them. (*He puts* CARLOS's *coin with others on table, sits down, and makes entry in his notebook.* CARLOS *passes out tarts to his sisters as they cross to the patio.*)

CARLOS (*offering tart to* PABLO): Have a bite?

PABLO: No, thank you, Carlos. You earned it—you eat it.

ISABEL: Pablo, why did Manuel say we should let you smell our tarts?

PABLO: Oh, he's annoyed, because every morning I stand here and enjoy the smell of his freshly baked pies and cakes when they are right out of the oven. Ah, what fragrance! It's as if the bakery has burst into bloom.

RAMONA: If you could be a beautiful smell, Pablo, instead of a man— would you like to be a beautiful bakery smell?

PABLO (*laughing*): Well, that's a new one on me! If I were a *smell* instead of a man? Of all the comical ideas!

INEZ (*explaining*): It's a game we play among ourselves. We ask each other what thing we'd like to be if we weren't a person—what color, what sight, what sound—

RAMONA: What sound would *you* like to be, Pablo, if you weren't a person?

PABLO: This minute?

RAMONA: Any minute.

PABLO: Let me think. (*Suddenly he slaps his knee.*) I have it! If I were a sound instead of a man, I'd choose to be a song! A happy little song in children's hearts. Or turning up in a boy's whistle—like this! (*He whistles a merry tune.*)

ISABEL: What sound do you think Manuel would like to be?

CARLOS: That's easy. He'd be the sound of gold pieces jingling in his own pocket.

ISABEL: I'm going to ask him. (*She goes to the table where* MANUEL *is putting his money back into cash box.*) Manuel, may I ask you a question?

MANUEL (*scowling*): What is it?

ISABEL: If you were a sound instead of a baker, what sound in the whole wide world would you choose to be?

MANUEL: Well, of all the idiotic nonsense! Clear out of here and stop bothering me! I have better things to do than to answer stupid questions. (ISABEL *returns to patio, and* PABLO *goes center.*)

PABLO: It has taken you a long time to count your money, Manuel.

MANUEL (*sneering*): It wouldn't take *you* long to count yours.

PABLO: That's right. I don't care much for money.

MANUEL: You're too lazy to earn it.

PABLO (*good-naturedly*): Oh, I work when I have to. But I'd rather sit in the sun and take advantage of all the small, everyday pleasures that life has to offer.

MANUEL: Like smelling my pastries, I suppose—without charge?

PABLO (*shrugging*): The air is free.

MANUEL: It's not as free as you think.

PABLO: What do you mean?

MANUEL: I'm going to make you pay for all the pastry smells I've supplied you with for many years.

PABLO (*smiling in disbelief*): You can't mean that!

MANUEL: But I do! You stand outside my bakery every day and smell my pies and cakes. To my mind, that is the same as taking them without paying for them. You are no better than a thief, Pablo Perez!

PABLO (*mildly*): I never took anything that didn't belong to me, and you know it. What's more, I haven't done your business any harm. Why, I've even helped it. People often stop when they see me standing here and go in to buy something. (*Children giggle, then begin to taunt* MANUEL *and run around him, sniffing.*)

ISABEL: I smell raisins!

RAMONA: I smell spice!

INEZ: How much does it cost to smell the flour on your apron?

CARLOS: May I smell your cap for a penny? (*He snatches baker's cap from* MANUEL's *head and sniffs it, laughing.*)

MANUEL (*angrily, snatching it back*): You'll laugh on the other side of your face when I get the Judge!

PABLO: When you get *who*?

MANUEL: The Judge. I'm going to tell him the whole story. I'll show you I'm not joking. The Judge will make you pay me. (*He grabs his cash box from table and exits left as* THREE WOMEN *enter right. They come downstage and question the children.*)

1ST WOMAN: What's the matter with Manuel?

2ND WOMAN: Will he be back soon? I want to buy a cake.

3RD WOMAN: So do I. What happened?

1ST WOMAN: He looked so angry. Where's he gone?

GIRLS (*excitedly, ad lib*): He's gone to get the Judge! He is angry! He is furious! (*etc.*)

1ST WOMAN: The Judge! What for?

CARLOS: He says Pablo will have to pay for smelling his cakes and pies.

2ND WOMAN (*to* PABLO): He wants you to pay him for doing *that*?

3RD WOMAN: He can't be serious!

PABLO: Oh, yes, he is! But I think it's very funny. (*He laughs, and the* WOMEN *join in.*)

1ST WOMAN: It's ridiculous! Everyone who goes by the shop smells his pastry.

2ND WOMAN: Is he going to take everyone in town to court? (*They are all in gales of laughter when* MANUEL *returns with* JUDGE, *followed by several* VILLAGERS.)

MANUEL (*to* JUDGE): There he is! (*points to* PABLO) There's the thief!

JUDGE: Calm yourself, Manuel. It has not yet been proved that Pablo is a thief. First he must have a fair trial. (*He sits down at table and motions for two chairs to be placed facing him.* VILLAGERS *and* THREE WOMEN *gather under tree and on patio with children. They whisper and talk together as they seat themselves.*)

1ST VILLAGER: In all my days, I've never heard of a case like this before.

2ND VILLAGER: How can a man steal the *smell* of anything?

3RD VILLAGER: I'm surprised the Judge would even listen to the baker's story. Money for smelling his cakes! How absurd!

2ND WOMAN: He sells as much bread and pastry as he can bake. What more does he want?

3RD VILLAGER: Manuel loves money and he figures this is a way to get more of it.

JUDGE (*rapping table with his gavel*): Quiet, everyone! Court is in session. I am ready to hear Manuel Gonzales, baker, against Pablo Perez, neighbor. I will hear the baker first. Manuel, tell your story.

MANUEL (*rising*): This man, Pablo Perez, comes and stands outside my bakery every day.

JUDGE: Does he block the way?

MANUEL: Not exactly.

JUDGE: Does he keep other people from going into your bakery?

MANUEL: No, sir, but—

JUDGE: Then what *does* he do?

MANUEL: He stands there, looking at my pies and cakes *and smelling them.*

JUDGE: That pleases you, doesn't it?

MANUEL: Pleases me! Far from it! Look here, your honor—every night I mix the flour and knead the dough and slave over a hot oven while that shiftless, good-for-nothing Pablo sleeps. Then he gets up in the morning, fresh as a daisy, and comes out here to smell the fine sweet pastry I've baked. He takes full value of this free, daily luxury. He acts as if it's his privilege. Now I ask you, Judge—is it right that I should work so hard to provide him with this luxury, without charge? No! He should pay for it!

JUDGE: I see. You may sit down, Manuel. Now, Pablo Perez, it is your turn. (PABLO *stands.*) Is it true that you stand in front of Manuel's bakery and smell his cakes and pies?

PABLO: I can't help smelling them, your honor. Their spicy fragrance fills the air.

JUDGE: Would you say you *enjoy* it?

PABLO: Oh, yes, sir. I am a man of simple pleasures. Just the smell of a bakery makes me happy.

JUDGE: But did you ever pay the baker for this pleasure?

PABLO: Well, no, sir. It never occurred to me that I had to pay him.

JUDGE: Pablo Perez, you will now put ten gold pieces on this table— for Manuel Gonzales. (VILLAGERS *gasp.* MANUEL *looks surprised and delighted.*)

PABLO (*stunned*): Ten gold pieces! For smelling the air near my own house?

JUDGE: Do you have that amount?

PABLO: I—I guess so, but it's my life's savings.

JUDGE: Where is it?

PABLO: In my house.

JUDGE: Get it and bring it here. (*Slowly* PABLO *crosses patio and exits left.* VILLAGERS *talk to each other disapprovingly.*)

1ST VILLAGER: The Judge shouldn't make Pablo pay.

1ST WOMAN: Pablo is an honest man.

2ND VILLAGER: I don't see how the Judge could rule in the baker's favor.

3RD VILLAGER: Why, he's richer than the Judge himself.

2ND WOMAN: And now he's going to get poor Pablo's savings.

3RD WOMAN: It's not fair!

JUDGE (*rapping with his gavel*): Silence in the court! (PABLO *returns sadly with purse, puts it on table before* JUDGE. MANUEL, *elated, rubs his hands together greedily.*)

MANUEL (*to* JUDGE): I knew your honor would do the right thing by me. Thank you, Judge. (*He picks up purse and starts to put it into his cash box.*)

JUDGE (*rising*): Not so fast, Manuel! Empty that purse on the table and count the gold pieces, one by one.

MANUEL (*grinning craftily*): Ah, yes, your honor. I must make sure I haven't been cheated. How kind of you to remind me! (*He empties purse and begins to count, excitedly.* JUDGE *watches* MANUEL *as he lovingly fingers each coin.*)

JUDGE: It gives you great pleasure to touch that gold, doesn't it, Manuel? You *enjoy* it.

MANUEL: Oh, I do, I do! . . . Eight . . . nine . . . ten. It's all here, your honor, and none of it false.

JUDGE: Please put it back in the purse. (MANUEL *does so.*) Now return it to Pablo.

MANUEL (*in disbelief*): *Return* it! But—but you just told Pablo to pay it to me.

JUDGE: No, I did not tell him to pay it to you. I told him to put it on this table. Then I instructed you to count the money, which you did. In doing so, you enjoyed Pablo's money the way he has enjoyed your cakes and pies. In other words, he has smelled your pastry and you have touched his gold. Therefore, I hereby declare that the case is now settled. (*He raps twice with his gavel.* MANUEL *shamefacedly shoves purse across table to* PABLO *and turns to leave.* JUDGE *stops him.*) Just a moment, Manuel! I hope this has been a lesson to you. In the future, think less about making money and more about making friends. Good friends and neighbors are better than gold. And now, if you please—my fee!

MANUEL: Yes, your honor. (*He opens his cash box willingly but* JUDGE *closes the lid.*)

JUDGE: Put away your money. There's been enough fuss over money already today. The fee I am asking is this—pies and cakes for everyone here—free of charge! (MANUEL *nods his head vigorously in assent.* VILLAGERS *and children cheer, then they rush to pastry counter and help themselves.* MANUEL *goes into bakery and reappears with more pastry piled high on tray.* PABLO *and* JUDGE *hold a whole pie between them and start to eat from opposite edges toward the center of pie, as the curtain closes.*)

THE END

About the Author
ADELE THANE

Although "The Baker's Neighbor" is a play that has been around a long time, it took a theater-minded woman like Adele Thane to bring it to life again. Adapting plays is just one way that Ms. Thane has been involved in the performance arts.

Ms. Thane started out as an actress in the New England Repertory Company, a theater group in Boston. During World War II, she entertained servicemen in hospitals and camps for the United Services Organization (USO). Later, she moved on to directing productions for theater and television and, finally, she made the step to writing and adapting plays.

Among her writings is the collection *Plays from Famous Stories and Fairy Tales*, which features adaptations of fairy tales originally told by Hans Christian Andersen, the Brothers Grimm, and others. She also has written an adaptation of *The Wizard of Oz* for the theater. Several of her one-act plays have been published in *Plays: The Drama Magazine for Young People*.

Reader Response

Open for Discussion

Suppose you are the judge in this play. Explain your ruling to the mayor of the town.

Comprehension Check

1. What would you say are the character traits of Manuel and of Pablo? Make a chart that lists their character traits.

2. Do most characters in the play agree with Manuel's point of view? Find three examples that show how characters other than Pablo respond to Manuel.

3. Suppose that in the future Manuel has a problem with a customer. How do you think he will act? Explain, using evidence from the play.

4. What do you think is the **theme** of this play? What evidence supports it? (Theme)

5. Think of other selections that have similar **themes.** How are they similar? (Theme)

Test Prep
Look Back and Write

Look back at page 618. If you didn't know what the word *miser* means, what clues would help you figure it out? Use details from the play to support your answer.

30

Test Prep

How to Read an Informational Article

1. Preview

- Read the title and look at the pictures. What do you think the pictures have to do with the title?

- The headings tell you the focus of each section. What do they have to do with the title?

2. Read and Find the Main Idea

- Read the article to find out what "all kinds of money" are. Jot brief notes under these headings:

Kind of Money	Where Used
shovels	China

- Find a sentence that sums up the main idea of the article.

3. Think and Connect

Look over your notes on "All Kinds of Money" and the statement of its main idea. Then look back at "The Baker's Neighbor" and answer these questions.

The Judge might have this main idea in mind when he gives his verdict. What has value for these characters? What do they agree to trade with?

All Kinds of Money

by Robert Young

Cowrie shells used as money among the Akan peoples of Ghana and the Ivory Coast

Growing Needs

Live without money? How could you do it? It would be very hard today, but it wasn't thousands of years ago. The earliest humans had simple needs: food, clothing, and shelter. Small family groups could take care of these needs themselves.

But in time, as the number of people increased, so did the need for food and other goods. Family groups often traveled together to find things to eat. On their travels, they met other families. These groups began to trade with each other. This made it easier for people to get the things they wanted.

Money of the Kissi peoples of Liberia; iron currency blade of the Ngbaka peoples of Liberia

Things of Value

Early money was often something people found useful. The early Greeks used oxen for money. People from Egypt and Crete used sheep. In England, during the times of Robin Hood, taxes were paid in horses.

Tools were very useful to people, so they were used as money too. Some African people used spearheads and knives as money. The Chinese used shovels. Early European settlers in North America used nails.

Salt has been another important form of money. That's right, the same kind of common salt we use in our saltshakers. But it wasn't always so common. Long ago salt was hard to get. Most of it was underground and had to be dug from deep within the earth.

Pretty Money

Some early money was whatever people considered pretty. That's why shells were used as money in many parts of the world. People from China, India, and Africa used the cowrie shell. Iroquois Indians used pieces of whelk shells and quahog clamshells to make beads called **wampum.** These beads were woven into belts and necklaces and used as money. Colonists used wampum made by Native Americans too. In 1626 Peter Minuit, governor of New Netherland, used shells

Learning to Trade

When people began to farm, they grew more food than they needed. They traded the extra food for goods and services from people who had other kinds of jobs, like making clothing, making tools, and protecting the community. This type of trade is called **barter.**

Bartering is still used when people want to make a trade or a payment without using money. But barter doesn't always work. It is often hard to make a fair trade using things that are different. How much corn is a knife worth? What if you have something to trade that nobody wants?

The simple answer is to use money. Money is anything that has value, can be saved, and that people agree to trade with.

to help buy Manhattan Island. He paid Indians about $25 worth of shells, beads, and knives. Some people believe that this was the best buy in the history of real estate.

Heavy Money

Some money was neither useful nor pretty. As late as the 1900s, people who lived on the Pacific islands of Yap used stones for their money. These weren't just any stones. The money was made from aragonite, a brownish white stone with large crystals like quartz. Since there was no aragonite on Yap, people paddled hundreds of miles to another island, Palau, to get the stones. The Yapese worked the stones into round shapes and drilled holes in the middle of them. Then they put sturdy sticks through the holes so that more than one person could help carry the stones. Some of the stones were as big as 12 feet across and weighed more than a ton!

Traditional Yapese money

People have used many other things as money over the years. Soap, cocoa beans, and elephant-tail hairs have been used. Grain, animal skins, fishhooks, and feathers have also been used. So have tea, tobacco, bird claws, and bear teeth.

Salt is important for many reasons: It is a mineral we need in order to stay healthy. For thousands of years, we've used it to season food. And before refrigerators were invented, salt was used to preserve food.

In the first century A.D., Roman soldiers were paid in salt. Our word *salary* comes from *sal*, which means "salt" in Latin.

Skill Lesson

Steps in a Process

- The actions you take to reach a goal or make something are the **steps in a process.**

- Sometimes steps in a process are shown by numbers or clue words such as *first, next, then,* and *last.* If there are no clues, use common sense to picture the steps.

- If you picture the result, you'll understand why each step is necessary.

- Identifying steps in a process will help you solve problems and follow directions.

Read "Beetle Research" from *Keeping Minibeasts: Beetles* by Barrie Watts.

Write About It

1. Identify the basic steps in collecting and caring for beetles. Use clue words or numbers to organize the order.

2. How does picturing the result of this experiment help you understand the steps?

BEETLE RESEARCH

by Barrie Watts

Some people enjoy collecting beetles in order to observe their behavior and learn about nature. The first step in beetle research is making a trap to catch the beetles.

A pitfall trap: A good way to collect ground beetles is to make a pitfall trap. You can set the trap in the woods or even in a garden. All you need is a jar or a plastic cup, four stones, and a small piece of wood. Bury the cup level with the surface and cover it with the wood and stones. Compare beetles caught at different times of the day. Put some food in the cup and see what attracts certain species. Always remove the traps when you have finished.

Handling: Beetles are easy to handle. Use a small paintbrush and a paper cup with the smaller ones because you can damage them if you pick them up in your hand. Larger ones can be picked up, but always be gentle. Do not worry if they give off a smelly fluid. This is their protection against predators.

Housing: An old aquarium with a net cover is the best container to keep beetles in. Ground beetles need a layer of earth in the bottom as well as pieces of wood and stones under which to hide. The lid must have plenty of holes, and the earth must be damp or the beetles will dry up. Make sure you put in a good supply of food. If you are keeping more than one beetle, make sure they are the same type, so they do not eat each other. A shady windowsill is the ideal place to put your beetle home.

Feeding: If the beetles are to stay healthy, you must provide the right food for them. Sometimes it is difficult to know what they eat, so watch them carefully before you collect them.

Releasing your beetles: When you have finished studying the beetles, always return them to the same habitat.

LOOK **AHEAD**

In "Andy's Secret Ingredient," Andy follows certain steps to use beetles in an altogether different kind of research.

Vocabulary

Words to Know

clenched   comparing   essay
cornmeal   primitive   grease
flyer

When you read, you may come across a word you don't know. To figure out its meaning, look for clues in the words and sentences around it. A clue might be a specific detail near the unknown word.

Notice *clenched* in the paragraph below and the detail in the same sentence. What do you think *clenched* means?

Unusual Foods

Today at lunch we discussed the essay we have to write about unusual foods. While comparing ideas, we noticed some unusual foods right in front of us. Rick was eating sunflower seeds and carrots. He said that in primitive times, people lived on seeds and roots. Jenny's lunch was eggs and dandelions. She found the recipe for it in a flyer at the health-food store. She made it by putting grease in a pan and adding eggs, cornmeal, and chopped dandelions. She offered me some, but I clenched my teeth and wouldn't open my mouth. Although I didn't taste anyone's food, I did get some ideas for my essay.

Talk About It

Talk about an unusual meal you've had. Use some or all of the vocabulary words.

Andy's Secret Ingredient

from *Beetles, Lightly Toasted*
by Phyllis Reynolds Naylor

Andy Moller desperately wants to win the Roger B. Sudermann essay contest for fifth grade. Unfortunately, this year's topic is conservation, which the fifth graders don't want to write about. When they stage a boycott against the essay contest, Andy's cousin Jack is the first to break it. Andy wonders how Jack will turn a strange experiment he does with hamburgers into an essay about conservation. Andy, who has always been competitive with Jack, comes up with a strange idea for his essay too.

Bon Appetit!

The way Andy figured it was this: If the population ever grew so big that there wasn't enough food to feed everybody, then people could save their lives by eating things they hadn't thought of eating before. Things like lizards and snakes and grasshoppers. Not that *Andy* would eat them, of course, but some day, if people were starving, *somebody* might.

Start with what you have and see how far you can stretch it, Mr. Sudermann had said. *Put your imaginations to work.* Maybe you didn't have to be starving. Maybe, if you were just poor or you wanted to save money on your grocery bill, you could find stuff to eat in your own backyard.

Andy knew that primitive tribes ate things like grubs, which was just like eating worms. He had heard about fancy stores selling chocolate-covered ants as a novelty item. But no one he knew, except the yellow cat, had ever made a meal out of beetles. The first thing he had to do was find out exactly what could be eaten safely. Wendell had told him once that a university was a place where you could find out anything you wanted to know, so Andy wrote a letter to Iowa State University:

Dear Sir:

I am writing an essay for a contest and I need to know what bugs and things you can eat. And worms too. How do you know if they are poison or not? How do you fix them? Please answer soon.

Yours truly,
Andy Moller

On the envelope he wrote, "Department of Bugs," and then he added the address he had copied from the catalog in Wendell's room, with his own address in the corner.

Aunt Wanda saw him putting on the stamp.

"Who's the letter to?" she asked, as she carried her jade plant to a sunny place on the window ledge.

"Oh, somebody," Andy told her.

"Well, most letters *are* to somebody," she said, and cast him a strange look.

Andy walked down to the end of the lane toward the mailbox. He was remembering once when he was about six years old, walking to the mailbox with Jack. Andy had been afraid of the Moller's turkey then—a big tom turkey which would suddenly take a dislike to you and come flapping and gobbling over to peck at your heels. For a while Andy had never gone outside unless the turkey was in its pen, but on that particular day, Jack had been visiting and told Andy that the turkey was locked up when it wasn't. They'd gotten only halfway down the drive to the mailbox when there came the old tom. Jack had laughed and climbed up a plum tree, but the turkey had chased Andy screaming back to the house, pecking at him all the way.

And what had Aunt Bernie said?

"Look how my Jack can climb!" That's what she'd said. She was always comparing the boys, and it was always Jack who came out ahead.

Andy put the envelope in the mailbox and raised the red flag so the mailman would know that there was a letter to be collected. Later, when he was doing his homework on the sun porch and had come into the dining room to get an eraser, he'd heard Aunt Wanda and Mother talking about him in the kitchen.

"Of course, I'm not going to ask him who that letter was to, and don't you go peeking in the mailbox, either," Mother was saying. "It's his business, after all."

"Well, who does he know he has to write a letter to, that he can't call up on the phone?" Aunt Wanda went on. "He's in a bit of trouble, if you ask me. Was caught taking something from the five-and-dime, I'll bet, and he's got to pay it back."

"Why on earth would you think a thing like that?" Mother demanded. "If you ask me, he's got a girl somewhere. That's the likeliest reason for a letter that I can think of."

For crying out loud! Andy said to himself, and went back out on the sun porch.

By the end of April, at least nine fifth graders had broken the boycott and were trying out for the contest. Dora Kray had rigged up some kind of funnel contraption on the roof of the Krays' garage to collect rainwater as a conservation measure. Andy thought this was probably the best idea anyone had thought of so far, until Mother told him that when she was a girl, they *always* collected water in a rain barrel, and used it to wash their hair. Russ, of course, to conserve land, was still trying to figure out a way to send garbage to outer space, but no one could figure out what Jack was trying to conserve.

On May 1, when Andy had about given up ever hearing from the University, there was a letter for him in the box, and he was glad he had found it before anyone else did:

Dear Andy:
   Your letter asking about bugs and things has been given to me for reply, and I hope I will be able to help. Probably most insects are edible, especially their larvae or pupae. But because some of them—especially brightly colored insects—might have poisons in their bodies, it would be best to stick with crickets, grasshoppers, and ordinary brown beetles.

   Ant and bee larvae are also a good source of fat and protein; meal worms, often found where grain is stored, are delicious, I understand, fried in garlic butter. To prepare insects for eating, put them on a diet of cornmeal for a few days to rid their digestive tracts of grit, then cook. Earthworms can also be put on a diet of applesauce, then simmered until tender. Grasshoppers, crickets, and beetles, lightly toasted, with the legs and wings removed, add crunch to a recipe, and can be used in place of nuts for brownies.

   If you don't like the idea of dropping live worms and insects in boiling water, you might put them in a covered box in the freezer first, then cook them later. Good luck on your essay, and bon appetit!

                         Cordially,
                         John Burrows, Entomologist

Andy understood the whole letter except the last two words before "cordially."

"Mom," he said that evening as he worked his arithmetic problems on the kitchen table, and she sat across from him going over her poultry and egg records, "What does *bon appetit* mean?"

"*Bon appetit?*" Mother looked up. "It's French, Andy. It means 'good appetite' or 'good eating.' 'Enjoy your meal'—something like that."

Andy kept one hand tightly over his mouth and said nothing.

One-half Cup of Nuts

On Saturday, Earl Moller went into town for a new auger motor for the silo, and took Andy with him. When they passed the Barths' farm, with its L-shaped patch of trees around the house, Andy asked, "How's Uncle Delmar's car doing? Did Jack's hamburgers hurt it any?"

"Another minute or so and they might have, but Del got the blamed things off in time," his father said. "Jack won't be trying that again soon, I can tell you." He looked at Andy and pushed back his cap, the one with the *Farley's Feed* emblem in front, two overlapping red F's against a white background. Almost all the men in Bucksville wore a cap from Farley's, except that the young farmers, like Wayne, wore the bill around in back instead. "How's *your* essay coming? You going to enter the contest too?"

"I'm thinking of it," Andy told him.

"Well, don't you go cooking lunch under *my* hood, or I'll set fire to your britches," Earl said with a smile.

The reason Andy couldn't tell his family what his essay was about was because, after he'd learned to cook the stuff he collected, he'd need somebody to taste it. He could just imagine what Lois would say if he asked her.

Are you nuts? That's what Lois would say.

He also had to find some recipes. He knew just what Aunt Wanda would say if he asked her how you fry meal worms in garlic butter.

You don't, she'd say. *Not in my skillets, you don't.*

After they bought the motor and Andy got some more three-ring notebook paper and a Magic Marker, Earl said, "You want to pick up a couple sandwiches somewhere?"

That's when Andy remembered the flyer from the Soul Food Kitchen and Carry-Out. He fished it out of his back pocket. "Two meals for the price of one, Dad," he said.

Mr. Moller's eyes scanned the menu there on the advertisement. "Looks pretty good to me," he said, and they drove down Main to North Street and to the little yellow frame building on the corner.

Soul Food Kitchen and Carry-Out, said a sign above the door, showing a smiling chicken at one end of the sign and a thick piece of pie at the other.

The first thing Andy saw in the little room with its green tables and yellow linoleum was Sam, who was putting silverware on the tables.

"Hi!" he called out when he saw Andy. He showed them to a little table by the wall and stood off to one side grinning while Mrs. Hollins came over to take their orders. She was a thin woman in a white uniform and white shoes with thick soles, and had a smile that stretched across her face, just like Sam's.

"How you doing?" she asked, and looked down at Andy. "You and Sam know each other from school?"

Andy nodded.

There was a sign above the grill that said, *Ask about our daily special.*

"What about the daily special?" Andy's father asked.

Mrs. Hollins smiled even wider. "Well, you are *some* kind of lucky today, because the special for Saturdays is catfish, all you can eat."

Andy's heart sank. Why couldn't it have been fried chicken or hot dogs or chili or hamburgers? "Catfish" sounded too much like "cat food" or "dog biscuits" or something.

"You order a Saturday special," Sam's mother went on, "and you get a plate of catfish, hush puppies, turnip greens, cornbread, and a big piece of rhubarb pie. All you can eat. You order Saturday special, you won't want *anything* till Sunday noon."

She laughed and Earl laughed and Sam's father over by the grill laughed too.

Andy's father pulled out the "two-for-the-price-of-one" flyer that Andy had shown him.

"That's right," said Sam's mother. "Neither *one* of you is going to want anything at all till church is over on Sunday."

"Could I . . . have chicken instead?" Andy asked.

"Of *course* you can have chicken," said Mrs. Hollins, as though it were the most reasonable request in the world. She didn't glare down at him as Aunt Wanda would have done and screech, "You don't like my *catfish?*"

"One Saturday special and one chicken platter," she called to her husband, and soon the little restaurant was filled with spicy smells and the sound of grease bubbling in the deep-fryer behind the counter.

"Ahhh!" said Earl, when the dinners arrived. As Mrs. Hollins poured more coffee in his cup, he said, "How's business?"

"Well, now that we put out those flyers, it's picking up some," Sam's mother told him. "Our older boy, Clay, is in business school, and we get a lot of good ideas from him. When he graduates he's going to help run the restaurant. Last year, when we first started, I wasn't sure how long there was going to *be* a restaurant, but now I think we're doing okay."

The way Earl tore into that catfish, shaking his head and smacking his lips, Andy knew it must taste pretty good. The chicken was good too. Aunt Wanda's chicken had never tasted this good. Not even Aunt Bernie's or Mother's. Andy grinned at Sam, who was watching them over by the counter.

What he was really thinking about, however, was earthworms, and whether they could be rolled in the Hollins' specially-flavored cornmeal and fried in hot grease. That would make one recipe for his essay.

After church on Sunday, when his chores were done, Andy spent the afternoon turning over logs to look for beetles. He worked until he had filled half a jar and took them up to his room, tucked inside his shirt. He put them in the little screened cage that he once used for his hamster, and carefully poured a small pile of cornmeal at one end.

For three days, Andy checked the cage, cleaning out the bottom and putting in fresh cornmeal. The brown beetles, looking fat and healthy, climbed up on each other's backs to get at the cornmeal. At the end of four days, Andy put the beetles in a small cookie tin with a tight lid and took it to the big freezer chest in the basement. He stuck it down in one corner beneath a stack of his mother's apple pies.

Saturday morning he checked again. The beetles were frozen solid. Some were on their backs with their legs in the air. Others looked as though they had frozen standing up. Andy peeled off all the wings and legs and threw them away, then chopped up the bodies into pieces until the little pile looked like a cup of black walnuts. Andy didn't mind this part. He didn't mind baiting a hook when he went fishing, either. It was the thought of eating the things that made his tongue curl. He simply did not allow himself to think about it, however. And every time his *throat* started to think about it, Andy told himself that only a far-out essay like this would win the contest. He put the beetles in a pan and toasted them in the oven for five minutes, then put them back in the jar. They gave off a sharp, pungent odor, and Andy kept the windows open while they were toasting.

"I want to make some brownies to take to school on Monday," he told his mother. "You give me the recipe, I'll make them myself."

"Now that's an offer I can't refuse," Mother told him. She took a recipe card from her box and showed him where she kept the flour and cocoa.

"He's got a girl, I'm sure of it," Andy heard her say to Aunt Wanda out on the sun porch. "Can't think of any other reason he'd be wanting to take brownies to school."

The batter was dark and moist. When the flour and eggs and sugar had been mixed, Andy put in a quarter of a cup of chopped walnuts and then, his teeth clenched, a quarter of a cup of chopped beetle.

All the time the brownies were baking, Andy wondered if he could smell the beetles. When the brownies were done, he took them out, cooled them for twenty minutes, then cut them into squares and piled them onto a platter. He was just washing out the bowl and spoon in the sink when Wendell came into the kitchen, a screwdriver hanging out of one pocket.

"Need me a 3/8-inch screw with a flat head," he said, rummaging around in the big drawer near the stove where Mother said you could find anything from toothpicks to flashlights. And then Wendell saw the brownies.

"Hey!" he said. "Don't mind if I do!" And he reached out one big hand, picked up a thick brownie, and took a bite.

Andy stood over by the wall, scarcely breathing. He saw Wendell's jaws go up and down, saw him swallow. Then another bite. Crunch. The jaws were moving again. Wendell held the brownie out in front of him, turning it around and around in his hand while he chewed, looking at it from all angles, then swallowed once more and popped the rest of it in his mouth.

"Good!" he said, wiping his hand on his jeans.

Andy silently collapsed in a chair by the table, his stomach queasy, but his heart pounding with relief.

About the Author
Phyllis Reynolds Naylor

During the Depression, when Phyllis Reynolds Naylor was very young, her family did not have money for a lot of extras. The family did have good books, though, and her mother would read to the children each evening. Ms. Naylor's parents also entertained the children with stories and songs they made up themselves.

Now that she is an adult, Ms. Naylor looks back on her childhood and considers herself one of the luckiest people she knows. Her upbringing, which was rich with literature and music, provided her with a wonderful foundation for becoming a writer. When Ms. Naylor is getting ready to write a new book, she is in a constant state of anticipation. "I never start writing a book until a character or setting or theme or plot ignites something within me," she said. "Then everything I see and hear seems to relate somehow to the work at hand, and I am constantly putting things together, like the pieces of a puzzle. My books are made up of things both imagined and remembered."

Several of Ms. Naylor's books deal with problems that young people face. *The Agony of Alice* deals with a young girl's search for a role model after the death of her mother. *Shiloh*, which won the Newbery Medal, portrays a boy who takes action to help an abused dog.

Reader Response

Open for Discussion

Do you think Andy will win the contest? Why or why not?

Comprehension Check

1. How do you think Andy feels when Aunt Bernie compares him to his cousin Jack? Do you think Andy's feelings about Jack have an effect on his interest in the essay contest? Use evidence from the story to explain.

2. Does the entomologist's letter have answers to all of Andy's questions? Tell how the letter affects what Andy thinks and does.

3. Do you think that Andy usually likes having new experiences? Give examples from the story to support your answer.

4. Before Andy chooses his project, he goes through the **process** of making a decision. List the **steps** Andy follows that lead up to his decision. (Steps in a Process)

5. What **steps** does Andy follow in his **process** of finding beetles and preparing them for cooking? (Steps in a Process)

Test Prep

Look Back and Write

Look back at pages 638-648. Andy, Jack, Dora Kray, and Russ all propose conservation projects that they can write essays about. Which project do you think would make the most difference to the way people live? Explain your evaluation.

Bug-a-licious!

by Ellen Florian

The food at the fair smelled delicious. People had crowded around to see what the chef was cooking, but so far, nobody had tasted it.

"Here, have some," the chef said with a smile, offering me a spoonful.

I hesitated, but decided to be polite and try it. Everyone watched as I raised the spoon to my mouth.

Closing my eyes, I took a deep breath and ate the contents all at once.

"Yuck!" said somebody.

"Eeeew!" said somebody else.

I began to feel queasy, but I wasn't about to let it show.

"Hey, not bad," I said as I walked away. But I had a sick feeling in the pit of my stomach. I had just eaten fried worms!

That spoonful of worms was just one of many delicacies I sampled at

CRISPY CRITTERS

Hug-a-Bug

A chef serves up a plate of yummy fried worms at Bug Bowl '97.

Bug Bowl '97 in West Lafayette, Indiana. Springtime is bug time, and every April, while the rest of us are getting out the insecticide, the folks in West Lafayette are celebrating bugs. I attended the three-day bugfest, sponsored by Purdue University, to see for myself what all the fuss was over creepy, crawly critters.

Like many people, I have *entomophobia,* a fear of insects. Insects are pests. They're ugly. They bite and sting and spread disease. They ruin plants. In other words, they deserve to be feared and sprayed to death, don't they? Not according to the people who run the Bug Bowl. "We want to get people excited to learn about insects," said Purdue's Al York, who is founder of the Bug Bowl and a professor of *entomology,* the scientific study of insects. "Insects are an important part of nature and a thing of beauty."

Bug Benefits

Cockroaches eat fallen leaves.

Termites recycle dead wood.

Bees provide honey.

Hug a Bug?

The entomologists at Purdue want to convince entomophobes like myself that bugs deserve a little more appreciation than they get. After all, insect species outnumber all other species on Earth combined.

"We should understand that they have a role in nature," said York.

Take cockroaches, for example. They may look disgusting, said York, but they eat fallen leaves in the forest and fertilize the soil with their dung. Similarly, termites are a big nuisance when they eat wood in houses, but they also consume dead wood in the wild, recycling it into soil on the forest floor. Bees sting, but they also provide honey.

Insects also play an important part in the food chain, say entomologists. Animals called *insectivores* rely solely on insects for food. Some other animals rely partially on insects for nourishment.

Insects pollinate about a third of all the plants we eat. In the United States alone, 100 major crops rely on animal pollinators, most of which are insects. For one out of every three bites of food you take, thank an insect.

"People say, 'Let's get rid of the insects because they cause problems for us,'" said Tom Turpin, also a professor of entomology at Purdue. "If we did, the Earth wouldn't be recognizable."

A Tasty Treat

Once I began to understand how important insects are, I approached the Bug Bowl with a more open mind. I set off to eat some bugs.

In the food tent, several chefs were preparing fancy bug cuisine, including caterpillar crunch, cricket fricassee, chicken breast coated with toasted mealworms, asparagus with white worm sauce, and critter corn fritters.

"I use only the finest critters in my fritters!" boasted chef Hubert Schmieder as he showed me a bowl of squirming worms.

A girl popped a fritter into her mouth. "M-m-m, good," she said.

I ate one too. It tasted fine.

Aside from being tasty, bugs are nutritious, said Turpin. "Insects are high in vitamins. They also have more protein than the meat we eat. In most countries, insects are an important part of people's diets as a source of protein."

Proteins are one of the three classes of food that people must have in their diet. The other two are fats and carbohydrates. Among other benefits, proteins function as building blocks for muscles and other tissues of the human body.

Nutritionists say that a prime cut of beef consists of about 20 percent protein. A grasshopper is about 60 percent protein. So, ounce for ounce, grasshoppers deliver three times the protein that beef provides.

Eat Safely

A word of caution: Before you dash out to collect insect recipes, know what you're eating. "Some bugs," said bug chef and graduate student Kathy Heinsohn, "can be dangerous."

Houseflies and cockroaches harbor bacteria that can make you sick, said Heinsohn. Brightly colored insects are usually poisonous. Those that have tiny hairs, or *cilia*, might irritate your mouth and throat. Generally, the safest insects to eat are pale in color and feed on green or brown plants, say entomologists.

Plot

- A **plot** includes the important events that happen in a story.

- Identifying the plot will help you understand the story better.

- A plot usually has a conflict or problem, rising action, climax, and an outcome or resolution.

- As you read, you can write the most important events on a story map to keep the plot structure organized.

Read "The Brahman and the Banker" from *More Stories to Solve* **told by George Shannon.**

Write About It

1. What are the most important events of this story?

2. Create a story map showing the problem, rising action, climax, and resolution of this story.

The Brahman and the Banker

TOLD BY GEORGE SHANNON

A Brahman (an upper-class person in India) and his wife once decided to go on a religious pilgrimage. To make certain that the small amount of money they had—seven hundred rupees—remained safe, they asked a banker friend to keep it for them. Because the banker declined several times before agreeing to keep it, the Brahman thought it would be an insult to ask him for a receipt.

Their trip went well. But when they got back home and went to get their money, the banker said they had never given him any to keep. Day after day, the Brahman asked the banker for his money, and day after day, the banker denied ever having received the Brahman's seven hundred rupees.

One day, while the Brahman was walking home from the banker's, a wealthy merchant's wife heard him crying.

When she learned his problem, she quickly thought of a plan to get his money back. She told the Brahman to return to the banker's the next day at a specific time and ask for his money again. She said that she would be there, too, but that he must pretend not to know her.

The following day, the woman went to the banker's a few minutes before the Brahman was to arrive. She told the banker she would like him to keep her many jewels while she was away. She was going to search for her husband, who was several weeks late coming home from a business trip. This time, when the Brahman came and asked for his money, the banker quickly gave it to him. A few moments later, the woman's maid came to announce that the woman's husband had just returned. Since she no longer needed to travel, the woman kept her jewels and the Brahman went home with his money. How did the woman's plan suddenly make the banker change his ways?

Eager to get his hands on the woman's jewels, the banker didn't want to frighten her away by appearing to have cheated a Brahman out of such a small sum of money.

LOOK AHEAD

In "In the Days of King Adobe," an old woman is too clever for the visitors who want to steal her ham. Follow the plot to see how she outsmarts them.

Vocabulary

Words to Know

fascinated   foolishness   rascals
generous   seldom

Many words have more than one meaning. To decide which meaning of a word is being used, look for clues in the surrounding sentences.

Read the paragraph below. Decide whether *generous* means "unselfish" or "large."

The Dinner Guest

Luisa <u>seldom</u> invited friends home to dinner, but today was different. Rose was coming. Luisa worried about how her little twin sisters would behave. Those two were always full of <u>foolishness</u>. Even Grandma called them <u>rascals</u>. But Luisa had nothing to worry about. Rose was a perfect dinner guest. She listened to the twins and acted as if everything they said <u>fascinated</u> her. One of the twins even offered Rose a <u>generous</u> helping of dessert. Luisa sighed with relief. She knew she'd ask Rose to come to dinner again.

Write About It

Make a list of table manners. Use as many vocabulary words as you can.

In the Days of King Adobe

as told by Joe Hayes

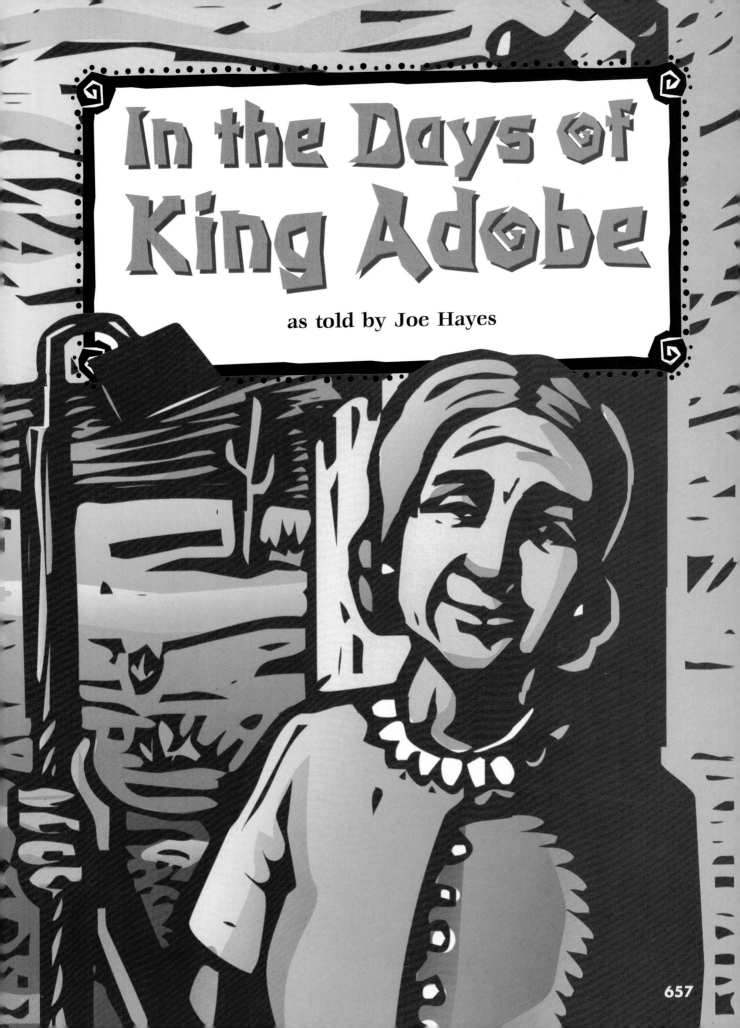

There was once an old woman who lived all alone in a tiny house at the edge of a village. She was very poor, and all she had to eat was beans and tortillas and thin cornmeal mush. Of course, she ate a few vegetables from her garden, but most of them she took into the village on market day to sell or trade for what little she needed for her simple life.

But the old woman was very thrifty, and by saving carefully—a penny a day, a penny a day—she was able to buy herself a big ham. She kept it hanging from a hook in a cool, dark closet behind the kitchen, and she only cut a thin slice from the ham on very special days—or if she was lucky enough to have company join her for a meal.

One evening a couple of young men who were traveling through the country stopped at the old woman's house and asked if they could have lodging for the night. The old woman had no extra beds, but she offered to spread a blanket on the floor for the young men to sleep on. They said that would be fine, and thanked the old woman for her kindness.

"It's nothing," the old woman told them. "I'm happy to have the company. I'll get busy and make us all a good supper."

She got out her pots and pans and then went to the closet and cut three slices from the ham—two thick, generous slices for the travelers and a thin one for herself.

The young men were delighted to see the old woman preparing ham for their supper. Seldom were they offered such good food in their travels. But those two young men were a couple of rascals, and right away a roguish idea came into their minds. They decided to steal the ham that night while the old woman was asleep.

After they had all eaten their fill, the old woman spread out a bed for the young men on the floor. She said good night and wished them good dreams and then went into her own room to sleep.

Of course, the young men didn't go to sleep. They lay on the floor joking and talking about how nice it was going to be to have a whole ham to eat.

When they felt sure the old woman was asleep, the young men got up and crept to the closet. They took the ham down from the hook and wrapped it in a shirt. One of the young men put the ham in his traveling bag. Then the two young men lay down to sleep with smiles on their faces. They had very good dreams indeed!

But the old woman hadn't gone to sleep either. In the many years of her life she had become a good judge of character, and she had noticed the rascally look in the young men's eyes. She knew she had better be on her guard. When she heard the young men getting up from their pad on the floor, she went to the door and peeked out. She saw everything the young men did.

Later that night, when the young men were sound asleep, the old woman crept from her room. She took the ham from the traveling bag and hid it under her bed. Then she wrapped an adobe brick in the shirt and put it in the traveling bag.

When the young men awoke in the morning, they were anxious to be on their way. But the old woman insisted they stay for a bite of breakfast. "It will give you strength," she told them. "You have a long day of walking ahead of you. And you may not have anything else to eat all day."

One of the young men winked at the other as he sat down at the table and said, "You're probably right, *abuelita*, but who knows? Last night I dreamed that today my friend and I would be eating good food all day long."

"Is that right?" the old woman replied. "Tell me more about your dream. I'm fascinated by dreams. I believe they are sometimes true."

The young man thought he'd really make fun of the old woman. He smiled at his friend and then said, "I dreamed we were sitting under a tree eating. It was in a beautiful land. And the king of that country was named Hambone the First."

"Aha!" spoke up the second young man. "Now I remember that I had the same dream. And I remember that the land in which Hambone the First was king was named Travelibag."

The young men had to cover their mouths to keep from bursting out laughing. But the old woman didn't seem to notice. In fact, she seemed to be taking them very seriously.

"I had a similar dream last night myself!" she exclaimed. "I was in a land named Travelibag, and Hambone the First was king of that country. But then he was thrown out by the good people and replaced by a new king named Adobe the Great. And for some people, that meant a time of great hunger had begun."

"Isn't that interesting," the young men said, biting their lips to keep from laughing. "Oh, well, it was just a dream." They hurried to finish their breakfast and then went on their way, laughing at the old woman's foolishness.

All morning long the two rascals joked about the old woman as they traveled down the road. As midday approached, they began to grow tired. They sat down under a shady tree to rest.

"Well, now," said the first young man as he leaned back and closed his eyes. "Don't you think it's time for dreams to come true? Here we are sitting under a tree, just as I dreamed. Open up the land of Travelibag. My stomach tells me I need to visit the king of that land."

"By all means," said the other. "Let's see how things are going with our old friend Hambone the First."

The young man opened his bag and pulled out the bundle wrapped in his shirt. Chuckling to himself he slowly unwrapped the shirt. Suddenly the smile disappeared from the young man's face. "Oh, no," he gasped. "The old woman knew more about dreams than we thought."

"What do you mean?" asked the other.

"Well," he said, "she told us Hambone the First had been thrown out, didn't she?"

"Yes."

"And do you remember who was put in his place?"

The young man laughed. "Adobe the Great! Where do you suppose she came up with a name like that?"

"Probably right here," said his friend. "Look."

The first young man opened his eyes. "I see what you mean," he groaned. "And I see what the old woman meant about the time of great hunger beginning. I'm starved!"

After several hungry days the two young men met another kind old woman who fed them a good meal. This time they didn't even think about trying to play any tricks.

About the Author
Joe Hayes

Joe Hayes is recognized as one of America's top storytellers. He says that his storytelling led directly to his writing. "In fact, most of the stories I've published were worked out orally long before I ever sat down to

write them." When asked how much time he spends writing a book, Mr. Hayes has two answers. "Well, I had been telling those stories for about four years before I wrote them down. So you could say it took four years. On the other hand, since I already had the stories in my head, it only took me about four hours to type them into my computer. So you could say it took four hours." He believes that he makes his stories sound natural because he writes them the way he tells them.

Mr. Hayes grew up in the southwestern United States. He developed an appreciation for Hispanic culture and the Spanish language from his Mexican American friends and schoolmates. Mr. Hayes taught high-school English before he discovered his talent as a storyteller. After listening to his stories, many people wanted to be able to read them too. His book *Watch Out for Clever Women!* from which the story "In the Days of King Adobe" is taken, is his fourteenth book. It was awarded the Southwest Book Award in 1995.

Reader Response

Open for Discussion

This is a storyteller's story. How would a storyteller tell the story to make it funny and exciting? Tell some parts of it as examples.

Comprehension Check

1. Compare the way the men act with the old woman to the way they act when they are alone. How do their thoughts about her change from the beginning to the end of the story? Find details to support your answer.

2. In what ways are the events of the story similar to both the men's and the old woman's dreams? How are they different?

3. What lesson do you think the storyteller wants the reader to learn? Use evidence from the story to explain.

4. At which point in the **plot** do you know what the conflict, or problem, is? What is the resolution of the conflict? (Plot)

5. What is the climax of the story? What events of the **plot** lead up to it? (Plot)

Test Prep

Look Back and Write

Look back at pages 658–662. Think of three words to describe the character of the old woman. Explain how each word accurately describes her, using evidence from the story.

One Day's Food

by Russell Ash

Every day . . . 7 million pizzas are eaten in America . . . one human heart pumps enough blood to fill 170 bathtubs . . . lightning strikes Earth 8 million times . . .

IT WOULD TAKE 75 SUPERTANKERS to carry one day's food for the entire planet. Most people rely on wheat, rice, and corn for their basic food. Adults need about 2,500 calories of food energy a day. However, while Westerners consume up to 4,000 calories a day, some Africans survive on barely 1,800 calories each. And every day, 35,000 people die of starvation.

FOOD CITY

This is what the world's daily helpings of some of its most nutritious foodstuffs would look like, delivered into the heart of a modern city.

THE FASTEST FOOD IN THE WORLD

Every day, Americans munch through 7 million pizzas, 4,400 tons of potato chips, 440 tons of pretzels, around 15 million burgers, 4 million gallons of ice cream, and 250 million sodas, as well as 5 French fries each.

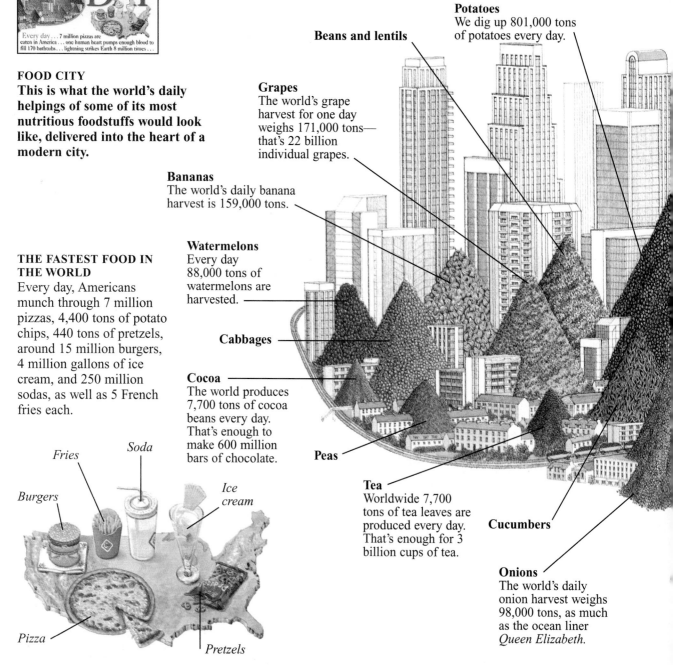

Potatoes
We dig up 801,000 tons of potatoes every day.

Beans and lentils

Grapes
The world's grape harvest for one day weighs 171,000 tons—that's 22 billion individual grapes.

Bananas
The world's daily banana harvest is 159,000 tons.

Watermelons
Every day 88,000 tons of watermelons are harvested.

Cabbages

Cocoa
The world produces 7,700 tons of cocoa beans every day. That's enough to make 600 million bars of chocolate.

Peas

Tea
Worldwide 7,700 tons of tea leaves are produced every day. That's enough for 3 billion cups of tea.

Cucumbers

Onions
The world's daily onion harvest weighs 98,000 tons, as much as the ocean liner *Queen Elizabeth*.

Fries

Soda

Ice cream

Burgers

Pizza

Pretzels

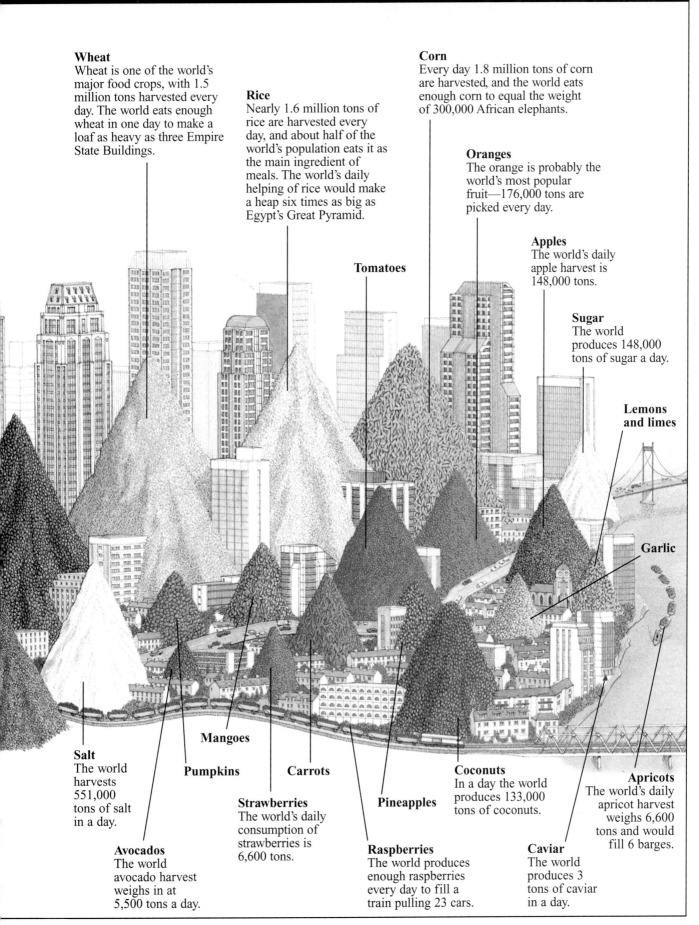

Wheat
Wheat is one of the world's major food crops, with 1.5 million tons harvested every day. The world eats enough wheat in one day to make a loaf as heavy as three Empire State Buildings.

Rice
Nearly 1.6 million tons of rice are harvested every day, and about half of the world's population eats it as the main ingredient of meals. The world's daily helping of rice would make a heap six times as big as Egypt's Great Pyramid.

Corn
Every day 1.8 million tons of corn are harvested, and the world eats enough corn to equal the weight of 300,000 African elephants.

Oranges
The orange is probably the world's most popular fruit—176,000 tons are picked every day.

Apples
The world's daily apple harvest is 148,000 tons.

Sugar
The world produces 148,000 tons of sugar a day.

Tomatoes

Lemons and limes

Garlic

Salt
The world harvests 551,000 tons of salt in a day.

Mangoes

Pumpkins

Carrots

Coconuts
In a day the world produces 133,000 tons of coconuts.

Apricots
The world's daily apricot harvest weighs 6,600 tons and would fill 6 barges.

Avocados
The world avocado harvest weighs in at 5,500 tons a day.

Strawberries
The world's daily consumption of strawberries is 6,600 tons.

Pineapples

Raspberries
The world produces enough raspberries every day to fill a train pulling 23 cars.

Caviar
The world produces 3 tons of caviar in a day.

Skill Lesson

Making Judgments

- **Making judgments** means forming opinions about someone or something. Characters, authors, and readers all make judgments.

- Characters make judgments about situations and other characters.

- Authors make judgments about the subject of their writing. Evaluate an author's judgments by asking if they are supported by evidence in the story or article.

- Readers make judgments about characters, authors, and ideas. A reader's judgment should be supported by evidence in the story or article.

Read "Can You Change Your School Lunch?" from *Zillions*.

Talk About It

1. What do you think of Justin's idea? What evidence in the article supports your judgment?

2. What is the author's judgment about how to change school lunches? How does the author support it?

Can You Change Your School Lunch?
from *Zillions*

Flavorless food? Cold main courses? These were one fifth grader's complaints, and he did something about it. Last year, Justin, ten, gathered a few fellow students at Alpharetta Elementary in Alpharetta, Georgia, and formed a youth advisory council to evaluate their school's lunches. "We also did a survey, and the kids told us their ideas," he said.

The group then shared their findings with their principal and the cafeteria manager. Justin also contacted Team Nutrition, a government program that provides nutrition information to schools and helps develop tasty and nutritious school lunches.

Team Nutrition sent three chefs to help create new meals. The "cold and flavorless" food was replaced with tasty meals such as oven-roasted turkey with vegetables, quesadillas, and apple strudel. "I'm very pleased with the results," Justin said.

If you want to change *your* school lunch, talk to your school's food-service manager and your principal. But keep in mind that school lunches must meet the government's nutritional goals. Also, food-service managers must often work with *commodities*— free food they get from the government. Commodities can include everything from pounds of peanut butter to loads of lentils. Or even *fig-nuggets*—pureed figs cooked into bite-sized squares. So food-service managers have to be very creative.

"You serve a kid fig-nuggets, he's going to look at you like you just gave him a plate of dog food," said Henry Biagi, school-district director of food services in Somerville, Massachusetts. Biagi solved the problem by mixing the fig-nuggets into cookies and trail mix.

Sound crazy? In San Francisco, schools mix pureed prunes into chocolate-chip cookies!

Ask your school's food-service managers what commodities *they* get, and see if *you* can come up with some creative recipes!

LOOK AHEAD

Just Telling the Truth
from Felicia the Critic by Ellen Conford

In "Just Telling the Truth," Felicia makes some judgments that get her in a bit of trouble. As you read, make judgments of your own about Felicia and her ideas.

Vocabulary

Words to Know

career	critical	efficient
maneuvered	opinion	resolved
shattered	survey	

When you read, you may come across a word you don't know. To figure out its meaning, look for clues in the words and sentences around it. A clue might be found in an explanation or definition given before or after the unknown word.

Read the paragraph below and notice *career*. Find an explanation or definition in the same sentence. Notice how this helps you understand what *career* means.

Career Choices

Dad wants me to be an auto mechanic and work with him in his shop someday. If I do, I hope I can be as efficient and careful as Dad. Once I helped him as he maneuvered a windshield so it fit perfectly on a car. If it had dropped, the shattered glass would have meant lost time and money. Sometimes I give Dad my opinion about improving the business. He listens and never says I'm being critical. Working at the shop may be the career for me, but I resolved to survey many jobs before making my decision.

Talk About It

Discuss a career that interests you. Use as many vocabulary words as you can.

672

Just Telling the Truth

from *Felicia the Critic*
by Ellen Conford

Felicia was sure it would be a good day. She was wearing her favorite sweater, and Cheryl was going to meet her at the corner, so she was sure she would have someone to walk to school with. Sometimes Cheryl's father drove her to school, like when she had to bring her bass viol for orchestra, and then Felicia often ended up walking alone.

Sometimes girls she knew would say, "Hi, Felicia," and that meant she could walk with them, but some days nobody said, "Hi, Felicia," and she had to walk by herself.

It wasn't that she didn't like to walk by herself. Lots of times, after school or during vacations, she went on walks alone, exploring blocks beyond her own, hoping that she would have some sort of adventure, or maybe even discover a completely uncharted, brand-new block that no one had ever seen before. (She hadn't discovered one as yet, and she didn't really think it was very likely that she would, but you never know.)

But somehow, walking to school alone was different from taking a walk.

Cheryl was not at the corner when Felicia got there. Felicia felt her stomach skitter with disappointment. Maybe Mr. Sweet had driven her to school after all. Or maybe Cheryl was sick, and not even coming to school today.

Felicia suddenly felt a little chilly under her sweater, and she shivered. Maybe she'd been wrong; maybe it wasn't a beautiful sweater day at all.

Then she saw Cheryl trotting up Decatur Street toward the corner. Felicia felt such a wave of relief wash over her that she wanted to grab Cheryl and hug her.

But instead she said, "You're late."

"Well, I couldn't help it," Cheryl panted, sounding a little annoyed. "I woke up late and my mother made me practice a whole half-hour anyway."

They started up Perry Street, walking slowly so Cheryl could catch her breath.

"If you got an alarm clock," Felicia suggested, "you could wake up on time."

"I have an alarm clock," Cheryl said. "I forgot to set it."

"Maybe if you put a little sign next to it, like, 'REMEMBER TO SET ME' or something—"

"For heaven's sake, Felicia," Cheryl broke in, "this is the first time in a whole year I overslept." She still sounded annoyed. She must be mad at her mother for making her practice even though she was late, Felicia thought. That *is* pretty unreasonable.

But that was the way Mrs. Sweet was. Not unreasonable—in fact, Mrs. Sweet thought herself *very* reasonable. She talked in a cool, reasonable tone of voice, and everything she said was reasonable. But she made Cheryl *do* a lot of things, and Cheryl wasn't sure she wanted to do all of them.

Like taking ballet lessons and going to French class at the Saturday morning Cultural Arts Community Workshop, and taking ice-skating lessons and having to practice the bass viol.

Although the bass really was a victory for Cheryl. Mrs. Sweet had wanted her to learn viola or violin in school, but once Cheryl saw the bass viol and heard the sounds it made, she was determined not to be talked out of it. And she had won. But since she had to practice a half hour every day, Felicia wasn't sure if she had really won anything.

They walked the rest of the way to school without saying very much, but that was all right. Felicia loved to talk, but sometimes Cheryl didn't. And it didn't matter, because they were friends. They could walk together without saying one word, and that was okay with Felicia.

The crossing guard stopped them just as they stepped off the curb to cross the street.

"Hold it there!" he ordered.

Felicia and Cheryl stepped back onto the sidewalk.

"Look at that," grumbled Felicia. "He's letting all those cars go by, and then he's going to let the other cars make their turns, and there are only two of us standing here, and we were practically halfway across the street anyway."

"It doesn't seem fair," Cheryl agreed.

"It's not just that it's not fair," Felicia complained, "but it's not *efficient*, either." "Efficient" had become one of Felicia's favorite words, ever since her father had pointed out to her that there were more *efficient* ways of getting her room cleaned up than by throwing everything into the bottom of the closet and then hoping that her mother wouldn't tell her she had to clean out the closet.

"The efficient way would be to let us cross because there are only two of us, and then let those three cars turn, and then the traffic going straight wouldn't have to stop at all after that. Because," Felicia glanced nervously around, "I think we're the last ones here."

The policeman stopped the traffic again and waved the two girls across the street.

"You see," Felicia said, hurrying into the school yard, "he just had to stop another whole line of cars to let us cross. Not efficient."

"Hurry up," urged Cheryl, sounding annoyed again. "We're going to be late."

At lunchtime, Felicia and Cheryl sat at a table with Phyllis Brody, Lorraine Kalman, and Fern Krinsky.

"Look at that Wendy Frank," Phyllis whispered. "Talking about her club. That's all she ever does. What's so great about her old club anyway?"

"What's so great about *any* club?" Felicia asked.

Phyllis looked at her disdainfully.

"Well, what do they do?" Felicia wanted to know. "What's the club for?"

"For?" echoed Fern. "What does it have to be for? It's a *club*."

"Well, shouldn't it be *for* something?" Felicia persisted. "You know, like stamp collectors, or ecology, or to feed starving children?"

"It's just a club, Felicia," Lorraine said, in the same patient-but-not-really-patient tone of voice Marilyn often used with her.

"I think a club should *do* something," Felicia went on doggedly. "Or else it's not a club, it's just a *group*."

Phyllis and Lorraine exchanged looks.

"*Anyway*," Phyllis continued, glaring at Felicia, "the way she's always whispering to people makes me sick."

"Maybe it wouldn't make you sick if she whispered to you sometimes," Felicia suggested, tearing open her bag of corn chips.

Phyllis scowled at her. "Eat your corn chips, Felicia," she said coldly.

But Phyllis's anger made Felicia's stomach jump. She pushed the cellophane bag to the center of the table. "Anybody want some?" she muttered, without looking up at the girls.

Nobody answered her, but Phyllis and Lorraine helped themselves to generous handfuls of the corn chips.

"Felicia, want to trade?" Cheryl asked. "I have bologna."

"Thanks," Felicia said gratefully. Cheryl always sensed the right thing to say.

"Here." Felicia handed Cheryl half of her sandwich.

Cheryl grinned. "But you have bologna too."

"But yours is on rye bread, and mine is on whole wheat," Felicia explained.

That wasn't really the reason. Felicia liked whole wheat bread almost as much as rye. She just wanted to trade with Cheryl today. It made her feel better.

"**W**here's Mom?" Felicia asked, dropping her schoolbooks on the kitchen table.

"Shopping," said Marilyn, not even looking up from her fingernails, which she was gloomily painting "Concord Grape."

Felicia opened the refrigerator door and peered inside.

"A good thing she is," commented Felicia, rummaging around through the shelves. "There isn't a thing in here to eat."

She took two slices of American cheese and a square of semisweet baking chocolate and put them on the table, along with a jar of peanut butter from the cabinet, and a spoon.

"You're going to get pimples if you keep on eating like that," Marilyn predicted.

Felicia took a spoonful of peanut butter and licked at it.

"Yecch," grimaced Marilyn. "How can you? Just watching you eat that makes me ill."

"Don't watch me, then," said Felicia reasonably.

"What do you think of this color?" Marilyn asked, holding up her hand so Felicia could see her nails.

The question was so unexpected that Felicia was startled. Marilyn never asked her opinion about anything, and half the time when Felicia said something to her sister, the reply was, "Who asked you?"

Felicia carefully peeled the plastic wrap off her cheese. Did Marilyn want to know the truth, or was she going to be sensitive and hurt if Felicia said she didn't like the color? Felicia sat, nibbling her cheese, hoping Marilyn would forget she'd asked.

"What do you think of this color?" Marilyn repeated irritably. "Aren't you listening?"

"I'm listening," Felicia said calmly.

"Well?"

"I think," Felicia said reluctantly, "that it looks like dried blood."

"Ohh!" Marilyn hissed. "You—"

Felicia jerked away from her sister, who looked as if she were about to lunge at her, and her arm hit the peanut butter jar, knocking it off the table to the floor, where it made a splattering smash.

"Ohh," groaned Felicia, looking at the mess of broken glass and peanut butter scattered over the kitchen.

"You'd better clean that up before Mother gets home," Marilyn warned. Felicia thought her sister looked almost glad about the mess on the floor.

Felicia went to the broom closet to get the broom and dustpan. The narrow closet was a jumble of cleaning equipment, all looking as if it would tumble out at you if you tried to remove anything. Felicia tugged at the broom, catching a sponge mop as it fell out at her and shoving it back in the closet. The dustpan was on the floor, with a pail of rags and a can of floor wax on top of it. Assorted spray cans, jars, and containers surrounded it on all sides. Carefully Felicia maneuvered things around till she could get the dustpan out.

"Whew," she breathed, forcing the closet door shut and leaning against it, "I'm tired before I've even started. What an inefficient closet."

She started to sweep up the shattered glass, but it was all mixed in with the peanut butter and Felicia realized she was smearing the stuff all over the floor.

"Oh!" she wailed. "Look at this!"

Marilyn looked disinterestedly. "You're making a bigger mess than before," she remarked.

The front door opened. "It's me," their mother called.

"Don't come in here with bare feet!" yelled Felicia.

"I don't usually go shopping in my bare—what happened here?" Mrs. Kershenbaum asked, standing in the kitchen doorway with two bags of groceries in her arms.

"It was an accident," Felicia said. "And I'm not doing too well getting it cleaned up."

"I can see that. Marilyn, take these bags, please, and be careful not to slip. I have three more out in the car you can help me with."

Marilyn sighed deeply and pulled herself up from her chair with a great effort. She took the bags from her mother and put them on the kitchen table.

"Wait, Felicia, I'll help you with that," her mother said. "I think you're just making it worse. Marilyn what *is* that on your fingernails?"

"Concord Grape," Marilyn said.

"Remove it, please," her mother said.

"*Mother,*" Marilyn began, in her most exasperated voice.

"I thought it looked like dried blood," Felicia said.

"Oh, forget it, Marilyn," her mother said. "Leave it on, leave it on. Just help me get those groceries in, please."

Grumbling, Marilyn followed her out to the car.

They came back in and plopped the bags down on the table.

"We'd better get this cleaned up first," said Mrs. Kershenbaum, taking off her coat, "or we'll kill ourselves."

She opened the broom closet door, and the mop fell out at her. She shoved it back in and pulled out a bag of sponges.

"Look, do it this way," she said, showing Felicia how to push the glass into one heap with the sponge and then wipe it all into the dustpan. "See, with the sponge you won't cut yourself and then when the glass is all cleaned up you can take care of the peanut butter."

"There," she said when Felicia was finished, "now we can walk in here without risk to life and limb. Where did Marilyn go? I wanted her to help me put the groceries away."

"Don't call her," Felicia said quickly. "I'll help you." She wanted an excuse to be alone with her mother. The way Phyllis, Lorraine, and Fern had talked to her at lunch had bothered Felicia all day. Even walking home with Cheryl hadn't made her forget the way she felt when Phyllis said, "Eat your corn chips, Felicia," in that cold, disdainful voice. Maybe her mother could explain why the girls had acted that way.

"So," Mrs. Kershenbaum said briskly when Felicia finished telling her the conversation as exactly as she could remember, "you got the feeling they were mad at you."

"It was no feeling," Felicia said positively. "They were mad at me, all right. But I don't know why."

Her mother looked at her for a long time. "Are you sure," she said finally, "you don't know why? You haven't even got an idea?"

"Well," Felicia hesitated, "I told the truth. Maybe they didn't like that."

"Felicia," her mother said gently, "there's a difference between truth and opinion. The truth is facts. Opinion is what you think. You told them what you thought."

"And they didn't like that. Shouldn't I say what I think?"

Her mother frowned. "Look, if you have a great idea for something and someone comes along and says, 'Boy, what a dumb idea, this is wrong and this is wrong,' wouldn't you feel bad?"

"I guess so," Felicia said uncertainly.

"Well, you see, you tend to be a little—critical. People don't like it when you tell them all their bad points, or all the things that are wrong with their ideas."

"It's bad to be critical?" asked Felicia, puzzled.

"Not that it's bad," her mother said. "But don't expect people to like it when you tell them what they're doing wrong, or why their plans won't work. Actually, there are people who make a career out of being critical."

"There are?"

"Sure. Critics."

"What do they do?" Felicia asked curiously.

"They read books and see plays and movies and concerts and television shows, and then they write their opinions about them. They explain what they thought was wrong and what they thought was right."

Felicia thought about this for a minute. Her mother said she tended to be critical, and there were actually people who got paid for being critical! Maybe . . .

"Maybe *I'll* be a critic some day," Felicia said thoughtfully.

"I wouldn't be surprised," her mother grinned. "But, in the meanwhile, you might try constructive criticism."

"Constructive criticism?"

"Instead of saying, 'This is lousy, this is lousy and this is lousy,' you point out how it could be better. See, constructive criticism is helpful. If you just tear something apart, you're being *destructive*. But if you show how it could be made better or done better, you're being *constructive*. And that's a very valuable talent to have, to be able to be a constructive critic."

A constructive critic! thought Felicia. That's what she was going to be from now on. Her parents always said that a child should develop his talents. A gift shouldn't be neglected, they said. It should be nourished, and practiced, till you got better and better at it.

Well, Felicia decided, criticalness is my talent, and I ought to develop it. There is no point, her mother always advised Marilyn, in trying to be something you're not. Just be the best you can at what you *are*.

That's what I'll do, Felicia resolved. I'll be the best critic I can. *Constructive* critic, she reminded herself.

"Do you mind," Felicia asked her mother, "if I make some constructive criticisms about the broom closet?"

"What?" asked her mother, perplexed.

"Well, I just decided I'm going to be a constructive critic and I think there might be some ways to make the broom closet more—efficient."

"Be my guest," her mother smiled. "Any constructive criticism about *that* disaster area will be appreciated."

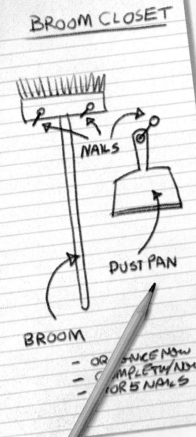

BROOM CLOSET

NAILS

DUST PAN

BROOM

- OR ONCE NOW
- COMPLETELY NOW
- FOR 5 NAILS

Felicia ran to get a magazine she had seen a couple of days ago. There was a picture in it of a "cleaning closet" that she remembered. Now if she could make her mother's broom closet look like that . . .

She found the picture she wanted and studied it for a while.

Then she took a pencil and paper, and biting her lip in concentration, began to scribble down her ideas.

"Now," she announced to her mother a while later, "I have here some suggestions about the broom closet. Some constructive criticism."

"Not right now, dear," Mrs. Kershenbaum said absently, running her finger down the cookbook index.

"Then can I do what I wrote on the list myself?"

"Yes, go ahead," her mother nodded.

"I need some nails and a hammer."

"In the basement."

Felicia got hammer and nails and took everything out of the broom closet.

"Look at this," her mother said angrily. "Just look at this! A four-pound roast, and a pound of it must be fat. They had it wrapped so you could only see the top and all the fat is on the bottom."

"Why don't you take it back?" Felicia said, standing in the broom closet and making little marks on the walls with a pencil.

"Oh, it's too much trouble," her mother grumbled. "Anyway, I want it for tomorrow, and it has to be marinated overnight."

Felicia started hammering.

"What are you doing?" her mother asked.

"Putting nails in to hang things up," Felicia replied.

"Oh. Well, be careful," she said dubiously.

"What is that NOISE?" Marilyn yelled from the stairs.

"Felicia is fixing up the broom closet," her mother yelled back over the noise of the pounding hammer.

"She'll probably break it," Marilyn said sourly, standing at the kitchen door to watch her sister.

"You can't break a broom closet," Felicia muttered, concentrating on her project.

"*You* could," retorted Marilyn. "Which one do you like best?" she asked her mother, holding up one hand with four fingernails painted different colors.

"That one," said her mother, pointing to the one pale fingernail on Marilyn's hand.

"I didn't put any polish on that one!" Marilyn wailed.

"Yes. I like that," her mother said firmly.

Felicia worked for almost an hour. When she was finished she stood back to survey the job. It's good, Felicia thought warmly. It's really good! It's neat, and organized and—*efficient.* She closed the door of the closet.

"I'm done," she announced. "Everybody come look."

Her father had come home while she was working and came into the kitchen now to see what she'd been doing.

"I'm here," her mother said, turning away from the stove to look.

"You too, Marilyn!" Felicia yelled.

"I do not have a consuming interest in broom closets!" Marilyn yelled back. "Hold the unveiling without me."

"Come on, Marilyn," Felicia insisted. "You were the one who said I'd break the closet."

"Oh, for heaven's sake," Marilyn complained, but she came, finally, into the kitchen too.

"Ready?" Felicia asked. "Da dum!" She flung open the door of the broom closet.

"It's gorgeous!" her mother gasped. "Felicia, it's wonderful."

"This is not our broom closet," declared Mr. Kershenbaum. "This is definitely not the broom closet I know and hate."

Felicia had put nails in the walls to hang up all the mops and brooms that had hooks on their handles. The ones that didn't have hooks hung with their handles downward on the wall, with two nails forming a sort of holder for them. The dustpan was also hung on a nail, and the pail, empty now, was hung by its wire carrying handle. The cleaning supplies, bottles, cans, were neatly arranged on the floor of the closet and the sponges were evenly stacked on the one small shelf at the top. Felicia had folded all the rags and put them on the shelf next to the sponges.

"I can't get over it," her mother marveled. "I've been meaning to do something about that closet for years . . . "

Felicia beamed with pride.

"Would you say that was constructive?" she asked her mother.

"Extremely."

This is a good start, Felicia thought happily. I'm going to make a fine critic.

After dinner, still glowing with the success of her broom closet project, Felicia went upstairs to her room and took out an old notebook. She tore all the used pages out of it and wrote on the first clean page: *Criticism Notebook*. She turned the page and wrote at the top of the next page: *Constructive Criticisms*.

Then she sat with her chin in her hand, nibbling on the end of her pen, thinking. She thought for quite a while, frowning with concentration, unaware of anything but the problem she was working on.

Finally, with a satisfied sigh, she bent over her notebook and began to write.

About the Author

Ellen Conford

Ms. Conford started writing books for young children when her own son was four years old. One day when she couldn't find anything suitable for him at the library, she went home and decided to write a book herself. The book became *Impossible, Possum*. She wrote two more picture books about the possum family before beginning to write for older children.

Not only do Ms. Conford's books entertain, but many of them are award winners. *Lenny Kandell, Smart Aleck* was named one of *School Library Journal's* Best Books of the Year. *Alfred G. Graebner Memorial High School Handbook of Rules and Regulations* was named a Best Book for Young Adults by the American Library Association.

It bothers Ms. Conford that there are so many young people and adults who never read just for pleasure. "I write the kinds of books for children and teenagers that I liked to read at their age," she says, "books meant purely to entertain, to amuse, to divert. I feel that I am competing with the television set for a child's mind and attention, and if I receive a letter that says, 'I never used to like to read until I read one of your books, and now I really enjoy reading,' I feel I've won a great victory."

Reader Response

When Felicia decides to be a constructive critic, she writes down her ideas about the broom closet on paper. If you were Felicia, what would you write?

Comprehension Check

1. In your own words, explain the difference between destructive and constructive criticism. Give an example of each from the story.

2. Most of the time, Felicia is sure that she is right. When does she show that she is not sure?

3. If the author had written her ideas about criticism in a short, nonfiction paragraph, would they have the same effect on you as they do in the story? Explain.

4. List three of Felicia's opinions. **Make judgments** about which you agree with and disagree with. Write your opinion next to each of Felicia's. (Making Judgments)

5. Look back at the lunchtime scene on pages 677–678. **Make** your own **judgment** about how all the girls could have gotten along better. (Making Judgments)

Test Prep

Look Back and Write

Look back at pages 675–678. Compare and contrast the characters of Cheryl and Felicia. Why do you think they are such good friends? Support your answer with evidence from the story.

How to Set Up a Home Study Center

from *School Power* magazine

Some people can study in the middle of blaring TVs and radios, ringing telephones, battling brothers and sisters, barking family dogs, and busy parents. Maybe you're one of these people, but probably you're not. You'll study better if you follow these guidelines.

Location

Try to find a quiet place that's free from distractions (no phone, no video games). Choose a place where you don't do other things. For example, if you study on your bed, you'll start thinking about falling asleep, and pretty soon . . . zzzzz . . .

Lighting

Some students like it bright, while others choose softer lighting. Natural light is best for you, but whatever light you use, make sure there's enough to read and work by without straining your eyes. **A lamp should shed light over your shoulder. It should not be aimed straight at the printed page.**

Seating

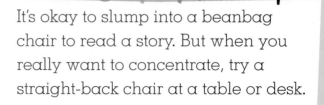

It's okay to slump into a beanbag chair to read a story. But when you really want to concentrate, try a straight-back chair at a table or desk.

692

Noise

Try to pick a place away from the center of activity. Post a personalized DO NOT DISTURB sign to let others know you're working.

Supplies

Many students waste valuable time searching for study supplies. You can be more efficient. Keep these things handy on your desk, in a shoebox, or in a plastic shopping bag.

✔ pencils
✔ pens
✔ erasers
✔ markers
✔ writing paper
✔ tape
✔ a hole punch
✔ a pencil sharpener
✔ glue or paste
✔ a ruler
✔ a stapler
✔ colored pencils
✔ paper clips
✔ index cards
✔ a calculator
✔ (anything else?)

Stocking a study center can get expensive. If there's something you need and don't have, talk it over with your teachers. They may have extra supplies on hand.

Bulletin Board

Use it to post calendars, important notices, and directions for special projects. Leave room for postcards, pictures, and cartoons. Your study center doesn't have to be boring.

References

Build a small personal library, with at least a dictionary and a thesaurus. Also useful: a one-volume desk encyclopedia, a set of encyclopedias (if your family has one), or access to an online encyclopedia through a computer service.

Add an almanac, an atlas, and other references as you need them. Example: if you're taking Spanish, you'll probably want a Spanish-English dictionary.

Michelle's tip for students on the go

Michelle is a competitive swimmer who practices 20 hours a week and goes to swim meets on a regular basis. To keep up with her schoolwork, she keeps a "study kit" in the family car. This kit includes many of the items on our Supplies list—plus a lapboard. This allows Michelle to study in the car on her way to practices and at meets while waiting for her event.

Visualizing

- **Visualizing** is creating a picture in your mind as you read.

- Pay attention to description, imagery, and sensory words that help you imagine what you are reading. Also think about what you already know about the places, people, and things being described.

- As you read and get more information, you may need to change the picture in your mind to match the new details.

- If you have a hard time visualizing, reread or read more slowly to get a better picture.

Read "Mrs. Middlesome-Merry's Art Studio" from *The Rainbow Watchers* **by Diana Hendry.**

Talk About It

1. What words does the author use to help you visualize Mrs. Middlesome-Merry?

2. Describe to a friend what you would see if you walked up the stairs and entered Mrs. Middlesome-Merry's art studio.

Mrs. Middlesome-Merry's
ART STUDIO

by Diana Hendry

Hannah half expected Mrs. Middlesome-Merry to look like a flower herself and to be wearing her violet hat, but when the door opened Hannah saw a small, chubby woman with yellow-going-gray hair and bluebell-blue eyes. She wore a big apron splodged with paint colors and soup colors, and the pocket of her apron was full of paintbrushes and soup ladles.

"Good morning," said Hannah's father, "my name is Thomas Knap and this is my daughter, Hannah. We live just down the street at number three twenty-five and yesterday I bought one of your paintings—*Red Tulips.*"

"Oh, how very nice!" said Mrs. Middlesome-Merry, turning red as the tulips. "Then come and see my other paintings," said Mrs. Middlesome-

Merry. "I have a studio at the top of the house, in the attic."

Climbing up to the studio was not easy for Hannah and her father because at the bottom of the stairs was a big brass tub and in the tub an ivy vine began; and the ivy went on and on, in and out of the banister rails in great loops and swirls, knots and jungle tangles as though it were trying to take over the whole house.

When they reached Mrs. Middlesome-Merry's attic they found that it was more like a garden than an attic. The room had a large skylight and beneath it a big wooden table. On the table were pots and pots of flowers—hyacinths in bowls, sweet peas in jugs, dog daisies in old milk bottles, lilies in a jam jar, poppies in a yogurt pot. And all round the walls were paintings of flowers—snowdrops and roses, dahlias and dizzy-lizzies, daffodils and delphiniums.

Hannah let her eyes have a very good drink and then she said, "I feel as if I'm back in the country in here."

LOOK AHEAD

As you read about trompe l'oeil art in "Is It Real?" notice how the author helps you visualize this particular style of art.

Vocabulary

Words to Know

artistic	**deceive**	**style**
realistic	**represent**	**viewer**
sculpture		

Words with similar meanings are called **synonyms.** You can often figure out the meaning of an unknown word by finding a clue in the words around it. Sometimes this clue is a synonym.

Read the paragraph below. Notice how *fool* helps you understand what *deceive* means.

Setting the Stage

How can you represent the real world on a stage? To create a setting for a play, you must deceive the audience. It's easy to design a realistic scene that will fool the viewer. A couch, a table, and a lamp can become a living room. If you want the style to be homey, add family photos and a fake fireplace. Shine a spotlight on orange foil to suggest flames. For a modern setting, put a sculpture next to simple chairs with bright cushions. It takes artistic talent to create a setting, and it also takes a trick or two.

Write About It

Use vocabulary words to describe the setting of a play you've seen or read.

Right: René Magritte,
La condition humaine, 1933.

Is It Real?

from *Artistic Trickery:*
The Tradition of
Trompe L'Oeil Art

by Michael Capek

When some people think about art, t___
___ntings in stuffy museu___
stern-faced folk___
___un. Thi___

1. Marilyn Levine,
   Black Gloves, 1987.

What Is Trompe L'Oeil?

When some people think about art, they think of old paintings in stuffy museums. They imagine artists as stern-faced folks who rarely laugh or have any fun. This image isn't true, of course. And the proof is trompe l'oeil.

Trompe l'oeil (pronounced *trump-LOY* or *trawmp-LOY*) is a French phrase that means "to trick or fool the eye"—and that's the whole point. Trompe l'oeil is a way of painting something so perfectly that the viewer is fooled into believing that what he or she sees is *real*.

Trompe l'oeil is different from realism, or still life painting, which tries to represent nonliving objects truthfully. An artist who works in the trompe l'oeil style wants to *deceive* the viewer. The viewer is supposed to think—at least for a minute—that the work is really the object being represented, instead of a painting or sculpture. Trompe l'oeil plays tricks on your visual sense, creating optical illusions. It's a kind of visual game. And the more familiar you become with the game, the more fun it is.

Throughout history, dozens of artistic movements and fads have come and gone. Many different artistic styles and techniques have been used to create trompe l'oeil. Contemporary super-realist artists, for example, whose paintings make us wonder "Is it a photograph or a painting?" are practicing trompe l'oeil.

2. Duane Hanson,
   Traveler, 1990.

Ceramic trompe l'oeil jokes have been around since people learned how to mold clay, fire it, and paint it to resemble anything from fish to handbags. For instance, when you look at *Black Gloves* (fig. 1) by Marilyn Levine, it's hard to believe they are not an actual pair of worn leather gloves but only cleverly painted ceramic. Even full-sized sculpture deceptions have been created from a variety of materials. Duane Hanson's 1990 sculpture, for example, *Traveler* (fig. 2), is a life-size portrayal of an exhausted tourist.

Artists have chosen to work with trompe l'oeil for a variety of reasons. Maybe painters want to challenge themselves and see how good they really are. Before the invention of the camera, artists used trompe l'oeil to capture events or people in a highly realistic way. Whatever their reasons for doing it, trompe l'oeilists—sometimes called illusionists—all have one thing in common: the desire to surprise.

Artists from many different countries have been *tromping* people's *oeils* for centuries. An ancient Roman mosaic floor discovered in a ruin is an early example of trompe l'oeil. The mosaic, sometimes referred to as *The Unswept Floor*, looks like it's covered with the remains of a great feast. There's even a mouse in the lower corner about to start its own feast. Other similar "littered" floors, even older than this one, date back to the second or third century B.C. Evidently the ancient Greeks appreciated the trompe l'oeil game before the Romans.

Interior designers still use trompe l'oeil to fool people's eyes. One interior design company (appropriately called Tromploy) came up with its own version of the old littered floor trick. The designers painted a floor with what appears to be a wrinkled scrap of paper lying near the door. Another designer, Charles Goforth, painted a canvas floor cloth (fig. 3) that looks like a beautiful Persian carpet with one corner turned up to reveal some dried leaves.

3. Charles Goforth,
   Kicked Carpet, 1989.

Food

Most of us love food. Food holds tremendous power over people. Trompe l'oeil artists like to play with our fantasies. They know the attraction of food will make viewers more susceptible to being tricked.

Audrey Flack's 1974 painting *Strawberry Tart Supreme* (fig. 4) seems so real you can almost taste the sweet chocolate icing, whipped cream, and strawberries. The gray border tells your eyes it's all fake, however. Flack does the same thing with fruit in *Spaced Out Apple*. Painted with slight flaws and looking like they were sliced just minutes ago, the apples and oranges seem to spill right out of the picture.

People have sworn they could smell peanuts while gazing at *Fresh Roasted* by John Haberle. The 1887 painting shows a wooden bin of roasted nuts and a tin measuring can—all behind that common trompe l'oeil device, broken glass. You want to reach out and pick up the peanut that seems to have fallen down to the edge of the bin.

Animals

Animals have occasionally been subjects for trompe l'oeil artists. But, the problem of making them appear lifelike, even for an instant, is difficult to overcome.

The 19th-century American painter Alexander Pope once painted a lion in a cage, which he exhibited in a fashionable New York hotel behind real iron bars. People from all over the country came to see the convincing illusion. A similar, though much more endearing, picture is Pope's *Pups in Transit*. It shows a crate of four sad-faced puppies. One sleepy pup sticks his nose through the wire. A sign above them reads "For Sale."

4. Audrey Flack,
   Strawberry Tart Supreme, 1974.

For people who want pets but don't want the responsibility, modern trompe l'oeil designers have the answer. One company, Decorative Arts, has created a dog that lies peacefully in a corner of a client's house (fig. 5).

The Tradition Continues

Tastes change, styles of art come and go, but trompe l'oeil remains popular. It's no mystery, really. Most of us love things that astonish us, make us shake our heads in wonder, or make us laugh, even at ourselves.

When people see Kent Addison's watercolor paintings, they often ask, "Are those real paper airplanes?" or "Why is a gum wrapper stuck onto that painting?" Of course, those items aren't real. Like so many trompe l'oeil artists before him, Addison likes to paint common objects. His *Still Life #1019* (fig. 6) focuses on paper—torn newsprint, folded brown wrapping paper, and notebook paper.

The trompe l'oeil game is old, but it remains fresh, and it will continue as long as artists delight in fooling our eyes and teasing our minds. Illusionists will keep on working their magic and making us exclaim, "That can't possibly be a painting!"

5. Decorative Arts, Inc.,
   trompe l'oeil mural, 1992.

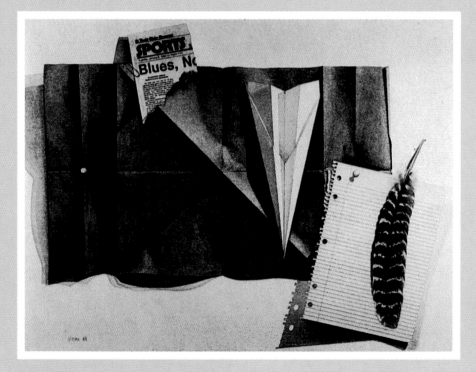

6. Kent Addison, *Still Life
   #1019*, 1982.

About the Author
Michael Capek

Michael Capek has always been a teacher. He has taught high school for thirty years, but even before that he loved to demonstrate new skills for others. "By nature I am a teacher," he has remarked. "I used to teach kids in the neighborhood where I grew up how to do all sorts of things—play basketball, find fossils, fish, whittle, whistle. You name it." Mr. Capek is convinced that his pleasure in teaching others is one of his main reasons for writing.

Artistic Trickery: The Tradition of Trompe L'Oeil Art was Mr. Capek's first book. Since then he has written another nonfiction work titled *Murals: Cave, Cathedral, to Street*. He finds writing nonfiction an enjoyable challenge "not because it's easy, but because it's hard to do well." Often he discovers that the real world is much more interesting than fiction. Besides writing books, Mr. Capek has written several articles for magazines such as *Adventure, Cricket, Teen, Ranger Rick,* and *Highlights for Children.*

One of the most enjoyable parts of writing a book, according to Mr. Capek, is researching the subject. He loves being around books. In fact, he can't imagine any better way of spending an afternoon than getting lost in the stacks of a library.

Mr. Capek lives in Kentucky with his family and his dog Jingle Bells.

Reader Response

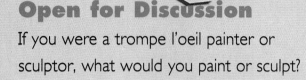

Open for Discussion

If you were a trompe l'oeil painter or sculptor, what would you paint or sculpt?

Comprehension Check

1. How would you know if a painting was done in the trompe l'oeil style? Use evidence from the selection to explain.

2. How might people be tromped by trompe l'oeil art? Give two examples from the selection.

3. Do you agree or disagree with the author that trompe l'oeil remains popular because most of us love things that astonish us? Why?

4. Not all of the works of art that are described are pictured. Find one such description and try to **visualize** the work of art as you read. Which details help create the picture in your mind? (Visualizing)

5. Choose one of the works of art to describe. In your own words, use imagery words to describe the picture so that someone else can **visualize** it. (Visualizing)

 **Test Prep**

Look Back and Write

Look back at pages 698–700. About how old is the idea and practice of trompe l'oeil? How can you tell? Support your answer with details from the selection.

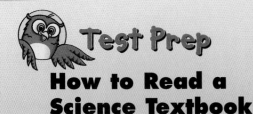

Test Prep

How to Read a Science Textbook

1. Preview

- The opening question and introductory paragraph tell you what you should learn from this lesson.

- What do the diagrams show? How will they help you understand the text?

2. Read and Note Information

- As you read, jot down information about how we see things and how we know what we're looking at.

  Light rays bounce off a banana.

  The light rays enter your eyes.

- Look also for what affects the brain. What can cause your brain to "see" what isn't really there?

3. Think and Connect

Think about "Is It Real?" Then look over your notes on "See the Picture!"

What information in "See the Picture!" can help you understand how trompe l'oeil plays tricks on your eyes?

See the Picture!

from *ScottForesman Science: Discover the Wonder*

How do your eyes work?

When you watch a movie in a theater, you know that the movie actors aren't really in the theater. Instead, they're just pictures on a screen. But what about your own eyes? Do the things you see live inside your head, or are they just pictures on a screen? Read on and find out.

Eyes for Seeing

Your eyes not only help you see motion when you watch movies, they also observe the objects around you. They quickly adjust to different amounts of light and see all the colors of the rainbow. Your eyes are like a camera.

Find the eye parts in the picture on page 709 as you read how your eyes help you find a snack. You're hungry, so you start looking for something to eat. Your eyes scan the kitchen table and stop at the banana. Light rays bounce off the

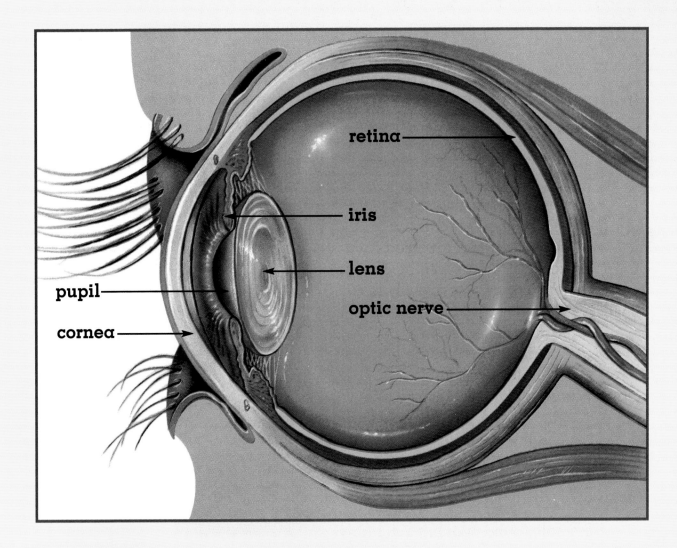

banana and travel to your eyes. But the rays must enter your eyes before you can see the banana.

The eyeball is covered with a tough, white layer, known as the white of the eye. However, on the seeing part of the eye, this layer is clear, and it is called the cornea. The cornea bends the banana's light rays as they enter the eye. Then the rays pass through the pupil—an opening in the eye that can expand and contract. The pupil looks like a tiny black dot, but it's really a hole.

The lens of your eye lies behind the pupil. Like the cornea, the lens bends the banana's light rays. After passing through the lens, the light rays form an upside-down image of the banana on the retina—the back part of the eye. The image is also reversed from left to right.

Thousands of tiny cells called rods and cones cover the retina. A bundle of nerves called the optic nerve connects the rods and cones to the brain. When light rays from the banana hit the retina, the rods and cones detect the rays and convert them into signals that the optic nerve carries to your brain. The signals carry information about the color, size, and shape of the image you're looking at.

Your brain interprets these signals and tells you that you're looking at a banana. It also lets you know that the banana isn't upside down and reversed from left to right. Your brain helps you see the banana as it really is.

Now that you can see the banana, you remember why you were looking for it in the first place. You reach out, take a banana off the table, and peel it. Thanks to your eyes, you've found something to eat.

Seeing Clearly

Light enters a camera through a small, round opening. On many cameras, you can control the amount of light entering the camera by making the opening larger or smaller. The colored part of your eye—the iris—is a doughnut-shaped muscle that does the same thing.

In bright light, your irises contract, and your pupils get smaller. So less light gets into your eyes. This is a good thing, because too much light can damage the retina. In dim light, your irises expand. The pupils get bigger and more light enters the eyes.

Other things besides light can change the size of the pupils. Strong emotions, such as fear or excitement, can make the pupils larger. Taking certain medicines can also change the size of the pupils, causing them to get larger or smaller.

Once light waves get in, the lenses help bring the light waves together, or focus them. Muscles make the lens thinner, to see distant objects, or thicker, to see nearby objects. Because the lenses can change shape, clear images form on your retinas, as shown in the top diagram.

In spite of this, some people still see fuzzy images. If you're nearsighted, images form in front of your retina. You can see things up close, but watching a fly ball in the distance is a problem!

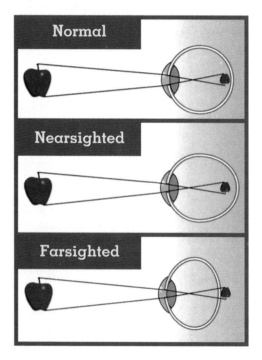

For normal vision, the image forms on the retina at the back of the eye. If a person is nearsighted or farsighted, the image doesn't form on the retina.

If you're farsighted, images form beyond your retina, as shown in the diagram. You have no problem tracking fly balls, it's threading a needle that bothers you!

Wearing eyeglasses or contact lenses usually corrects both sight problems. Putting a glass or plastic lens close to the eye makes the image focus on the retina, where it's supposed to be.

Now You See It, Now You Don't

Some pictures trick your eyes into seeing something that isn't there! Let's take a look at some "tricky" pictures.

What do you notice about the spiraling lines? Can you tell where the spirals begin and end?

If you can't tell where the spirals begin and end, there's a reason. The spirals aren't spirals—they're circles! The design around each circle makes you think you're looking at spirals. Trace one spiral with your finger, and you'll see!

Look at the pairs of up and down lines. Are the pairs of lines crooked or straight?

If you put a ruler on the lines in each set, you'll see that all the lines are parallel. The short slanted lines drawn on each up and down line make the lines look crooked.

You rely on your eyes to give you accurate information about the world. But colors, patterns, and motion can affect what your brain perceives. You can't always believe what you see!

Tube Time

by Eve Merriam

I turned on the TV
and what did I see?

I saw a can of cat food talking,
a tube of toothpaste walking.

Peanuts, popcorn,
cotton flannel.
Jump up, jump up,
switch the channel.

I turned to station B
and what did I see?

I saw a shampoo bottle crying,
a pile of laundry flying.

Peanuts, popcorn,
cotton flannel.
Jump up, jump up,
switch the channel.

I turned to station D
and what did I see?

I saw two spray cans warring,
a cup of coffee snoring.

Peanuts, popcorn,
cotton flannel.
Jump up, jump up,
switch the channel.

I turned to station E
and what did I see?

I saw dancing fingers dialing,
an upset stomach smiling.

Peanuts, popcorn,
cotton flannelette:
jump up, jump up,
turn off the set.

Meow!

Meow!

713

One Blue Door

by Pat Mora

To make a poem
listen: crow calls.
Rain paints a door,
blue in the sky.

To make a poem
you need the door
blue and lonely
swinging in the rain.

To make a poem
you need to leap
through that blue door
onto a crow.

To make a poem
you need to glide
on crow's black *caw,*
skimming the trees.

To make a poem
you need to taste
petals of rain.
Open your mouth.

To make a poem
you need to hear
fountains sprouting
in your hands.

Leap through one blue door
onto crow's black call.
Catch rain's petal-fall.
Music in your hands.

Leap through one blue door.

Artist to Artist

by Davida Adedjouma

I write books, now, because my father wanted
to be an artist when he grew up & he was good
at it, too. Drew people with meat on their bones
in flesh-colored tones from my 64-colors box
of crayons. But
every night—& sometimes even weekends & holidays—
he dressed in the blue uniform & black shoes
of many other fathers who also weren't doctors or lawyers,
teachers or preachers, & rode the 10:00 p.m. bus
to the downtown post office. Sorted mail by zip code—
60620, 60621, 60622. He sorted mail all night &
into the day because we had bills to pay. For 30 years
my father rode the bus feeling black and blue. He
never drew & his degrees in art & education sat
hardening on a shelf along with his oils
& acrylics. But
along with his gapped teeth, his bow legs & his first name
with an A at the end, he gave me the urge to create
characters with meat on their bones, in flesh-colored tones
written in words as vivid as a 64-colors box of crayons.
I write, he drew. Daddy, thank you!
& now that you're
retired . . .

         . . . what do you want to be?

Wrap-Up

How do we find a new way?

The Flash of Creativity

Draw a Web

The characters and artists in these selections all have flashes of creativity. In cartoons, a creative idea is often shown as a light bulb. When the light goes on, an idea is born.

1. Choose a character or artist in this unit. **Think** about the creative idea this person has.

2. **Draw** the person's head. Over it, draw a light bulb. Write the creative idea in the light bulb.

3. Use the light bulb as the center of a web. **Extend** the web by adding light bulbs connected by lines. In the bulbs, write your own ideas or else what might happen because of the original idea.

The Big Moment

Construct a Diorama

Which selection in this unit has the most dramatic moment? Illustrate that moment with a diorama.

1. **Plan** your design. What are the characters doing at this moment?

2. **Design** the characters and a background. Cut out the characters and position them in front of the background.

3. **Present** your diorama to classmates by reading some lines from the story that your scene represents.

The Trickster Tricked

Write a Ballad

"The Baker's Neighbor" and "In the Days of King Adobe" are adapted from folk tales. One form of folk tale is the *ballad,* a popular song that tells a story. The lines of a ballad usually rhyme, and it often has a *refrain—* several lines that are repeated after each verse.

1. With a partner, choose a tale and **outline** the events of the plot.

2. **Write** a ballad of 2–3 verses based on the tale. Add a refrain. You may choose to write new words to a song you already know.

3. **Perform** your ballad for listeners.

How To . . .

Write Instructions

"Andy's Secret Ingredient" and "In the Days of King Adobe" are about recipes and food preparation. "Just Telling the Truth" is about arranging a closet. These activities can be described in a how-to article. Choose an activity or another one that you know how to do.

1. **Analyze** the steps needed to do the activity.

2. **Write** a how-to article. Number the steps 1, 2, 3, and so on. Have a friend read your article to be sure the steps are clear.

Test Talk

Answer the Question

Score High!

A scoring checklist shows you what makes up a good answer to a test question. You can learn how to write answers that score high by using a scoring checklist.

Read the scoring checklist at the right.

A test about "See the Picture!" pages 708–711, might have this question.

Test Question 1

What controls the amount of light that enters a person's eyes? Use details from the article to support your answer.

Look at the First Try answer on page 719. Then see how the student used the scoring checklist to improve the answer.

Scoring Checklist

✓ **The answer is correct.** It has only correct details from the text.

✓ **The answer is complete.** It has all the necessary details from the text.

✓ **The answer is focused.** It has only details from the text that answer the question.

First Try

It's not focused enough. The detail about a camera doesn't belong.

It's not complete. It's missing the fact that emotions play a part.

Light enters a camera through a small, round opening. A person's pupils control the amount of light that enters the eyes. Bright light makes the pupils get smaller, so less light enters the eyes. Dim light makes the pupils get bigger. Strong medicines can also make the pupils smaller or bigger.

It's not all correct. It's not strong medicines. It's certain medicines.

Improved Answer

Tell why this is a better answer. Look back at the scoring checklist for help.

A person's pupils control the amount of light that enters the eyes. Bright light makes the pupils get smaller, so less light enters the eyes. Dim light makes the pupils get bigger, so more light enters. Strong emotions can make the pupils bigger, so more light enters. Some medicines can also change the size of the pupils.

Try it!

Now look at the First Try answer below. Then rewrite the answer and improve it. Look back at the scoring checklist for help.

Test Question 2

How does the brain receive the pictures that enter the eye? Explain, using details from the article.

First Try

The lens of the eye focuses upside-down pictures on the cornea. Thousands of tiny cells called rods and cones change the pictures into signals that carry information about color, size, and shape of things. You can't believe what you see because motion makes straight lines crooked.

Glossary

How to Use This Glossary

This glossary can help you understand and pronounce some of the words in this book. The entries in this glossary are in alphabetical order. There are guide words at the top of each page to show you the first and last words on the page. A pronunciation key is at the bottom of every other page. Remember, if you can't find the word you are looking for, ask for help or check a dictionary.

The entry word is in dark type. It shows how the word is spelled and how the word is divided into syllables.

The pronunciation is in parentheses. It also shows which syllables are stressed.

Abbreviated part-of-speech labels show the function or functions of an entry word and any listed form of that word.

re•trace (ri trās′), *v.* to go back over: *We retraced our steps to where we started.* ❏ *v.* **re•traced, re•trac•ing. —re•trace′a•ble,** ADJ.

Sometimes, irregular and other special forms will be shown to help you use the word correctly.

The definition and example sentence show you what the word means and how it is used.

720

Aa

a•bun•dance (ə bun′ dəns), N. quantity that is a lot more than enough: *There is an abundance of apples this year.*

ac•quaint (ə kwānt′), *v.* be acquainted with; to have personal knowledge of; know: *I have heard about your friend, but I am not acquainted with him.*

ad lib (ad lib′), ADV. on the spur of the moment; freely: *The jazz band played ad lib.* ❏ *v.* **ad libs, ad libbed, ad lib•bing.**

a•do•be (ə dō′bē), N. brick made of clay baked in the sun: *They built a house of adobe.*

ad•vise (ad vīz′), *v.* to give advice to; offer an opinion to; counsel: *I advised them to be cautious. I shall act as you advise.* ❏ *v.* **ad•vised, ad•vis•ing.**

ag•ate (ag′it), N. a playing marble with colored stripes or clouded colors: *She used the milky agate as her shooter.*

a•gen•cy (ā′jən sē) N. a person or company that has the authority to act for another: *Employment agencies help people get jobs.*

a•gree•ment (ə grē′mənt), N. an understanding reached by two or more persons, groups of persons, or nations among themselves. Nations make treaties and individuals make contracts; both are agreements.

al•ter•nate (ȯl′tər nāt), *v.* to happen by turns: *The signals on the stoplight alternate between red and green.* ❏ *v.* **al•ter•nat•ed, al•ter•nat•ing.**

Alz•heim•er's disease (älts′hī mərz), disease of the brain. Alzheimer's disease causes confusion and gradual loss of memory.

a·mend·ment (ə mend′mənt), N. change made in a law, bill, or motion by addition, omission, or alteration of language: *The Congressman proposed an amendment to the Constitution.*

an·chor (ang′kər), N. the last person to run or swim on a relay team: *When the anchor finishes, the race will be over.*

an·kle (ang′kəl), N. joint that connects the foot with the leg.

an·nounc·er (ə noun′sər), N. person who makes announcements, introduces programs, reads news, or describes sports events on radio or TV.

an·tic·i·pa·tion (an tis′ə pā′shən), N. act of anticipating; looking forward to; expectation: *In anticipation of a cold winter, they cut extra firewood.*

ap·pli·cant (ap′lə kənt), N. person who applies for something, such as a loan, a job, or admission to a school: *There are many applicants for this job.*

ap·ply (ə plī′), V. to make a request; ask: *She applied for a summer job.* ❑ V. **ap·plied, ap·ply·ing.**

ar·tis·tic (är tis′tik), ADJ. of art or artists: *That museum has many artistic treasures.* **–ar·tis′ti·cal·ly,** ADV.

a·shore (ə shôr′), ADV. on the shore; on land: *The sailor had been ashore for months.*

assembly line, row of workers and machines along which work is passed until the final product is made: *Most cars are made on an assembly line.*

as·sent (ə sent′), N. acceptance of a proposal, statement, etc.; agreement: *She gave her assent to the plan.*

ath·lete (ath′lēt′), N. person trained in sports and exercises of physical strength, speed, and skill. Baseball players, runners, boxers, and swimmers are athletes.

ath·let·ic (ath let′ik), ADJ. having to do with active games and sports: *an athletic association.* **–ath·let′i·cal·ly,** ADV.

at·mo·spher·ic (at′mə sfir′ik), ADJ. of or about the air that surrounds the Earth: *atmospheric conditions, atmospheric pressure.*

awe (ȯ), N. great fear and wonder; fear and great respect: *The sight of the great waterfall filled us with awe.*

B b

bal·lot (bal′ət), N. piece of paper or other object used in voting: *cast a ballot.*

ban·dan·na (ban dan′ə), N. a large handkerchief, often worn on the head or neck: *Helen tied a bandanna around her neck.* ❑ N., PL. **ban·dan·nas.**

ban·ner (ban′ər), N. piece of cloth with some design or words on it: *Our championship banners hang in the school gym.*

barb (bärb), N. point sticking out and curving backward from the main point of an arrow, fishhook, etc.: *When I cast my fishing lines, the barb caught in a fish's mouth.*

bar·na·cle (bär′nə kəl), N. any of various small saltwater shellfish that attach themselves to rocks, the bottoms of ships, the timbers of wharves, etc.

bar·ter (bär′tər), N. trading by exchanging one kind of goods for other goods without using money.

be·hav·ior (bi hā′vyər), N. manner of behaving; way of acting: *Her sullen behavior showed that she was angry.*

a	hat	ė	term	ô	order	ch	child		a in about
ā	age	i	it	oi	oil	ng	long		e in taken
ä	far	ī	ice	ou	out	sh	she	ə	i in pencil
â	care	o	hot	u	cup	th	thin		o in lemon
e	let	ō	open	u̇	put	ŦH	then		u in circus
ē	equal	ȯ	saw	ü	rule	zh	measure		

bel·fry (bel′frē), N. tower for a bell or bells: *We rang the bells in the belfry of the church.* ❑ N., PL. **bel·fries.**

bit·ter (bit′ər), ADJ. showing pain or grief: *bitter tears.* harsh or cutting: *bitter words.* —**bit′ter·ly,** ADV. —**bit′ter·ness,** N.

blocks (bloks), N., PL. objects that a runner's feet are placed on at the start of a race: *Lynn positioned her feet on her blocks and waited for the race to begin.*

blood·hound (blud′hound′), N. a large, powerful dog with a keen sense of smell: *The bloodhounds tracked the lost child.*

bob·ber (bob′ər), N. a float attached to a fishing line: *Our bobbers floated gently on the lake.*

body language, way a person moves and stands and the expression on a person's face, which give clues to what a person is thinking and feeling.

bound (bound), ADJ. under some obligation; obliged: *I feel bound by my promise.*

breed (brēd), V. to raise or grow, especially to get new or improved kinds: *to breed new varieties of corn, to breed cattle for market.* N. group of animals or plants looking much alike and having the same ancestry: *Collies and German shepherds are breeds of dogs.* ❑ V. **bred, breed·ing.** —**breed′a·ble,** ADJ.

brim (brim), N. edge or border of anything; rim: *Don't go near the brim of the canyon.* —**brim′less,** ADJ.

Brit·ish (brit′ish), N., PL. the people of Great Britain: *The British support their king.*

bruised (brüzd), ADJ. injured under the skin, showing a mark or discoloration: *He couldn't sleep on his bruised shoulder.*

Cc

ca·ble (kā′bəl), N. an insulated bundle of wires that carries an electric current or electric signals.

caf·e·ter·i·a (kaf′ə tir′ē ə), N. restaurant, dining room in a school, and the like, where people serve themselves. ❑ N., PL. **caf·e·ter·i·as.**

ca·reer (kə rir′), N. way of living; occupation or profession: *I plan to make law my career.*

car·go (kär′gō), N. load of goods carried by a ship, plane, truck or the like: *The freighter had docked to unload a cargo of wheat.* ❑ N., PL. **car·goes** or **car·gos.**

cause (kȯz), N. subject or movement in which many people are interested and to which they give their support: *World peace is the cause she works for.*

cem·e·ter·y (sem′ə ter′ē), N. place for burying the dead; graveyard. ❑ N., PL. **cem·e·ter·ies.**

cent (sent), N. penny. One hundred cents make one dollar. ■ Another word that sounds like this is **scent.**

center field, in baseball, the section of the outfield between left field and right field.

ce·ram·ic (sə ram′ik), ADJ. of or about a material made of baked clay, such as pottery, earthenware, or porcelain: *He made a ceramic vase in art class.*

cerebral palsy (sə rē′brəl pȯl′zē) N. paralysis caused by damage to the brain before or at birth. Persons suffering from cerebral palsy have trouble coordinating their muscles.

chal·lenge (chal′ənj), V. to call in question; doubt; dispute: *Are you challenging my statement that Montana is a coastal state?*

cham·pi·on·ship (cham′pē ən ship), N. position of a champion; first place: *My mom won the golf championship.*

cha·os (kā′os), N. very great confusion; complete disorder: *The tornado left the town in chaos.*

char·i·ty (char′ə tē), N. fund or organization for helping the sick, the poor, and the helpless: *She gives money regularly to the Red Cross and to other charities.*

check·point (chek′point′), N. place of inspection on a road, at a border, etc.: *We had to stop at the border checkpoint and show our identification.*

chirr (chėr), V. a shrill, trilling sound: *The raccoons were chirring last night.* ❑ V. **chir·ring, chirred.**

cho·ral (kôr′əl), ADJ. of a choir or chorus: *Our choral society meets on Wednesdays.*

civ·il (siv′əl), ADJ. polite; courteous: *I pointed out the way in a very civil manner.*

clamp (klamp), N. a device for holding things tightly together: *She used a clamp to hold the arm on the chair until the glue dried.*

clench (klench), V. to grasp firmly: *I clenched the bat and swung at the ball.*

cling (kling), V. to stick or hold fast; adhere: *The child is clinging to his mother's hand.* ❑ V. **clung, cling·ing.**

col·lapse (kə laps′), V. to break down in vital energy, stamina, or self-control through exhaustion or disease: *Joe collapsed after the hard race.* ❑ V. **col·lapsed, col·laps·ing. –col·laps′i·ble,** ADJ.

col·li·sion (kə lizh′ən), N. act of hitting or striking violently together; crash: *The car was badly damaged in the collision.*

col·o·ny (kol′ə nē), N. group of living things of the same kind, living or growing together: *a colony of ants, a coral colony.* ❑ N., PL. **col·o·nies.**

com·mu·ni·cate (kə myü′nə kāt), V. to give or exchange information or news by speaking, writing, and so on; send and receive messages: *We communicate by sending letters to each other.* ❑ V. **com·mu·ni·cat·ed, com·mu·ni·cat·ing. –com·mu′ni·ca′tor,** N.

com·mu·ni·ca·tions (kə myü′nə kā′shənz), N. system of giving or exchanging information or news by telephone, radio, television, and so on: *A network of communications links most parts of the world.*

com·mu·ni·ty (kə myü′nə tē), N. all the people living in the same place and subject to the same laws; people of any district or town: *This lake provides water for six communities.* ❑ N., PL. **com·mu·ni·ties.**

com·pare (kəm pâr′), V. to find out or point out how persons or things are alike and how they are different: *While comparing my answers with the teacher's, I found I had made a mistake.* ❑ V. **com·pared, com·par·ing.**

com·pass (kum′pəs), N. device for showing directions, having a needle that points to the North Magnetic Pole.

con·cen·trate (kon′sən trāt), V. to pay close attention; focus the mind: *Concentrate on your reading so that you understand the story.*

con·dense (kən dens′), V. to change from a gas or vapor to a liquid: *If steam touches cold surfaces, it condenses or is condensed into water.* ❑ V. **con·densed, con·dens·ing. – con·den′sa·ble,** ADJ.

a	hat	ė	term	ô	order	ch	child	
ā	age	i	it	oi	oil	ng	long	a in about
ä	far	ī	ice	ou	out	sh	she	e in taken
â	care	o	hot	u	cup	th	thin	ə⟨ i in pencil
e	let	ō	open	ù	put	ŦH	then	o in lemon
ē	equal	ȯ	saw	ü	rule	zh	measure	u in circus

con·di·tion (kən dish′ən), N. state in which someone or something is: *The condition of the house is better than when I bought it.*

con·fi·dent (kon′fə dənt), ADJ. having confidence; firmly believing; certain; sure: *I feel confident that our team will win.* **–con′fi·dent·ly,** ADV.

con·fu·sion (kən fyü′zhən), N. condition of being perplexed or bewildered: *His confusion over the exact address caused him to go to the wrong house.*

con·spire (kən spīr′), V. to plan secretly with others to do something unlawful or wrong; plot: *The spies conspired to steal secret government documents.*

con·sti·tu·tion·al (kon′stə tü′shə nəl), ADJ. of, in, or according to the constitution of a nation, state, or group: *The Supreme Court must decide whether this law is constitutional.*

con·struc·tive (kən struk′tiv), ADJ. helping to improve; useful: *During my report the teacher gave some constructive suggestions that helped me think of ideas I had overlooked.* **–con·struc′tive·ly,** ADV. **–con·struc′tive·ness,** N.

con·sume (kən süm), V. to eat or drink up: *We will each consume at least two sandwiches on our hike.* ❑ V. **con·sumed, con·sum·ing.**

contour map, map showing heights above sea level by means of contour lines that have the same elevation at all points.

con·tract (kən trakt′), V. to become shorter or smaller; shrink: *Wool fibers contract in hot water.*

con·ven·ience (kən vē′nyəns), N. anything handy or easy to use; thing that saves trouble or work: *A folding table is a convenience in a small room.*

con·ver·sa·tion (kon′vər sā′shən), N. talk; exchange of thoughts by talking together.

co·op·e·rate (kō op′ə rāt′), V. to work together: *Everyone cooperated in helping to clean up after the class party.* ❑ V. **co·op·e·rat·ed, co·op·e·rat·ing.**

corn·meal (kôrn′mēl′), N. coarsely ground dried corn.

cor·ri·dor (kôr′ə dər), N. a long hallway; passage in a large building into which rooms open: *There are three main corridors in our school.*

coun·cil (koun′səl), N. group of persons elected by citizens to make laws for and manage a city, town, community, or school group. ■ Another word that sounds like this is **counsel.**

coun·sel (koun′səl), N. advice: *A wise person gives good counsel.* ■ Another word that sounds like this is **council.**

count·er (koun′tər), N. **1** a long, flat, raised surface in a store, restaurant, bank, and the like, on which money is counted out, and across which goods, food, or drinks are given to customers. **2** thing used for counting. The beads on an abacus are counters.

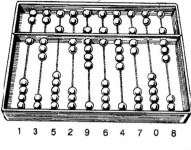

1 3 5 2 9 6 4 7 0 8

counter

course (kôrs), N. area marked out for races or games: *a golf course, a race course.*

crit·ic (krit′ik), N. person who makes judgments of the good and bad points of books, music, pictures, plays, acting, etc.: *We went to see the movie because we read that the critics liked it.*

crit·i·cal (krit′ə kəl), ADJ. inclined to find fault or disapprove: *a critical disposition.* **–crit′i·cal·ly,** ADV.

cross-stitch (krôs′stich′ *or* kros′stich′), N. embroidery made with one stitch crossed over another, forming an X: *Grandma worked on her cross-stitch while she talked with me.*

crypt (kript), N. an underground room or vault: *The crypt beneath the main floor of a church was formerly used as a burial place.*

cul·prit (kul′prit), N. person guilty of a fault or crime; offender: *Someone broke the window; are you the culprit?*

cus·to·di·an (ku stō′dē ən), N. person who takes care of a building or offices; janitor: *a school custodian.*

cut (kut), V. to remove someone from a team, group, and so on: *The coach had to cut four players from the soccer team.* ❑ V. **cut, cut·ting.**

D d

dam·age (dam′ij), N. harm or injury that lessens value or usefulness: *The accident did some damage to the car.*

dart (därt), V. to move suddenly and swiftly: *The deer saw us and darted away.*

de·ceive (di sēv′), V. to make someone believe as true something that is false; mislead; fool: *His excuse deceived me until I learned the truth.* ❑ V. **de·ceived, de·ceiv·ing.**

de·fi·ance (di fī′əns), N. act of defying; standing up against authority and refusing to recognize or obey it; open resistance to power: *The colonists' defiance of the king led to war.*

de·lay (di lā′), N. period of time when something is put off or held up: *After several delays, the plane took off.*

de·liv·er·y (di liv′ər ē), N. an act of carrying and giving out of letters, goods, and the like: *There are two deliveries of mail a day in our city.*

❑ N., PL. **de·liv·er·ies.**

dem·on·stra·tion (dem′ən strā′shən), N. an act of showing or explaining something by carrying out experiments or by using samples or specimens: *A compass was used in a demonstration of the Earth's magnetism.*

de·pot (dē′pō), N. railroad or bus station: *Depots are crowded at this time of day.*

de·sert·er (di zėr′tər), N. member of the armed forces who leaves without permission or intention to return.

des·per·ate (des′pər it), ADJ. ready to try anything; ready to run any risk: *He hadn't worked in a year and was desperate for a job.* **—des′per·ate·ly,** ADV.

de·spite (di spīt′), PREP. in spite of: *We walked despite the rain.*

de·tect (di tekt′), V. to find out; discover; catch: *Can you detect any odor in the room?* **—de·tec′tion,** N.

de·ter·mined (di tėr′mənd), ADJ. firm; resolute: *Her determined look showed that she had made up her mind.* **—de·ter′mined·ly,** ADV. **—de·ter′mined·ness,** N.

di·ar·y (dī′ər ē), N. book for keeping a daily account of activities, thoughts, and so on. ❑ N., PL. **di·ar·ies.**

dip·lo·mat (dip′lə mat), N. person whose work is to manage the relations between his or her nation and other nations: *The U.S. diplomat went to a meeting in China.*

dis·count (dis′kount), ADJ. selling goods at prices below those suggested by manufacturers: *a discount store.* **—dis·count′a·ble,** ADJ. **—dis′count′er,** N.

a	hat	ė	term	ô	order	ch	child		a in about
ā	age	i	it	oi	oil	ng	long		e in taken
ä	far	ī	ice	ou	out	sh	she	ə {	i in pencil
â	care	o	hot	u	cup	th	thin		o in lemon
e	let	ō	open	ù	put	ᵀH	then		u in circus
ē	equal	ȯ	saw	ü	rule	zh	measure		

dis·dain·ful·ly (dis dān′fəl ē), _ADV._ in a way or manner that feels or shows pride and scorn: _The teacher stared disdainfully at the child who threw an eraser._ **–dis·dain′ful,** _ADJ._

dis·grace (dis grās′), _v._ to cause disgrace to; bring shame upon: _I read about an embezzler disgracing her family._ ❑ _v._ **dis·graced, dis·grac·ing. –dis·grac′er,** _N._

dis·may (dis mā′), _v._ to trouble greatly; make afraid: _The thought that she might fail the test dismayed her._

dis·o·bey (dis′ə bā′), _v._ to refuse to follow orders or instructions; fail to obey: _The stubborn student disobeyed the teacher._ ❑ _v._ **dis·o·beyed, dis·o·bey·ing.**

dis·patch (dis pach′), _v._ to send off to some place or for some purpose: _Extra fire trucks were dispatched to the site of the blaze._

display case, a glassed enclosure for viewing: _The jewelry is in a display case at the front of the store._

dis·trac·tion (dis trak′shən), _N._ thing that draws away the mind, attention, etc.: _Noise is a distraction when you are trying to study._

dol·phin (dol′fən), _N._ any of numerous sea mammals related to the whale, but smaller. Dolphins have beaklike snouts and remarkable intelligence.

do·mes·ti·ca·tion (də mes′tə kā′shən), _N._ a change from a wild to a tame or cultivated state: _The domestication of plants and animals began thousands of years ago._

dom·i·nant (dom′ə nənt), _ADJ._ most powerful or influential; controlling: _She was a dominant figure in local politics._

do·nate (dō′nāt), _v._ to give money or help, especially to a fund or institution; contribute: _We donate food to the community shelter every Thanksgiving._ ❑ _v._ **do·nat·ed, do·nat·ing.**

doom (düm), _v._ to condemn to an unhappy or terrible fate: _Poor health doomed my cousin to an inactive life._

Doppler radar (dop′lər rā′där), _N._ type of radar that measures the speed of moving objects.

down·pour (doun′pôr′), _N._ a heavy rain.

drib·ble (drib′əl), _v._ **1** to flow or let flow in drops or small amounts; trickle: _Gasoline dribbled from the leak in the tank._ **2** to move a ball along by bouncing it or giving it short kicks: _dribbling a basketball or soccer ball._ ❑ _v._ **drib·bled, drib·bling. –drib′bler,** _N._

E e

e·col·o·gy (ē kol′ə jē), _N._ the sum of relationships between organisms and an environment: _a threatened ecology._

ef·fi·cient (ə fish′ənt), _ADJ._ able to produce the effect wanted without waste of time, energy, and so on; capable: _An efficient worker makes good use of his or her skills._ **–ef·fi′cient·ly,** _ADV._

eld·er·ly (el′dər lē), _ADJ._ somewhat old; beyond middle age: _Tim helped the elderly lady cross the street._ **–el′der·li·ness,** _N._

em·bed (em bed′), _v._ to enclose in a surrounding mass; fasten or fix firmly: _Precious stones are often found embedded in rock._ ❑ _v._ **em·bed·ded, em·bed·ding.** Also, **imbed.**

e·merge (i mėrj′), _v._ to come into view; come out; come up: _The sun emerged from behind a cloud._ ❑ _v._ **e·merged, e·merg·ing.**

en·to·mol·o·gist (en′tə mol′ə jist), _N._ a person who studies insects: _The entomologist showed us a rare beetle._

en·to·mol·o·gy (en′ tə mol′ ə jē), _N._ branch of biology that deals with insects. **–en′to·mol′·o·gist,** _N._

erode (i rōd′), *v.* to eat or wear away gradually; eat into: *Running water eroded the soil.* ❑ *v.* **e·rod·ed, e·rod·ing. –e·rod′i·ble,** *ADJ.*

es·say (es′ā), *N.* a short written composition.

e·vac·u·ate (i vak′yü āt), *v.* to withdraw; remove: *All civilians were told to evacuate the war zone.*

ewe (yü), *N.* a female sheep: *The ewe is in the pen next to her lambs.*

ex·cur·sion (ek skėr′zhən), *N.* a short trip taken for interest or pleasure, often by a number of people together: *Our club went on three excursions this year.*

ex·tin·guish (ek sting′gwish), *v.* to put out: *Water extinguished the fire.* **–ex·tin′guish·a·ble,** *ADJ.*

ex·tract (ek strakt′), *v.* to pull out or draw out, usually with some effort: *extract a tooth, extract iron from the Earth.* **–ex·tract′a·ble,** *ADJ.* **–ex·tract′tor,** *N.*

F f

faith (fāth), *N.* belief without proof; trust: *We have faith in our friends.*

fal·con·ry (fȯl′kən rē *or* fal′kən rē), *N.* sport of hunting with falcons, swift flying hawks.

fas·ci·nate (fas′n āt), *v.* to interest greatly; attract very strongly; charm: *She was fascinated by the designs and colors in African art.* ❑ *v.* **fas·ci·nat·ed, fas·ci·nat·ing. –fas′ci·nat·ing·ly,** *ADV.*

fate (fāt), *N.* your lot or fortune; what happens to a person, group, and so on: *History shows the fate of many nations.*

fear·less (fir′lis), *adj.* without fear; afraid of nothing; brave; daring. **–fear′less·ly,** *ADV.* **–fear′less·ness,** *N.*

feel·er (fē′lər), *N.* a special part of an animal's body for sensing by touch. Insects, crabs, lobsters, shrimp, and the like, have feelers on their heads.

fluke (flük), *N.* a lucky stroke in games, business, or life: *It was a fluke that she won three games in a row.*

fly·er (flī′ər), *N.* a small notice or advertisement, usually printed on one page, that is to be handed out to people; flier.

fo·cus (fō′kəs), *v.* to make an image clear by adjusting a lens, the eye, and so on. ❑ *v.* **fo·cused, fo·cus·ing** *or* **fo·cussed, fo·cus·sing.**

fool·ish·ness (fü′lish nis), *N.* behavior that is unwise, silly, or without sense: *Their foolishness got the children into trouble.*

fo·rag·er (fôr′i jər), *N.* one that hunts or searches for food: *The foragers brought back some berries.*

fra·grance (frā′grəns), *N.* a sweet smell; pleasing odor: *the fragrance of flowers, the fragrance of perfume.*

frame (frām), *N.* a wooden structure within a hive that holds sheets of wax: *He removed frames of wax from the beehive.*

freak (frēk), *N.* something very odd or unusual: *Snow in summer would be called a freak of nature.*

fu·gi·tive (fyü′jə tiv), *ADJ.* like a runaway: *a fugitive serf.*

G g

gale (gāl), *N.* **1** a very strong wind. A gale blows with a velocity of 32 to 63 miles (51 to 101 kilometers) per hour. **2** a noisy outburst: *The joke caused gales of laughter.*

a	hat	ė	term	ô	order	ch	child	ə {	a in about
ā	age	i	it	oi	oil	ng	long		e in taken
ä	far	ī	ice	ou	out	sh	she		i in pencil
â	care	o	hot	u	cup	th	thin		o in lemon
e	let	ō	open	u̇	put	ŦH	then		u in circus
ē	equal	ȯ	saw	ü	rule	zh	measure		

gen•er•ous (jen′ər əs), ADJ. **1** willing to share with others; unselfish: *a generous giver. Our teacher is always generous with his time.* **2** large; plentiful: *a generous piece of pie.* —**gen′er•ous•ly,** ADV.

ges•ture (jes′chər), V. to make or use a movement of any part of the body to help express an idea or feeling: *She gestured to her brother to stand up straight.* ❑ V. **ges•tured, ges•tur•ing.**

gid•dy (gid′ē), ADJ. having a whirling feeling in one's head; dizzy: *It makes me giddy to go on a merry-go-round.* ❑ ADJ. **gid•di•er, gid•di•est.** —**gid′di•ly,** ADV. —**gid′di•ness,** N.

glim•mer (glim′ər), N. a faint, unsteady light.

grease (grēs), N. soft, melted animal fat used in cooking.

gren•a•dier (gren′ə dir′), N. a member of a specially chosen unit of foot soldiers: *The grenadiers marched down the road.*

gri•mace (grim′is *or* grə mās′), N. a twisted expression of the face; ugly or funny smile: *He grimaced from the pain of his broken leg.* ❑ V. **gri•maced, gri•mac•ing.** —**gri•mac′er,** N.

ground ball, baseball hit so as to bounce or roll along the ground; grounder.

gut (gut), V. to remove the intestines of; disembowel: *We gutted the fish and then Mom fried them for dinner.* ❑ V. **gut•ted, gut•ting.**

Hh

head•line (hed′līn′), N. words printed in heavy type at the top of a newspaper article telling what it is about: *Today's headlines look interesting.*

hearing aid, a small battery-powered device which amplifies sounds, worn by people who cannot hear well.

he•ro•ic (hi rō′ik), ADJ. of, like, or suitable for a hero; brave, great, or noble: *the heroic deeds of*

our firefighters. —**he•ro′i•cal•ly,** ADV.

hob•by•ist (hob′ē ist), N. person who is very interested in a hobby or hobbies: *The hobbyists met to view each other's stamp collections.*

home•less (hōm′lis), ADJ. without a home: *a stray, homeless dog.*

home•stead (hōm′sted′), N. public land granted to a settler under certain conditions by the U.S. government.

home•y (hō′mē), ADJ. homelike: *My aunt's house is very homey.* ❑ ADJ. **hom•i•er, hom•i•est.** —**hom′ey•ness,** N.

hor•ri•fy (hôr′ə fī), V. to cause to feel a shivering, shaking fear: *The scary movie horrified us.* ❑ V. **hor•ri•fied, hor•ri•fy•ing.**

house•hold (hous′hōld), N. all the people living in a house: *Everyone in our household helps with the chores.*

hov•er (huv′ər *or* hov′ər), V. to stay in or near one place; wait nearby: *The dogs hovered around the kitchen door, hoping to be fed.*

hur•ri•cane (hėr′ə kān), N. storm with violent wind and, usually, very heavy rain. Hurricanes are common in the West Indies and the Gulf of Mexico. The wind in a hurricane blows with a speed of more than 75 miles (121 kilometers) per hour.

hurricane

Ii

i•den•ti•fy (ī den′tə fī), V. to recognize as being, or show to be, a particular person or thing;

prove to be the same: *She identified the wallet as hers by describing it.* ❑ v. **i·den·ti·fied, i·den·ti·fy·ing. —i·den/ti·fi/a·ble,** ADJ. **—i·den/ti·fi/a·bly,** ADV.

il·lu·sion·ist (i lü/zhə nist), N. person who produces things that appear to be different from what they really are: *The illusionists made it seem as if the pencils were floating in the air.*

i·mag·i·nar·y (i maj/ə nər/ē), ADJ. existing only in the imagination; not real: *Elves are imaginary. The equator is an imaginary circle around the earth.*

im·pres·sion (im presh/ən), N. effect produced on someone: *Punishment seemed to make little impression on the stubborn child.*

in·au·gu·rate (in ȯ/gyə rāt/), v. to make a formal beginning of; begin: *The invention of the airplane inaugurated a new era in transportation.* ❑ v. **in·au·gu·rat·ed, in·au·gu·rat·ing.**

in·be·tween (in/bi twēn/), ADJ. being or coming in the space or time separating two objects or places.

in·di·cate (in/də kāt), v. to point out; make known; show: *The arrow on the sign indicates the right way to go.* ❑ v. **in·di·cat·ed, in·di·cat·ing.**

in·flam·ma·tion (in/flə mā/shən), N. a diseased condition of some part of the body, marked by heat, redness, swelling, and pain: *A boil is an inflammation of the skin.*

in·hale (in hāl/), v. to breathe in; draw air, gas, tobacco smoke, etc., into the lungs: *He inhales the fresh mountain air.* ❑ v. **in·hales, in·haled, in·hal·ing. –in/ha·la/tion,** N.

in·jured (in/jərd), ADJ. wounded or harmed; hurt: *an injured arm.*

in·ju·ry (in/jər ē), N. hurt or loss caused to or endured by someone or something; harm; damage: *The car accident resulted in few injuries.* ❑ N., PL. **in·jur·ies.**

in·sec·ti·cide (in sek/tə sīd), N. any substance for killing insects.

in·sec·ti·vore (in sek/tə vôr), N. any animal or plant that feeds mainly on insects. Moles and mantises are insectivores.

in·spect (in spekt/), v. to look over carefully; examine: *The engineer inspects the new dam.*

in·stinct (in/stingkt), N. a natural feeling, knowledge, or ability, such as that which guides animals; inborn tendency to act in a certain way: *Birds build their nests by instinct.*

in·stinc·tive·ly (in stingk/tiv lē), ADV.. acting according to a natural feeling, knowledge, or ability; caused or done by instinct; born in an animal or person, not learned: *Spiders instinctively know how to spin webs.* **–in·stinc/tive,** ADJ.

in·sult (in sult/), v. to say or do something very scornful, rude, or harsh to: *She insulted me by calling me a liar.* **–in·sult/ing·ly,** ADV.

in·ter·pret (in tėr/prit), v. to explain the meaning of: *She interprets the movie for her friends.*

in·ter·pret·er (in tėr/prə tər), N. someone who interprets foreign languages, sign language, and so on.

in·tes·tine (in tes/tən), N. Also, intestines, PL. part of the digestive system. Partially digested food passes from the stomach into the small intestine, a winding, narrow tube, where digestion is completed and nutrients are absorbed by the blood. The small intestine empties into the large intestine, a wide tube, where water is absorbed and wastes are eliminated.

a	hat	ė	term	ô	order	ch	child	⎧ a in about
ā	age	i	it	oi	oil	ng	long	e in taken
ä	far	ī	ice	ou	out	sh	she	ə ⎨ i in pencil
â	care	o	hot	u	cup	th	thin	o in lemon
e	let	ō	open	ů	put	ŦH	then	⎩ u in circus
ē	equal	ȯ	saw	ü	rule	zh	measure	

in·va·sion (in vā′zhən), N. act or process of invading; entering by force or as an enemy; attack.

in·ven·tion (in ven′shən), N. something new or made for the first time: *Television is a twentieth-century invention.*

is·sue (ish′ü), V. to send out; put forth: *This magazine is issued every week. The government issues money and stamps.* ❑ V. **is·sued, is·su·ing.**

J j

jew·el·ry (jü′əl rē), N. ring, bracelet, necklace, or other ornament to be worn, usually set with imitation gems or made of silver, gold, and the like.

jum·ble (jum′bəl), V. to mix or confuse: *She jumbled everything in the drawer while hunting for her other blue sock.* ❑ V. **jum·bled, jum·bling.**

L l

lar·va (lär′və), N. the wormlike early form of an insect from the time it leaves the egg until it becomes a pupa or adult. A caterpillar is the larva of a butterfly or moth. *The silkworm is a larva.* ❑ N., PL. **lar·vae** (lär′vē), **lar·vas.**

league (lēg), N. association of sports clubs or teams: *baseball leagues.* ❑ V. **leagued, lea·guing.**

le·gal·ly (lē′gə lē), ADV. done according to law; in a lawful manner: *My brother and I are legally adopted.*

lei·sure (lē′zhər *or* lezh′ər), ADJ. free; not busy: *leisure hours.*

lib·er·ty (lib′ər tē), N. condition of being free; freedom; independence: *The American colonies won their liberty.*

lime·stone (līm′stōn′), N. a sedimentary rock made mostly of calcium carbonate, used for building and for making lime. Marble is a kind of limestone.

lin·ger (ling′gər), V. to stay on; go slowly, as if unwilling to leave: *He often lingers after the others leave.*

lobe (lōb), N. a rounded part that sticks out or down. The lobe of the ear is the lower rounded end.

lo·co·mo·tive (lō′kə mō′tiv), N. engine that moves from place to place under its own power. Locomotives are used to pull railroad trains.

locomotive

lodge (loj), N. place to live in; house, especially a small or temporary house: *My aunt rents a lodge in the mountains for the summer.*

long·house (lȯng′hous′), N. a large, rectangular dwelling of certain North American Indians, especially the Iroquois: *Many families lived together in one longhouse.* ❑ N., PL. **long·hous·es** (lȯng′houz′iz).

low-rent, of a residential area where rents are typically low: *Many people wanted to move into the new low-rent housing project.*

Mm

mag·ni·fy (mag′nə fī), v. to cause something to look larger than it actually is; increase the apparent size of an object: *The microscope magnified the bacteria so that they could be seen and studied.* ❏ v. **mag·ni·fied, mag·ni·fy·ing. —mag′ni·fi·ca′tion,** N.

magnifying glass, lens or combination of lenses that causes things to look larger than they really are: *Grandpa used a magnifying glass to read the small print.*

ma·neu·ver (mə nü′vər), v. to move or handle skillfully: *I maneuvered the car through the heavy traffic with ease.* **—ma·neu′ver·a·bil′-i·ty,** N. **—ma·neu′ver·a·ble,** ADJ.

marsh (märsh), N. low, soft land covered at times by water. Such plants as reeds, rushes, and sedges grow in marshes, but trees do not. ❏ N., PL. **marsh·es. —marsh′like′,** ADJ.

ma·tron (mā′trən), N. a woman who manages the household affairs or supervises the inmates of a school, hospital, dormitory, or other institution: *The matron told the students to go to bed at nine.*

may·on·naise (mā′ə nāz′), N. a salad dressing made of egg yolks, vegetable oil, vinegar or lemon juice, and seasoning, beaten together until thick: *I ordered my hamburger with extra mayonnaise.*

me·di·um (mē′dē əm), ADJ. having a middle position, quality, or condition; moderate: *He is of medium height.*

men·in·gi·tis (men′in jī′tis), N. a very serious bacterial disease in which the membranes surrounding the brain or spinal cord become inflamed. Meningitis can be fatal.

mid·day (mid′dā′), N. the middle part of the day; noon: *We call our midday meal "lunch."*

might·y (mī′tē), ADJ. showing strength or power; powerful; strong: *a mighty opponent, the mightiest ruler.* ❏ ADJ. **might·i·er, might·i·est. —might′i·ness,** N.

mi·li·tia (mə lish′ə), N. army of citizens who are not regular soldiers but who undergo training for emergency duty or national defense.

mi·rac·u·lous (mə rak′yə ləs), ADJ. marvelous; wonderful: *The famous actor gave a miraculous performance.* **—mi·rac′u·lous·ly,** ADV.

mi·ser (mī′zər), N. someone who loves money for its own sake; one who lives poorly in order to save money and keep it: *The old man was a miser and paid his employees very little.*

mis·sion (mish′ən), N. errand or task that people are sent somewhere to do: *a diplomatic mission.*

mois·ture (mois′chər), N. slight wetness; water or other liquid suspended in very small drops in the air or spread on a surface. Dew is moisture that collects at night on the grass.

muf·fle (muf′əl), v. to dull or deaden a sound: *The wind muffled our voices.* ❏ v. **muf·fled, muf·fling.**

mush·er (məsh ər), N. one who travels through snow driving a dogsled: *The musher urged the dogs on with a whistle.*

Nn

nav·i·gate (nav′ə gāt), v. to move, walk, or swim about: *I can barely navigate with this sprained ankle.* ❏ v. **nav·i·gat·ed, nav·i·gat·ing.**

Na·zi (nä′tsē or nat′sē), N. member or supporter of the Nationalist Socialist Party, a fascist political party in Germany, led by Adolf Hitler. ❏ N., PL. **Na·zis.**

a	hat	ė	term	ô	order	ch	child		a in about
ā	age	i	it	oi	oil	ng	long		e in taken
ä	far	ī	ice	ou	out	sh	she	ə	i in pencil
â	care	o	hot	u	cup	th	thin		o in lemon
e	let	ō	open	ů	put	ŦH	then		u in circus
ē	equal	ȯ	saw	ü	rule	zh	measure		

nec·tar (nek′tər), N. a sweet liquid found in many flowers. Bees gather nectar and make it into honey.

neur·on (nŭr′on), N. one of the cells forming the brain, spinal cord, and nerves; nerve cell. Neurons conduct nerve impulses.

night crawler, any of various large earthworms that come to the surface of the ground at night: *Night crawlers make good bait for fishing.*

nu·tri·tious (nü trish′əs), ADJ. valuable as food; nourishing.

Oo

ob·sess (əb ses′), V. to fill someone's mind; keep the attention of: *I was obsessed with the fear that I might fail.* **–ob·ses′sor,** N.

ob·sta·cle (ob′stə kəl), N. something that prevents or stops progress; hindrance: *Bad weather and poor roads were obstacles that we faced on our last trip.*

o·ce·an·ic (ō′shē an′ik), ADJ. of or in the ocean: *oceanic islands, oceanic fish.*

o·pin·ion (ə pin′yən), N. what you think; belief not based on actual knowledge or proof; judgment: *In my opinion, their plan will never succeed.*

op·po·nent (ə pō′nənt), N. person who is on the other side in a fight, game, or discussion; person fighting, struggling, or speaking against another: *She defeated her opponent in the election.*

op·ti·cal (op′tə kəl), ADJ. of or about the eye or the sense of sight; visual: *Nearsightedness is an optical defect.* **–op′ti·cal·ly,** ADV.

or·deal (ôr dēl′), N. a severe test or experience: *I dreaded the ordeal of going to the dentist.*

or·gan·ize (ôr′gə nīz), V. to put into working order; get together and arrange: *We organized a trip to the city zoo with our teacher.* ❏ V. **or·gan·ized, or·gan·iz·ing. –or′gan·iz′er,** N.

or·phan·age (ôr′fə nij), N. home for children who are without parents.

o·ver·came (ō′vər kām′), V. past tense of **overcome;** conquered: *I finally overcame my fear of snakes and held one in science class.*

o·ver·take (ō′vər tāk′), V. to catch up with: *Watch as she overtakes that runner.* ❏ V. **o·ver·took, o·ver·tak·ing.**

Pp

pan·ic (pan′ik), V. to affect or be affected with a sudden, uncontrollable fear that causes an individual or entire group to lose self-control and take wild flight: *The audience panicked when the fire broke out.* ❏ V. **pan·icked, pan·ick·ing.**

par·lor (pär′lər), N. formerly, a room for receiving or entertaining guests; sitting room.

pas·try (pā′strē), N. piece of baked food made with dough rich in butter or shortening: *We bought a dozen pastries at the bakery.* ❏ N., PL. **pas·tries.**

pave·ment (pāv′mənt), N. a covering or surface for streets, sidewalks, and the like, made of asphalt, concrete, gravel, stones, and the like.

pem·mi·can (pem′ə kən), N. dried meat pounded into a paste with melted fat. It is lightweight and stays good for a long time, so it is useful on journeys.

pe·nin·su·la (pə nin′sə lə), N. piece of land almost surrounded by water, or extending far out into the water. Florida is a peninsula. ❏ N., PL. **pe·nin·su·las. –pe·nin′su·lar,** ADJ.

per·mis·sion (pər mish′ən), N. consent; leave: *My sister gave me permission to use her camera.*

pig·gy·back (pig′ē bak), ADJ., ADV. on the back: *to ride piggyback.*

pig·let (pig′lit), N. a young pig: *The piglet squealed when it was taken away from its mother.*

pi·o·neer (pī′ə nir′), N. person who settles in a part of a country, preparing it for others: *The pioneers of the American West included trappers, explorers, and farming families.*

plan·ta·tion (plan tā′shən), N. a large farm or estate, especially in a tropical or semitropical region, on which cotton, tobacco, sugarcane, rubber trees, and the like, are grown. The work on a plantation is done by laborers who live there.

pleas·ure (plezh′ər), N. something that pleases; cause of joy or delight: *Eating candy and watching movies are two of my favorite pleasures.*

pole (pōl), V. to make a boat go with a pole: *The man poled the boat down the canal.* ❏ V. **poled, pol·ing.**

po·lite·ness (pə līt′nes), N. state of having or showing good manners: *My mother was impressed with your politeness at dinner.*

polls (pōlz), N. PL. place where votes are cast and counted: *The polls will be open all day.*

pon·der (pon′dər), V. to consider carefully; think over: *He pondered the problem.*

pop·u·la·tion (pop′yə lā′shən), N. people of a city, country, or district.

por·ta·ble (pôr′tə bəl), ADJ. capable of being carried; easily carried: *a portable typewriter, a portable radio.*

pos·ses·sion (pə zesh′ən), N. something owned; property: *The autographed baseball is my most prized possession.*

pouch (pouch), N. bag or sack: *a mail pouch.* ❏ N., PL. **pouch·es.**

pre·cinct (prē′singkt), N. a part or district of a city: *an election precinct, all police precincts.*

pre·dict (pri dikt′), V. to tell beforehand; prophesy; forecast: *The Weather Service predicts rain for tomorrow.* **–pre·dict′a·ble,** ADJ. **–pre·dict′a·bly,** ADV.

pres·sure (presh′ər), N. the continued action of a weight or other force: *Hurricanes can occur when there is low atmospheric pressure over warm oceans.*

prey (prā), N. SING. *or* PL. animal or animals hunted and killed for food by another animal: *Mice and birds are the prey of cats.*

prim·i·tive (prim′ə tiv), ADJ. of or about early times; of long ago: *Primitive people often lived in caves.* **–prim′i·tive·ly,** ADV.

priv·i·lege (priv′ə lij), N. a special right, advantage, or favor: *My sister has the privilege of driving the family car.*

pro·duc·er (prə dü′sər), N. someone or something that produces. Producers often grow or manufacture things that are used by others.

proj·ect (proj′ekt), N. group of apartment buildings built and run as a unit, especially with government support.

pros·per (pros′pər), V. to be successful; have good fortune; flourish: *Our business prospered.*

pro·tein (prō′tēn), N. any of the many complex substances containing nitrogen that are necessary parts of the cells of animals and plants. Proteins are a necessary part of human and animal diets. Meat, milk, cheese, eggs, and beans contain protein. A protein is made of several or many amino acids.

a	hat	ė	term	ô	order	ch child	a in about
ā	age	i	it	oi	oil	ng long	e in taken
ä	far	ī	ice	ou	out	sh she	ə i in pencil
â	care	o	hot	u	cup	th thin	o in lemon
e	let	ō	open	ù	put	ᵺ then	u in circus
ē	equal	ȯ	saw	ü	rule	zh measure	

Q q

Quak·er (kwā′kər), N. member of a Christian group called the Society of Friends. Quakers favor simple religious services and are opposed to war and to taking oaths.

quan·ti·ty (kwän′tə tē), N. a large amount; large number: *The baker buys flour in quantity. She owns quantities of books.* ❏ N., PL. **quan·ti·ties.**

quea·sy (kwē′zē), ADJ. inclined to nausea; easily upset: *a queasy stomach.* ❏ ADJ. **quea·si·er, quea·si·est. –quea′si·ly,** ADV. **– quea′si·ness,** N.

quick·en (kwik′ən), V. to move more quickly; hasten: *He quickened his pace.*

R r

rack·et (rak′it), N. loud noise; loud talk; din.

raid (rād), N. a sudden attack: *The pirates planned a raid on the harbor.* **–raid′er,** N.

ramp (ramp), N. a sloping way connecting two different levels of a building, road, and so on; slope.

ras·cal (ras′kəl), N. a bad, dishonest person: *The rascals stole our garbage cans.*

re·act (rē akt′), V. to act in response: *Dogs react to kindness by showing affection.*

realistic

re·al·is·tic (rē′ə lis′tik), ADJ. like the real thing; lifelike: *The speaker gave a very realistic picture of life a hundred years ago.* **–re′al·is′ti·cal·ly,** ADV.

re·call (ri kȯl′), V. to call back to mind; remember: *I can recall stories told to me when I was a small child.*

reck·less (rek′lis), ADJ. behaving or acting in a careless way, regardless of possible dangerous effects or results; not careful: *Reckless driving causes many accidents.* **–reck′less·ly,** ADV. **–reck′less·ness,** N.

re·cord (rek′ərd), N. **1** a thin, flat disk, usually of vinyl or other plastic, with narrow grooves on its surface, used on a phonograph. Variations in the grooves of records are picked up by the needle of a phonograph and transformed into sound. **2** the known facts about a person, group, organization, subject, and so on: *records department.*

re·cov·er (ri kuv′ər), V. **1** to get well; get back to a normal condition: *She recovered from her cold.* **2** to get back something lost, taken away, stolen, or sent out: *After the argument, I needed time to recover my temper. The police recovered the stolen car.*

reel[1] (rēl), V. to draw in or wind on a roller or spool: *She reeled in a fish.* **–reel′er,** N.

reel[2] (rēl), V. to suddenly sway or stagger from shock: *She reeled when the ball struck her.*

ref·e·ree (ref′ə rē′), N. person who rules on the plays in some games and sports: *a football referee.* ❏ N., PL. **ref·e·rees;** V. **ref·e·reed, ref·e·ree·ing.**

ref·u·gee (ref′yə jē′ *or* ref′yə jē′), N. person who flees for refuge or safety, especially to a foreign country, in time of persecution, war, or disaster: *Refugees from the war were cared for in neighboring countries.* ❏ N., PL. **ref·u·gees.**

re·lay (rē′lā), N. race in which each member of a team runs, swims, and so on, only a certain part of the distance: *relay race.*

rep·re·sent (rep′ri zent′), V. to show in a picture, statue, carving, and the like; give a likeness of; portray: *This painting represents the seasons.*

rep·re·sent·a·tive (rep′ri zen′tə tiv), N. person appointed or elected to act or speak for others: *Our club has two representatives at the convention.*

res·cu·er (res′kyü ər), N. someone who saves someone or something from danger, capture, harm, and so on: *The rescuers managed to save the young child from the river.*

res·i·dent (rez′ə dənt), ADJ. of or about a person living in a place: *My parents serve on the resident council of our apartment building.*

re·solve (ri zolv′), V. to make up your mind; determine; decide: *I resolved to do better work in the future.* ❏ V. **re·solved, re·solv·ing.**

re·spon·si·ble (ri spon′sə bəl), ADJ. having the duty or obligation of taking care of someone or something: *You are responsible for keeping your room cleaned up.* **—re·spon′si·bly,** ADV.

re·trace (ri trās′), V. to go back over: *We retraced our steps to where we started.* ❏ V. **re·traced, re·trac·ing. —re·trace′a·ble,** ADJ.

re·trieve (ri trēv′), V. to find and carry back to someone: *I threw the ball, and my dog retrieved it.* ❏ V. **re·trieved, re·triev·ing. —re·triev′a·ble,** ADJ. **—re·triev′a·bly,** ADV.

right (rīt), N. a just claim; something that is due to someone: *Each member of the club has a right to vote. I demand my rights.*

ro·guish (rō′gish), ADJ. of or like rogues; dishonest; rascally: *The roguish boy tried to steal her money.* **– ro′guish·ly,** ADV. **–ro′guish·ness,** N.

ruf·fle (ruf′əl), V. to destroy the smoothness of; make rough or uneven: *A breeze ruffled the lake.* ❏ V. **ruf·fled, ruf·fling.**

rug·ged (rug′id), ADJ. covered with rough edges; rough and uneven: *rugged ground, rugged rocks.* **–rug′ged·ly,** ADV. **–rug′ged·ness,** N.

run·a·way (run′ə wā′), ADJ. running away; having run away: *runaway slaves.*

rus·tler (rus′lər), N. a cattle thief: *The police caught the rustlers before they got away with our cattle.*

S s

sap·phire (saf′īr), N. a clear, hard, usually blue, precious stone.

sapphire

saw grass, grass that has sharp-edged leaves: *The little girl cut her leg on the saw grass.*

scal·lion (skal′yən), N. a young onion that has no large, distinct bulb.

scent (sent), N. a smell: *The scent of roses filled the air.* ■ Another word that sounds like this is **cent.**

sched·ule (skej′ül *or* skej′əl), N. the time fixed for doing something, arrival at a place, and so on: *The bus was an hour behind schedule.*

a	hat	ė	term	ô	order	ch	child		a in about
ā	age	i	it	oi	oil	ng	long		e in taken
ä	far	ī	ice	ou	out	sh	she	ə{	i in pencil
â	care	o	hot	u	cup	th	thin		o in lemon
e	let	ō	open	ù	put	ŦH	then		u in circus
ē	equal	ò	saw	ü	rule	zh	measure		

scowl (skoul), *v.* to look angry or sullen by lowering the eyebrows; frown: *Stop scowling at your little brother!*

sculp•ture (skulp′chər), *N.* piece of art made by carving, modeling, casting, and so on. A sculpture may be cut from blocks of marble, stone, or wood, cast in bronze, or modeled in clay or wax.

seep (sēp), *v.* to leak slowly; trickle; ooze: *Water seeped through the sand.*

sel•dom (sel′dəm), *ADV.* not often; rarely: *I am seldom ill.*

se•lect (si lekt′), *v.* to pick out; choose: *Select the book you want.*

sen•si•ble (sen′sə bəl), *ADJ.* having or showing good sense or judgment; wise: *She is far too sensible to do anything foolish.* **–sen′si•bly,** *ADV.*

shaft (shaft), *N.* long, slender stem of an arrow, spear, etc.: *The shaft of the spear was 3 feet long.*

shat•tered (shat′ərd), *ADJ.* broken into pieces: *The shattered glass was all over the floor.*

sheath (shēth), *N.* case or covering for the blade of a sword, knife, and the like. ❏ *N., PL.* **sheaths** (shēᴛʜz *or* shēths).

shel•ter (shel′tər), *N.* a temporary place of shelter for poor or homeless people, or for animals without owners: *a homeless shelter.* **–shel′ter•er,** *N.* **–shel′ter•less,** *ADJ.*

shoot•er (shüt′ər), *N.* a playing marble used to hit other marbles: *The shooter knocked two marbles out of the circle.*

sign (sīn), *v.* 1. to use sign language: *She signed her part of the conversation.* 2. to make gestures or motions that mean, stand for, or point out something: *She signed that he should be silent.* **–sign′er,** *N.*

ski (skē), *v.* to glide over snow or water on a pair of long, flat, slender pieces of hard wood, plastic, or metal that are fastened to your shoes or boots: *My family skied in Colorado last year.* ❏ *v.* **skied, ski•ing.** **–ski′er,** *N.*

skid (skid), *v.* to slip or slide sideways while moving: *The car skids on slippery roads.* ❏ *v.* **skid•ded, skid•ding.**

slav•er•y (slā′vər ē), *N.* practice of holding people against their will and forcing them to work without pay.

smudge (smuj), *N.* a dirty mark; smear.

snag (snag), *v.* to catch on a snag: *She snagged her sweater on a nail.* ❏ *v.* **snagged, snag•ging.**

so•ci•e•ty (sə sī′ə tē), *N.* group of persons joined together for a common purpose or by a common interest. A club, a fraternity, a lodge, or an association may be called a society. ❏ *N., PL.* **so•ci•e•ties.**

som•ber (som′bər), *ADJ.* having deep shadows; dark; gloomy: *A cloudy winter day is somber. It was a somber room with dark furniture and heavy black wall hangings.*

so•nar (sō′när), *N.* device for finding the depth of water or for detecting and locating underwater objects. Sonar sends sound waves into water, and they are reflected back when they strike the bottom or any object.

sou•ve•nir (sü′və nir′ *or* sü′və nir), *N.* something given or kept for remembrance; memento; keepsake: *She bought a pair of moccasins and a hat as souvenirs of her trip out West.*

spec•ta•tor (spek′tā tər), *N.* a person who looks on without taking part: *There were many spectators at the game.*

splat•ter (splat′ər), *v.* to splash or spatter: *splattered with paint.*

sprain (sprān), N. injury caused by a sudden twist or wrench: *The sprain took a long time to heal.*

sprin·kler (spring′klər), N. device for scattering water on gardens and lawns: *Dad uses sprinklers to water the lawn when it doesn't rain.*

sprint (sprint), V. to run at full speed, especially for a short distance.

sprouts (sproutz), N., PL. the first stalks of germinating beans, alfalfa seeds, and the like, sometimes eaten as a vegetable.

squish (skwish), V. to press something soft and wet, or to move in a soft, wet, oozing way: *The mud squished between my toes.*

steed (stēd), N. horse, especially a riding horse.

stock·ing (stok′ing), N. a close-fitting, knitted covering of wool, cotton, silk, nylon, and the like, for the foot and leg: *Green stockings were part of her costume for the play.*

stor·age (stôr′ij), ADJ. of or about being put away for later use: *storage area.*

strad·dle (strad′l), V. to walk, stand, or sit with the legs wide apart. ❑ V. **strad·dled, strad·dling. – strad′dler,** N.

strength·en (strengk′thən), V. to make or grow stronger: *Exercise strengthens muscles.* **–strength′en·er,** N.

stress (stres), N. great pressure or force, especially a force that can cause damage to a structure: *The roof collapsed under the stress of the heavy snow.*

strike (strīk), V. to stop work to get better pay, shorter hours, etc.: *The coal miners will strike if the company refuses to improve safety conditions in the mines.* ❑ V. **struck, struck or strick·en, strik·ing.**

stun (stun), V. to daze; bewilder; shock; overwhelm: *She was stunned by the news of her friend's death.* ❑ V. **stunned, stun·ning.**

style (stīl), N. manner; method; way: *She learned several styles of swimming.*

sub·mis·sive (səb mis′iv), ADJ. yielding to the power, control, or authority of another; obedient.

suf·fra·gist (suf′rə jist), N. person who favors giving the right to vote to more people, especially to women.

su·pe·ri·or (sə pir′ē ər), N. person who is higher in rank, position, or ability: *The officer asked his superiors for advice.*

sur·vey (sər vā′), V. to look over; view; examine: *The buyers surveyed the goods offered for sale.* ❑ V. **sur·veyed, sur·vey·ing.**

sus·pi·cious (sə spish′əs), ADJ. causing one to suspect; questionable: *A man was hanging about the house in a suspicious manner.* **–sus·pi′cious·ly,** ADV. **–sus·pi′cious·ness,** N.

swamp (swämp), N. wet, soft land; marsh: *the swamp along the river's edge.*

switch (swich), N. **1** a change; shift: *A switch in dates on the schedule confused the passengers.* **2** device for making or breaking a connection in an electric circuit. ❑ N., PL. **switch·es.**

swol·len (swō′lən), ADJ. grown or made bigger; swelled: *a swollen ankle.*

swoop (swüp), V. to come down with a rush, as a hawk does; sweep rapidly down upon in a sudden attack: *He saw bats swooping down from the roof of the cave.* **–swoop′er,** N.

Tt

tar·get (tär′git), V. to specify something as a problem or goal; single out: *He targeted my spelling as an area for improvement.*

a hat	ė term	ô order	ch child
ā age	i it	oi oil	ng long
ä far	ī ice	ou out	sh she
â care	o hot	u cup	th thin
e let	ō open	ů put	ᴛʜ then
ē equal	ȯ saw	ü rule	zh measure

ə { a in about / e in taken / i in pencil / o in lemon / u in circus }

tech·nique (tek nēk′), N. a special method or system used to accomplish something: *She has her own techniques for painting portraits.*

ten·don (ten′dən), N. a tough, strong band or cord of tissue that joins a muscle to a bone or some other body part.

thrift shop, shop in which secondhand items are sold at low prices.

thrift·y (thrif′tē), ADJ. careful in spending; economical; saving: *a thrifty shopper.* ❑ ADJ. **thrift·i·er, thrift·i·est. –thrift′i·ly,** ADV. **thrift′i·ness,** N.

thrill (thril), N. a shivering, exciting feeling: *I get a thrill whenever I see a parade.*

tie (tī), N. a heavy piece of timber or iron placed crosswise to form a foundation or support. The rails of a railroad track are fastened to ties about a foot apart. ❑ V. **tied, ty·ing.**

tilt (tilt), V. to tip or cause to tip; slope; slant; lean: *You tilted your head forward when you bowed. This table tilts.* **–tilt′a·ble,** ADJ. **–tilt′er,** N.

toast (tōst), N. act of drinking to the health or success of someone or something: *They drank a toast to the new year.*

tor·rent (tôr′ənt), N. heavy downpour: *The rain came down in torrents during the thunderstorm.*

tor·til·la (tôr tē′yə), N. a thin, flat, round cake made of cornmeal, commonly eaten in Spanish America. It is baked on a flat surface and served hot. ❑ N., PL. **tor·til·las.**

track meet, series of contests in running, jumping, throwing, and similar sports.

tra·di·tion (trə dish′ən), N. custom or belief handed down from one generation to the next: *Our family has many traditions for celebrating holidays.*

trans·con·ti·nen·tal (tran′skon tə nen′tl), ADJ. crossing a continent: *transcontinental flights.*

trans·late (tran slāt′ *or* tranz lāt′), V. to change from one language into another: *He translated a book from French into English.* ❑ V. **trans·lat·ed, trans·lat·ing. –trans·lat′- a·ble,** ADJ.

tread (tred), N. act or sound of stepping: *the tread of marching feet.*

tri·al (trī′əl), N. a formal examination and deciding of a case in court: *The suspect was brought to trial.*

trig·ger (trig′ər), V. to initiate; start: *The burglar's movement triggered the alarm to go off.*

trol·ley (trol′ē), N. an electrically powered vehicle for public transportation. ❑ N., PL. **trol·leys.**

tro·phy (trō′fē), N. any prize, cup, and the like, awarded to a victorious person or team: *The champion kept her tennis trophies on the mantel.* ❑ N., PL. **tro·phies.**

trop·i·cal (trop′ə kəl), ADJ. of or like the tropics: *tropical heat. Bananas are a tropical fruit.* **–trop′i·cal·ly,** ADV.

tu·tor (tü′tər), N. a private teacher: *A tutor comes once a week to help me with mathematics.*

U u

ul·ti·ma·tum (ul′tə mā′təm), N. a final offer or demand, given with the threat of severe penalties if refused.

un·clench (un klench′), V. to open or become opened from a clenched state: *unclench your fists.*

un·con·scious (un kon′shəs), ADJ. not conscious; not able to feel or think: *knock unconscious, unconscious from anesthetic.* **–un·con′- scious·ly,** ADV. **–un·con′scious·ness,** N.

un·der·brush (un′dər brush′), N. bushes and small trees growing under large trees in woods or forests; undergrowth; understory: *Many animals live in the underbrush of a forest.*

un·ex·pect·ed (un′ek spek′tid), ADJ. not known beforehand; unforeseen: *an unexpected difficulty, an unexpected change in the weather.* **–un′ex·pect′ed·ly,** ADV. **–un′ex·pect′-ed·ness,** N.

un·for·tu·nate (un fôr′chə nit), ADJ. not lucky; having bad luck: *She had an unfortunate accident.* **–un·for′tu·nate·ly,** ADV.

up·right (up′rīt′), ADV. straight up; in a vertical position: *Hold yourself upright.* **–up′right′ly,** ADV. **–up′right′ness,** N.

V v

val·u·a·ble (val′yü ə bəl or val′yə bəl), ADJ. having value; being worth something: *valuable information, a valuable friend.*

val·ue (val′yü), N. power to buy: *The value of the dollar lessened from 1980 to 1990.*

ven·om (ven′əm), N. the poison of snakes, spiders, and the like.

view·er (vyü′ər), N. person who watches or looks at something.

vi·o·la (vē ō′lə), N. a stringed musical instrument like a violin, but somewhat larger and lower in pitch: *Maritza plays the viola in the orchestra.* ❑ N., PL. **vi·o·las.**

vi·sa (vē′zə), N. an official signature or endorsement upon a passport, showing that it has been examined and approved. A visa is granted by the consul or other representative of the country to which a person wishes to travel. ❑ N., PL. **vi·sas.**

vis·u·al (vizh′ü əl), ADJ. received through the sense of sight: *visual impressions.* **–vis′u·al·ly,** ADV.

vol·un·teer (vol′ən tir′), N. someone who offers his or her services by choice: *We asked for volunteers to help us clean up the park.*

vow (vou), N. a solemn promise: *marriage vows.*

W w

wet·land (wet′land′), N. Often, **wetlands,** swamps, marshes, or other lands that are soaked with water but where plants continue to grow.

wil·der·ness (wil′dər nis), N. a wild, uncultivated, or desolate region with few or no people living in it. ❑ N., PL. **wil·der·ness·es.**

wince (wins), V. to draw back suddenly; flinch slightly: *I winced when the dentist's drill touched my tooth.* ❑ V. **winced, winc·ing.**

wind·up (wind′up′), N. in baseball, a swinging movement of the arms while twisting the body just before pitching the ball.

with·drew (wiтн drü′ or with drü′), V. past tense of **withdraw;** removed: *The coach withdrew the player from the game when he was hurt.*

wok (wok), N. a metal cooking bowl, used for stir-frying.

Y y

young·ster (yung′stər), N. child: *Those youngsters are still in kindergarten.*

a	hat	ė	term	ô	order	ch	child		a in about
ā	age	i	it	oi	oil	ng	long		e in taken
ä	far	ī	ice	ou	out	sh	she	ə {	i in pencil
â	care	o	hot	u	cup	th	thin		o in lemon
e	let	ō	open	ů	put	тн	then		u in circus
ē	equal	ȯ	saw	ü	rule	zh	measure		

Handbook of Reading Skills

How to Use This Handbook

The following reading skills and definitions are found throughout this book. Understanding these skills can help you as you read. In this section, the skills are arranged in alphabetical order. Use these pages to help you review the terms and definitions. When reading, refer back to these pages as often as needed.

Author's Purpose

- **Author's purpose** is the reason or reasons an author has for writing.
- Authors often have more than one purpose for writing and don't usually state their purposes.
- Four common purposes are to persuade, inform, entertain, and express.
- Predicting an author's purpose can help you match how you read to what you read. For example, if an author wants to explain a difficult idea, you may decide to read slowly. But when an author's purpose is to entertain, you may want to read quickly.

Author's Viewpoint

- **Author's viewpoint** is the way an author thinks about the subject of his or her writing.
- To learn an author's viewpoint, think about the author's opinion and choice of words.
- Unbalanced, or biased writing, happens when an author presents only one viewpoint. Balanced writing presents both sides of an issue equally.

Cause and Effect

- A **cause** is why something happens. An **effect** is what happens.
- A cause may have more than one effect, and an effect may have more than one cause.
- Clue words, such as *because* and *since,* signal a cause and effect relationship. Sometimes there are no clue words.
- Sometimes the author does not tell a cause, and you need to think about why something happened.

Character

- **Characters** can be people or animals in stories.

- You can learn about characters by noticing what they think, say, and do.

- You can also learn about characters by thinking about how other characters treat them and what other characters say about them.

- When you read, think of what you already know about real people and what you have learned about the characters so far. Use this to decide what a character's actions mean and what a character might do next.

Compare and Contrast

- **Comparing** is telling how two or more things are alike. **Contrasting** is telling how two or more things are different.

- Authors sometimes use clue words, such as *similar to, like,* or *as,* to compare things. They may use clue words, such as *different from, but,* or *unlike,* to contrast things.

- When there are no clue words, compare and contrast by asking, "What does this remind me of?"

Context Clues

- **Context clues** are words that help explain an unfamiliar word.

- Context clues can appear just before or after an unfamiliar word. Sometimes they are in a different part of the story or article, far from the unfamiliar word.

- When reading, look for specific context clues such as definitions, explanations, examples, and descriptions.

- Using context clues will help you read and understand information more quickly.

Drawing Conclusions

- When you form opinions based on facts and details, you are **drawing conclusions.**

- To draw conclusions, think logically. Also use clues from what you've read and your own knowledge and experience.

- To check your conclusions, ask yourself if they make sense. Are there any other possible conclusions?

Fact and Opinion

- A **fact** can be proved true or false. Statements of fact can be proved through observation or research.

- An **opinion** tells a person's ideas or feelings. It cannot be proved true or false, but it can be supported or explained.

- Some statements of opinion begin with clue words such as *I believe* or *in my opinion.*

- Some paragraphs have both facts and opinions.

Generalizing

- **Generalizing** is making a statement about what several people or things have in common.

- *Many people like popcorn* is a generalization. Clue words, such as *many* and *most,* can signal generalizations.

- A valid generalization is supported by facts and logic. A faulty generalization is not.

Handbook of Reading Skills

Graphic Sources

- A **graphic source** is something that shows information visually. Pictures, charts, graphs, and maps are graphic sources.

- Graphic sources help you understand what you read because they provide a lot of information quickly.

- Before you read, look for graphic sources that could give you an idea of what the article or story is about.

- As you read, compare the written words to the graphic sources for a better understanding of the main ideas.

Main Idea and Supporting Details

- The topic is what a paragraph, article, or story is about.

- The **main idea** is the most important idea about the topic.

- Sometimes the main idea is stated. When it is not, you have to decide what is most important and put it into your own words.

- **Supporting details** tell more about the main idea.

- Knowing the main idea will help you better understand and remember what you read.

Making Judgments

- **Making judgments** means forming opinions about someone or something.

- Authors make judgments about the subject of their writing. Evaluate an author's judgments by asking if they are supported by evidence in the story or article.

- When reading, you should support your judgments about characters or situations with evidence from the text.

Paraphrasing

- **Paraphrasing** is explaining something in your own words. When you paraphrase, you should include only the author's ideas and opinions.

- Check your paraphrasing by asking yourself, "Did I use my own words? Did I keep the author's meaning?"

- Use paraphrasing as a strategy when you study for tests and when you need to give information in oral or written reports. Putting information into your own words will help you remember ideas.

Plot

- A **plot** includes the important events that happen in a story.

- A plot usually has a conflict or problem, rising action, climax, and an outcome or resolution.

- *Conflict* is the story's main problem. The conflict can be within a character, between two characters, or between a character and nature.

- During the *rising action,* one event follows another. Each event adds interest or suspense to the conflict.

- The *climax* is the high point where the main character faces the problem directly.

- The *resolution* is where the conflict is resolved.

Predicting

- **Predicting** is giving a statement about what you think might happen next in a story or come next in an article. The statement you give is a **prediction.**

- You can make predictions based on what you already know and what has already happened in a story or an article.

- After you predict something, continue reading to check your prediction. As you learn new information, you might need to change your prediction.

Sequence

- **Sequence** is the order in which things happen.

- Words such as *then* and *after* are often clues to the sequence. Words such as *meanwhile* and *during* show that several events can happen at once.

- By arranging events in sequence, you can see how one thing leads to another.

Setting

- The **setting** is the time and place in which a story happens.

- In some stories, the author tells exactly when and where the story takes place. In other stories, the author tells about the setting through details, and you have to figure out the time and place.

- Sometimes the author tells only one part of the setting, either the time or the place.

- In some stories, the setting is very important. It affects what happens in the story and why. In other stories, it isn't important.

Steps in a Process

- The actions you take to make something or to reach a goal are **steps in a process.**

- Sometimes steps in a process are shown by numbers or clue words, such as *first, next, then,* and *last.* If there are no clue words, think about what you already know about how the process might be done.

- If you picture the result, you'll understand why each step is necessary.

- Identifying steps in a process will help you solve problems and follow directions.

Summarizing

- **Summarizing** means telling just the main ideas of an article or the plot of a story.

- A good summary is brief. It does not include unnecessary details, repeated words or thoughts, or unimportant ideas.

Text Structure

- **Text structure** is the way a piece of writing is organized.

- There are two main kinds of writing—fiction and nonfiction. Each is read in a different way. Identifying the text structure will help you choose the best reading strategy.

- Fiction is often organized in chronological order.

- Nonfiction can be organized in chronological order, by main ideas and supporting details, or by relationships such as cause and effect, problem and solution, and comparison and contrast.

Theme

- **Theme** is an underlying meaning or message of a story. A story can have more than one theme.

- Themes can be statements, lessons, or generalizations that stand on their own, such as *Life is what you make of it.*

- Sometimes the author states the theme directly. Readers may have to figure out the theme by asking, "What did I learn by reading this story?"

- Look for evidence in the story to support the theme or themes.

Visualizing

- **Visualizing** is creating a picture in your mind as you read.

- Pay attention to description, imagery, and sensory words that help you imagine what you are reading. Also think about what you already know about the places, people, and things being described.

- As you read and get more information, you may need to change the picture in your head to match the new details.

- If you have a hard time visualizing, reread or read more slowly to get a better picture.

Spelling Lists

From the Diary of Leigh Botts

army	starve	scar	garbage	argue
apartment	guitar	Arkansas	hamburger	return
purpose	surface	curl	purse	furniture
courage	journal	courtesy	nourish	journey

Faith and Eddie

heavy	ahead	measure	already	jealous
meadow	weapon	said	again	against
degree	cheese	succeed	speech	breeze
goalie	piece	believe	thief	chief

Looking for a Home

choice	noisy	spoil	poison	Illinois
loyal	destroy	annoy	oyster	voyage
powder	towel	downtown	drown	growl
amount	our	outside	couch	surround

Meeting Mr. Henry

brain	plain	claim	complain	favorite
stranger	aliens	vacation	sidewalk	slide
survive	crime	bowling	owner	arrow
snowball	whole	globe	antelope	slope

Eloise Greenfield

choose	school	broom	scoop	booth
threw	crew	drew	jewel	future
music	usually	humor	Utah	taught
naughty	daughter	laundry	sausage	launch

Unit 2

The Diver and the Dolphins

major	subject	junior	judge	lodge
ridge	ledge	legend	general	Georgia
character	chorus	orchestra	mechanic	chord
raccoon	occur	accurate	occasion	accuse

The Fury of a Hurricane

knowledge	know	knew	knuckle	knitting
knapsack	numb	bomb	tomb	climber
plumbing	ghost	spaghetti	aghast	glisten
listening	fasten	hustle	mistletoe	whistle

Dwaina Brooks

mailbox	nearby	into	sometimes	sunset
anything	daylight	something	haircut	notebook
earthquake	hideout	textbook	volleyball	horseback
handwriting	kickstand	rattlesnake	fireplace	housework

Everglades

handle	perhaps	anger	accident	adventure
before	because	decided	pretend	belong
possible	solve	problem	lobster	python
swung	jungle	shuttle	blood	flood

Missing Links

discovered	disorder	disappoint	disobey	disapprove
unsure	unclear	unable	unbuckle	unlimited
midweek	midyear	midway	midnight	midstream
pretest	preschool	precook	prepaid	prerecorded

Unit 3

Going with the Flow

months	friends	grades	cowboys	valleys
donkeys	missiles	costumes	pictures	mornings
matches	bushes	benches	speeches	passes
kisses	dresses	batteries	companies	centuries

Kate Shelley: Bound for Legend

radios	videos	pianos	patios	banjos
heroes	potatoes	echoes	tornadoes	tomatoes
cuffs	cliffs	beliefs	hoofs	roofs
themselves	lives	leaves	loaves	halves

The Marble Champ

can't	wouldn't	don't	weren't	I'm
I'll	let's	that's	there's	what's
she's	you're	they're	who's	we're
I've	you've	should've	could've	we've

From Bees to Honey

Houston	Alaska	Kentucky	Little Rock	Duluth
Arizona	Miami	Indiana	Alabama	Baltimore
Detroit	Florida	Los Angeles	Hawaii	Memphis
Virginia	Oregon	Pittsburgh	Texas	South Carolina

Babe to the Rescue

friend's	today's	Dad's	Mom's	sister's
sisters'	child's	children's	person's	people's
grandmother's	uncle's	grandfather's	uncles'	doctor's
doctors'	cousin's	cousins'	woman's	women's

Unit 4

The Yangs' First Thanksgiving

write	right	buy	by	to
too	bored	board	it's	its
threw	through	knead	need	main
mane	past	passed	allowed	aloud

The Jr. Iditarod Race

answer	minute	happened	library	opened
length	getting	when	finished	maybe
mystery	dentist	actually	width	caramel
pumpkin	quarter	sandwich	grabbed	frightening

The Night Alone

followed	following	lighter	lightest	tried
trying	cuter	cutest	excited	exciting
amused	amusing	bigger	biggest	wrapped
wrapping	earlier	earliest	easier	easiest

The Heart of a Runner

manager	president	different	terrible	finally
really	supposed	probably	California	especially
balance	constant	innocent	realize	opportunity
pollute	prisoner	celebrate	grocery	elevator

The Memory Box

either	another	computer	calendar	solar
particular	evil	fossil	civil	cancel
label	channel	quarrel	eaten	frozen
siren	curtain	captain	fountain	bargain

Spelling Lists

Unit 5

I Want to Vote!

strong	nothing	everything	clothing	among
sting	hanger	lightning	blank	trunk
thought	chipmunk	shrink	they	north
then	without	though	Thanksgiving	there

The Long Path to Freedom

comfortable	reasonable	washable	agreeable	valuable
responsible	convertible	flexible	sensible	reversible
contestant	defiant	observant	servant	occupant
student	urgent	confident	resident	opponent

from Chester Cricket's Pigeon Ride

famous	nervous	joyous	marvelous	humorous
mysterious	dangerous	selection	instruction	attraction
rejection	education	inflation	decoration	information
organization	conversation	imagination	admiration	preparation

Passage to Freedom: The Sugihara Story

bookshelf	someone	everybody	nowhere	cupcake
wristwatch	everyone	blindfold	typewriter	grandparent
home run	each other	hot dog	all right	high school
pen pal	living room	peanut butter	no one	first aid

Paul Revere's Ride

please	pleasant	cloth	clothes	sign
signature	dream	dreamt	part	partial
moist	moisten	breathe	breath	create
creature	elect	election	practice	practical

Unit 6

The Baker's Neighbor

of	off	except	accept	which
witch	where	were	weather	whether
plant	planet	bounds	bounce	desert
dessert	rise	raise	dinner	diner

Andy's Secret Ingredient

until	went	enough	TV	one
didn't	a lot	want	doesn't	always
necklace	exact	burglar	equipment	chimney
exist	rumbling	upon	athlete	examine

In the Days of King Adobe

aware	prepare	share	declare	spare
beware	dairy	stairway	prairie	repair
dear	beard	appear	weary	smear
volunteer	career	cheery	pioneer	reindeer

Just Telling the Truth

lonely	hundred	friend	built	beautiful
heard	radio	their	caught	bored
guard	pierce	shrieked	receive	horrible
jewelry	tumble	northern	acre	museum

Is It Real?

column	columnist	face	facial	voice
vocal	limb	limber	fast	fasten
wise	wisdom	cycle	bicycle	human
humane	stable	stability	final	finality

Acknowledgments

Text

Dorling Kindersley (DK) is an international publishing company specializing in the creation of high quality reference content for books, CD-ROMs, online, and video. The hallmark of DK content is its unique combination of educational value and strong visual style—this combination allows DK to deliver appealing, accessible, and engaging educational content that delights children, parents, and teachers around the world. Scott Foresman is delighted to have been able to use selected extracts of DK content within the Scott Foresman Reading program.
122–123: "A City Street Today" from *A Street Through Time* by Anne Millard, illustrated by Steve Noon. Copyright © 1998 by Dorling Kindersley Limited; **232–233:** "Detectives" from *Crime and Detection.* Copyright © 1998 by Dorling Kindersley Limited; **324–325:** "People and Animals" from *DK Nature Encyclopedia* © 1998 by Dorling Kindersley Limited; **400–401:** "Dogs in Sports" from *Dog* by Juliet Clutton-Brock. Copyright © 1991 by Dorling Kindersley Limited; **578–579:** "1939" from *Children's History of the 20th Century.* Copyright © 1999 Dorling Kindersley Limited; **668–669:** "One Day's Food" from *The World in One Day* by Russell Ash. Text copyright © 1997 by Russell Ash. Compilation and illustration copyright © 1997 Dorling Kindersley Limited.

20: "Nothing New Under the Sun (Hardly)" from *Homer Price* by Robert McCloskey. Copyright 1943, renewed © 1971 by Robert McCloskey. Used by permission of Viking Penguin, a division of Penguin Putnam, Inc.; **22:** "From the Diary of Leigh Botts" from *Dear Mr. Henshaw* by Beverly Cleary. Text copyright © 1983 by Beverly Cleary. Used by permission of HarperCollins Publishers; **37:** "The Rampanion" from *The Kids' Invention Book* by Arlene Erlbach. Copyright © 1997 by Arlene Erlbach. Reprinted by permission of The Lerner Group; **40:** From *Lost and Found* by Jean Little. Copyright © 1985 by Jean Little. Reprinted by permission of Penguin Books Canada Limited; **42:** From *Faith and the Electric Dogs* by Patrick Jennings. Copyright © 1966 by Patrick Jennings. Reprinted by permission of Scholastic, Inc.; **62:** "Say What?" by Tracey Randinelli. Copyright © 1998 Sesame Workshop (New York, New York). All rights reserved. Reprinted with permission from *Contact Kids Magazine;* **64:** From *We Don't Look Like Our Mom and Dad* by Harriet Langsam Sobol. Copyright © 1984 by Harriet Langsam Sobol. Used by permission of Coward-McCann, Inc., a division of Penguin Putnam, Inc.; **66, 81:** From *Orphan Train Rider: One Boy's True Story* by Andrea Warren. Copyright © 1996 by Andrea Warren. Reprinted by permission of Houghton Mifflin Company. All rights reserved; **86:** From "The Yankee Doodle Shortstop" by Helen J. Hinterberg, *Cricket,* July 1996. Reprinted by permission of the author; **88:** *Finding Buck McHenry* by Alfred Slote. Copyright © 1991 by Alfred Slote. Used by permission of HarperCollins; **104:** From "Analysis of Baseball" by May Swenson. Copyright © 1971 by May Swenson. Used with permission of the Literary Estate of May Swenson; **106:** From *Alesia* by Eloise Greenfield and Alesia Revis. Text copyright © 1981 by Eloise Greenfield and Alesia Revis. Reprinted by permission of Scott Treimel New York; **108:** "Eloise Greenfield" from *Childtimes: A Three-Generation Memoir* by Eloise Greenfield. Copyright © 1979 by Eloise Greenfield and Lessie Jones Little. Used by permission of HarperCollins Publishers; **124:** "Curb Your Cloud" by Richard Garcia; **125:** "Since Hanna Moved Away" by Judith Viorst. Reprinted with the permission of Margaret K. McElderry Books, an imprint of Simon & Schuster Children's Publishing Division from *If I Were in Charge of the World and Other Worries* by Judith Viorst. Copyright © 1981 Judith Viorst; **126:** "August 8" by Norman Jordan from *My Black Me,* ed. by Arnold Adoff. Puffin Books, 1974; **127:** "You and I" from *My Song Is Beautiful* by Mary Ann Hoberman. Copyright © 1994 by Mary Ann Hoberman, copyright © 1994 by Little, Brown and Company, Inc. (illustrations). By permission of Little, Brown and Company, Inc.; **134:** "Do You Know Your (first-aid) ABCs?" *Current Health 1,* April 1994. Copyright 1994 by Weekly Reader Corporation. Further reproduction is prohibited without permission from Weekly Reader Corporation. All rights reserved; **136:** From *Dolphin Adventure: A True Story* by Wayne Grover. Text copyright © 1990 by Wayne Grover. Used by permission of HarperCollins Publishers; **153:** From "Family, Friends, and Dolphin Neighbors" by Denise Herzing and Patricia Warhol from *Dolphin Log,* March 1993. Reprinted by permission; **156:** "Hurricane Season Peaks in September," *USA Today* Weather Page; **158:** From *Hurricanes: Earth's Mightiest Storms* by Patricia Lauber. Copyright © 1996 by Patricia Lauber. Reprinted by permission of Scholastic, Inc.; **175:** "My Life's Work: Hurricane Flier" by Robert Bahr from *Boys' Life,* April 1993, pp. 42–43. Reprinted by permission of the author; **178:** "Reach Out & Make a Difference," *Current Health 1,* December 1994. Copyright 1994 by Weekly Reader Corporation. Further reproduction is prohibited without permission from Weekly Reader Corporation. All rights reserved; **180:** From *It's Our*

World, Too! by Phillip Hoose. Copyright © 1993 by Phillip Hoose. By permission of Little, Brown and Company; **194:** "Lighting Up Hope" © 2000 Consumers Union of U.S., Inc. Yonkers, NY 10703-1057, a nonprofit organization. Reprinted with permission from the Zillions® for educational purposes only. No commercial use or photocopying permitted. Log onto www.Zillions.org.; **196:** "Conservation Efforts" by Gary Chandler and Kevin Graham from *Kids Who Make a Difference,* pp. 15–16. Reprinted by permission of The Millbrook Press Inc.; **198:** *Everglades* by Jean Craighead George. Text copyright © 1995 by Jean Craighead George. Illustrations copyright © 1995 by Wendell Minor. Used by permission of HarperCollins Publishers; **214:** "Everglades" text from *The World Book Encyclopedia.* © 2001 World Book, Inc. By permission of the publisher. www.worldbook.com; **216:** From "The Case of Granny and the Alien Bandit" by Michael Manley from *Ranger Rick,* September 1994. Reprinted by permission of the author; **218:** "Missing Links" from *Flute Revenge: Plus Two More Mysteries* by Andrew Bromberg. Copyright © 1982 by William Morrow & Company, Inc. By permission of Greenwillow Books, a division of William Morrow & Company, Inc.; **234:** "Thistles" from *The Rose on My Cake* by Karla Kuskin. Copyright © 1964, renewed 1992 by Karla Kuskin. Reprinted by permission of Scott Treimel New York; **235:** "De colores" from *De Colores and Other Latin American Folk Songs* by José-Luis Orozco. Copyright © 1994 by José-Louis Orozco. Used by permission of Dutton Children's Books, a division of Penguin Putnam, Inc.; **236:** "Valuables" by X. J. Kennedy. Copyright © 1991 by X. J. Kennedy. First appeared in *The Kite That Braved Old Orchard Beach,* published by Margaret K. McElderry Books, a division of Simon & Schuster Books for Young Readers. Reprinted by permission of Curtis Brown, Ltd.; **237:** "To You" from *Collected Poems* by Langston Hughes. Copyright © 1994 by the Estate of Langston Hughes. Reprinted by permission of Alfred A. Knopf, Inc.; **244:** Excerpt from *Ride the Red Cycle* by Harriette Gillem Robinet. Copyright © 1980 by Harriette Gillem Robinet. Reprinted by permission of Houghton Mifflin Company. All rights reserved; **246:** From *Going with the Flow* by Claire Blatchford. Copyright 1998 by Claire Blatchford. Published by Carolrhoda Books, Inc., a division of Lerner Publishing Group. Used by permission of the publisher. All rights reserved; **260:** "Drive" from *Rimshots: Basketball Pix, Rolls, and Rhythms* by Charles R. Smith, copyright © 1999 by Charles R. Smith. Used by permission of Dutton Children's Books, an imprint of Penguin Putnam Books for Young Readers, a division of Penguin Putnam Inc.; **262:** *The Spectacular Trains: A History of Rail Transportation* by John Everds. Hubbard Press, 1973; **264:** From *Kate Shelley* by Robert San Souci, illustrated by Max Ginsburg. Text Copyright © Robert D. San Souci, 1995. Published by arrangement with Dial Books for Young Readers, a division of Penguin Putnam, Inc.; **283:** "The Last Western Frontier" from *Scott Foresman Social Studies—America: Yesterday and Today.* Copyright © 1988 Scott, Foresman and Company; **286:** "Anything You Set Your Mind To" from *One-Minute Birthday Stories* by Shari Lewis and Lan O'Kun. Copyright © 1992 by Richard Rehbein. Used by permission of Random House Children's Books, a division of Random House; **288:** "The Marble Champ" from *Baseball in April and Other Stories,* copyright © 1990 by Gary Soto, reprinted/recorded by permission of Harcourt, Inc.; **302:** "The Big Ouchie" by Jordan Brown in *3-2-1 Contact Magazine,* October 1994. Copyright © 1994 by Children's Television Workshop (New York, New York). All rights reserved; **306:** "Bee Bodies" excerpted from *The World Book Encyclopedia.* © 2001 World Book, Inc. By permission of the publisher. www.worldbook.com; **308:** From *A Beekeeper's Year* by Sylvia Johnson. Copyright © 1994 by Sylvia Johnson (text), 1994 by E. M. Peterson Books (illustrations). Reprinted by permission of Little, Brown & Company; **326:** "What Do Animals Say?" by Deborah Hammons from *The Christian Science Monitor,* May 26, 1998. Reprinted by permission of the author; **328:** From *Babe: The Gallant Pig* by Dick King-Smith, copyright © 1983 by Dick King-Smith. Used by permission of Crown Children's Books, a division of Random House, Inc.; **347:** "Cry Wolf" from *Cry Wolf and Other Aesop Fables,* retold by Naomi Lewis. Text copyright © 1988 by Naomi Lewis. Reprinted by permission; **348:** "Stars" from *Canto Familiar,* copyright © 1995 by Gary Soto, reprinted by permission of Harcourt, Inc.; **350:** "Remember" from *It's Raining Laughter* by Nikki Grimes. Copyright © 1997 by Nikki Grimes. Used by permission of Dial Books for Young Readers, a division of Penguin Putnam, Inc.; **351:** "A tutor who tooted the flute" by Carolyn Wells from *Call Down the Moon: Poems of Music,* ed. by Myra Cohn Livingston. New York: Simon & Schuster, 1995; **351:** "A bugler named Dougal MacDougal" from *Primrose Path* by Ogden Nash. Copyright © 1935 by Ogden Nash. By permission of Little, Brown and Company; **358:** "The Origami Truce" from *Lucky Charms and Birthday Wishes* by Christine McDonnell. Copyright © 1984 by Christine McDonnell. Used by permission of Viking Penguin, a division of Penguin Putnam, Inc.; **360:** From *Yang the Third and Her Impossible Family* by Lensey

Artists

Photographs

Every effort has been made to secure permission and provide appropriate credit for photographic material. The publisher deeply regrets any omission and pledges to correct, in subsequent editions, errors called to its attention.

Unless otherwise acknowledged, all photographs are the property of Scott Foresman, a division of Pearson Education. Page abbreviations are as follows: **(t)** top, **(c)** center, **(b)** bottom, **(l)** left, **(r)** right, **(ins)** inset, **(s)** spot, **(bk)** background.

1, 2, 62(tr, cr, br), 63(all), 88(c), 89(tr), 308, 458(bl), 459(cl), 476, 534(l), 544(bk), 633(b), 651(cr), 652(tl), 653, 692: PhotoDisc; **17, 447:** Sharon Bell Mathis-Marcia C. Bell/Courtesy, HarperCollins Publishers/Courtesy Sharon Bell Mathis; **37–39 (bk), 40–41, 64–65 (bk), 102–103, 108–121, 286–287, 300–301, 348–351, 358–359, 454–455, 470–471, 560–561, 580–581, 602–605, 654–655, 694–695, 706–707, 714–715:** Sharon Hoogstraten; **37, 38(tl):** Alison DeSmyter Courtesy the family; **38(bc), 39(tr):** Houston Chronicle Library; **60(t):** Jacket photo copyright © 1996 by Alison Kaplan/Courtesy Scholastic; **62(cl):** Tim Mantoani/Zephyr Images; **64–65:** Patricia Agre; **66–67(bk), 284(bl):** Kansas State Historical Society; **71, 73(t), 78:** Courtesy Lee & Novelle Nailling; **79:** Aneal Vohra for Scott Foresman; **82(t):** Marcelle de Leleu Hopper Courtesy Yvonne Watson & Marcelle Hopper; **83(l):** Courtesy Orphan Train Heritage Society; **83(r):** Public Domain; **104:** © Paul A. Souders/Corbis; **108(cl), 109(b), 118–119:** Courtesy Eloise Greenfield; **115(all):** UPI/Corbis-Bettmann; **122–123, 324(t), 324(b), 325(tl), 325(tr), 325(b), 400(tl), 400(tl), 401(c), 401(c), 579(br), 668–669:** © Dorling Kindersley; **132–133:** Zigy Kaluzny/Stone; **151(t):** Courtesy Wayne Grover; **153–154(bk):** Michel Verdure; **154(ins):** Denise Herzing; **155(bk):** Bob Talbot; **156–157(bk):** Greg Vaughn/Stone; **158–159(bk), 174(bk):** Courtesy of the Rosenberg Library, Galveston, TX; **161(bk):** John Turner/Stone; **163, 175(bl), 177(r), 726(c):** NASA; **165(bu):** Weatherstock; **166(b):** Patrick Farrell/Miami Herald; **167(bk), 169(bk), 446:** AP/Wide World; **167(ins-c):** John Berry; **169(ins-tc):** Jeff Cory/Sipa Press; **169(ins-bc):** Raul De Molina/Corbis Sygma; **170(c):** Joe McDonald/Animals Animals/Earth Scenes; **170(tl):** Ken Cole/Animals Animals/ Earth Scenes; **171(bk):** Claudine Laabs; **172(cl):** Robert Lubeck/Animals Animals/Earth Scenes; **173(cr):** Courtesy Patricia G.Lauber; **175(br), 176–177(t):** Ted Carlson/Check Six; **176(cr), 177(b):** Acey Harper Photography; **182(t):** Courtesy, Little, Brown and Company; **192(t):** Richard Connelly/Rosenstone/Wender; **194(br), 195(tr):** From "Lighting Up Hope," *Zillions Magazine,* Vol. 9, No.6, May/June 1999/Consumers Union; **212(b):** Courtesy Jean Craighead George; **215(b):** Randy Wells/Stone; **232(bl):** Roger-Viollet/© Topham/The Image Works, Inc.; **232(cr), 232(bc), 233(tr):** Natural History Museum/© Dorling Kindersley; **232(c), 401(cl):** Mary Evans Picture Library; **233(tl):** *The Long Goodbye,* Courtesy Lion's Gate Films/Ronald Grant Archive/The Cinema Museum; **233(tc):** © Topham/The Image Works, Inc.; **233(cr):** © Touchstone Pictures/The Kobal Collection; **233(b):** G. Bassignac/Gamma/Frank Spooner Pictures Ltd.; **242–243(c):** Lori Adamski Peek/Stone; **258:** Courtesy Claire Blatchford; **281(b):** Courtesy Max Ginsburg; **281(t):** East Bay Photo Lab/Courtesy Bantam Doubleday Dell Books; **285(cr):** Courtesy Southern Pacific Railroad; **300:** Courtesy Carolyn Soto; **304(l), 305(r):** © David Madison; **304(r):** © Tom DiPace; **305(l):** Al Tielemans/Duomo Photography Inc.; **308–309, 322–323(bk):** Mary L. Lanford/Elizabeth M. Peterson; **311(b), 315(t), 316(t), 318(cl), 319(tl), 320(tl), 321(b):** from *The Beekeeper's Year* by Sylvia Johnson. Copyright © 1994 by Sylvia A. Johnson (text), Illustrations (photos) © 1994 by E.M. Peterson Books. By permission of Little, Brown and Company; **313(t):** Vanessa Serra/Liaison Agency; **324(cl):** Barnaby's Picture Library; **324(cr):** Paul van Gaalen/Bruce Coleman Collection; **324(b):** Geoff Tompkinson/SPL/Photo Researchers, Inc.; **325(cl):** Planet Earth Pictures; **325(br):** Simon Everett/Natural Science Photos; **345(t):** Photo: Michael Dyer Associates/Courtesy, Candlewick Press; **356–357:** Peter Timmermans/Stone; **377:** Photo: Don Perkins/Courtesy Lensey Namioka; **384–399:** Ted Wood Photography; **400(c):** Allsport; **401(cr):** Powerstock Zefa/Index Stock Imagery; **419:** Courtesy, Greenfield Review Press; **433:** Bob Martin/Allsport; **437:** USOC/Allsport; **445:** Hulton Deutsch/Allsport; **449(r):** © Bettmann/Corbis; **452(c), 453(tr):** Michael Zirkle; **470(t):** Courtesy Mary Bahr Fritts; **470(b):** Courtesy Albert Whitman & Company; **482–483:** Stock Illustration Source; **484–485(bk), 631, 651(bl):** SuperStock; **502:** Courtesy Zibby Oneal; **527(t):** Courtesy Kate McMullan; **534–536(bk):** M. Angelo/Corbis; **554(t):** Photo: Marcia Johnson/Courtesy Farrar, Straus & Giroux, Inc.; **554(b):** Courtesy Garth Williams; **556(bc):** Wolfgang Kaehler; **557(tr):** Richard Du Toit/BBC Photo; **557(cl):** Michael Fogden/DRK Photo; **557(br):** Roger de la Harpe/ABPL Anthony Bannister Photo Library; **558(t):** Franklin J. Viola/Viola Photo; **558(ins-ltr):** Norbert Wu/DRK Photo; **558(bl):** Howard Hall/Howard Hall Productions; **559(tr):** © Clay Bryce; **559(bl):** Gerry Bishop; **561(cl):** Wade Spees; **576(all):** Courtesy, Lee & Low Books; **578(tl, tr):** Popperfoto; **578(bc):** *The Wizard of Oz,* Courtesy Turner Entertainment/MGM/Ronald Grant Archive/The Cinema Museum; **578(bl):** AKG London Ltd.; **578(br):** Sonia Halliday; **579(tl):** FPG/Robert Harding; **579(cr):** © UPI/Bettmann/Corbis; **579(bl):** *Gone With the Wind,* courtesy Turner Entertainment/MGM/Ronald Grant Archive/The Cinema Museum; **596(b):** Courtesy William Morrow; **601(r):** Courtesy of Putnam County, photo by Dennis Sant; **603:** Telegraph Colour Library 1999/FPG International LLC; **604:** Stone; **604–605:** Mariko Abe/Photonica; **610–611:** John Lund/Stone; **631–632:** Aldo Tutino/Art Resource, NY; **633(t):** © Jack Fields/Corbis; **649:** Phyllis Reynolds Naylor Photo by Katherine Lambert/Courtesy Phyllis Reynolds Naylor; **651—bug eating:** Steve Liss/Corbis Sygma; **651, 652—ant:** Raymond A. Mendez/Animals Animals/Earth Scenes; **651, 653—cicada:** A. Shay/O.S.F./ Animals Animals/Earth Scenes; **652—meal worm larva:** Louis Quitt/Photo Researchers Inc.; **652—cockroach:** Norm Thomas/Photo Researchers Inc.; **652—termite:** Noble Proctor/ Photo Researchers Inc.; **652—bee:** D. Wilder/TOM STACK & ASSOCIATES; **652—earthworm:** Oxford Scientific Films/Animals Animals/Earth Scenes; **666:** Courtesy Joe Hayes; **690(t):** *1999* by Ellen Conford Reprinted by permission of the author and/McIntosh and Otis, Inc.; **692:** Stone; **692:** Rene Magritte, *La condition humaine,* Gift of the Collectors Committee, © 1998 Board of Trustees, National Gallery of Art, Washington; **698:** Marilyn Levine, *Black Gloves,* 1987 painted ceramic 14.50 x 12.50 x 3 inches; O. K. Harris Works of Art, New York, NY/O. K. Harris Works of Art; **699:** Duane Hanson, *Traveler,* 1990, Courtesy Duane Hanson; **701:** Charles Goforth, *Kicked Carpet,* 1989, Courtesy Charles Goforth; **703:** Audrey Flack, *Strawberry Tart Supreme,* 1974, Allen Memorial Art Museum, Oberlin College, Ohio; National Endowment for the Arts Museum Purchase Plan and Fund for Contemporary Art, © Audrey Flack, 1974/Allen Memorial Art Museum, Oberlin College, Ohio; **705(t):** Decorative Arts, Inc., *trompe l'oeil,* 1992: © Jimmy M. Prybil/Reflected Images, Friendswood, TX; **705(b):** Kent Addison, *Still Life #1019,* 1982; **706:** Courtesy Lerner Publishing Group; **722:** Bob Daemmrich; **727(t):** Gary J. Benson; **730:** Christie's, London/SuperStock; **731:** Gemmedia; **733:** Eric Howden.

Glossary

The contents of the glossary have been adapted from *Thorndike Barnhart Intermediate Dictionary.* Copyright © 1999 Addison Wesley Educational Publishers, Inc., Glenview, Illinois.